THE LIMITS OF CONSTITUTIONAL DEMOCRACY

THE UNIVERSITY CENTER
FOR HUMAN VALUES SERIES

CHARLES R. BEITZ,
EDITOR

THE LIMITS OF CONSTITUTIONAL DEMOCRACY

Jeffrey K. Tulis and Stephen Macedo, editors

PRINCETON UNIVERSITY PRESS   PRINCETON AND OXFORD

Library of Congress Cataloging-in-Publication Data

The limits of constitutional democracy / edited by Jeffrey K. Tulis and Stephen Macedo.
     p. cm. — (University Center for Human Values series)
   Includes index.
   ISBN 978-0-691-14734-5 (hardcover : alk. paper) — ISBN 978-0-691-14736-9
(pbk. : alk. paper)
  1. Democracy—United States.   2. Constitutional history—United States.
3. Constitutional law—United States.   I. Macedo, Stephen, 1957–   II. Tulis, Jeffrey.
   JK1726.L56 2010
   321.8—dc22

                                                                          2010007375

British Library Cataloging-in-Publication Data is available

This book has been composed in Sabon

Printed on acid-free paper. ∞

press.princeton.edu

Printed in the United States of America

10 9 8 7 6 5 4 3 2 1

Contents

Constitutional Boundaries

JEFFREY K. TULIS AND STEPHEN MACEDO

OUR LARGE THEME IS FAILURE and success in constitution making, or the limits of constitutional democracy. The convergence of recent scholarly work in political science and law and political events throughout the world make this a timely project inside and outside of the academy. The number of new constitutional texts written in support of regime formation in the past thirty years is astonishing. The profusion of ideas and scholarship on constitution making also marks a milestone for social science, which had long neglected the study of laws and constitutions, and for legal studies, which recently added the study of constitutional design to its usual emphasis on constitutional interpretation and analyses of court doctrine.

This worldwide effort in political and academic arenas is, however, marked by a kind of ambivalence. On the one hand, there is considerable optimism that constitutional democracy represents a high point, if not a culmination, in the history of political life. The attractiveness of this political idea is so powerful that even countries such as Russia, whose long anticonstitutional pedigree continues to shape politics as it is experienced there, claim to be constitutional democracies. On the other hand, for all the attractiveness of the idea of constitutional democracy, establishing it in practice has proved difficult in many new regimes throughout the world, as the Russian case and the conflicts in Iraq and Afghanistan vividly illustrate. Constitutional democracy is at once an attractive idea and a daunting enterprise. There are limits to the possible establishment, to say nothing of the flourishing, of the idea of constitutional democracy.

This book takes up the concern about the limits of constitutional democracy by returning to its most basic questions: What is constitutional democracy? What does it mean for constitutional democracy to succeed or fail? To address issues so fundamental that they are often overlooked or taken for granted means that one can no longer assume the attractiveness of the idea of constitutionalism but must interrogate the meaning, limits, and appeal of the constitutional idea. Our usual way of talking about the limits of constitutional democracy is to discuss the variety of indigenous circumstances—ethnic and tribal traditions, lack of commitment to a rule of law, religious strife—that hinder its development. For many who adopt this usual approach, constitutional democracy itself is unlimited in its appeal, but circumstances limit its establishment. In this book, we reverse the lens on these phenomena. Here we ask: What are the limits of constitutional democracy under minimally plausible circumstances for its establishment? What can we expect of constitutional democracy even under hospitable social circumstances? In a political order in which the citizenry is committed to constitutional democracy and its basic tenets, such as the rule of law properly conceived, what can constitutional democracy accomplish and what will it fail to accomplish? This is another way of asking what constitutional democracy is, what its *theoretical boundaries* are. Can this sort of regime adequately contend with emergencies? Can constitutional democracies conduct war effectively and still remain constitutional democracies? Can constitutional democracy cope with global interdependence?

This distinction between the conventional understanding of limits and the approach of this book is intentionally overdrawn. Studies of political and social circumstances inevitably run up against the question of the limits of constitutional democracy per se. And our analyses of constitutional democracy will inevitably raise questions about indigenous political and social circumstances or prerequisites. But in each case there is a distinct emphasis that colors the presentation. Our emphasis here is on the meaning and the limits of constitutional democracy itself.

This project was inspired by a remarkable recent study that offers an account of the creation, maintenance, and change of constitutional democracy. In *Constitutional Democracy: Creating and Maintaining a Just Political Order*, the late Walter F. Murphy developed a constitutional theory that was unusually comprehensive. Murphy showed how the problems of constitutional creation and maintenance could be illuminated by conjoining literatures and fields that rarely spoke to one another. He brought together the concerns of legal academics who study constitutions with political scientists who study law in one overarching account. It may be surprising to the general reader that these intellectual communities often work separately even though they study the same subject. To be sure, legal academics and political scientists usually raise different questions and often deploy different methods. Yet there is much to learn from each community, and Murphy's book transcended that divide. Within political science, Murphy synthesized literatures from warring conceptual and methodological approaches and from diverse subfields—ranging from comparative politics to American political development, from theories of rational choice to studies of political behavior, and from political theory to political history. The result is a modern version of an Aristotelian idea that constitutional theory could be architectonic.

We decided to bring the spirit of Murphy's approach to a topic mentioned but not developed at length in his book. Murphy attended to the problems of constitutional creation, maintenance, and change but only obliquely dealt with the issues of failure and limit. Like the earlier contrast between two understandings of limits, this distinction—between constructive constitutionalism and the limits of constitutionalism—is a matter of emphasis. Murphy emphasized the constructive capacity of constitutionalism but necessarily discussed limits as a subsidiary theme. The scholarship gathered in this book takes up the theme of constitutional limits and constitutional failure as our central theme but, of course, necessarily discusses success and constitutional capacity as well.

What Is Constitutional Failure?

Part I includes four chapters that treat the issue of constitutional failure or success as a theoretical problem. What is constitutional failure or success? All four authors bring original, thought-provoking, counterintuitive answers to this question. Sotirios Barber argues that a healthy constitution requires a group of diverse and self-critical citizens "who see each other as moral equals and parts of one community of abstract interests conceived as real interests." These citizens and the politicians among them are contestants regarding the meaning of the common good and the most effective means to secure it. Because he shows these political attitudes to be more constitutive of success for a constitutional democracy than institutional capacities and pathologies, Barber upends the conventional understanding of constitutional failure. For Barber, the Articles of Confederation was not a failure (as is usually assumed in historical accounts) because the peaceful constitutional revolution occasioned by institutional breakdown and economic crisis revealed potent civic attitudes capable of constitutional revision and redesign. On the other hand, the long-term stability of the U.S. Constitution and the American political system it created (usually interpreted as evidence of constitutional health) may portend failure to the extent that it is symptomatic of a mentally inert citizenry no longer capable of self-critical constitutional reflection and debate.

Like Barber, James Fleming seeks to challenge the conventional understanding of success and failure. He surveys the growing literature on constitutional breakdown in the United States in order to show that most constitutional critics mislabel institutional, policy, or cultural problems as constitutional crises or constitutional failures. Fleming urges greater care in distinguishing constitutional failures from other sorts of failure by delimiting the constitutional sort to those that can be tied explicitly to the constitutional text. Because the text is subject to plausible but divergent interpretations, Fleming argues that the American political order has been marked by numerous "successful failures": that is, plausible but faulty interpretations that would have undermined the health of our polity have frequently lost out in the course of American political development.

It might be thought that the most successful constitution would be like a well-wrought urn, perfectly coherent with all parts contributing to a harmonious whole. Gary Jacobsohn argues that successful constitutions require disharmony, as elements in tension or even contradiction form a dialogical relation that allows constitutions to develop over time while maintaining an identifiable identity. He reveals the difficult puzzle of constitutional design to be not so much to overcome disharmony but rather to constitute it. He illustrates this argument with examples that span the globe.

The final chapter in this part, by Will Harris, takes Jacobsohn's insight to a higher level of abstraction. Harris shows how political design can bind two projected worlds—one of success, the other of failure in mutual constitution. He argues that constitutional democracy requires these two constitutions of failure and of success as part of its life as well as its origin. Indeed, in the American case, Harris argues that the deep structure or grammar of constitutional politics can be found in two failures and two successes corresponding to the negative and positive constitutional visions of the Federalists and Antifederalists. Harris shows that America invented or brought to self-consciousness a new form of regime, replacing what used to be called a "mixed constitution" with what he calls a regime of contending "multiple constitutions."

How Can Constitutional Democracy Contend with Emergency?

Tools used to fight the war on terror include military commissions, enhanced interrogation techniques, and limitless detention along with extraordinary measures devised to contend with economic crises. These measures have raised anew the question of how and whether constitutions can work in emergencies. Are constitutions best preserved by forcing emergency action outside of the constitutional order until the emergency has passed? Or should constitutions provide mechanisms within their design to contend with unforeseen emergencies? In part II, three essays provide contending answers.

Most discussions of this topic recur to the classic account of "prerogative" in John Locke's *Second Treatise on Government*, where it is argued that unanticipated emergencies require executives to go beyond the law, sometimes against the law, to preserve the polity and its legal system.

Locke wrote before the distinction between a written constitution and ordinary law had become commonplace, so he did not address the question of whether the necessity to go beyond law in emergencies requires an executive to go beyond the constitution as well.

Ben Kleinerman argues that emergency power must be exercised outside of the legal and constitutional order for constitutions to preserve their compositional and moral integrity and to prevent extreme action from becoming routine. In his account, appeals to necessity that are ratified by the people or by the legislature can bring extralegal action back under a constitution—but all extralegal emergency actions are initially extraconstitutional as well. Kleinerman insists on this conceptualization to force the polity to confront necessity as the determining issue and to avoid any sense that emergency action is authorized by normal processes. He illustrates the importance of this extraconstitutional conceptualization by comparing Lincoln's actions and arguments under its auspices with those of Woodrow Wilson in World War I, who sought legal authorization for illegal acts with the deleterious consequence of normalizing the extreme.

Jeffrey Tulis shows that Locke's problem of prerogative is more vexing than Locke acknowledged because, as Carl Schmitt argued, extreme emergencies raise the possibility of actions beyond all familiar normative orders. A people may be rendered incapable of bringing an executive back under a constitution in such circumstances. Tulis's solution to this problem is to broaden the reach of constitutions to encompass emergency power and to preserve the operation of separation of powers through emergency, while narrowing the classic conception of statesmanship at the same time. He also argues that this Hamiltonian solution is the best reading of the U.S. Constitution.

Finally, Kim Scheppele surveys emergency actions throughout the world in recent history to suggest that neither the extraconstitutional approach nor the intraconstitutional approaches have worked. Whether one attempts to force executives beyond the constitution in emergency or to temporarily expand the constitution in emergencies and retract it in normal times, all recent exercises of extraordinary power have been made part of the normal operations and expectations of governance. Scheppele's solution is to thicken the constitution to better anticipate emergencies or to at least normalize the processes through which emergencies are discussed, addressed, and limited. In her view, greater attention to the mechanisms of emergency power can actually better preserve the distinction between emergency power and normal political action. One might describe this approach as challenging the Lockean problematic itself by suggesting that law can comprehend the power and institutional mechanisms needed to contend with all future emergencies.

How Can Constitutional Democracy Contend with War?

Closely related to the question of emergency is the limit of constitutional democracy in war. Are constitutional democracies adequate for the successful prosecution of war? Does the conduct of war necessarily undermine constitutional cultures? These questions are taken up in part III. Unlike the previous two parts, these essays do not offer contending answers to the same question. Instead, they use this topic to generate an array of new questions and their distinct answers show just how important these hitherto neglected questions are for the large issue of constitutional democracy and war.

Adrian Vermeule argues that the commander in chief's power needs to be understood not only as designating the head of the armed forces but as the constitutional marker for "an economy of glory." He shows how Machiavelli can inform this understanding of the commander in chief's power and also argues that the economy of glory helps us understand the relationship between the executive and the legislature. Mariah Zeisberg argues that debates over the war powers in the U.S. Constitution are fundamentally miscast because they treat the issue as one of legal settlement. Instead, she develops and illustrates a "relational" understanding of constitutional power that accommodates the competing needs of legislative and executive powers. Joseph Bessette revisits Justice Jackson's opinion in the *Youngstown* case, upon which almost all current understandings of the limits of presidential power are built. In an essay sure to provoke debate, Bessette shows how Jackson's classic opinion is fundamentally mistaken because it transmutes a separation-of-powers principle into one of legislative supremacy. Finally, Mark Brandon notes that the United States has been engaged in various wars most of the time since World War I. Brandon argues that this state of affairs has serious constitutional costs, costs that extend beyond civil liberties to the mental state and civic capacities of ordinary citizens. Brandon raises the profound question whether contemporary circumstances mean that war is no longer an external circumstance with which constitutions must contend. Is war now becoming a normal feature of constitutional democracy itself?

How Can Constitutional Democracy Contend with Globalization?

The final section of the book, part IV, takes up the challenges that globalization and interdependence pose to the future of state-based constitutional democracy. The phenomenon is so new that there is no classic account or even set of questions to revisit and develop. Like the authors in the preceding part, these scholars define and address a set of distinct questions that, taken together, begin to map a subject—in this case, the problems globalization pose for constitutional theory.

Jan-Werner Müller argues that the limits and possibilities of constitutionalism are best revealed by three paradigmatic responses to the facts of globalization and interdependence. Müller describes these as "constitutional closure" focused on sequestering state-based constitutional regimes from the pressures of internationalization; "limited mutual constitutional opening" or "constitutional tolerance" in which state-based constitutions are preserved but altered somewhat to accommodate the requirements of interdependence; and, finally, a global constitution, replacing altogether state-based constitutional democracy. Müller develops normative standards to evaluate these three paradigms, moving back and forth between the paradigms and the standards in a kind of reflective equilibrium.

Is orthodox Islam compatible with constitutional democracy? Ran Hirschl offers a fundamentally new approach to this issue. In *Democracy in America*, Alexis de Tocqueville made the troubling claim that the Islamic faith was incompatible with constitutional democracy. Some contemporary theorists have pondered the ways in which Islam could be incorporated into modern constitutional democracies much as orthodox versions of Christianity have been absorbed by, and perhaps transformed in, the American constitutional tradition. Hirschl argues that a new political form, a new regime, is emerging in late modernity. He calls this "constitutional theocracy" in which a principle of separation of powers is incorporated—with roles for religious and secular authority separate and distinct—but at the same time a very robust role for an established religion is preserved. This powerful original essay shows the challenges posed and the limits for constitutional democracy revealed by the religious resurgence throughout the world today.

Rogers Smith extends the idea of interdependence to include foreign peoples whose lives have been importantly constituted by the actions of constitutional democracies. In this provocative chapter, Smith argues that constitutional democracies whose actions and policies alter the lives of aliens incur an obligation to offer citizenship to affected peoples who desire it. Making good on this obligation will be constrained by circumstances and other obligations, but Smith makes a strong case for a new and extraordinary principle of inclusion.

The problem of terrorism and the proliferation of nuclear weapons pose new challenges to constitutional democracies. In the final chapter of part IV, Daniel Deudney defends an unorthodox proposition he labels "'nuclear constitutional internationalism,' which holds that the survival of limited constitutional government, particularly in the United States, is coming increasingly to depend upon the strength of the international arms control system." Deudney establishes the first intellectual bridge between, on the one hand, the theory and practice of constitutional design and, on the other hand, international arms control. In his view, this conjunction is the last hope for state-based constitutional democracy, which otherwise may need to be replaced with a new form of governance altogether, such as global constitutionalism.

Christopher Eisgruber's conclusion nicely knits the essays together and draws out several basic themes. Eisgruber gets to the core argument of many of the chapters in his acute restatement of their theses. He shows how these chapters speak to each other not only within the four broad categories in which we have arranged them but also in other conjunctions that span the book. For examples: he shows how Deudney's essay on the implications of global forms of war speaks to issues in Brandon's essay on the constitutional culture of war; he sees a similar logic in Zeisberg's arguments about the relation of Congress and the presidency on war power and Scheppele's cross-national account of the need for constitutionalized emergency power; and he reflects on the different intellectual purposes for which Lincoln is invoked in many of the essays.

Yet Eisgruber's conclusion on "Constitutional Engagement and Its Limits" offers more than an acute closing commentary: it advances its own constructive argument about the nature of constitutionalism. Drawing on the entire set of essays, he redescribes the limits of constitutional democracy as "a series of four tensions, two internal and two external: personal freedom–civic virtue, political order–sustained argument, state sovereignty–constitutional sovereignty, and equality–membership. All eight poles of these dyads correspond to essential constitutional aspirations." He shows how each of these four tensions is a potential source of constitutional failure, yet a well-designed constitutional order cannot flourish, indeed cannot exist, without these tensions. It would be hard to imagine a more astute summary and elaboration of the idea that there are limits inherent in the enterprise of making and sustaining a constitutional order.

We would like to thank the several institutions and many individuals who made this project possible and contributed to its development. In February 2007 Princeton's Law and Public Affairs Program, under the direction of Kim Scheppele, hosted a small conference to celebrate and discuss the publication of Walter Murphy's book *Constitutional Democracy: Creating and Maintaining a Just Political Order*. The participants included, Sotirios Barber, James Fleming, Robert George, Jeffrey Tulis, and Stephen Macedo. Everyone noted that Murphy's book is unusually significant—an assessment confirmed a year later when that book was named the Best of the Social Sciences by the American Association of Publishers. The group decided that another conference was warranted. This second conference would not be a celebration of Murphy's book, nor would it produce a *Festschrift* in his honor. Instead, we designed a conference of original research that would emulate the project that Murphy began and carry it forward to subjects meriting new or renewed attention. Stephen Macedo and Jeffrey Tulis brought together leading scholars in political science and law working on questions of constitutional design, maintenance, and change. It was decided that this second conference would probe the problem of constitutional failure.

Sponsored and funded by Princeton's University Center for Human Values (UCHV), directed by Stephen Macedo; the Law and Public Affairs Program, directed by Kim Scheppele; the James Madison Program in American Ideals and Institutions, directed by Robert George; and the Mamoudha Bobst Center for Peace and Justice, directed by Jennifer Widner, this large conference convened in February 2008. All of the authors in this book participated, joined by a stunning array of talent in constitutional theory and law including John Ferejohn, Cindy Skatch, James Ceaser, Keith Whittington, John McGinnis, Mark Graber, Sanford Levinson, Mark Tushnet, Stanley Katz, Ian Shapiro, Mary Dudziak, Ellen Kennedy, Rolf Poscher, Leslie Gerwin, Paul Starr, Jennifer Widner, and Robert George. This book was developed out of that remarkable assembly. We are very grateful to all these scholars for their comments on the work presented here as well as for sharing their own ongoing projects on cognate themes. We also appreciate the support and useful suggestions from referees for Princeton University Press.

We thank the staff of UCHV for all its administrative assistance, especially Erum Syed and Susan Winters. We appreciate the continued support from the new director of UCHV, Charles Beitz. Valuable research assistance was provided by Evan Oxman at Princeton and Loren Rotner and Emily Hawthorne at the University of Texas at Austin. Chuck Myers, Deborah Tegarden, and Brian MacDonald, our editors at Princeton University Press, have been exceptionally helpful. We appreciate all of their assistance and also the interest and support of the Press's Director, Peter Dougherty.

Finally, we would like to acknowledge the late Walter F. Murphy, whose scholarly career continues to set the agenda for so many important studies of constitutional democracy in our time, and who provided constructive criticism and helpful encouragement for the present project. We learned of Walter's death just as this volume was going to press. Our deep sadness at the loss of a good friend is tempered by the hope that this book will constitute one of many testaments to his enduring legacy.

Part I

WHAT IS CONSTITUTIONAL FAILURE? ⎯⎯⎯⎯⎯⎯⎯⎯⎯⎯⎯

1

Constitutional Failure: Ultimately Attitudinal

SOTIRIOS A. BARBER

As ideological divisions widen and continue to weaken the common ground of the nation's civic life, American constitutional theorists and social scientists have reopened a recurring question: is the Constitution adequate to its ends? Alan Wolfe laments the moralistic populism and public cynicism that has all but destroyed Congress's institutional integrity and democratic accountability.[1] Sanford Levinson shows how "hard-wired" constitutional provisions like the Electoral College and the composition of the Senate contribute to bad policies and institutional decay.[2] Ronald Dworkin proposes a theory of human dignity as common moral ground for rescuing American politics from ideological warfare and restoring genuine political debate.[3] In the most pessimistic work of this expanding genre, Sheldon Wolin argues that a constitutionalism of "limited and modest ambitions" cannot control a regime whose sources of power are inherently expansive "capital, technology, and science" and whose aims are corporate profits in a global economy and security from terrorism that its economic and cultural expansion provokes.[4]

Is the U.S. Constitution (government under the Constitution) failing, then? In what ways might it be failing? Was it programmed to fail from the beginning, as Wolin suggests? Or is it repairable, as Levinson, Dworkin, and Wolfe assume? These are the first-order questions of constitutional failure: the whether, why, and how of constitutional failure as a present reality. But there are prior questions, including the question of what might be meant by "constitutional failure"—the questions we should debate when deciding whether the constitution is failing. I address parts of this complicated issue here and submit that (1) constitutional failure is at bottom as much

---

1. Alan Wolfe, *Does American Democracy Still Work?* (New Haven: Yale University Press, 2006), 1–24.

2. Sanford Levinson, *Our Undemocratic Constitution* (New York: Oxford University Press, 2006), 49–62, 81–97.

3. Ronald Dworkin, *Is Democracy Possible Here?* (Princeton: Princeton University Press, 2006).

4. Sheldon Wolin, *Democracy Incorporated: Managed Democracy and the Specter of Inverted Totalitarianism* (Princeton: Princeton University Press, 2008), 100.

or more an attitudinal than an institutional matter, (2) constitutional failure centrally involves a failure to maintain a "healthy politics," and (3) a
successful constitution would provide for the probable failure of formal
institutions by equipping its people for the task of institutional reform.

Failure to Do What?

Talk of constitutional failure presupposes a notion of constitutional
success.[5] What, then, is the U.S. Constitution supposed to accomplish?
Americans generally assume that their formal constitution aims to secure
negative rights against government, to maintain processes of popular
choice, and to pursue substantive ends beyond rights and democratic
processes. Yet theorists differ on which of these aims to emphasize. Negative constitutionalists including Randy Barnett[6] and Michael Zuckert[7]
emphasize negative rights over constitutional processes and substantive
ends like national security and the general welfare. Procedural consti-

---

5. Adrian Vermeule challenged this proposition in the Princeton conference of February 2007, at which I presented a draft of this paper. He claims constitutional failure does
not presuppose a notion of constitutional success because discussants can agree only on
what counts as constitutional failure, not success. Professor Vermeule and I disagree across
the board. First, I would expect little disagreement with a test of constitutional success
described at a high level of abstraction, such as "adequa[cy] to the exigencies of government and the preservation of the Union," to borrow from Congress's charge of 1787 to the
Philadelphia Convention, which Madison renders in *Federalist* No. 45 as adequacy "to the
public good, the real welfare of the great body of the people." Second, I would not expect
universal agreement on what counts as constitutional failure, perhaps short of a violent
revolution. The founding generation reached no consensus on whether the Articles of Confederation had failed. Opposing the changes proposed by the Philadelphia Convention,
some Antifederalists claimed that mere (Article XIII) amendments augmenting Congress's
powers would suffice to correct the Confederation's deficiencies. Finally, and centrally, an
outside observer like Professor Vermeule might contend that disagreement over whether the
Constitution (government under the Constitution) is adequate to "the people's welfare" is
disagreement either about nothing at all or about something that does not admit of truly
better or worse understandings. But should the disagreeing parties themselves reach either
conclusion, they would cease to be disagreeing parties. The mere fact of disagreement about
either constitutional success or failure would hardly indicate either that there's nothing to
disagree about, or that no one answer is better than any other, or that discussants should
not seek the better answer, or that they should not reflect on what they are looking for
before they start the quest.
6. Randy Barnett, *Restoring the Lost Constitution* (Princeton: Princeton University Press,
2003), 33–38.
7. Michael P. Zuckert, "On Constitutional Welfare Liberalism: An Old–Liberal Perspective," in *Liberalism: Old and New,* ed. Ellen Frankel Paul, Fred D. Miller, and Jeffrey Paul
(New York: Cambridge University Press, 2007), 313–15.

tutionalists like John Hart Ely emphasize democratic processes and associated values and conditions (political freedoms mostly) over goods like
national security and prosperity.[8] Ends-oriented, or, as I prefer, welfare
constitutionalists, such as Martin Diamond,[9] Stephen Elkin,[10] Lawrence
Sager,[11] Cass Sunstein,[12] and Walter Murphy,[13] place equal or greater
emphasis on preambular ends like the common defense and the general
welfare.

A welfarist accepts Madison's claim in *The Federalist* that "the supreme
object" of any legitimate government is the people's "real welfare" and
that "no form of Government whatever, has any other value, than as it
may be fitted for the attainment of this object."[14] My previous argument
for welfare constitutionalism relies on moral readings (in Ronald Dworkin's sense) of *The Federalist* and other historical sources, like the Declaration of Independence, the opinions of John Marshall, and the speeches
of Abraham Lincoln.[15] My leading point against a constitutionalism centered on negative rights against the state is its inability to explain why
reasonable persons would establish a government for the *chief* purpose of
limiting it or why they would establish government if they thought harm
from that government more likely than benefits.[16] I claim that constitutionalists who say that all is process cannot imagine, much less identify,
a normative process that, like a road to nowhere, is connected in no way
to a substantive public good of some sort, like national security or, more

8. John Hart Ely, *Democracy and Distrust* (Cambridge: Harvard University Press, 1980),
88–101.

9. Martin Diamond, *As Far as Republican Principles Will Admit* (Washington, DC: AEI
Press, 1992), 352–68.

10. Stephen L. Elkin, *Reconstructing the Commercial Republic: Constitutional Design
after Madison* (Chicago: University of Chicago Press, 2006), 5–14, 127–39.

11. Lawrence Sager, *Justice in Plain Clothes* (New Haven: Yale University Press, 2004),
5–10, 70–83.

12. Cass R. Sunstein, *The Second Bill of Rights: FDR's Unfinished Revolution and Why
We Need It More Than Ever* (New York: Basic Books, 2004), 175–92.

13. Walter F. Murphy, *Constitutional Democracy: Creating and Maintaining a Just Political Order* (Baltimore: Johns Hopkins University Press, 2007), 7–8, 334–41, 516–17.

14. Alexander Hamilton, James Madison, and John Jay, *The Federalist*, ed. Jacob E.
Cooke (Middletown, CT: Wesleyan University Press, 1961), No. 45, 309.

15. See Sotirios A. Barber, *Welfare and the Constitution* (Princeton: Princeton University
Press, 2003), 8–22, 92–100. For a defense of Ronald Dworkin's approach to constitutional
interpretation, see Sotirios A. Barber and James E. Fleming, *Constitutional Interpretation:
The Basic Questions* (New York: Oxford University Press, 2007), 155–70. Dworkin's origi-
nal theory was set forth in Ronald Dworkin, *Taking Rights Seriously* (Cambridge: Harvard
University Press, 1971), 132–37.

16. Herbert J. Storing, *What the Anti-Federalists Were For* (Chicago: University of Chicago Press, 1981), 69; Sotirios A. Barber, "Fallacies of Negative Constitutionalism," *Fordham Law Review* 75 (2006): 653–57.

broadly, officials who try to do the right thing. Thus, in *The Federalist*, Madison conceives the procedural concept of checks and balances as a "policy of supplying by opposite and rival interests, the defect of better motives."[17] Nor can road-to-nowhere proceduralists explain why one process, like deliberative democracy, is better than others, like consulting the Delphic Oracle. Welfarists are thus obliged to submit theories of substantive constitutional ends. Corollary to any such theory would be a theory of constitutional failure or success, and in view of the Constitution's undeniable features, a welfarist theory of failure or success would accommodate the negative libertarian's view of failure as chronic disregard of constitutional rights and the proceduralist's view of failure as institutional breakdown.

Notwithstanding the Constitution's legal aspect, explicit in Article VI's declaration that the Constitution is "supreme Law," welfare constitutionalism emphasizes the instrumentalism implicit in the Preamble: the Constitution as means to ends like the common defense and the general welfare. Though Levinson might not call himself a welfarist, welfarists would agree with him that the Preamble is the Constitution's most important part.[18] Allowing for all but inevitable and (as we shall see) necessary disagreements about the practical meanings of preambular ends in changing historical circumstances, we can say, as a first approximation, that the Constitution fails to the extent that the government it establishes *and* the social order that the government both reflects and enables fail to inspire (1) a general sense of progress toward (2) a reasonable version of the ends of government. This definition combines both a consensual or subjective element and a real or objective element: the former refers to what some population believes, and the latter refers to what is objectively true. The public generally has to believe (more often than not and over some specified period of time) that both the country and its elected leaders are headed in the right direction, and observers asking the question of constitutional failure or success have to judge for themselves whether the public is approximately right. This two-part requirement (first describing and then assessing the public's perception of government's performance) reflects the responsible government to which *The Federalist* aspires: government that reconciles the public to what is right—government that educates the public to its true interests.[19] This aspiration expresses itself in practice as a "healthy politics," and, I claim, a healthy politics is the ultimate test of constitutional success.

17. *Federalist* No. 51, 349.
18. Levinson, *Undemocratic Constitution*, 4.
19. *Federalist* No. 63, 423–25; and No. 71, 482–83.

The Welfare Theory of Constitutional Failure or Success

A welfarist definition of constitutional failure or success faces at least three problems: in America's present political climate, a healthy politics seems utopian, and emphasizing ends or policy results seems to depreciate constitutional rights and constitutional institutions. These objections run deep, and though a conclusive response to them is too much to claim, I have attempted one elsewhere.[20] Here I can invoke only the presuppositions of everyday life, presuppositions that seem ineluctable. Ordinary political actors take their disagreements about things like fairness and goodness seriously. They assume that particular conceptions of normative ideas can be wrong and that good-faith debate aims to find which side is favored by an unprejudiced assessment of the evidence.[21] Because political actors assume that the ends of government are *real and approachable ends*—goods about whose meaning and conditions people can err (with some people erring more than others)—welfare constitutionalism requires consensus on neither the meaning of ends nor the most affordable means. Far from guaranteeing constitutional success—that is, reasonably arguable progress toward real ends—consensus about either ends or means hastens constitutional failure by obviating debate through which error is revealed and progress maintained. This fact argues for a reasonable measure of philosophic and cultural diversity and social experimentation within a single community of interests abstractly conceived—abstract interests, like security and well-being, conceived, again, as real ends about whose meaning the community as a whole and its individual members can err. This diversity should produce disagreement about ends and means—reasonable and civil disagreement, in the ideal—and the value that welfarists must place on reasonable diversity and civil disagreement answers the charge that welfarism is utopian. Though a politics of reasonable and civil conflict is visionary, it is no more so than any other constitutional aspiration, like national security and the general welfare. It is not otherworldly in a way that would make it unapproachable.[22]

Nor need welfarism depreciate either constitutional rights or constitutional institutions—at least not functional constitutional rights and institutions. Fallible actors who pursue real ends require institutions for collecting and assessing the evidence of diverse experiences and giving

20. Barber, *Welfare and the Constitution*, chaps. 2–4.

21. David O. Brink, *Moral Realism and the Foundation of Ethics* (Cambridge: Cambridge University Press, 1989), 23–24.

22. Barber, *Welfare and the Constitution*, 55–64.

legal form to those conclusions that the evidence favors. Fallible actors require institutions to administer the law and collect the resources that administration requires. They require rights of inquiry, expression, and participation on which public accountability depends and through which errors are exposed and corrected. They require rights of property and personal autonomy prerequisite to the formation and expression of diverse opinions. Clearly, therefore, a constitution devoted to real ends fails to the extent that its government fails to honor negative liberties and maintain representative institutions that permit (as negative liberties do) and enable (as representative institutions do) public debate about the direction and the conduct of public policy.[23] So at least some institutions and negative liberties are integral to the collective pursuit of real goods, and a task of constitutional theory and citizenship is debating which rights and institutions are functional to this enterprise.

Human fallibility, the attraction of real goods like security and well-being, and the resulting case for a reasonable political diversity thus enable us to say that *a constitution is successful if the government it establishes maintains arguable fidelity to its terms and arguable progress (relative to resources over the mid- to long term) toward (what all responsible elements of society can regard as) publicly reasonable versions of constitutional ends.* Defined this way, constitutional success is marked not by a consensus that reaches from preambular ends all the way down to concrete policies; it is marked by a certain quality of debate, *a healthy politics*, together with the social preconditions of a healthy politics.

A healthy politics features reasonable differences among political contestants who see each other as moral equals and parts of one community of abstract interests assumed to be real goods. These contestants see each other as engaged in good-faith disagreements about the common good and how to pursue it and about the true understandings and applications of constitutional principles and provisions. The immediate preconditions of a healthy politics include religious moderation (i.e., either the privatization of religious conviction or its subordination to a secular reasonableness); equal political, economic, and social opportunity; a general perception of economic fairness; and realistic prospects for economic growth at the collective and individual levels. This specification of conditions reflects a theory of the ends of government that builds on authorities like Lincoln and *The Federalist.*[24] Writers like Dworkin, Wolfe, Levinson, and Wolin are

23. *Federalist* Nos. 44–53.

24. See Walter Berns, *The First Amendment and the Future of American Democracy* (New York: Basic Books, 1976), 64–66; Martin Diamond, *The Founding of the Democratic Republic* (Belmont, CA: Thompson/Wadsworth, 1981), 72–76; Barber, *Welfare and the Constitution*, 100–106.

responding to the erosion of these conditions in America since the 1970s. Though I deny that some of these conditions (especially economic fairness and equal opportunity) are utopian in a strict sense, I concede that they are beyond reasonable expectations, or at least any that I can defend.[25] For numerous reasons—environmental, social-psychological, geopolitical— one can doubt also that unlimited economic growth is either possible or productive of human well-being.[26] But the question of this essay is what is meant by constitutional failure or success, not whether the Constitution has failed or is failing, and, I contend, the chief measure of constitutional success is the quality of civic debate.

Constitutional Failure as (Mostly) a Matter of Attitude

If the heart of constitutional success is a "healthy politics," constitutional success remains at least partly an institutional matter because a "healthy politics" is itself an informal institution whose activities and aims (e.g., law making and laws) are enabled by formal institutions—hence, the overlap of welfare constitutionalism and procedural constitutionalism. But a healthy politics is not an enactment of any sort; it is a social practice that expresses an attitude of individual citizens toward self in relation to others. Conceiving constitutional success as a healthy politics deemphasizes the breakdown of formal institutions as the essence of constitutional failure, for formal institutions can break down even when parties disagree with civility and in good faith. Yet most of us associate constitutional failure with institutional failure, as the framers did, and formal institutional failure is one way a constitution can fail. Nevertheless, I doubt that *formal* institutional failure is sufficient grounds for declaring constitutional failure, or at least unequivocal constitutional failure. Let me explain by first reviewing the importance of constitutional attitudes to constitutional success.

Madison claims in *The Federalist* that the social and institutional checks that he describes are adequate to "supply the defect of better motives"[27]— motives or attitudes that he claims for himself and his generation, even

---

25. Pessimism is justified in view of conditions of the large commercial republic beyond the immediate conditions specified above. These broader conditions include inexhaustible natural resources, nations that peacefully accept the cultural convergence that comes with the unlimited economic expansion of one member or group (i.e., cultures that walk quietly to their deaths), prospects for economic fairness within the expanding member and its partners, prospects for economic fairness within some nations without war (instead of trade) with other nations, the rationality of nuclear war, and technological advance that doesn't create more vulnerabilities than it can compensate for.

26. Murphy, *Constitutional Democracy*, 131–32.

27. *Federalist* No. 51, 349.

as he abandons a strategy of cultivating those attitudes in future generations.[28] Madison thus departs from a tradition that stretches from Aristotle to the Antifederalists and beyond. This tradition holds, in effect, that
no mere arrangement of offices and decisional procedures can adequately
"supply the defect of better motives." It holds (pace Justice Holmes) that
because no constitution can be made for people with *fundamentally* different views, successful institutions will actively cultivate the attitudes
and virtues that support the institutions and, better, the principles that
the institutions embody. Aristotle maintains that a viable constitutional
arrangement will reflect the personal commitments of a community's
politically most powerful element.[29] In a popular system like the United
States, this would mean either a population generally devoted to public
purposes in ways that respect individual rights and institutional norms or
a population not so privatized that it cannot produce and support leaders with the requisite virtues and concerns. In a pluralist system (justified,
again, not as an end in itself but as a condition for the pursuit of real
ends by fallible actors—pluralism or diversity as instrumental to political
truth), the leaders in question would constitute a leadership stratum (in
Congress, the professions, the military, the clergy, the media) composed
of members whose disagreements remained civil from a mutual sense of
each other's good faith.

Though Madison's depreciation of virtue and public-purposefulness
resonates with modern writers from Holmes to Rawls, Aristotle and the
tradition were right: there is no substitute for "better motives." Madison
himself all but conceded as much when, both in the Constitutional Convention and at the end of his presidency, he proposed a national university to cultivate a national (and nationalizing) leadership community that
would promote "those liberal sentiments and those congenial manners"
at the "foundation" of the political system.[30] Hamilton made a related
concession when he said in *The Federalist* that "whatever fine declarations may be inserted in any constitution," the security of constitutional
rights "must altogether depend on public opinion, and on the general
spirit of the people and of the government."[31]

Additional support for the traditional emphasis on attitudes comes
from postwar writers of the "liberal virtues" persuasion, like Diamond,[32]

28. *Federalist* No. 49, 340–41.
29. Ernest Barker, *The Politics of Aristotle* (Oxford: Oxford University Press, 1970), 110, 233.
30. Marvin Myers, *The Mind of the Founder: Sources of the Political Thought of James Madison* (Indianapolis, IN: Bobbs-Merrill, 1973), 387.
31. *Federalist* No. 84, 580.
32. Diamond, *As Far as Republican Principles Will Admit*, 337–68.

Pangle,[33] Macedo,[34] Sandel,[35] Galston,[36] and Elkin.[37] Indirect support for the classical position derives from the new literature on constitutional failure. Wolfe identifies zealous partisan gerrymandering as a major factor in the emergence of a Congress that no longer satisfies standards of democratic accountability; he also describes how the public's ignorance of public policy and cynicism toward politics contribute to the nation's political ills.[38] Further support for the classical position lies also in modern advances in the theory of constitutional interpretation. Dworkin and Moore have shown how a self-critical and public-spirited quest for presumed truth, moral and nonmoral, (e.g., about both the abstract meaning and concrete applications of normative ideas like liberty and property) is essential to the faithful application of the Constitution in concrete cases.[39] The Constitution can hardly displace "better motives" if fidelity to the Constitution as written—fidelity to the Constitution as positive law— depends on "better motives."[40] Support for the classical position lies also in the nation's experience with constitutional emergencies. Distinguished from mere political emergencies (unanticipated challenges to the nation like Pearl Harbor, 9/11, and Hurricane Katrina), *constitutional* emergencies occur when officials believe they have no politically workable option that does not violate some constitutional rule or principle. Lincoln's case is the leading example; it illustrates how constitutional failure is more attitudinal than institutional.

Lincoln claimed that his suspension of habeas corpus in the border states was essential to holding those states in the union, an imperative of his duty faithfully to execute the union's laws.[41] Lincoln's action belies

---

33. Thomas L. Pangle, *The Spirit of Modern Republicanism: The Moral Vision of the American Founders and the Philosophy of Locke* (Chicago: University of Chicago Press, 1988).

34. Stephen Macedo, *Diversity and Distrust* (Cambridge: Harvard University Press, 2000).

35. Michael J. Sandel, *Democracy's Discontent: America in Search of a Public Philosophy* (Cambridge: Harvard University Press, 1996).

36. William Galston, *Liberal Purposes: Goods, Virtues, and Purposes in the Liberal State* (Cambridge: Cambridge University Press, 1991).

37. Elkin, *Reconstructing the Commercial Republic.*

38. Wolfe, *Does American Democracy Still Work?*, 40–49, 53–56.

39. Dworkin, *Taking Rights Seriously*, 134–37; Michael S. Moore, "A Natural Law Theory of Interpretation," *Southern California Law Review* 58 (1985): 277–398. See also, Barber and Fleming, *Constitutional Interpretation*, 155–70.

40. More generally, and *pace The Federalist*, the rule of law cannot substitute for the rule of human beings where law represents and flows from a commitment to public reasonableness, a virtue. For an argument that public reasonableness is essential to liberalism, see Stephen Macedo, *Liberal Virtues: Citizenship, Virtue, and Community in Liberal Constitutionalism* (Oxford: Clarendon Press, 1990), 40–45.

41. Roy P. Basler, *Abraham Lincoln: His Speeches and Writings* (New York: Gosset & Dunlap, 1946), 599–601.

Justice Salmon Chase's famous proposition in *Ex Parte McCardle* (1867)[42] that the Constitution is adequate to all contingencies. Chase's claim, though false, is understandable as an attempt to deny unsettling truths: foresight is limited; conventions run out; constitutional leadership can demand extraconstitutional acts, despite the risk that extraconstitutional acts by a Lincoln will serve as precedents for exploitation by lesser figures in constitutionally governable situations. Extraconstitutional acts in constitutionally governable situations are, of course, unconstitutional. But because "ought" implies "can," it is hard to hold leaders responsible to the Constitution when circumstances preclude constitutional action. The best leaders can do under these circumstances, from a constitutionalist point of view, is to restore constitutional conditions, as Lincoln did. Lincoln's experience indicates that notwithstanding the extraconstitutional acts that they justify, constitutional emergencies cause (total) constitutional failure only if the nation's leadership lacks a vision of constitutional conditions and the willingness and ability to restore those conditions. Whether existing or emerging leaders have the requisite vision, motives, and prospects involves a mix of moral and nonmoral questions: what the right vision is and the capacities, commitments, and prospects for success. These questions may be impossible to answer with much confidence in particular circumstances, because of the paucity of evidence regarding both the motives of the actors involved and the course of historical change together with questions regarding the best overall conception of preambular ends. But these difficulties do not invalidate the questions or preclude evidence favoring some answers over others in particular circumstances; nor do they cancel the duty to seek the best evidence.

Constitutional Success and Constitutional Reform

Returning to our three models of the Constitution as a whole—negative, welfarist, and procedural—we can confidently dismiss the negative model.[43] It makes no sense to establish government for the sake of limiting it or if prospects of harm from government outweigh prospects of benefits. This leaves us with the positive and procedural models, and if we view procedures as means to abstract ends, we can assume the validity of either model for present purposes. Starting with the positive model, we can say that judgments of constitutional failure presuppose concep-

---

42. 74 U.S. (7 Wall.) 506 (1869).

43. Dismissing the negative-rights model of the Constitution as a whole does not mean dismissing the value of negative rights, for, as already observed, some negative rights are functional to the pursuit of real ends.

tions of constitutional success and therewith conceptions of the social state of affairs that constitutional government is obligated to achieve. Writers about constitutional failure are thus obliged to defend their versions of this state of affairs. The conception I have defended elsewhere as a working hypothesis is the one that Diamond and Berns described as "the large commercial republic"—a regime committed to, for example, growth, equal opportunity, and fairness.[44] The soundness of this conception is irrelevant for present purposes; writers have challenged it over the years, on moral and historical grounds, and my point here depends on its fallibility. The ends of the Preamble considered holistically are neither semantically nor metaphysically reducible to "the large commercial republic." Justice, the common defense, and domestic tranquillity, for example, taken together do not *mean* "large commercial republic." Nor do the elements of the large commercial republic *constitute* the Preamble's ends taken together in the manner that, say, three legs and a seat, suitably formed, constitute a three-legged stool. The Preamble's ends taken as a whole may be summarized as Madison does in *The Federalist* where he says that "the real welfare of the great body of the people . . . is the supreme object to be pursued."[45] Alternatively, he refers in the same paragraph to "the happiness of the people," and later he says, famously, "Justice is the end of government" and "It ever has been, and ever will be pursued until it be obtained, or until liberty be lost in the pursuit."[46] Summarize preambular ends as you will, however, and there is still no reducing or equating them to "large commercial republic."

"Large commercial republic" can thus be no more than a mere conception of the ends of government. The same holds for any conception of the general welfare, the public's happiness, or justice. Any such conception can be wrong or inferior to alternative conceptions that are materially affordable and politically feasible. The modern Republican Party thus rejects "the large commercial republic" that Diamond attributed to the framers. Though the Party of Reagan promotes commerce, it rejects religious privatization and an active governmental commitment to economic fairness, as Diamond, extrapolating from *The Federalist* and anticipating Rawls, understood economic fairness.[47] The Reagan view of constitutional ends may prove politically feasible and morally more attractive than that of the American founding, as Diamond interpreted the founding. I mention this conflict here to illustrate both the contentious nature of any specific conception of constitutional ends, regardless of its pedigree, and the feasibility of alternative conceptions.

44. Barber, *Welfare and the Constitution*, 100–106.
45. *Federalist* No. 45, 309.
46. *Federalist* No. 51, 352.
47. See Barber, *Welfare and the Constitution*, 103.

While every judgment of constitutional failure presupposes a conception of constitutional ends, human fallibility makes every concrete theory of constitutional ends debatable and therewith provisional—sound as far as the present weight of the evidence. Theories of structural means are also debatable (except perhaps for the structure of debate itself). "Separation of powers" names one set of structural means, yet "separation of powers" attracts competing conceptions; one would restrain government, the other would enhance its competence.[48] "Federalism" names another structural arrangement, yet "dual federalism" competes with "national federalism." "Responsibility" names a relationship between institutional actors, yet responsibility *to* the electorate competes with responsibility *for* the public interest, in the face of public pressure if need be. Majoritarian democracy competes with constitutional democracy. And the procedural, negative, and positive versions of constitutional democracy compete with each other. All structural notions of any normative force attract competing conceptions, and the constitutional status of no such conception is beyond reasonable challenge.[49]

The provisional nature of structural arrangements is evinced by the actions of the framers themselves and in the way the Constitution presents its institutions. The Preamble offers the arrangements it prescribes as instruments of its ends, and the framers openly subordinated means to ends when they exceeded Congress's charge and proposed a new constitution and ratification by a provision other than mandated by the Articles. Antifederalists judged these decisions unconstitutional and declared that the framers' lawlessness would serve as an example for the subjects of the new constitution. Madison at least feigned a different view; he described the convention's choices as lawful. He observed in *The Federalist* that Congress had charged the convention with (1) "revising" the Articles in a manner (2) "adequate to the exigencies of government" and "the preservation of the Union." He reasoned that since the parts of this charge were "irreconcilably at variance with each other," the convention had to decide "which was the more important, which the less important part." Because

48. Gary Wills, *A Necessary Evil: A History of American Distrust of Government* (New York: Simon & Schuster, 1999), 73–75.

49. Barber and Fleming, *Constitutional Interpretation*, 117–33. This generalization would not hold for what could be the institutional notions of "reason" and "public reasonableness," for one cannot have a reason for rejecting reason or a public reason for rejecting public reasonableness. (One person or a few persons could of course have reasons for restricting the circle of persons to whom they give reasons.) Reservations in reason's behalf could in turn favor some institutional theories over others. An example might be national federalism over dual federalism. I argue to this effect in a work in progress, borrowing from my previous writings and from recent works like Malcolm M. Feeley and Edward Rubin, *Federalism: Political Identity and Tragic Compromises* (Ann Arbor: University of Michigan Press, 2008), esp. 103–23.

"the establishment of a government adequate to the national happiness was the end at which these articles [the Articles of Confederation] themselves originally aimed," and because experience under the Articles had proved that the nation's happiness required a real national government and a ratification procedure other than Article XIII (which, said Madison, risked "the absurdity" of putting the nation's fate in the hands of one-sixtieth of its population) the convention had acted consistently with its charge. What made this conduct lawful, said Madison, were "two rules of construction, dictated by plain reason as well as founded on legal axioms": "that every part of the [legal] expression ought, if possible, to be allowed some meaning, and made to conspire to some common end," and "that where the several parts cannot be made to coincide, the less important should give way to the more important part; the means should be sacrificed to the end, rather than the end to the means."[50]

Though Madison's claim of fidelity to Congress's charge has seemed disingenuous to observers over the years, his challenge remains: How can one obey a command whose elements conflict? What reasoning can support sacrificing ends to means when the means in question serve no equal or superior end and implicate no moral principle? Indeed, why sacrifice ends to means when doing so would offend a moral principle that is central to the nation's self-understanding, namely, that when a government ceases to be an instrument of its ends, "it is the Right of the People to alter or to abolish it." This twofold right (to alter and to abolish) makes *amendability* a moral imperative of liberal constitutionalism, an implication of practical reason itself.[51] Though the Articles of Confederation provided for amendments in Article XIII, Madison and everyone else knew that by requiring unanimous consent of the states, Article XIII made the nation's formal constitution virtually unamendable. That is, under the circumstances of the founding period, the particular content of Article XIII offended the very principle that Article XIII embodied, and fidelity to the principle was morally imperative.

Amendability thus complicates our view of fidelity to the Constitution or any constitution that is consistent with liberal principles. Because the Constitution provides for amendments and for legitimacy's sake must do so, fidelity to the Constitution cannot mean simple fidelity to the document as it might stand at any given moment. No one would say that the oath to preserve and defend the Constitution is an oath to oppose any and all constitutional amendments. Amendments are justified on instrumentalist grounds: the Constitution or some part of it is inadequate to,

---

50. *Federalist* No. 40, 258–60, 263.
51. Sotirios A. Barber, "Congress and Responsible Government," *Boston University Law Review* 89 (2009): 702–3.

perhaps even destructive of, the ends of government. If the will in the country is sufficient to achieve needed change in the officially prescribed way, the Constitution remains amendable and therewith consistent with its background principles. If the will and the official way lapse into chronic failure to coincide, as was the case in 1787, the Constitution ceases to be serviceable to its ends and loses thereby its morally obligatory force. [52] In these circumstances, the only constitutionalist course is extraconstitutional means to constitutional change—"changes ... instituted by some *informal and unauthorized propositions*, made by some patriotic and respectable citizens," as Madison put it.[53]

One need not agree with Madison's argument to acknowledge its respectability. Allowing merely this much has implications for the nature of constitutional failure. Most would say today as in 1787 that the Articles failed. *The Federalist* opens with a declaration of that failure and later describes the proposed changes as fundamental—"an alteration in the first principles and main pillars" of the Confederation.[54] But that the Confederation failed in all respects and that its failure amounted to total constitutional failure are debatable. Madison claimed, in effect, that fidelity to a lawful charge of the Confederation Congress opened the way to constitutional reform. And because the Confederation Congress was a creature of the Articles of Confederation and acted consistently with the Articles when it charged the Philadelphia Convention, one could say the Articles of Confederation itself was open to reform. The Philadelphia Convention, the Congress, and the state ratifying conventions can be seen as agents of constitutional reform acting under institutional understandings (Madison's interpretive "axioms" and the principle of amendability itself) that permitted such reform. A continuity of sorts can describe the change from the Articles to the Constitution. One can reasonably say that the latter succeeds the former in a line of succession constituted by one set of principles, the principles of the Declaration of Independence. Unequivocal constitutional failure would have occurred had the nation proved incapable of constitutional reform.

The experience of Lincoln and the framers shows that, given the "exigencies of government," the successful pursuit of ends like national security and the general welfare must allow for criticism of the nation's institutional arrangements and civic culture, the pursuit of truly constitutional conditions, and, if need be, constitutional change. Murphy thus treats the moral and intellectual capacity to make, maintain, and reform,

---

52. I defend this view of constitutional obligation in *On What the Constitution Means* (Baltimore: Johns Hopkins University Press, 1984), chap. 3.

53. *Federalist* No. 40, 265 (emphasis in original).

54. *Federalist* No. 1, 3; and No. 15, 93.

constitutions—as distinguished from fidelity to any given constitution—as the preeminent constitutional virtue.[55] This assessment fits the nation's view of Lincoln and the framers as the exemplars of republican statesmanship. Human fallibility and the reasons for adopting and maintaining constitutions make the capacity to reform them (even to remake them) as essential to the general welfare.[56] Define a constitution in terms of the aspirations and principles that justify its institutional arrangement "to a candid World," and one can argue that this constitution-making capacity literally *is* the constitution.[57] In any event, a constitution that leaves its people incapable of constitutional reform is at best a failure in progress.

Prospects for a Healthy Politics (Constitutional Success)

From the theory of constitutional success sketched here, it follows that a good constitution preserves doubt about its own success even as it works (with arguable success) to approximate its ends and maintain the capacity for constitutional reform. For these reasons, the current wave of commentary on constitutional failure renews a conversation without concluding it, and this conversation is a sign of constitutional health.

Yet the "capacity for constitutional reform" is the active and self-regarding virtue of a community; *The Federalist* calls it the capacity for "establishing good government from reflection and choice," rather than depending "on accident and force."[58] As a virtue of the community, the capacity for constitutional reform requires multiple actors in different roles. Publius says, we recall, that when institutions fail it is "essential that . . . changes be instituted by some *informal and unauthorized propositions*, made by some patriotic and respectable citizen or number of citizens."[59] He also says that "frequent reference of constitutional questions to the decision of the whole society" is a bad idea because in normal times the "spirit of party" will be connected to "the changes to be made." Submission to the people worked in revolutionary times, he says, largely because external dangers "repressed the passions most unfriendly to order and concord," "stifled the ordinary diversity of opinions on great national questions," created "a universal ardor for new and opposite

55. Murphy, *Constitutional Democracy*, 15–16, 522–36.

56. Barber, *Welfare and the Constitution*, 122–26.

57. Borrowing from Macedo on "public reasonableness" (*Liberal Virtues*, 41–45) and Diamond's view (from Aristotle) that "each political order is literally constituted by the kind of human character it aims . . . to form" (*As Far as Republican Principles Will Admit*, 340). I argue to this effect in "Congress and Responsible Government," 698–703.

58. *Federalist* No. 1, 3.

59. *Federalist* No. 40, 265 (emphasis in original).

forms," and fostered "an enthusiastic confidence of the people in their patriotic leaders."[60] Here, then, is the public and a competent segment thereof joined by relationships of loyalty and trust that are sustained by threats to the nation that all sides view in the same way, even as they disagree how best to respond to those threats.

At present the nation seems very far from any such situation. The nation's problems are there; what is missing is a leadership stratum that enjoys broad public trust—a leadership community that the public's major parts recognize as committed to addressing the nation's problems. The nation's present ideological divisions preclude both the formation and the recognition of such leaders. The root cause of these divisions may lie in some incorrigible features of the human condition, like a universal need for, and an inability to believe, stories about things like creation and redemption as hedges against an uncontrollable natural world of which mankind seems an insignificant part. Short of ultimate causes would be forces in modern life that defeat the sense of fallibility that a healthy politics presupposes. These forces include religious fundamentalism and its supposed opposites, the various forms of academic moral skepticism. They include secular dogmas like the laws of "history" and "the market." Tragically for the United States, given the framers' strategy against intoler- ance, they include the tendency of a commercial society to foster narrow conceptions of self and to substitute them for broad conceptions of self— "self-interest" for the "public interest" and "personal responsibility" for "social responsibility." Why debate ultimate practical questions if there are no ultimate practical questions—if, that is, you know what you want and pursuing your wants is a matter not of debating others but of bargain- ing with them? Why debate in good faith if you are certain of God's truth or history's truth or the market's truth? Why debate if there is no truth or approximate truth that can provide a good reason for what to do, perhaps even what to believe? Why debate if there is no truth or only your truth or as many truths as positions in the debate? Why debate in good faith if truth is an artifact of power or agreement secured through power?

The renewed concern for a healthy politic thus faces daunting challenges.

60. *Federalist* No. 49, 340–41.

2

Successful Failures of the American Constitution

JAMES E. FLEMING

What Is Constitutional Failure?

What is constitutional failure? Does it presuppose a conception of constitutional success and of the preconditions for constitutional success?[1] How does a constitutional failure differ from or relate to other constitutional misfortunes, such as an imperfection in the constitutional document (e.g., the imperfect provision for affirmative liberties, which has led to decisions like *Dandridge v. Williams, San Antonio v. Rodriguez, Harris v. McRae,* and *DeShaney v. Winnebago County*);[2] a decision in constitutional law that has horrible consequences for the lives of particular citizens or groups and for the way of life of the polity (e.g., *Dred Scott v. Sandford, Plessy v. Ferguson,* and *Korematsu v. United States*);[3] a decision that has disastrous consequences for interpretive method and for the development of doctrine in important areas (e.g., *Slaughter-House Cases* and *Bowers v. Hardwick*);[4] or a decision that makes a travesty of our constitutional order (e.g., *Buckley v. Valeo,* which reduces our political system from a fair scheme of equal participation to a veritable

I prepared an earlier draft of this article for the conference on "The Limits of Constitutional Democracy," held at Princeton University, February 14–16, 2008. I am grateful to Chris Eisgruber for his thoughtful comments on the draft on that occasion as well as to Sot Barber, Sandy Levinson, Steve Macedo, and Jeff Tulis for helpful communications about the article. I also benefited from presenting a subsequent draft in a faculty workshop at Boston University School of Law. I have incorporated an adapted version of part II in my article, "Toward a More Democratic Congress?" *Boston University Law Review* 89 (2009): 629.

1. Sotirios A. Barber, "Constitutional Failure: Ultimately Attitudinal," chapter 1 in this volume.

2. *Dandridge v. Williams,* 397 U.S. 471 (1970); *San Antonio v. Rodriguez,* 411 U.S. 1 (1973); *Harris v. McRae,* 448 U.S. 297 (1980); *DeShaney v. Winnebago County Dep't of Social Servs.,* 489 U.S. 189 (1989).

3. *Dred Scott v. Sandford,* 60 U.S. (19 How.) 393 (1857); *Plessy v. Ferguson,* 163 U.S. 537 (1896); *Korematsu v. United States,* 323 U.S. 214 (1944).

4. *Slaughter-House Cases,* 83 U.S. 36 (1872); *Bowers v. Hardwick,* 478 U.S. 186 (1986). Fortunately, *Bowers* was overruled by *Lawrence v. Texas,* 539 U.S. 558 (2003).

marketplace of ideas)?[5] Finally, how does a constitutional failure differ from or relate to a constitutional stupidity (e.g., the fact that the entire Bill of Rights did not apply to the states from the beginning) or a constitutional tragedy (e.g., the Supreme Court's holding in *Washington v. Glucksberg* that the Constitution does not protect the right to die, including the right of terminally ill persons to physician-assisted suicide)?[6]

We might also ask, how does a constitutional failure differ from or relate to other types of failure—for example, a moral, political, or institutional failure or a failure of policy? However we answer these questions, it seems clear that we have no dearth of constitutional misfortunes. Without purporting to answer them in this essay, I begin by making some observations about the discourse of failure that is in the air at the present time; then sketch the conceptions of constitutional success and failure that are implicit in my Constitution-perfecting theory of securing constitutional democracy; distinguish three possible sites of constitutional failure: creation, maintenance, and change; and discuss a phenomenon I call successful failures of the American Constitution.

Discourse of Failure in the Air

Whatever failure is, there is considerable talk of it in the air these days. Just consider these titles:

- Bruce Ackerman, *The Failure of the Founding Fathers: Jefferson, Marshall, and the Rise of Presidential Democracy*
- Ronald Dworkin, *Is Democracy Possible Here? Principles for a New Political Debate*
- Alan Wolfe, *Does American Democracy Still Work?*
- Sanford Levinson, *Our Undemocratic Constitution: Where the Constitution Goes Wrong (and How We the People Can Correct It)*[7]

5. *Buckley v. Valeo*, 424 U.S. 1 (1976).

6. See William N. Eskridge Jr. and Sanford Levinson, eds., *Constitutional Stupidities, Constitutional Tragedies* (New York: New York University Press, 1998), in particular, James E. Fleming, "Constitutional Tragedy in Dying: Or Whose Tragedy Is It, Anyway?" (ibid., 162). I have drawn the opening paragraph in this article from that essay.

7. Bruce Ackerman, *The Failure of the Founding Fathers: Jefferson, Marshall, and the Rise of Presidential Democracy* (Cambridge: Harvard University Press, 2005); Ronald Dworkin, *Is Democracy Possible Here? Principles for a New Political Debate* (Princeton: Princeton University Press, 2006); Alan Wolfe, *Does American Democracy Still Work?* (New Haven: Yale University Press, 2006); and Sanford Levinson, *Our Undemocratic Constitution: Where the Constitution Goes Wrong (and How We the People Can Correct It)* (New York: Oxford University Press, 2006).

Consider also:

- John Dean, *Broken Government: How Republican Rule Destroyed the Legislative, Executive, and Judicial Branches*
- Thomas Mann and Norman Ornstein, *The Broken Branch: How Congress Is Failing America and How to Get It Back on Track*
- Larry Sabato, *A More Perfect Constitution: 23 Proposals to Revitalize Our Constitution and Make America a Fairer Country*
- Robert Kuttner, *The Squandering of America: How the Failure of Our Politics Undermines Our Prosperity*
- Sheldon Wolin, *Democracy Incorporated: Managed Democracy and the Specter of Inverted Totalitarianism*[8]

Before this recent spate of books, there was:

- Mark Brandon's *Free in the World: American Slavery and Constitutional Failure*
- John Finn's *Constitutions in Crisis: Political Violence and the Rule of Law*
- Ellen Kennedy's *Constitutional Failure: Carl Schmitt in Weimar*[9]

I should also mention Will Harris's *The Interpretable Constitution* and Sotirios Barber's *On What the Constitution Means*, for both of these works prefigure the discussion of failure today.[10] Doubtless there are other examples as well, but this list should serve to illustrate the range of discourse about failure.[11]

8. John Dean, *Broken Government: How Republican Rule Destroyed the Legislative, Executive, and Judicial Branches* (New York: Viking, 2007); Thomas Mann and Norman Ornstein, *The Broken Branch: How Congress Is Failing America and How to Get It Back on Track* (New York: Oxford University Press, 2006); Larry J. Sabato, *A More Perfect Constitution: 23 Proposals to Revitalize Our Constitution and Make America a Fairer Country* (New York: Walker, 2007); Robert Kuttner, *The Squandering of America: How the Failure of Our Politics Undermines Our Prosperity* (New York: Alfred A. Knopf, 2007); and Sheldon Wolin, *Democracy Incorporated: Managed Democracy and the Specter of Inverted Totalitarianism* (Princeton: Princeton University Press, 2008).

9. Mark Brandon, *Free in the World: American Slavery and Constitutional Failure* (Princeton: Princeton University Press, 1998); John Finn, *Constitutions in Crisis: Political Violence and the Rule of Law* (New York: Oxford University Press, 1991); and Ellen Kennedy, *Constitutional Failure: Carl Schmitt in Weimar* (Durham, NC: Duke University Press, 2004).

10. William F. Harris II, *The Interpretable Constitution* (Baltimore: Johns Hopkins University Press, 1993); Sotirios A. Barber, *On What the Constitution Means* (Baltimore: Johns Hopkins University Press,1984).

11. Mark Brandon has offered a useful typology, distinguishing four distinct types or domains of constitutional failure: a failure of constitutionalism; a failure of a constitution; a failure of constitutional order; and a failure of constitutional discourse. Brandon strikingly observes that success in one domain can contribute to failure in another, and vice versa. Brandon, *Free in the World*, 18–22. I would add that we might even conceive of successful failures: features of a constitution that fail to work as contemplated or designed (from the

We should ask, are these authors really arguing that we are experienc-
ing a *constitutional* failure, as distinguished from a moral failure, a political failure, an institutional failure, or a failure of policy that may or may
not be directly related to the Constitution? To be talking about distinctly
constitutional failure, I submit, one has to be talking about failures *of*
the Constitution, failures *caused by* the Constitution, failures *stemming
from* a feature or defect of the Constitution, even failures *required by* the
Constitution, or the like. For example, if a filibuster in the Senate somehow were to cause a breakdown of the federal government and the constitutional order, that would not be a constitutional failure because the
Constitution does not require the availability of filibusters (and, indeed,
some have argued that they are unconstitutional). On the other hand,
if the Supreme Court's decision in *Bush v. Gore*,[12] resulting in the victory of George W. Bush in the Electoral College, somehow had provoked
a democratic revolution and the overthrow not only of President Bush
and the Supreme Court but indeed of the entire constitutional order, that
would be a constitutional failure, because the Constitution requires the
election of the president through the Electoral College system and thus
the Supreme Court's decision in *Bush v. Gore* is directly related to it.

The striking fact of the matter is that, for all the ominous talk of failure,
it is for the most part not talk of constitutional failure in this sense. Instead,
it is talk of other sorts of shortcomings or failure: a moral failure (e.g., in
which a people prove to lack the public reasonableness and religious moderation necessary for a morally pluralistic constitutional democracy);[13] a
political failure (e.g., the emergence of a new form of democratic politics
that prompts analysts to ask whether American democracy still works);[14]
an institutional failure (e.g., the developments leading to the diagnosis of
the institution of Congress as "the broken branch");[15] or a failure of policy (e.g., a policy that has unintended bad consequences or indeed makes
a problem worse rather than helping to solve it).

Some readers may see this as an overly limited, legalistic, or formalistic
understanding of "constitution" and constitutional failure. My account is
indeed formalistic, as Christopher Eisgruber has suggested.[16] It is in fact

---

standpoint of some interpretations) but nonetheless work tolerably well or even better than
contemplated or designed and in that sense are successful. I say more about this in the final
section.

12. 531 U.S. 98 (2000).

13. See, e.g., Dworkin, *Democracy*, 52–55; James E. Fleming, *Securing Constitutional
Democracy: The Case of Autonomy* (Chicago: University of Chicago Press, 2006), 226.

14. See Wolfe, *Democracy*.

15. See Mann and Ornstein, *Broken Branch*.

16. Christopher L. Eisgruber, "Comments for Panel on 'Philosophical and Theoretical
Perspectives on Constitutional Failure and Success,'" presented at the conference on "The
Limits of Constitutional Democracy," Princeton University, February 15, 2008.

proudly formalistic. I think that drawing these distinctions is the most clear-headed way to proceed in thinking about constitutional failure. To be sure, we might expect that any constitutional failure is likely to be accompanied by moral failure, political failure, institutional failure, or failures of policy (though not necessarily so), but that is not to say that moral failure, political failure, institutional failure, or failures of policy are necessarily accompanied by constitutional failure. Even if these types of failure may be interrelated, they are not the same thing.

Thus, it appears that the worrisome states of affairs diagnosed are not failures of the Constitution, failures required by the Constitution, or failures directly attributable to the Constitution. Of course, it could be the case that these types of failure are ultimately attributable to the Constitution in the sense that they are made more likely by our constitutional design. This seems to be the suggestion of Barber's criticism of Madison's (and our Constitution's) eschewal of the Aristotelian tradition of "supplying the defect of better motives" by inculcating moral and civic virtues in favor of a strategy of private incentives.[17] Moreover, it could be the case that long-term or endemic failures of institutions, or a decay in the political culture, are ultimately attributable, indirectly, to the Constitution, if only in the sense that the Constitution did not establish better institutions or better mechanisms for inculcating and maintaining a healthy political culture.[18] But, again, it seems more clear-headed to see such failures as institutional failures or moral failures rather than as constitutional failures as such.

Let me illustrate my claim with a few observations about Levinson's recent book, *Our Undemocratic Constitution: Where the Constitution Goes Wrong (and How We the People Can Correct It)*. I think his book is the closest thing we have in mainstream constitutional scholarship to an argument that the U.S. Constitution has failed or is in serious danger of failing. Levinson is talking about potential constitutional failure in my formal sense: failures *of* the Constitution, failures *directly attributable to* the Constitution, indeed perhaps failures *required by* the Constitution—these would be failures *caused by* the "hard-wired" features of the structural Constitution that he criticizes. However, he does not talk about actual failure but about serious defects, problematic dysfunction, and "hard-wired" features of our structural Constitution that could contribute to a crisis if not a failure.[19] Nowhere does he say our Constitution has failed. Indeed, much of his gripe with the Constitution and our constitutional culture concerns the extent to which we venerate the

17. Barber, "Constitutional Failure."
18. I want to thank Steve Macedo and Jeff Tulis for pressing this possibility.
19. Levinson, *Undemocratic Constitution*, 22–24.

Constitution and view it as a success. Thus, he laments how difficult it is to arouse people about the need for a constitutional convention to make basic changes in the structural Constitution.[20] He is frustrated that it is such a struggle to get people to see, as he puts it in his title, "where the Constitution goes wrong." It is even more difficult to motivate them to press for a constitutional amendment, let alone a constitutional convention, to correct it.

What exactly is Levinson's indictment of the U.S. Constitution? He argues that it is seriously *undemocratic* as measured by a normative theory of democracy that is more majoritarian than the arrangements established in the Constitution. His criticism also includes a number of empirical propositions in support of the view that the constitutional order is dysfunctional, if not broken.[21] He fears that the undemocratic features of our structural Constitution he criticizes may contribute to constitutional crises, and he tells us about a number of crises that we have narrowly averted (including some about which we did not even know). For example, in 1976, had only 5,559 voters in Ohio and 3,687 voters in Hawaii voted for Gerald Ford instead of Jimmy Carter, Ford would have had 269 electoral votes to Carter's 268 and Reagan's 1, and that would have sent the choice to the House of Representatives.[22]

But his analysis, focusing as it does on the "hard-wired" features of our structural Constitution that have been in place since the beginning,[23] could have been written at nearly any time during the nation's history,

---

20. Ibid., 167–80.

21. Levinson told me in an email that he had proposed to Oxford University Press the title of "Our Broken Constitution," but they declined because they had already used "broken" in the title of the Mann and Ornstein book, *The Broken Branch*. Mann and Ornstein diagnose the institutional failure of Congress. For what it is worth, I think it is a good thing that Oxford did not let Levinson use that title, because it would not have fit his book as well as the title they agreed upon does.

22. Levinson, *Undemocratic Constitution*, 94. See also Sanford Levinson and Jack M. Balkin, "Constitutional Crises," *University of Pennsylvania Law Review* 157 (2009): 707.

23. The Constitution, even if not perfectly democratic, is still standing, and so these "hard-wired" features of the structural Constitution have not caused failure yet. And so, if Levinson's diagnosis is one of constitutional failure, it presumably is an argument that the seeds of failure were planted by mistakes at the very beginning and that these seeds are ripening into possible failure at some point in the future. In any case, he is not arguing that the Constitution, however woefully undemocratic, has failed. (Quite apart from Levinson's analysis of the "hard-wired" features of the structural Constitution, I hasten to acknowledge that some have argued that the Constitution did fail during the Civil War, in part because of the seeds of failure that were planted at the very beginning. See, e.g., Brandon, *Free in the World*; Mark A. Graber, *Dred Scott and the Problem of Constitutional Evil* [New York: Cambridge University Press, 2006].)

and certainly any time during the twentieth century.[24] Granted, the presidential election controversy culminating in *Bush v. Gore*,[25] shifts in population resulting in the disproportionate influence of small states in the Senate and the Electoral College, and the emergence of the red states–blue states phenomenon (with small red states having disproportionate influence in the Senate and presidential elections) give the book a special urgency at the present time. Nonetheless, even if George W. Bush had easily carried Florida in the 2000 presidential election and Al Gore had conceded defeat on election night, Levinson still would have viewed the outcome as a travesty that demonstrates one important place where the Constitution goes wrong (and what We the People should do to correct it). After all, Gore still would have won the nationwide popular vote by a considerable margin and still would have lost in the Electoral College, 271–267. And so, Levinson still would have called for the abolition or reform of the Electoral College in favor of direct popular vote and a requirement that, to be elected, a presidential candidate must win a majority of the popular vote.[26]

Thus, Levinson's book is not simply a diagnosis of constitutional failure at the present time. Instead, it is a descendant of writing during the Progressive Era castigating the Constitution for being undemocratic and for not embodying more features of a British-style system of parliamentary supremacy. Not surprisingly, he praises this Progressive Era literature and the Progressive movement for constitutional change. Woodrow Wilson could have written much of this book (in fact, Levinson concludes his book with a quotation from Wilson himself).[27]

In sum, Levinson does not so much argue that the Constitution has failed as that the Constitution is seriously imperfect from the critical standpoint of a normative political theory of majoritarian democracy that is not embodied in the Constitution. He criticizes the conception of democracy—with all its limitations on majority rule and one person, one vote—established by the Constitution. Thus, his book is notably different from the other books about failure in an important respect: the other books are clearly for and about our present predicament—for example, Alan Wolfe's *Does American Democracy Still Work?*, the title of which implies that it used to work but no longer does. Now I turn from Levinson's argument that the Constitution is imperfectly democratic to my own Constitution-perfecting theory of securing constitutional democracy.

24. I say that this analysis could have been written at any time during the twentieth century because I recognize that some of the features of our practice that he criticizes, such as policy-based presidential vetoes and filibusters in the Senate, developed over time.

25. 531 U.S. 98 (2000).

26. See Levinson, *Undemocratic Constitution*, 81–97.

27. Ibid., 181.

Constitutional Failure from the Standpoint of a Constitution-Perfecting Theory

Anyone who knows my work may ask, what am I doing writing about constitutional failure? After all, in my book, *Securing Constitutional Democracy*, I put forward a "Constitution-perfecting theory," a theory that strives to interpret the American Constitution so as to make it the best it can be.[28] And I might be accused of subscribing to the "perfect Constitution" view that Henry Monaghan famously derided (and that Eisgruber has cleverly analyzed).[29] That makes me seem like an unlikely candidate for a being a contributor to a book on constitutional failure. But there is no inconsistency between propounding a Constitution-perfecting theory and believing that the American Constitution as it stands is seriously flawed. Similarly, there is no inconsistency between Ronald Dworkin's propounding a moral reading of the Constitution and a view of constitutional interpretation that aspires to "happy endings,"[30] while also writing a book that asks "Is Democracy Possible Here?"[31] A Constitution-perfecting theory does not entail that the Constitution is the best a constitution can be. Rather, it entails that in interpreting whatever imperfect constitution we have, we should strive to make it the best it can be.

I plan to sketch the conceptions of constitutional success and failure that are implicit in my Constitution-perfecting theory of securing constitutional democracy. I want to begin by suggesting three possible sites of constitutional failure. Here I draw from Walter F. Murphy's *Constitutional Democracy: Creating and Maintaining a Just Political Order*. In that book, Murphy does not develop a theory of constitutional failure as such. Instead, he focuses on constitutional creation, maintenance, and change.[32] Nonetheless, we can infer from his analysis three principal possible sites of constitutional failure, to wit: creation, maintenance, and change.

A. Failure in Creating a Constitution

First, a constitution or constitutional order might fail in its very *creation*. It might be analogous to a product that is botched in its very design. It might prove to be wholly inadequate to pursuing its own ends, much

28. Fleming, *Securing Constitutional Democracy*, 4, 16, 210–11.

29. Henry P. Monaghan, "Our Perfect Constitution," *New York University Law Review* 56 (1981): 353; Christopher L. Eisgruber, "Justice and the Text: Rethinking the Constitutional Relation between Principle and Prudence," *Duke Law Journal* 43 (1993): 1, 7.

30. Ronald Dworkin, *Freedom's Law: The Moral Reading of the American Constitution* (Cambridge: Harvard University Press, 1996), 38.

31. Dworkin, *Democracy*.

32. Walter F. Murphy, *Constitutional Democracy: Creating and Maintaining a Just Political Order* (Baltimore: Johns Hopkins University Press, 2007).

less any desirable ends worthy of a people aspiring to constitutional self-government. The Articles of Confederation, Barber points out, failed in this way.[33] He adds, though, that the Articles were not a total constitutional failure. We the People, after all, proved capable of constitutional reform, of forming "a more perfect union" through adopting the Constitution.

B. Failure through Inadequate Maintenance

Second, a constitution or constitutional order might fail because of improper or inadequate *maintenance*. In *American Constitutional Interpretation*, Murphy, Barber, Stephen Macedo, and I conceive the enterprise of constitutional interpretation on the basis of three fundamental interrogatives: What is the Constitution, who may authoritatively interpret it, and how ought it to be interpreted?[34] Murphy's idea of constitutional interpretation as constitutional maintenance,[35] which I share, fosters a more comprehensive and comprehending view of all three interrogatives—*what*, *who*, and *how*—than do conventional accounts of constitutional interpretation, especially originalist accounts.

What is the Constitution? On our view, the Constitution includes not only the constitutional document but also the broader constitutional order: original meaning or understanding, underlying political theories of democracy and constitutionalism, previous interpretations as the constitutional order has developed, settled practices, traditions, and aspirations. Furthermore, the constitutional document and constitutional order encompass purposes such as those set forth in the Preamble. *Who may interpret?* Instead of judicial monopoly, we embrace departmentalism, that is, dividing yet sharing interpretive authority among courts, legislatures, executives, and the citizens. *How to interpret?* Quite unlike a "clause-bound interpretivism" or narrow originalism, I have defended a philosophic approach to and Constitution-perfecting theory of constitutional interpretation.[36]

I want to make three points about the idea of constitutional maintenance in relation to the idea of constitutional failure. My first point concerns the idea of maintenance itself: it underscores that the Constitution is not "a machine that would go of itself." Instead, it is a scheme that requires maintenance and repair to make it work, to keep it from failing. To be sure, the departmentalism that I have defended is hospitable to the

---

33. Barber, "Constitutional Failure."

34. Walter F. Murphy, James E. Fleming, Sotirios A. Barber, and Stephen Macedo, *American Constitutional Interpretation*, 4th ed. (New York: Foundation Press, 2008), 1–21.

35. Murphy, *Constitutional Democracy*, 460–96.

36. Sotirios A. Barber and James E. Fleming, *Constitutional Interpretation: The Basic Questions* (New York: Oxford University Press, 2007); Fleming, *Securing Constitutional Democracy*.

view that constitutional norms are self-enforcing through the operation of the political processes to a greater degree than is acknowledged by conventional court-centered accounts.[37] Such accounts mistakenly think that the protection of constitutional norms comes only from courts enforcing them against the political processes. But Murphy's and my accounts emphasize the place of courts in the larger institutional scheme of courts, legislatures, and executives sharing authority and responsibility to interpret the Constitution so as to maintain the system. Furthermore, our idea of maintenance is more comprehensive and comprehending than interpretation conceived in narrow originalist fashion as doing backward-looking historical research into relatively concrete original meanings and then preserving those meanings against encroachment or change.

The second point stems from the fact, already noted, that the idea of constitutional interpretation as constitutional maintenance encourages a broader view of *what* and *how* than do conventional accounts, in particular, originalist accounts. It fosters a salutary concern for furthering the purposes of the constitutional order instead of being focused in a backward-looking way with interpreting narrowly conceived clauses in isolation or with taking a litigation-oriented perspective.

Originalists typically claim that they have a monopoly on the classical, interpretive justification of judicial review: courts are to interpret the Constitution and to *preserve* it against encroachment by legislative and executive encroachment.[38] Originalists might say that they, too, believe in constitutional maintenance in this sense of *preservation*. For example, Scalia likes to say that the point of the Constitution is to preserve the original meaning of the Constitution and to prevent change. Indeed, he has written that the Constitution's "whole purpose is to prevent change." According to Scalia, "A society that adopts a bill of rights is skeptical that 'evolving standards of decency' always 'mark progress,' and that societies always 'mature,' as opposed to rot."[39] For a society or a constitution to "rot" sounds like a form of failure.

But narrow originalism, if scrupulously practiced, would be a poor form of constitutional maintenance. It would shackle us to the relatively concrete original meanings, expectations, and applications of the framers and

37. Fleming, *Securing Constitutional Democracy*, 70–71, 74, 167–70; James E. Fleming, "The Constitution Outside the Courts," *Cornell Law Review* 86 (2000): 215; James E. Fleming, "Judicial Review without Judicial Supremacy: Taking the Constitution Seriously Outside the Courts," *Fordham Law Review* 73 (2005): 1377.

38. See Fleming, *Securing Constitutional Democracy*, 20–21, criticizing Robert H. Bork, *The Tempting of America* (New York: Free Press, 1990), 143–60, and Antonin Scalia, "Originalism: The Lesser Evil," *University of Cincinnati Law Review* 57 (1989): 849, 862–64.

39. Antonin Scalia, *A Matter of Interpretation* (Princeton: Princeton University Press, 1997), 40–41.

ratifiers.[40] Indeed, thankfully for the sake of maintenance, originalism is honored more in the breach than in the observance. If you have any doubts on this score, I would point out that originalists' common complaint is that judicial decisions have not followed the original meaning of the Constitution as they understand it.[41] I daresay that we would not have originalism as a polemical movement if our practice were in fact originalist.

The third point concerns the fact that the idea of constitutional interpretation as constitutional maintenance fosters a broader view of *who* than do conventional accounts. It fosters a healthy, vigorous departmentalism, as opposed to conventional accounts of judicial monopoly or at least judicial supremacy, especially the hubristic view of the Rehnquist Court (and possibly the Roberts Court). Despite the claims of judicial monopoly or judicial supremacy, the actual practice of most arrangements in fact produces some form of departmentalism. Some form of departmentalism is healthier than having courts be the ultimate if not the exclusive interpreter of the Constitution. We should, with Murphy, situate interpreters as political actors in the political system and conceive interpretation as part of the operation of the political system, not simply as the peculiar province of judges divining and enforcing the original meaning of a legal document.[42] This conception of constitutional maintenance at once broadens what courts' constitutional responsibilities are and broadens what legislative and executive responsibilities are. Legislatures and executives share in the responsibilities of both interpretation and maintenance. Under such a departmentalist arrangement, a constitutional order may be more successful at constitutional maintenance that staves off decline, breakdown, and failure than under a system of judicial monopoly that ignores the imperatives of constitutional statesmanship and drives out the idea of taking the Constitution seriously outside the courts.

C. Failure through Change or Reform

Third, a constitution or constitutional order might fail with respect to *change* or *reform*. I distinguish two types of such failure. One, a people might lose the very capacity to change or reform. For a people committed to constitutional self-government, this clearly would be a form of failure.[43] There may be implicit in Levinson's criticism of our undemocratic

40. See Barber and Fleming, *Constitutional Interpretation*, 79–98.

41. See ibid., 79–98; Michael C. Dorf, "Integrating Normative and Descriptive Constitutional Theory: The Case of Original Meaning," *Georgetown Law Journal* 85 (1997): 1765; James E. Fleming, "Fidelity to Our Imperfect Constitution," *Fordham Law Review* 65 (1997): 1335, 1347.

42. Murphy, *Constitutional Democracy*, 460–96.

43. Barber, "Constitutional Failure"; Murphy, *Constitutional Democracy*, 17–19, 497–529.

Constitution and, in particular, Article V's onerous procedures for amendment the charge that they have enervated or destroyed our very capacity to change or reform through constitutional amendment.

Two, a constitution or constitutional order might breach the limits of legitimate constitutional change, for example, by adopting what Murphy would conceive as an unconstitutional amendment,[44] or by adopting what my theory of securing constitutional democracy would conceive as an amendment repudiating fundamental preconditions for the trustworthiness and legitimacy of our constitutional democracy.[45] Those, too, would be forms of failure or breakdown. We should distinguish, with Murphy, between *amending* a constitutional order (correcting, adjusting, or modifying it) and *repudiating* it (destroying it and creating another one).[46] Amendments repudiating unalienable rights or constitutive principles would signal a repudiation or breakdown of the existing regime or a change of identity to a new regime by destroying an existing constitutional order and creating another one.

My Constitution-perfecting theory of securing constitutional democracy presupposes a conception of constitutional success and of the preconditions for constitutional success. I develop a guiding framework with two fundamental themes: first, securing the basic liberties that are preconditions for *deliberative democracy* to enable citizens to apply their capacity for a conception of justice to deliberating about and judging the justice of basic institutions and social policies as well as the common good; and, second, securing the basic liberties that are preconditions for *deliberative autonomy* to enable citizens to apply their capacity for a conception of the good to deliberating about and deciding how to live their own lives. Together, these themes afford everyone the status of free and equal citizenship in our morally pluralistic constitutional democracy. They reflect two bedrock structures of our constitutional scheme: deliberative political and personal self-government. Each theme would secure preconditions for the trustworthiness of the outcomes of the political process in our constitutional democracy. That is, to be trustworthy, a constitutional democracy must secure and respect a scheme of basic liberties that guarantees the preconditions not only for deliberative democracy but also for deliberative autonomy.[47]

What would constitute a failure or breakdown with respect to these preconditions for a trustworthy and successful constitutional democracy?

---

44. Murphy, *Constitutional Democracy*, 18–19, 516–21. I should also mention Harris's rich and subtle analysis of the limits of textual amendability. Harris, *Interpretable Constitution*, 164–208.

45. Fleming, *Securing Constitutional Democracy*, 10, 73–74.

46. Murphy, *Constitutional Democracy*, 506–8.

47. Fleming, *Securing Constitutional Democracy*, 10, 73–74.

I certainly do not wish to suggest that every time the government fails to respect a basic liberty—for example, the Supreme Court's failure to recognize the right to die, including the right of terminally ill persons to physician-assisted suicide[48]—that the Constitution or constitutional order has failed. What, then, would constitute a failure or breakdown with respect to the preconditions for deliberative democracy and deliberative autonomy? To illustrate the two together, I offer an example drawn from Bruce Ackerman's defense of "dualist democracy" as the best account of our Constitution in his *We the People: Foundations*.[49]

Ackerman contends that our Constitution, unlike the German Basic Law, is open to "morally disastrous" amendments repealing fundamental rights.[50] To test this contention, he conjures up two hypothetical Christianity amendments. The first establishes Christianity as the state religion of the American people, thereby repealing the fundamental right to liberty of conscience. (Liberty of conscience is a precondition for deliberative autonomy.) The second forbids repeal of the first, thereby entrenching it and in effect repealing freedom of speech and dualist democracy itself.[51] (Freedom of speech is a precondition for both deliberative democracy and deliberative autonomy.) Ackerman states that "dualist democrats" like himself would accept these amendments as valid, while "rights foundationalists" (a view he attributes to John Rawls, Ronald Dworkin, Walter Murphy, and me) would reject them as unconstitutional. Asserting that in America, unlike Germany, "almost all lawyers" would consider "absurd" or "preposterous" the idea that an amendment to the Constitution might be unconstitutional, Ackerman claims that his theory of dualist democracy better fits our constitutional order than does rights foundationalism.[52]

Yet Ackerman himself does not say simply that the hypothetical amendment repealing liberty of conscience is valid because it has been

---

48. *Washington v. Glucksberg*, 521 U.S. 702 (1997), criticized in Fleming, *Securing Constitutional Democracy*, 220–26.

49. Bruce Ackerman, *We the People: Foundations* (Cambridge: Harvard University Press, 1991). I have developed a fuller analysis of Ackerman's argument in James E. Fleming, "We the Exceptional American People," in *Constitutional Politics: Essays on Constitution Making, Maintenance, and Change*, ed. Sotirios A. Barber and Robert P. George (Princeton: Princeton University Press, 2001), 91.

50. Ackerman, *We the People*, 14–15.

51. Ibid., 14–15 and 15–16 n.

52. Ibid., 15 and 15 n. Ackerman states: "I doubt, moreover, that one may find many American lawyers who seriously disagree—even among those who presently wrap themselves up in foundationalist rhetoric." Ibid., 14–15. He does, however, mention Walter Murphy as "a constitutionalist who may have the courage of his foundationalist convictions." See Bruce Ackerman, "Constitutional Politics/Constitutional Law," *Yale Law Journal* 99 (1989): 453, 470 n. 28, citing Walter F. Murphy, "*Slaughter House*, Civil Rights, and the Limits on Constitutional Change," *American Journal of Jurisprudence* 32 (1987): 1.

ratified through Article V procedures. Instead, he concedes that it would inaugurate a "deep transformation" of our Constitution: "on more or less the same order, though of a very different kind," as the transformations to new "regimes" within dualist democracy achieved by the Reconstruction Republicans and New Deal Democrats.[53] Nor does Ackerman say simply that the hypothetical amendment entrenching such a repeal is valid, because the voice of the People has duly spoken. Rather, he states that it would amount to a "repeal of dualist democracy itself."[54] That is, the latter amendment would go beyond the former's deep transformation within dualist democracy to a repeal of that order. From the standpoint of my theory, Ackerman's hypothetical amendments would amount to a constitutional breakdown or revolution, ushering in a new constitutional order altogether.[55]

These two hypothetical amendments illustrate the possibility of breakdown or failure through repudiation of unalienable basic liberties that are preconditions for deliberative democracy and deliberative autonomy. What about the possibility of breakdown or failure with respect to the structural features or principles of the Constitution? Are there structural features and principles that are similarly constitutive, indeed unalienable, such that either their failure to work as originally contemplated or their repudiation through constitutional amendment would signal constitutional breakdown or failure? I take up the second by briefly analyzing Levinson's proposed amendments to the structural Constitution. Then

53. Ackerman, *We the People*, 14. For Ackerman's argument for a "regime perspective," or for conceiving our constitutional history in terms of three regimes or republics (those inaugurated by the Founding, Reconstruction, and the New Deal), see ibid., 58–67.

54. Ibid., 15–16 n. Ackerman's implicit distinction between "deep transformations" within dualist democracy and a "repeal of dualist democracy itself" bears a resemblance to Murphy's distinction between amending a constitutional order (correcting, adjusting, or modifying it) and repudiating it (destroying it and creating another one). See, e.g., Walter F. Murphy, "An Ordering of Constitutional Values," *Southern California Law Review* 53 (1978): 703, 757. The Supreme Court of California, drawing a distinction between "amendment" and "revision," struck down a state constitutional amendment, adopted by referendum, that would have required state judges, when interpreting the state constitution, to follow the United States Supreme Court's interpretations of similarly worded clauses in the national constitutional document. See Walter F. Murphy, "Merlin's Memory: The Past and Future Imperfect of the Once and Future Polity," in *Responding to Imperfection*, ed. Sanford Levinson (Princeton: Princeton University Press, 1995), 163, 177, discussing *Raven v. Deukmejian*, 801 P.2d 1077 (Cal. 1990). The Court reasoned that such a change "would so fundamentally transform California's status as a member of a federal union as to effect a constitutional revision; and the [constitutional] text provided that 'revisions' could be accomplished only by special conventions."

55. John Rawls, *Political Liberalism* (New York: Columbia University Press, 1993), 239; Samuel Freeman, "Original Meaning, Democratic Interpretation, and the Constitution," *Philosophy & Public Affairs* 21 (1992): 3, 41–42.

I consider the first by discussing what I call successful failures of the American Constitution.

Would any of the amendments that Levinson hopes for repudiate any unalienable principles of deliberative democracy? I am assuming that we would not have a constitutional convention (contrary to Levinson's hopes),[56] but that we nonetheless would adopt several amendments he would support to eliminate or mitigate the undemocratic features of the Constitution he condemns. For example, we might abolish the Electoral College in favor of direct popular election of the president and a requirement that, to be elected, a presidential candidate must win a majority of the popular vote. And we might amend Article V to eliminate the role of the states in amending the Constitution and to make it easier for the people to amend it, for example, in favor of requiring proposal by 60 percent of the federal legislators and ratification by 60 percent of the voters in a national referendum. (I chose 60 percent to make the process more onerous than requiring only a simple majority but less burdensome than requiring the present proposal by two-thirds of both houses of Congress and ratification by three-fourths of the states.) We might even abolish the Senate in favor of unicameralism. (Article V does say that "no state, without its consent, shall be deprived of its equal suffrage in the Senate," but it does not say that we have to have a Senate. Arguably we could repeal Article I's provisions establishing a Senate.) We could come up with many other changes to the "hard-wired" features of the structural Constitution that Levinson might support.

Would any of these amendments go beyond the limits of legitimate constitutional change and signal a breakdown or failure? I think not. None of them would be incompatible with, much less destroy, our scheme of constitutional democracy. To be sure, some of the changes would make the Constitution more of a majoritarian "representative democracy" as distinguished from a "constitutional democracy."[57] But such changes would not move us so far on the continuum from constitutional democracy to majoritarian representative democracy as to make it appear that we had alienated our "unalienable" rights or repudiated our basic principles, that is, renounced principles that are the essence of our constitutional democracy. This should come as no surprise, because Levinson's concern is with changing certain "hard-wired" details of our structural Constitution,[58] not with repudiating fundamental rights protecting the dignity, liberty, or equality of individuals or groups. The latter are what we more commonly think of as "unalienable rights" or fundamental, constitutive principles

56. Levinson, *Undemocratic Constitution*, 11–24.
57. Murphy et al., *American Constitutional Interpretation*, 45–64.
58. Levinson, *Undemocratic Constitution*, 22, 108.

that are preconditions for the success of our constitutional democracy. Repudiating them might rise to the level of failure or breakdown because doing so might repudiate the constitutional order itself.

Successful Failures of the American Constitution

Again, Barber points out that any theory of constitutional failure presupposes a conception of constitutional success and of the preconditions for constitutional success.[59] We should also recognize the possibility of successful failures. Sometimes, features of a constitution or constitutional order fail to work as contemplated or designed, but that failure turns out to be a good thing. For things work differently than contemplated, but they still work tolerably well or even better, all things considered, than they would have if they had worked as contemplated. Let me mention several examples of such successful failures.

The first three examples involve situations where there are two fundamentally different, yet plausible, interpretations of the Constitution's original meaning or strategy available. I concede for the sake of argument that one (the weaker interpretation) was the original meaning, suggest that it has failed in the sense that we have not followed it, and then suggest that the Constitution has succeeded by following the other (the better interpretation). These examples are deliberately counterfactual (some readers might say, perversely so) in the sense that I do not believe that the Constitution, on its best interpretations, was in fact originally designed to operate in the ways contemplated by them. My point is twofold. First, if the Constitution in fact had operated in these ways, in accordance with these plausible but weaker interpretations, it might well have failed by now. And, second, because the Constitution in fact has not operated in these ways, but rather has operated in accordance with the better interpretations, it has been tolerably successful. When there are two radically different competing, plausible understandings of the Constitution, sometimes the better interpretation succeeds, and we avert the failure that might have ensued had the weaker interpretation been adopted.

First, consider the successful failure of the strategy of enumerated federal powers. Assume for the sake of argument—with the Antifederalists and the Federalist Society today—that the original Constitution's strategy was to conform rigidly to a principle of limited and enumerated federal powers. It is a good thing that, beginning at least with *McCulloch v. Maryland* (1819),[60] we have not rigidly followed such a principle. For

59. Barber, "Constitutional Failure."
60. 17 U.S. 316 (1819).

under such a scheme our federal government today surely would be inadequate to pursuing the Constitution's ends and, indeed, the Constitution might well have failed by now. Even though the Rehnquist Court to some extent tried to revive this strategy, its federalism counterrevolution seems to have been largely symbolic and seems to have retreated somewhat in the end.[61] And 9/11, Hurricane Katrina, and the financial crisis beginning in 2008 demonstrated even to "new federalism" Republicans the need for a strong federal government with powers not specifically enumerated in the Constitution.

Second, consider the successful failure of the strategy of enumerated constitutional rights. Here assume for the sake of argument—with the narrow originalists—that the original Constitution's strategy was to enumerate all the constitutional rights we have and (contrary to the implication of the Ninth Amendment) to exclude the protection of rights not enumerated in the text. It is a good thing that we have not followed such a principle but instead have interpreted our Constitution to secure many "unenumerated" basic liberties that are preconditions for a trustworthy and successful constitutional democracy.[62] For our Constitution and constitutional law would be far less protective of our basic liberties, and far less worthy of our affirmation and support, under such an arrangement. Indeed, it might have failed by now.

Third, and relatedly, consider the successful failure of the judiciary to apply originalism to limit constitutional interpretation to enforcing the relatively specific original meanings or understandings of the framers and ratifiers. Assume for the sake of argument—again, with the narrow originalists—that there was an original understanding (or design) that the Constitution should be interpreted according to the principles of narrow originalism. It is a good thing that in practice courts have eschewed such a programmatic originalism in favor of what Barber and I have called a fusion of approaches to constitutional interpretation[63] and what Murphy has called constitutional interpretation as constitutional maintenance. Otherwise, the Constitution might have failed by now.

Fourth, consider the successful failure of the Electoral College. I hasten to say that Levinson puts forward powerful criticisms of the Electoral College[64] and that I would support a constitutional amendment to abolish it or at least to alter it to a system of proportional allocation of each state's electoral votes instead of the largely winner-take-all system

---

61. See, e.g., Mark Tushnet, *The New Constitutional Order* (Princeton: Princeton University Press, 2003).

62. Fleming, *Securing Constitutional Democracy*.

63. Barber and Fleming, *Constitutional Interpretation*, 189–92.

64. Levinson, *Undemocratic Constitution*, 81–97.

we currently have. In speaking of the successful failure of the Electoral College, I refer to the failure of the Electoral College to work as might have been contemplated: with electors of each state, exercising independent judgment, really choosing the president (without being bound by the popular vote of the state). Instead, as things have turned out, the electors largely ratify the choice of the statewide electorate. This is a more defensible state of affairs than contemplated. And so, I would say that, though the Electoral College is imperfect, it has worked tolerably well on the whole. Let us remember that the problems of the presidential election controversy leading up to *Bush v. Gore* were not in the first instance problems of the Electoral College; instead, they were problems of the Florida voting system, with its variety of voting machines from county to county and all the rest of it.[65]

My examples of successful failures acknowledge that, to some extent, one person's success is another's failure, and vice versa (or success from one theoretical standpoint is failure from another). We can also see this phenomenon in the First Things symposium some years ago in which conservatives lamented the "end of democracy"[66] through Supreme Court decisions like *Planned Parenthood v. Casey*[67] and *Romer v. Evans*,[68] at the same time that many liberals celebrated these same decisions as confirming the status of equal citizenship of women and gays and lesbians in our constitutional democracy.[69] Such is the character of successes, failures, and successful failures of the American Constitution.

---

65. I should also mention the successful failure of the founding fathers to anticipate the rise of parties and the rise of presidential democracy (here, of course, I allude to Bruce Ackerman's recent book). See Ackerman, *Failure*.

66. The 1996 First Things symposium is reprinted in Mitchell S. Muncy and Richard John Neuhaus, eds., *The End of Democracy: The Celebrated First Things Debate with Arguments Pro and Con and "The Anatomy of a Controversy"* (Dallas: Spence Publishing, 1997).

67. 505 U.S. 833 (1992).

68. 517 U.S. 620 (1996).

69. See, e.g., Fleming, *Securing Constitutional Democracy*, 2–4, 96, 192.

3

The Disharmonic Constitution

GARY JEFFREY JACOBSOHN

CONSTITUTIONS MAY BE VIEWED as instruments through which "a nation goes about defining itself."[1] This is often attempted in preambles—but in other parts as well—wherein all manner of noble intentions are detailed in lofty and inspiring prose. However genuine may have been the intentions of the authors of this kind of language, experience leads us to anticipate a substantial disconnect between word and deed as constitutional development unfolds. But if our response to this nearly certain story line is to abandon the idea that constitutions have significant expressive value, we may be asking language to bear more weight than it can or should. We may be investing words with an overly declarative meaning, as if the identities of constitutions could be deduced from inscription alone. Such an investment also yields a static view of constitutional identity, fixing its content in the codified affirmations of a specific time and place. But a more modest understanding of the constitution's expressive function is compatible with the position taken in this chapter. Thus, I argue for a fluid concept of identity, in which constitutional assertions of self-definition are part of an ongoing process entailing adaptation and adjustment as circumstances dictate. It is not fluidity without boundaries, however, and textual commitments such as are embodied in preambles often set the topography upon which the mapping of constitutional identity occurs.

As a political document the identity of a constitution is inescapably controversial, and thus too, one could argue, is the very analytical value of the concept. "'[W]ho we are,'" as Mark Tushnet has noted, "is often—perhaps always—contestable and actively contested."[2] I contend that the dissonance within and around constitutions is in fact key to understanding their identity. Far from being fatal to the inquiry, the contestability of constitutional identity is a crucial element in our attempt

---

1. Mark Tushnet, "Some Reflections on Method in Comparative Constitutional Law," in *The Migration of Constitutional Ideas*, ed. Sujit Choudhry (Cambridge: Cambridge University Press, 2006), 82.
2. Ibid.

to comprehend it. Thus, in what follows I press for a dialogical understanding that incorporates an easily overlooked feature of the universal
constitutional condition, which is that in one way or another all constitutions confront or embody the problem of *disharmony*.[3] Sometimes this
condition exists in the form of contradictions and imbalances internal to
the constitution itself, and sometimes in the lack of agreement evident in
the sharp discontinuities that frame the constitution's relationship to the
surrounding society.[4] The question of identity is prominently implicated
in the various permutations of the disharmonic constitution, embodied principally in the determination to eliminate or maintain its discordant aspects.[5] Disharmony is a precondition for change, and efforts to
reduce or defend it reveal that constitutional identity is not a static or
fixed thing. To appreciate the phenomenon is to see its dynamic quality,
which results from the interplay of forces seeking either to introduce
greater harmony into the constitutional equation or to create further
disharmony. One could imagine the latter development culminating in a

3. As far as I know the specific idea of disharmony as applied to political things originated with the scholar of Indian society André Béteille, who was prominently followed
in his usage of the term by Samuel Huntington in his 1981 study, *American Politics: The
Promise of Disharmony* (Cambridge: Harvard University Press, 1981). For Huntington,
disharmony refers to the gap between promise and performance, and the attempt to close
this gap is the main explanation for social change in the United States. In his account, the
United States is the most disharmonic of all polities, because the existential and normative
orders are necessarily inconsistent with one another, given the presence of a high degree of
ideological consensus and the inevitable failure of the society to measure up to its principled
commitments. As explained below, my use of the term as applied to constitutional orders
is a more expansive understanding that imagines different forms of disharmony, of which
Huntington's version is only one.

4. The latter form of disharmony is what André Béteille had in mind in distinguishing between harmonic and disharmonic societies. "A disharmonic society . . . shows a lack
of consistency between the existential and the normative orders: the norm of equality is
contradicted by the pervasive existence of inequality." André Béteille, *The Idea of Natural Equality and Other Essays* (Delhi: Oxford University Press, 1987), 54. For Béteille, a
scholar of caste in India, the 1950 Indian Constitution, with its promise of a casteless and
classless society, exemplifies the disharmonic circumstance. I use the term more broadly to
accommodate other kinds of contradictions as well, including those preventing a constitution—for example, Israel's—from being harmoniously composed.

5. This constitutional predicament includes, according to William F. Harris II in chapter 4
of this volume, a further disharmonic antinomy, which he characterizes as the positive and
negative constitutions. "Any distinct constitution will have specific traits of failure matched
of itself, as negative *attributes*, which, when assembled 'coherently' and made interactive,
set up a comprehensively negative alternative constitution." Harris traces this opposition
to Aristotle, who "matched good and bad constitutions as an essential part of 'constitution' itself." These two constitutions—in the United States, a Constitution of Order and a
Constitution of Disorder—illuminate each other as they function in tandem with each other
over time. For our purposes, this persistent interplay is one manifestation of the dialogical
unfolding of constitutional identity.

rupture of the constitutional continuity necessary for achieving the unity that sustains identity, thereby setting in motion a process with a goal of reconstituting the polity. But even in cases of radical transformation, the shaping of a new constitutional identity is never simply a matter of "reflection and choice."[6]

In this I am in partial agreement with the philosopher Michael Kenny, who says of "[t]he presumption that a cultural community possesses a core or bedrock identity" that it "encourages the idea that group identities can be grasped in isolation from wider social and cultural processes."[7] As applied more specifically to constitutional communities, I am less skeptical than Kenny of the supposition concerning the existence of a core, believing with Aristotle that the specific end toward which the community aspires is critical to the concept of identity; but I embrace the idea that a dialogical engagement between a document's core commitment(s) and its external environment is crucial to the formation and evolution of a constitutive identity. Of course, the balance of political forces at any given time is always a key variable in how this all plays out. Whether in Turkey, where secular and nonsecular (or at least less-secular) parties compete for recognition as the authentic voice of traditional values; in Israel, where a persistent and fragile political equilibrium is traceable to the dual commitments of the nation's founding; in India, where a dominant, inclusive nationalist outlook has been relentlessly challenged by another with strong ethnic aspirations, the course of constitutional identity is impelled by the discord of ordinary politics within limits established by profound commitments from the past.

Continuities of Conflict

According to Alasdair MacIntyre, "We enter upon a stage which we did not design and we find ourselves part of an action that was not of our making."[8] It is an illusion to think that personal identity can be abstracted from the larger historical narrative of which it is a part, and so too with constitutions. The story of a life has a broader sweep than what is included within the span of a lifetime. "I am born with a past; and to try to cut myself off from that past . . . is to deform my present relationships. The possession of an historical identity and the possession of a social

6. Alexander Hamilton, John Jay, and James Madison, *The Federalist*, ed. Jacob E. Cooke (Middletown, CT: Wesleyan University Press, 1961), Nos. 1, 3.

7. Michael Kenny, *The Politics of Identity: Liberal Political Theory and the Dilemmas of Difference* (Cambridge: Polity, 2004), 101.

8. Alasdair MacIntyre, *After Virtue: A Study in Moral Theory* (Notre Dame: University of Notre Dame Press, 1981), 199.

identity coincide."[9] But does the past render identity so beholden to the historical narrative to which it is tethered as to leave it without agency, without the means of altering or transcending the story line within which it is a character?

This, of course, is a question with considerable importance for constitutional identity, where the balance between organic and agency-driven development looms large in critical constitutional calculations of design and growth, perhaps nowhere more pointedly than in episodes of dramatic regime transformation. General Douglas MacArthur's belief that American governing principles and institutions were "fit for all peoples everywhere" drove the process of constitutional imposition in Japan, but how much of the subsequent success of that venture resulted from the rightness of his vision or the fact that, as one study of Japanese political reconstruction contends, the "commitment to democratic constitutionalism . . . rested on deep cultural foundations"?[10] The same question may be asked of societies whose foundations are more discordant, for example, India, where the imposition of Anglo-Saxon law over an extended period of time by a British administration resolutely committed to the moral superiority and transferability of its governing ideas confronted an indigenous cultural and legal tradition of markedly dissimilar convictions. According to MacIntyre, "What I am . . . is in key part what I inherit, a specific past that is present to some degree in my present."[11] How are we to understand the remarkable achievement of Indian constitutional democracy: as the welcome, if surprising, outgrowth of a conflicted inheritance; as the proof that what is inherited, no matter its significance for personal identity, is not an inevitable constraint in shaping a constitutional identity; or, as Lloyd and Susanne Rudolph have I think rightly suggested, as evidence that when the conflicting strands of a divided inheritance engage one another dialectically rather than dichotomously, good things can happen?[12]

Consider in this context Edmund Burke, the most eloquent and persistent critic of British imperialism in India. Burke saw constitutions as embodiments of unique histories and circumstances. The nation was

9. Ibid., 205.

10. Ray A. Moore and Donald L. Robinson, *Partners for Democracy: Crafting the New Japanese State under MacArthur* (Oxford; Oxford University Press, 2002), 14, 34. In relation to this exercise, Walter Murphy writes that, "to maximize the constitutional enterprise's chances, founders must take their past into account. They cannot, at will, erase myths and memories. . . . To minimize trauma, the language of the new or revised institutions and aspirations must demonstrate respect for much of what the society has historically cherished." Walter Murphy, *Constitutional Democracy: Creating and Maintaining a Just Political Order* (Baltimore: Johns Hopkins University Press, 2007), 201.

11. MacIntyre, *After Virtue*, 206.

12. Lloyd I. Rudolph and Susanne Hoeber Rudolph, *The Modernity of Tradition* (Chicago: University of Chicago Press, 1967), 10.

a "moral essence," in the apt phrase of one of Burke's interpreters, "a cultural personality in time."[13] At the core of his theory of the constitution was the principle of inheritance, more familiarly known as *prescription*.[14] "[A] nation," said Burke, "is not an idea of local extent, but is an idea of continuity, which extends in time as well as in numbers, and in space. . . . [It] is a deliberate election of ages and generations; it is a Constitution . . . made by the peculiar circumstances, occasions, tempers, dispositions, and moral, civil, and social habitudes of the people that disclose themselves only in a long space of time."[15]

As the key to constitutional identity, prescription represents what endures through the changes occurring within the natural progression of any society. But, as the Indian, Irish, and American controversies that so defined Burke's political career make very clear, prescription need not be a code word for the status quo. Indeed, the commitment to established institutions (including the rule of law) may require—as was true in these three cases—a quite energetic program of reform that belies Burke's reputation for stodgy conservatism. Burke often distinguished between reform (healthy) and innovation (problematic), the latter having more to do with change that is disconnected from principles engrained in the prescriptive constitution.

But suppose it is innovation that is in fact required. A theory of constitutional identity that cannot account for the more radical departures from constitutional continuity is an incomplete theory. Again, MacIntyre is clarifying. Indeed, just at the point in his argument when he appears most Burkean—invoking the historical narrative, the importance of tradition, and the constraints of inheritance—he turns on Burke with surprising vehemence, saying, "[W]hen a tradition becomes Burkean, it is

13. Gerald W. Chapman, *Edmund Burke and the Practical Imagination* (Cambridge: Harvard University Press, 1967), 90.

14. The prescriptive constitution has been the subject of insightful scholarly treatment. See, in particular, Francis P. Canavan, *The Political Reason of Edmund Burke* (Durham, NC: Duke University Press, 1960); Chapman, *Edmund Burke and the Practical Imagination*; and Michael Freedman, *Edmund Burke and the Critique of Political Radicalism* (Chicago: University of Chicago Press, 1980).

15. Edmund Burke, "Speech on a Motion Made in the House of Commons, the 7th of May 1782, for a Committee to Inquire into the State of the Representation of the Commons in Parliament," in *On Empire, Liberty, and Reform*, ed. David Bromwich (New Haven: Yale University Press, 2000), 274. Or, as Laurence Tribe, whatever his skepticism concerning the concept of constitutional identity, has eloquently pointed out: "To be free is not simply to follow our ever-changing wants wherever they might lead. . . . to make . . . choices without losing the thread of continuity that integrates us over time and imports a sense of our wholeness in history, we must be able to . . . choose in terms of commitments we have made." Laurence Tribe, "Ways Not to Think about Plastic Trees: New Foundations for Environmental Law," *Yale Law Journal* 83 (1974): 1315, 1326–27.

always dying or dead."[16] MacIntyre's reasons for distinguishing his views on tradition from Burke's infuse the concept of identity with a dynamic quality that broadens its applicability to the constitutional experience.

These reasons center on tradition itself or, with reference to Burke, the unfortunate contrast between conflict and stability. Burke's conception of tradition lacks adversarial vitality; the weight of habit and routine represents continuity without conflict; constitutional identity comes to be identified with, and rigidified in, the dominant will in the community. Slavery in the United States, for example, may have produced a body of settled law, but its incompatibility with other parts of the American historical narrative—formal and informal—rendered its status as a constitutionally sanctioned inheritance fatally suspect. The argument over its presumptive validity was a way of addressing the question of whether the peculiar institution had any purchase in a fair account of American constitutional identity. This identity is, as the American case illustrates, often shaped through the creative interaction between divergent strands within an ongoing tradition; whatever ultimate convergence to universal norms of constitutionalism emerges will continue to bear the imprint in practice of distinctive primary sources. The disharmonic constitutional self embodies the specific components of an identity that evolves as these elements play off against each other within limits of the national historical narrative.

To bring together the key elements in these reflections on constitutional identity, I highlight two interrelated themes: aspirational content and dialogical articulation. Framing them are the two ubiquitous ideas that drive the process of constitutional identity: prescription and disharmony. The first has a verb form that can mean either *to recommend* or *to impose*. One way to interpret the MacIntyre critique of Burke is to see it as an effort to soften the determinative power of prescription by moving it away from imposition toward recommendation, stopping somewhat short of the latter. Thus, the past cannot be excised from the developmental path of constitutional identity, but it need not establish its precise direction. It is the second idea—disharmony—that infuses an element of uncertainty into the future course of constitutional identity and gives it its dynamic quality.

Aspirational Content

Seventeenth- and eighteenth-century philosophers (e.g., John Locke and Thomas Reid) maintained that continuity in consciousness is the key to establishing the identity of a person. One of the difficulties, however, in

---

16. MacIntyre, *After Virtue*, 206.

moving from the personal to the political is that nations, more so than persons, have conflicting self-understandings. How, as we asked earlier, are we to talk about a nation's constitutional identity if it is contestable? While this question will resonate in many places, one need go no further than the United States where, as Mark Graber has reminded us, "Slavery was embedded in a way of life that most Southerners and some Northerners thought intrinsically valuable and expressive of the highest constitutional aspirations."[17]

That they so believed may call into question the significance of aspiration as a constitutionally viable concept. Graber, for instance, finds that the presence of competing aspirational commitments provides dubious interpretive standing for the idea. "Racist and other ascriptive ideologies are as rooted in the American political tradition as liberal, democratic, and republican ideals."[18] To anoint one ideal over another—as one would by assigning it special meaning in distinguishing constitutional identity— is an arbitrary intrusion into a constitutional process that, properly conceived, should not be identified with a specific aspirational agenda.

The problem with this view is that it makes an erroneous inference from the presence of a disharmonic constitutional tradition. It assumes that a conflicted constitutional tradition deprives all sides to the conflict of any legitimate claim to speak *for* the constitution. But in his critique of the *Dred Scott* decision, Abraham Lincoln disagreed, articulating a theory of aspiration in which eighteenth-century principles of natural right were at the core of constitutional meaning and hence a standard for evaluating the work of the Court.[19] Chief Justice Roger Taney had, Lincoln thought, denuded the Declaration of any constitutive significance by transforming it into a positivist document of no moral consequence. But for its signers, "They meant simply to declare the *right* [to human equality], so that the *enforcement* of it might follow as fast as circumstances should permit."[20] The failure to achieve unity of purpose was less an indication that the aspiration to human equality was of no constitutive meaning than it was evidence for the inability of many of the framers immediately to solidify its content within the folds of the constitutional identity they were shaping. In declaring that people of African descent should not expect enforcement of a right to which they were ascriptively excluded, Taney had failed to understand how the aspirations of the Constitution defined

17. Mark A. Graber, *Dred Scott and the Problem of Constitutional Evil* (Cambridge: Cambridge University Press, 2006), 83.

18. Ibid., 78.

19. I pursue this Lincolnian theory in *The Supreme Court and the Decline of Constitutional Aspiration* (Totowa, NJ: Rowman & Littlefield, 1986).

20. Roy Basler, ed., *The Collected Works of Abraham Lincoln* (New Brunswick, NJ: Rutgers University Press, 1953), 2: 406.

Americans as a people, and thus his ruling obligated other actors—principally Congress—to challenge it politically. Indeed, a constitution of aspiration is incompatible with the idea that the Supreme Court exercises an interpretive monopoly over the document. *We the People* were unable (and, in many cases, unwilling) contemporaneously to extend the justice of the Constitution to all those who fell under its sway, but the posterity of the excluded would in due course see their promised constitutional entitlement fulfilled, with or without the help of the Court.

Constitutions provide structures to mediate among conflicting political aspirations, but that they must or can be neutral with respect to them does not necessarily follow. As Walter Murphy has noted, "Every society has its own values, traditions, and customs. Leaders who try to transform a people operate under conditions of restricted choice. The [constitutional] text's values and aspirations must build on some of the existing culture's norms and will likely have to repudiate others."[21] All of this building and repudiating, incorporating and negating, is consistent with the primacy of particular aspirations within an ongoing dynamic of disharmonic contestation. This contestation can result in the further legitimation and entrenchment of the aspirations—for example, the adoption of the post–Civil War amendments—or it can lead to their delegitimation and erosion in the name of alternative aspirations that are intelligible in light of the broader historical narrative that sustains both. Radical constitutional transformation may be conceptualized as the replacement of one aspirational agenda for another, an ascendance—for example, the adoption of the postwar German Basic Law, or the adoption of the new South African Constitution—that invariably retains much from constitutional antecedents in a given nation's prescriptive constitution.

---

21. For Murphy, these aspirations serve to reconstitute a people and provide them with a common creed. Constitutional theorists must consider the degree to which these aspirations rely on the past as opposed to a rejection of that past. Bruce Ackerman, *The Future of Liberal Revolution* (New Haven: Yale University Press, 1992). Frederick Schauer, emphasizing the close relationship between constitutions and national identity, views the making of a constitution as a critical step in the establishment of independence. While this means relying on indigenous constitutional sources, to what degree they should also be independent from past practices is not entirely clear. Frederick Schauer, "On the Migration of Constitutional Ideas," *Connecticut Law Review* 37 (2005): 907. Michel Rosenfeld argues, "Constitution making involves an act of negation, a break with a preconstitutional past." Michel Rosenfeld, "The European Treaty-Constitution and Constitutional Identity: A View from America," *International Journal of Constitutional Law* 3 (2005): 316, 318. Rosenfeld contends that the construction of a constitutional identity usually entails a conscious act of negation coupled with unconscious acts of incorporation from the past—that "both negation and reincorporation are essential for a constitution to materialize in form and substance." Ibid., 320.

Dialogical Articulation

Charles Taylor, like Alasdair MacIntyre, has proposed that we understand identity "dialogically," as an interactive process in which a person develops a self in response to an environment consisting of religion, state, family, and so on. The dialogical view also functions in the constitutional arena in interpretive and political activity occurring in courts, legislatures, and other places public and private. Such activity will be most evident where the responsibility for constitutional development is not clearly identified with the judiciary—where, that is, the notion of a court as principal shaper and articulator of constitutional identity is not reflexively assumed. It will, for example, be more prominently revealed in many European countries where practices such as abstract review facilitate greater legislative engagement in the determination of substantive constitutional meanings.[22]

Pursuing identity along dialogical paths may thus require reconsideration of the juri-centric model that has long dominated contemporary constitutional theorizing, exemplified in the work of Ronald Dworkin, whose considerable achievements have not, it must be said, flowed from their attention to comparative issues. In this model, the judge, idealized in Dworkin's Herculean philosopher-jurist, is guardian and expositor of the moral principles that structure and guide the nation's constitutional development.[23] Dworkin has not convincingly incorporated the untidy realities of disharmonic constitutional traditions into his theory.[24] To be sure, the quest for unity, central to the idea of constitutional identity, is fully compatible with his commitment to law as integrity, but realizing that commitment through the exercise of judicial unilateralism is problematic, and perhaps more so in places where a nation's historical narrative remains deeply contested. Think again of *Dred Scott*.

In India, to take another example, there are two powerful claims on constitutional identity, both firmly rooted in centuries of conflict and contestation. Since independence, one of these claims—for a secular composite culture nation—has been in ascendance, but the other—for a Hindu nation—has influenced the aspirational content of constitutional identity, and at times posed a distinct threat to the predominant view. The identity that has emerged from this extended discordant chronicle reflects the entrenched realities of both visions; the constitutional text embodies them, though by no means equally, as does the history of constitutional construction and interpretation. Along the way there have been efforts

---

22. Alec Stone-Sweet, *Governing with Judges* (Oxford: Oxford University Press, 2000).

23. Ronald Dworkin, *Taking Rights Seriously* (Cambridge: Harvard University Press, 1977).

24. Ibid., 579, 574.

to reinvent the past, most notably by Hindu nationalists seeking to create a history expunged of the truths that complicate their ethnoreligious story. The prescriptive constitution, however, places limits on these inventions, and the process of dialogical interaction ultimately determines the substance of identity. The process is open to various possibilities, but reconsideration of ends and commitments cannot be boundless and totally open-ended; thus the development of a constitutional self must be constrained in its grasp of future possibilities by what "the past has made available to the present."[25]

Much of the aspirational content of a nation's specific constitutional identity consists of goals and principles that are shared by other nations and that are indeed part of a common stock of aspirations we have come to associate more generally with the enterprise of constitutionalism. Such norms need to be reconciled with the particularistic commitments of local traditions and practices; the contours of constitutional identity will to a large extent reflect how these disharmonies get resolved. South Africa, with its persistent attention to the interaction of local participation and international influences, provides a textbook example. But as the deliberative process that culminated in a new constitution made abundantly clear, separating from the past is not so easily accomplished, whatever the benefits associated with it. Incorporating international standards— for example, equal treatment of individuals under law—within the set of newly mandated constitutional aspirations would still require reconciliation with a quite different aspirational legacy that was as intractable as the historical narrative from whence it derived.[26]

---

25. So too the Israeli case. Ruth Gavison has observed that "the conflicts within Israeli society . . . translate to deep debates about the identity and the legitimacy of the state itself." These conflicts refer to the nation's dual aspirational commitments to develop the polity as both Jewish and democratic. The discordant notes in the Israeli constitutional tradition have provided the backdrop for a judicial commitment to complete what may be conceptualized as an unfinished or complex revolution. The success of Israel's "constitutional revolution" is, to be sure, an oft-debated story; how one evaluates it depends on one's judgment about the Supreme Court's management of the constitutional disharmony bequeathed to it by the nation's divided historical legacy. But as Gavison, echoing MacIntyre, rightly points out, "Ultimately, it is the interplay of deep cultures that make legal traditions robust and solid, because they are then based on deep sources of meaning and continuity." Ruth Gavison, "Law, Adjudication, Human Rights, and Society," *Israel Law Review* 40 (2007): 13, 30.

26. The South African Constitution, like its Indian counterpart, can be characterized as a "militant" constitution in the sense that it was intended by its framers to confront and challenge critical aspects of the existing social and economic structure. But this ambition was quickly tempered by a set of realities carried over from the old regime. A very different angle on the challenge to constitutional design posed by the tension between universalistic and particularistic demands appears in the effort to adopt a constitution for Europe. The issue here is also one of identity, not so much how extranational precepts and principles are to be integrated into the jurisprudence of nations possessing unique histories and ways of

Applications

Some of these thoughts can be applied to two polities, South Africa and India. Both are known for the depth of their societal divisions and possessed of constitutions reflecting conscious efforts to create separation from the past without entirely escaping it.

South Africa

The South African Constitution has often been referred to as "the birth certificate of a nation." One of the participants in its creation describes it as "the growing soul of a nation."[27] In this account, it represents the "discovery of nationhood."[28] While references like these reflect an understandable sense of pride in a remarkable achievement, they also serve to call attention to the question of how a constitution comes to acquire a specific identity. Such terms as birth, soul, and discovery frequently come up in discussions of personal identity. Does the story of one of the most important constitutional developments of our time expand the significance of their application to polity-level questions of identity?

In 1996 the Constitutional Court of South Africa delivered a judgment in a case that it properly referred to as unprecedented. Pursuant to a provision of the Interim South African Constitution of 1993, the Court's ruling concerned certification of the newly adopted permanent Constitution. Was the new document in compliance with criteria set out in language from the earlier constitution's preamble, which had stipulated that "in order to secure the achievement of this new goal, elected representatives of all the people of South Africa should be mandated to adopt a new Constitution in accordance with a solemn pact recorded as Constitutional Principles"? To reach its decision the Court was required to assess the provisions of the new document in light of the thirty-four Constitutional

doing things, but how—or whether—the distinctive political and legal cultures of a diverse group of nations can be incorporated within an overarching framework of international governance such as to create a constitutional identity for the new entity as a whole. So far the effort has been more encouraging for constitutional theorists than for politicians. See, for example, the entries in the special issue on the proposed European Constitution published in the *International Journal of Constitutional Law* in May 2005. On the problem of creating a European constitutional identity in the face of extraordinary diversity, see the debate between Jürgen Habermas and Dieter Grimm. For example: Dieter Grimm, "Does Europe Need a Constitution?" *European Law Journal* 1 (1995): 282; and Jürgen Habermas, "Remarks on Dieter Grimm's 'Does Europe Need a Constitution?'" *European Law Journal* 1(1995): 303.

27. Hassen Ebrahim, *The Soul of a Nation: Constitution-Making in South Africa* (Cape Town: Oxford University Press, 1998), 256.

28. Ibid., 4.

Principles enumerated in the 1993 iteration. It was unlikely that any of the judges could have minimized the significance of this undertaking, for they all knew, in accordance with the express language of the governing constitutional directive, that a decision to certify would be final and could never again be raised in any court of law, including their own.

The power exercised by the Court was as extraordinary as it was unprecedented: to legitimate (or not) a governing code by which a people commit to the structuring of a constitutional way of life. Indeed, this was the first and only occasion when a court had been given the responsibility of certifying a constitutional text.[29] Of the constitutional principles that were the touchstone for the certification exercise, the Court said: "[They] must be applied purposively and teleologically to give expression to the commitment 'to create a new order' based on a 'sovereign and democratic constitutional state' in which 'all citizens' are 'able to enjoy and exercise their fundamental rights and freedoms.'" The judges and the Constitution's drafters were constrained in their creative efforts by guidelines adopted several years earlier, but within the broad parameters of these directives they had considerable leeway in designing and shaping constitutional policy.[30]

In what sense, if at all, may the culmination of this judicial exercise be understood as having shaped a constitutional identity? Did the mandate to pursue a purposive and holistic application of enumerated principles suggest the presence of a unified vision of constitutional practice that represents the core of this identity? Would compliance with the commitments of the drafters of the interim document of 1993 be evidence for the successful construction of a constitutional identity in 1996?

The "birth certificate" of a nation would constitute a misleading marker if it conveyed the idea that a document—any document—could bring into the world some constitutional article whose identity was discernible

29. Namibia in 1989 also incorporated a set of constitutional principles, but unlike in South Africa, these were to serve only as guidelines for the final document.

30. The certification process was well within the spirit of the negotiating process among various groups and interests that guided the entire constitution-making arrangements. For an analysis of the process that discusses certification in light of competing models—consociationalism and justice—see Siri Gloppen, *South Africa: The Battle over the Constitution* (Aldershot: Dartmouth Publishing, 1997). Firoz Cachalia also looks at the contrasting models and makes a passionate argument for adopting a Rawlsian interpretation of South Africa's Constitution, which he finds "especially valuable in societies that are 'deeply divided' by competing identities." Firoz Cachalia, "Constitutionalism and Belonging," in *The Post-Apartheid Constitutions: Perspectives on South Africa's Basic Law*, ed. Penelope Andrews and Stephen Ellmann (Johannesburg: Witwatersrand University Press, 2001), 367. Cachalia advocates forging "a distinction between constitutional identity and cultural identity," although it is difficult to perceive the constitutional process in South Africa as having culminated in a solution in which the former has been made separate from the latter.

in the details of its very existence. Who would say, for example, that the constitutional identity of the former Soviet Union was discernible within the folds of its governing charter? Nor would the idea that a constitutional "soul" existed independent of the larger environment surrounding the entity within which it was contained capture the interactive reality of the identity-forming process.

Thus, all that we know about the constitution-making exercise in South Africa supports the conclusion that the declaratory act of enumerating principles that are subsequently incorporated in a final governing legal code did not in itself establish or confirm the existence of something we might call a constitutional identity. The political context within which the principles were adopted suggests the fallacy of understanding constitutional identity either as a purely wrought product of the theoretical imagination *or* as the inevitable outgrowth of a fixed and essentially unalterable nature. The actual course of South African constitutional design did not occur in a vacuum; indeed, an extensive public record reveals a very complex and nuanced political process culminating in a final constitutional product. The constitutional principles enunciated in the 1993 document were neither discovered nor invented; rather, in the dying days of the old apartheid regime these principles became the focus of a deliberate effort to incorporate contradictory visions—in other words, disharmony—within the project of constitutional design. The Constitutional Court was then given the assignment of mediating these conflicting aspirations so as to leave space for all major parties to accept the legitimacy of the new arrangements while engaging the political process in developing a coherent vision of a constitutional future for the country.

Concurrently, the constitutional framers (and subsequent judges on the Constitutional Court) participated in a systematic and comprehensive effort to incorporate the experience of other nations in the provisions of, and interpretive approaches to, their newly constituted arrangements.[31] The South African Court quickly developed a distinctive "dialogical" interpretive approach to structure the judicial appropriation of foreign materials into its constitutional jurisprudence.[32] In some cases this led to an emulation and transplantation of the foreign experience, in others to a conscious rejection. The engagement with other constitutional cultures and practices has sharpened the understandings of South Africans about their own legal culture, while making clear that this culture is not developmentally tethered to an indigenous core requiring only discovery and nurturing.

31. Article 35.

32. Sujit Choudhry, "Globalization in Search of Justification: Toward a Theory of Comparative Constitutional Interpretation," *Indiana Law Journal* 74 (1999): 819.

India

Probably more than any tribunal in the world, the Indian Supreme Court has been deeply committed to the concept of constitutional identity. It has done so mainly through elaboration of the controversial doctrine of "basic structure," in which it has designated a number of constitutional features to be of such importance that it would be prepared to challenge any action, including an amendment to the Constitution, perceived as a threat to their existence.[33] Moreover, in the spirit of the multilateralism that serious engagement with the problem would seem to require, it has upheld extraordinary actions by other institutions—such as the dismissal of elected state governments by the central government in New Delhi—that were motivated by a proper regard for constitutional identity.

Much of the debate in India over judicial enforcement of the basic structure doctrine has concerned its application to the issue of secularism. The Indian Constitution was adopted against a backdrop of sectarian violence that was only the latest chapter in a complex centuries-old story of Hindu–Muslim relations on the Asian subcontinent. Much of that history had been marked by peaceful coexistence; nevertheless, the bloodbath that accompanied Partition reflected ancient contestations and insured that the goal of communal harmony would be a priority in the constitution-making process.[34] But it was not the only priority. If not as urgent, then certainly as important, was the goal of social reconstruction, which could not be addressed without constitutional recognition of the state's interest in the "essentials of religion."[35] So deep was religion's penetration into a social structure that was by any reasonable standard grossly unjust that the framers' hopes for a democratic polity meant that state intervention in the spiritual domain could not be constitutionally foreclosed. The design for secularism in India required a creative balance between socioeconomic reform that could limit religious options and political toleration of diverse religious practices and communal develop-

---

33. The doctrine has been described in many works. See, in particular, A. Lakshminath, *Basic Structure and Constitutional Amendments: Limitations and Justiciability* (New Delhi: Deep & Deep Publications, 2002), and Paras Diwan and Peeyushi Diwan, *Amending Powers and Constitutional Amendment*, vol. 2 (New Delhi: Deep & Deep Publications, 1997). It has been passionately debated in Pran Chopra, ed., *The Supreme Court versus the Constitution: A Challenge to Federalism* (New Delhi: Sage Publications, 2006).

34. "We have accepted [secularism] not only because it is our historical legacy and a need of our national unity and integrity but also as a creed of universal brotherhood and humanism. It is our cardinal faith." *S. R. Bommai v. Union of India*, 3 SC 1 (1994), 148.

35. Gary Jeffrey Jacobsohn, *The Wheel of Law: India's Secularism in Comparative Constitutional Context* (Princeton: Princeton University Press, 2003).

ment.[36] Taken together, the ameliorative and communal provisions demonstrate a constitutional purpose to address the social conditions of people long burdened by the inequities of religiously inspired hierarchies.

Over the years, this constitutional goal has come under repeated assault from different locations along the political spectrum, with the greatest challenge issuing from the Hindu right. The Supreme Court's main response has been to declare secularism a "part of the basic structure of the Constitution and also the soul of the Constitution."[37] Describing the commitment to secularism in this dramatic way suggested that the same concern with constitutional identity that lay behind the Court's earlier rulings on unconstitutional amendments generated the outcome in the secularism case. To be sure, there is no reason to think that a judicial reference to the "soul of the Constitution" was used with any awareness of debates in the seventeenth and eighteenth centuries (or, indeed, as far back as Plato) over the significance and place of the soul in determining personal identity, but there is every reason to suppose that its usage was intended to mark secularism as critical to Indian constitutional identity.

Indian secularism, however, poses an interesting challenge for a theory of identity. We might call it the "presumption in favor of settled practice" problem, which I referred to earlier in connection with Burke and the

36. This balance is inscribed in several constitutional provisions that express the limits and possibilities of secularism in India. Thus, the ameliorative aspiration of Indian secularism is embodied in Article 25, which, after providing for religious freedom, declares that the state shall not be prevented from "regulating or restricting any economic, financial, political or other secular activity which may be associated with religious practice." "Providing for social welfare and reform" is explicitly included within the parameters of the guaranteed freedom. This constitutional strand underscores the transformative dimension of Indian nationalism, the commitment to social reconstruction as the path to creating one nation out of a multiplicity of peoples. Additional provisions are designed to accommodate the other principal facet of Indian social reality, the entrenched character of communal affiliation. Under Article 26, religious denominations are granted the right to establish and maintain institutions for religious and charitable purposes, and the same right is extended to the creation and administration of religiously based educational structures in Article 30.

37. *S. R. Bommai v. Union of India*, at 143. This is the leading Indian case on secularism. In it the Court upheld the authority of the central government to dismiss the elected governments in three states because of the alleged failures of their administrations in implementing and respecting the constitutional commitment to secularism. By upholding the deployment of emergency powers under Article 356, the Court agreed that these governments had not acted "in accordance with the provisions of the Constitution." Article 356 had been modeled after the American Guaranty Clause (Article IV, Section 4), but the willingness of the Indian Court to confront the question of identity contrasts sharply with the U.S. Supreme Court's reluctance to engage it. Indeed, the judicial practice of invoking the "political question" doctrine to avoid difficult constitutional questions began in *Luther v. Borden,* which was in essence a case of political identity, in which the Supreme Court refused to say what it was that the republican guaranty clause guaranteed.

prescriptive constitution. We want to retain the idea of prescription without having to embrace a logic that requires us to extend the legitimacy of the constitution to the society of which it is a part. When reviewing the debates about religion and politics at the Constituent Assembly and the various judicial pronouncements on the subject over the years, one sees very clearly that a principal purpose behind the Indian commitment to secularism was to challenge an entrenched way of life and to modify it in the direction of a democratic way of life rooted in equality. In a very real sense, the constitutional "soul" was intended to be ornery, projecting an identity that was at once confrontational and emblematic of the document's abiding commitments. In both the early philosophical ruminations about consciousness and the Burkean reflections on nationhood and prescription, the concept of identity is associated with the idea of continuity rather than transformation. How then are we to explain the expansive ambitions of the soulful concept at the core of Indian constitutional design?

Mindful of our earlier reflections, there are two points to be made here. First, constitutional identity can accommodate an aspirational aspect that is at odds with the prevailing condition of the society within which it functions. Burke's prescriptive constitution might suggest that what is must be (identity as pure discovery), but, as MacIntyre demonstrated, a strictly positivistic inference need not be drawn from the principle of inheritance. In the case of India's constitutional framers, the prevailing social structure, while deeply rooted in centuries of religious and cultural practice, was contestable in accordance with sources from within the Indian tradition that are also a part of the prescriptive constitution.[38] History revealed disharmony within established traditions and between the dominant strand and the society. "One of the remarkable developments of the present age," wrote Nehru shortly before independence, "has been the rediscovery of the past and of the nation."[39] Nehru was one of several delegates at the Constituent Assembly to invoke the name of Ashoka, the legendary leader from the third century B.C., whose famous edicts have endured as a source of moral and ethical reflection for more than a millennium. Used both as an emulative model for behavior toward society's

38. As H. Patrick Glenn has observed, "Opposition to a tradition may be . . . conducted within the tradition itself, using both its language and its resources (the struggle from within)." H. Patrick Glenn, *Legal Traditions of the World* (Oxford: Oxford University Press, 2000), 17. This is particularly the case in Hinduism, which stands out among the world's religious traditions for the heterodox character of its teachings. "What distinguishes Hinduism from other traditions, religious and other, is that informal tradition is recognized generally as having priority even over the sacred texts." Ibid., 269.

39. Jawaharlal Nehru, *The Discovery of India* (Oxford: Oxford University Press, 1997), 515.

destitute and as a basis for criticizing the Hindu nationalist rejection of Indian nationhood as rooted in a composite culture, the Ashokan example shows how continuity in the construction of a constitutional identity can draw upon alternative (and even dissenting) sources within one tradition, and then reconstitute them to serve at times as a reproach to other strands within the same tradition. In MacIntyre's terms, it exemplifies "continuities of conflict."

The process by which this concept of secularism emerged as a mark of constitutional identity, then to be extended protected status under the Court's basic structure jurisprudence, is roughly analogous to the dialogical formation of personal identity, which is developed, as Charles Taylor argued, "only against the background of things that matter." Much as a self evolves interactively within the specific contours of its environment, India's constitutional identity, as refracted through the determinative lens of secularism, is the product of historically conditioned circumstances in which choices are limited by the dual realities of complex communalism and religiously inspired societal inequality.[40] The nation as an "idea of continuity," in which, as Burke said, a constitution discloses itself "only in a long space of time," can go far to explain how the main outlines of a secular identity are discoverable as a contingent part of the political and moral order. But within these broad outlines is considerable space for inventive statesmanship.

Conclusion

There is, of course, much more that could be said about these cases. That they are both commonly viewed as success stories is no doubt partly attributable to the enormity of the challenges confronting their respective constitutional experiments. Like so much else in India and South Africa that is jarring in the magnitude of their incongruities, the histories of intercommunal hostility and conflagration in these polities coexist with stories of democratic constitutionalism that are remarkable for having unfolded as impressively as they have within such distinctly inhospitable environments. But the conflicts out of which the constitutional identities of these nations have come into being are exceptional only in their

40. As Anthony D. Smith has observed, "A national identity is fundamentally multidimensional; it can never be reduced to a single element." Anthony D. Smith, *National Identity* (Reno: University of Nevada Press, 1991), 14. The same applies to constitutional identities. Thus, Smith's discussion of the Indian case appropriately invokes the communal question as one of the relevant dimensions. "The Indian example reveals the importance both of manufactured political identity and of preexisting ethno-religious ties and symbols from which such an identity can be constructed." Ibid., 113.

extremity; their emergence conforms to the model of disharmonic contestation that is present in the shaping of all such identities.

The intensity of the contestation may not be present in many places, and even when it is, it may not manifest itself in quite the same way as in the above instances. Thus, there are two dimensions along which conflict fuels the development of constitutional identity: the first is internal to the document (assuming one exists) and includes alternative visions or aspirations that may embody different strands within a common historical tradition; the second entails a confrontational relationship between the constitution and the social order within which it operates. Most constitutions are fundamentally acquiescent in the sense that their framing is not likely to culminate in a document antagonistic to the very societal structures of stability that provide ballast for the constitutional enterprise. But even these constitutions—the American being a good example—may take on a militancy at some point in its history, as the tensions within the first dimension create a dynamic of change that proves ultimately transformative in the evolution of the nation's constitutional identity.

Thus, the debate in the United States over the post–Civil War amendments, a debate that was all about the substance of American constitutional identity, implicated both of these dimensions of disharmonic contestation. Those who have held that the amendments essentially completed the Constitution, that they represented, in Frederick Douglass's famous metaphor, the removal of the scaffolding surrounding the "magnificent [basic?] structure" of constitutionally designed liberty, must nevertheless acknowledge the tensions remaining in the document after the additions had been incorporated. These discordant parts—involving mainly the locus of power within a federal system of governance—have provided occasions for institutional conflict in which political actors (including judges) have pursued their competing aspirational agendas. As George Thomas says of American constitutionalism, it is "primarily about countervailing power and not about the legal limits enforced by courts."[41] He rightly views this as a result of constitutional planning: "In attempting to balance agonistic principles, which furnish the basis for a workable and contained political order, the Madisonian framework necessarily invites struggles over constitutional meaning and identity."[42] The second dimension of contestation—confrontation between constitution and social order—came into play in the course of the ongoing struggle to apply the amended document to the massive problem of racial inequality,

41. George Thomas, *The Madisonian Constitution* (Baltimore: John Hopkins University Press, 2008), 2.
42. Ibid., 38.

by efforts either to denude it of any real significance or to enable it to begin the process of social reconstruction.

The channeling of conflict in the American Constitution around a set of agonistic institutions and principles may, as Thomas suggests, reflect a calculated feature of constitutional design, but one may also understand it as a refined and carefully crafted version of a phenomenon that presents itself—if in less structured ways—in the experience of other nations as well. The African statesman Julius K. Nyerere has observed that "any constitution must take account of divisions within the society without entrenching them—or it must allow the institutions it establishes to do these things."[43] To describe a specific constitutional identity requires familiarity with the history and culture of a given society, for it is out of custom and tradition that a people acquires the materials from which the rules and aspirations that shape future governance spring. But there is nothing immutable in what emerges; the past always remains a part of the present, yet identity develops as a dialogically unfolding process of adaptation, appropriation, and overcoming of the past. In the end, constitutional identity will be fashioned—and refashioned—through the struggle *over* constitutional identity.

43. Mwalimu Julius K. Nyerere, "Reflections on Constitutions and African Experience," in *Constitutions and National Identity*, ed. Thomas J. Barron, Owen Dudley Edwards, and Patricia J. Storey (Edinburgh: Quadriga, 1993), 19. This understanding, in which disharmony is both necessary and troubling, parallels Jonathan Marks's interpretation of Rousseau's political thought, in which "the human good [is viewed] not as a unity but as a set of disharmonious attributes or tendencies that must somehow be arranged in a life so as not to tear the human being apart." Jonathan Marks, *Perfection and Disharmony in the Thought of Jean-Jacques Rousseau* (New York: Cambridge University Press, 2005), 87.

4

Constitution of Failure

THE ARCHITECTONICS OF A WELL-FOUNDED
CONSTITUTIONAL ORDER

WILLIAM F. HARRIS II

> The advice nearest to my heart and deepest in
> my convictions is, that the Union of the States
> be cherished and perpetuated. Let the open
> enemy to it be regarded as a Pandora with her
> box opened, and the disguised one as the serpent
> creeping with his deadly wiles into Paradise.
> —James Madison, "Advice to My Country," 1834

I

At its simplest, a constitution is a proposition against failure.

Historically and analytically, this observation reflects the disposition of the constitutional Founding in the United States. The theoretical reciprocity between the Constitution (as the construction of a world of success) and Failure (as the projection of an alternative world of collapse[1]) is the key to the architectonics of a founded constitutional order.

In more particular terms, the Founding of Constitutional America encompasses a Constitution of Order substantially corresponding to a Constitution of Disorder. The two exist side by side as the comprehensively established possibilities of the American civic world. From the beginning,

---

1. As Alexander Hamilton describes the allied intellectual and political tendencies of the Confederation that the proposed Constitution is designed to displace: "These were suggestions [of self-serving noncooperation among jealous States] which human selfishness could not withstand, and which even speculative men, who looked forward to remote consequences, could not, without hesitation, combat. Each State, yielding to the persuasive voice of immediate interest or convenience, has successively withdrawn its support, till the frail and tottering edifice seems ready to fall upon our heads, and to crush us beneath its ruins." Alexander Hamilton, John Jay, and James Madison, *The Federalist*, ed. Jacob E. Cooke (Middletown, CT: Wesleyan University Press, 1961), No. 15.

the successful Constitution of the United States was set out with its negative twin. And the two continue to exist, radically separated but constitutively adjacent—matched alternatives that give meaning and force to each other. But for this country's dual sets of founders, each has its own positive and negative regimes: For the Federalists, the Constitution of the United States and the Constitution of the Disunited States; for the Antifederalists, the Constitution of Liberty and the Constitution of Oppression.

With constitutions, failure—like success—is not something that "happens"; it is something that is made. "Ideas" (for James Madison, "mental pictures") configure worlds. Bad ideas, set out with public commitment, engender bad worlds.

Constitution Making at the Edge of Failure

In every age across two centuries of American experience with the Constitution, its most earnest advocates and protectors have been inclined to say that we are on the brink of losing it, or having it fail. The appreciation of this fear is intensified by the fact that most of the framers had very severe doubts at the end of their lives that the Constitution they had made would survive. Such *constitutional* fear has been so consistent and repeated that it is possible to say that it is characteristic of the enterprise. This is as it should be.

One might say (and might properly have said at most points in America's history) that the Constitution of the United States is on the verge of being made a lie—that the propositions of its text concerning a present future have been, or are about to be, falsified. One might quite as readily, however, say that the Constitution is just at the limits of being made true, that its future present is almost here, and even that the truthfulness of its vision is a surprise beyond the anticipations of its framers. This would be so because the political world made possible by the Constitutional text has set up further potential, not fully contained in its words but generated by them. It is astounding to reflect that this prospect for the Constitution's *promise* to be more than its *statement* may be owing in large part to the threatening ongoing presence of the Negative Constitution.

After all, it is not that strange to say, in conventional terms, that great success is dependent on being susceptible to great failure. Neither set of the Constitution's founders—Federalist or Antifederalist—disputed that the new enterprise of constitution making was risky business. Both realized that the greater the ambition, the greater the risk. What might it look like, however, to see this conventional wisdom not merely as a historical occurrence but as a reflection of a more fundamental theory of constitutionalism itself? Conventional wisdom—if it sustains the meaning of its label—may suppress a perplexing profundity with a cover of ordinariness.

This elemental balance between the lie and the truth, failure and success, of the Constitution contains the germ of a constitutional theory.

An Alternative "System"

In the broader context of a theory of constitutional founding, "failure" is not merely a condition where something is broken and needs to be fixed, even if that specifiable condition of brokenness is quite consequential or pervasive. This essay offers an argument about the theoretical status and constitutional character of Failure. It is not an account of intractable deficiencies that impede governmental functioning, or of exigent challenges that threaten to undermine a constitutional scheme, or of recalcitrant issues that give rise to the need for a new political form. Indeed, each of these may be incorporated into the larger design of a Constitution of Failure. Instead, this Constitution of Failure is an alternative "system" (or, more properly, a fully *formed* antiorder) that exists beside constitutional order. In important respects, this antiorder of Failure may be incorporated within the constitutional enterprise itself.

The overall purpose of this essay is to begin to frame a characterization of the Constitution of Failure—that is, one conceived of as a "constitution" on its own terms—working it into a useful theoretical scheme that can aid understanding of constitutionalism more profoundly.

ANTI-CONSTITUTION VERSUS THE UNCONSTITUTIONAL

The Constitution of Failure, moreover, is not a matter of some aspects of the Constitution becoming frayed or worn out, disused or abused. It is not the realm of the "unconstitutional," conceived of in terms of actions taken or conditions maintained under the Constitution that are violative of it. These are important concerns, indeed. But they are, in fact a reflection of the internal coherence of the Positive Constitution itself—by their analytical critique against an accepted standard, reinforcing the integrity of the Positive Constitution on its own terms. In this sense, the mere recognition of "unconstitutionality" is itself an assertion of the purported Constitution's true character. Eventual problematics such as these are the subject of constitutional enforcement, amendment (on a smaller scale of refining the periphery, well short of constitution making), or internal self-reformation (on a larger scale of recovering the core of what was originally set up). Still, the *systematic* "unconstitutional" may arise from the Constitution of Failure, masquerading as authentic "constitutional" because it does derive from a sort of constitution—and one that has also, in an important sense, been made in the course of a founding.

As a crucial aspect of the overall American constitutional enterprise to found and sustain a well-ordered community—a universal exemplar with a destiny of prosperity and acclaim[2]—the Constitution of Failure is the Constitution's *comprehensive* alternative. As such, it has the capacity to offer at least as much substantive meaning to the constitution-making project as the words and structure of the Constitutional Document or the design of civic life that the text of this Constitution anticipates. Nevertheless, because of its formal resemblance to the Constitution, and its alignment with the Constitution, the negative alternative may at times be mistaken for the real thing. Unhappily—a word that the Founding generation might have chosen for this situation—over time and through a deficit of theoretical perspicacity, some of a Constitution's purported adherents may slip into that Negative Constitution unawares. In that role, they attempt to vindicate the principles of the Negative Constitution as earnestly as they might have faithfully honored their oath to the Constitution itself. That is, their deficiency of vision may well coexist with a surfeit of sincerity or a plenitude of zeal.

CONCURRENT NEGATIVE AND POSITIVE

A constitution is not established simply in reaction to a prevailing set of problematic conditions sustaining the presence or possibility of failure that might exist in a country, although this might also be a plausible claim. (At least this may indeed seem to be so, often in retrospect, as the eventual success of a constitution retrospectively defines the conditions it was supposed to address.) That is to say, its founding is not solely a problem-solving venture to counter prospects of difficulty or woe. Quite beyond these compelling practical considerations, the basic architectonics of a founding incorporates the holistic establishment of both the Negative and the Positive constitutions. A world of Failure is as much an artifact of a constitution making as a world of Success. Both worlds are *formed*, so that there is a "form of order" and a "form of disorder"—as in the co-presence of matter and antimatter—and both

---

2. Moses tells his People of how they will be honored by the rest of the world for their distinguishing rule of law:

> Behold, I have taught you statutes and judgments. . . . Keep therefore and do them; for this is your wisdom and your understanding in the sight of the nations, which shall hear all these statutes, and say, Surely this great nation is a wise and understanding people. . . . And what nation is there so great, that hath statutes and judgments so righteous as all this law, which I set before you this day? (Deuteronomy 5, 6, and 8 [King James Version]).

occupy the same space in the projections of a founding's anticipated possibilities.[3] When either of them "happens," we *know* it. This is a phenomenon of constitutional *recognition*, even if it has not been seen like this before.

NOT ENDEMIC OR SUCCESSIVE, BUT COGNATE AND PARALLEL

The theoretical idea of a matched system of Failure is also more than an acknowledgment of the crucial insight that every true constitution contains within itself pathologies endemic to its very character even (or especially) at its best—pathologies that challenge it over time and may weaken or strengthen it, depending on how they are dealt with. The theoretical proposition that every particular constitution has its own authentic and holistic negative—precisely because of its overarching constitutiveness—takes this profound initial insight about pathology to another level.[4] What can then be seen is that the simultaneous presence of this comprehensive negative adds at the same time to the threatened status and to the promised outcome of the Constitution.

The Negative Constitution may come to seem incidental, a mere artifact of the fears that provoke or sustain the Positive Constitution. Or, more consequentially, as the success of the Positive Constitution over time accrues a quality of political naturalness or historical inevitability, the Negative Constitution may achieve something of the same status—as the set of natural conditions or evolved historical circumstances whose problematics are presumed in retrospect to have given rise to the making of the Positive Constitution. Thus, this Positive Constitution may seem even more necessary or inevitable. At the extremes of such a process of founding, carried into its elaborated effects over time, a successful constitution may come to seem the very embodiment of authentic politics and good government, while a failed constitution may serve as the epitome of disorder and corruption.

In this theoretical sense, the architectonic relationship is the one between the Constitution and its negative ("Constitution" and "Anti-Constitution"), and not between the Constitution and its absence ("Constitution" and

---

3. It is interesting to consider the image of Nature here as a prototype for *constitution*, but one might question which way the metaphor goes: whether "matter and antimatter" may be rather more a constitutional theory of the universe. Thus, as Aristotle would have it, Nature itself reflects the constitutional enterprise.

4. And it may add to this insight an inclination toward homeopathy, as it seems to have done in the case of Madison when he writes in *Federalist* Nos. 10 and 51, arguing that sources of potential political devastation like factionalism and conflict should be built into the genetic composition and the ongoing processes of the Constitution.

"Non-Constitution").[5] Though there might be considerable theoretical dispute whether chaos can have constitutional character at all, there can be very little empirical disagreement that disorder can be so total as to reflect the workings of a comprehensive system. Today we call this a "failed state." In its completeness of disorder and in its generativeness of violence, it is something well beyond the natural unruliness of an unformed entity, or of a preconstitutional nonorder.

Negation as Constitutive

A real constitution knows its negation. It is founded on this knowledge. This is partly because that negation is the artifact of the making of a constitution and partly because a constitution is the artifact of an awareness of the negation. One of the defining characteristics of a real constitution is that it constantly anticipates its own failure. It articulates the contours of its demise. In fact, what it might mean for a real constitution to operate is that it exists on the edge of failure, as an attribute of its animating spirit.

In the broader theory of constitutionalism—the architectonics of the well-founded constitutional order—the awesome agenda of a constitution is to domesticate even its negation, and it can do so the more plausibly because this negative has been encompassed in its founding. What an extraordinary constitutiveness that a constituted order would predefine the terms of its own failure—to be sure, a failure in its own image. This may be why the Negative is so *systematic* or, rather, so *comprehensively negative* of the Constitution.

There are two senses in which it can be true that the validity of a constitution is dependent on a continuing knowledge of its negation and on the sustaining spirit of comprehending its demise.

ESTABLISHMENT BY CONTRAST

The success or effectiveness of a constitution may be assessed in contrast to its failing. In this sense, purportedly, the failure of constitution is the

---

5. The biblical parallel to this proposition occurs at the beginning of the book of Genesis, where Creation is set out in response to an earth, formless and empty. To counter such a nonstate, the first stage of this founding is to create light and to separate it from darkness, drawing limits that leave the two to constitute day and night, the order of time. The American minimalist Barnett Newman strove to capture the image of this prior state of nonconstitution in his painting, *Day before One* (1951). Everything after—the positive and the negative—serves to displace the absence of creation, or constitution.

Constitution of Failure. This would be an accomplishment of a tightly wound constitutional theory.

Similarly, for example, in regard to political theory generally, Thomas Hobbes's Kingdom of Darkness (a "Kingdom" indeed) or State of Nature (a "State," for sure) remains a constantly *possible* outcome of attempts to achieve an authoritative, well-ordered human community. By *constitutive contrast*, these negative regimes determine the state of political order, or Commonwealth—its domain and its character. In *Leviathan*, the disorder of Nature is comprehensive and thoroughly articulated— that is, it is fully "constitutional," though in this negative sense. By the time Hobbes begins to describe his Commonwealth, it has already been completely prefigured in the negative by the characteristics set out for the disordered State of Nature. More specifically in the exposition of his theory, Commonwealth is itself *set up, established* in contrast to its absence and failure—as a constituted displacement of the preexisting realm of disorder. To be successful, it must meet the compositional standard already exhibited in the negative realm. Substantively, one might elaborate his entire affirmative model of Commonwealth by systematically negating the constituent traits of the State of Nature (i.e., reasoning by double negative). For Hobbes, whose universe of reasoning is founded on the rule of either-or—the law of noncontradiction—a theory instituting a regime of political authority can be expounded twice, in sequence: first in the negative (the Kingdom of Darkness) and then in the positive (Commonwealth).

Comparably from the perspective of a more concrete constitutional theory, *The Federalist*, as part of its overall strategy of argument (which is, largely, a program of *exposition as advocacy*) and from the present point of that text, sets out two Americas. Both of them are elaborated as potential, systematically ordered futures—the Union of the American People and the Disunited States of America. In this case, however, the two parallel worlds are intertwined in the text as it is written, and the heroic vitality of the Positive Constitution interactively takes energy from the catastrophic doom of the Negative Constitution. Both are projections into the future, as consequences of constitution making. They reflect the interaction of parts composed well or poorly. But, in this case differently from Hobbes, though the two constitutional alternatives are finely balanced against each other, it may not be possible to produce either as a straightforward analytical negation of the other. In the greater nuance of their reinforcement of each other, the two are more comprehensively interrelated, and permanently so. The constituted "state" here is more firmly grounded in a *nature* of *contradiction*, which would be consistent with *The Federalist*'s mixed view of *human* nature (and of nature at large).

DEFINITION BY FAILURE

A constitution determines the traits of its own potential demise. This is especially so as it operates through the *experience* of a people in *constitutional* time—where history itself is framed by that constitution and where a people's own history is best understood by using that constitution as a template for the significance of events. These are the particular failures appropriate to itself, "definitive failures." And, thus, some failures are characteristically *definitive* of a specific constitutional order.

Ultimately, this is an aspect of what makes a constitution *constitutive*: it constitutes its own negative, and is mutually constituted by it. Any particular constitution will have specific traits of failure matched to itself, as negative *attributes*, which—when assembled "coherently" and made interactive—set up a comprehensively negative alternative constitution. This theoretical effect is a quality of the completeness of its *making*—in which it makes a system that includes its appropriate negation.

It is not, however, the case that the Negative Constitution is repudiated and disabled as a result of a constitution making. Instead, both constitutions are set in motion at the Founding. And they evolve together, so that both are elaborated over time. A constitution is mutually defined by and generatively defining of failure, and one of the chief means by which such a constitution sustains itself—engendering the terms of its ongoing *ratification* after the period of explicit "consent"—is by its (tentatively) controlling embrace of this reciprocal failure. In this respect, through articulating and thereby controlling the terms of its own demise, a constitution is sustained and reinforced by the very seeming fragility of its ever-apparent susceptibility to failing—in its own way.

At the same time, it advances its own success by elaborating an increasing capacity for organizing human endeavor and for increasing differentiation in its efficacy at prompting productive problems, across an expanding range of tests that threaten it. In such a manner, a constitutional order is not so much susceptible to the depredations of a "natural" history beyond its ordering, which might throw up events randomly. However much a challenge to the Constitution may be characterized as an emergency, what at times appears to be a pressing need to respond to external crisis will most likely turn out to have been a predictable urgency—the culmination of characteristic difficulties, with a strong sense later that "we've seen this before." The pattern repeats. When the threat has subsided or after it has been dealt with, it will be understood that the Constitution has been subjected, once again, to the challenges of its own already configured worst fears. Or at least it is interpreted that way. The threat only seemed to occur as a surprise because of the forgetfulness of founding that accompanies any successfully constitutional establishment over time. The challenge was erroneously perceived as an incident or exigency, rather than a manifestation of a built-in continuing possibility or liability.

The survivalist impetus of a successful constitutional enterprise is to establish a closed system. But, to provide a system big enough, this constitution making has to be a complex and extensive project, with a capacity for internal self-reformation; the project can be accomplished only by incorporating both the Negative Constitution and an openness to change on the Constitution's own terms, in response to that ongoing embrace.

II

The constitutive reciprocity between Positive and Negative constitutions is, at its most basic, a reflection of the fundamental grammar of political theory in both of the traditions from which constitutionalism arises, the classical-social compact and the biblical. This grammar is so thoroughly taken for granted that it may not be articulated very often for its own sake as the matrix of our political understandings. But stating what goes without saying, with an awareness of the deeper design behind it, is a crucial phase and a defining trait of constitutional theory, which might then take that understanding of what lies behind the obvious and *make something* of it.

Constitutions, Good and Bad

This fundamental grammar can be shown in Aristotle's systematic relationship between good and bad constitutions. Each analytical type of constitutional form (government by the one, the few, or the many) is precisely matched to its negative, in a sequence so routinely retold that we may not notice its underlying significance. This classic understanding of *matched* good and bad constitutions is an essential quality of the very idea of "constitution" itself. This sequence, moreover, reflects a very long-standing habit of constitutional thinking that is a manifestation of a more profound mutuality of the two constitutions. They are matched to each other indeed, but they are also *mutually constitutive*, reflexively defining by negation, analytically canceling out each other precisely, so that the presence of qualities of the one is the absence of qualities of the other. They are good and bad in respect to each other, partaking of the same form—where one is holistic and the other partialistic, but both are coherent.

The good and bad versions of the same constitutional form are both "constitutions," Aristotle holds, though there may be incomplete manifestations of either. Nevertheless, there is an extreme form of government, epitomizing disorder itself, which is so systematically factionalistic as to be no constitution at all, only an imposter in its pretense to have the part count absolutely for the whole. Tyranny is, in its plenary partialism and instability, a contradiction within itself. It is nonconstitutional. And another form of political order, using judicious mixture and balance as a means for approximating a stable holism, takes on the characterizing names of the enterprise itself: "polity," and "constitutional government."

The first foundation of a substantive theory of constitutionalism can be seen in Aristotle's contrast between "constitutional government" and "no constitution at all."

The later, social compact version of this most basic scheme in political theory is reflected in Hobbes's two mutually sustaining worlds, as noted earlier. The "state" of Nature as the pervasive condition of "war of all against all" is matched to the *state* of Commonwealth as the establishment of sovereign authority that represents a "real unity of them all," founded on an "everyone" created by a covenant of every one with every one.

Covenants, Honored or Violated

In the biblical tradition, Moses concludes the most archetypal founding of them all, organizing it around a twofold promise of blessing and curse that depends upon the People keeping or not keeping the Covenant. And so, in the book of Deuteronomy, the two parallel future possibilities are presented in detail, fully articulated as alternative future worlds constituted by the Covenant in its positive and negative consequences. The final speech of Moses to his People embraces benediction and malediction, in tandem.[6]

Later on in the Bible, this duality takes up the sequence of the destruction of the Temple and of Jerusalem, and the Exile of the People, as a systematic *way of living* in failure and desperation, followed by the Return, the recovery of Jerusalem, with the rebuilding of the Temple and the structured ways that ennoble it. The New Testament's account of Crucifixion and Resurrection (each annexed to a world that parallels

---

6. The interleaving of parallel worlds described in detail, one of Light and one of Darkness, *arising from two covenants*—the Covenant with God and the Covenant with Evil—provides the expositional and theoretical structure of the book of Isaiah. Here the simultaneity of the two possibilities is so strong that the worlds shift in a jittery juxtaposition even within sentences. Isaiah, however, complicates the theoretical project by saying—more like *The Federalist* will—that at times what seems to be light is in fact darkness. The Prophet is also a theorist.

the other) reflects very much the same model of explanation, with Jesus declaring that the "temple" will be destroyed but restored in three days.[7]

In significant respects, the overarching argumentative strategy of *The Federalist,* with its covenantal preoccupations in both name and substance,[8] follows Moses in its portrayal of a choice between a world of blessing (where weaknesses will be stabilizing) and a world of curse (where strengths will be destructive).[9] The bottom-line message of *The Federalist,* like that of Moses in his valedictory, is: "You choose."

III

The juxtaposition of two parallel worlds of alternative possibility is a powerful but conventional structure of analytical *thinking* and rhetorical *exposition.* In the context of the American Founding, however, it is also a structure of constitutional *making.* It is the genetic matrix of the American constitutional enterprise. One crucial shift from classical to Federalist thought, found in the comparative purposes for articulating the paired worlds, is the move from generic (a means of disclosing the character of the types of political form) to generative (a means of creating new forms of polity). This is a shift from preservative (knowing something constitutionally which already exists, so that it can be maintained, or appreciated as it is being lost) to transformative (understanding the science of how things are made, so that something new can be achieved, or can come to be in the future).

A Founding of Multiple Constitutions

As part of a strategic agenda for a founding, explicitly conceived, James Madison lays out a comprehensive account of past and present regimes of federation, disclosing their intrinsic problematics or "vices" as a functional match to their "constitutions." He uses this elaborated set of

7. In the book of Mark, the juxtaposition of worlds encompasses the Kingdom of Heaven and the Kingdom of Earth in the same space, at the same time—a strategy that James Madison uses in *The Federalist,* where he suggests that the new world of Constitutional America has in its essence already occurred. It is fully present for those who can see it and live according to its ways. It simply needs to be apprehended (seen for what it is) and given form (so that it can be used and preserved).

8. See Madison's prefiguring of Abraham Lincoln's Gettysburg Address in *Federalist* No. 14: "[T]he mingled blood which they ["American Citizens"] have shed in defense of their sacred rights consecrates their Union. . . ."

9. In a similar manner, the English constitutional theorist John Milton structures his poetic account of the order of time: *Paradise Lost* and *Paradise Regained.*

accounts (one from outside and one from inside America) as the negative order to which a new system of politics is to be analytically juxtaposed.[10] The inventiveness of his constitutional proposals during the Convention for what will become the Federalists' Positive Constitution is a function, in multifaceted ways, of the insightfulness of his (now Federalist) Negative Constitution. Later, during the ratification process, the even greater imaginativeness of Madison and Hamilton's interpretive arguments on behalf of the proposed Positive Constitution[11] is generated substantially through taking into account the opposing matched pair of Negative and Positive constitutions of the Antifederalists (and, at times, the Federalists' strategic depiction of the two Antifederalist constitutions).

That is to say, in the first stage, a propositional creativity is prompted by insightful *negation* (of the Federalist Anti-Constitution). And, in the second stage, a ratifying imagination is derived from constructivist *opposition* (to the twofold Antifederalist constitutions). In the first stage, comprising the period just before and during the drafting Convention of 1787 in Philadelphia, Madison is focused on countering the Federalist Negative Constitution of national disunion and majority tyranny. In the second stage, at the time of the ratification debate, *The Federalist Paper's* Positive Constitution is set out in close conjunction with this Federalist Negative Constitution. In addition, crucially, it is *developed* as an imaginative *comprehensive* alternative, in opposition to the Antifederalists' Positive and Negative constitutions.

The latter pair is generally marked by the contrast between simple, responsive versus complicated, repressive government. The choice between these two Antifederalist options might well have looked like all there was to decide. But what *The Federalist* puts forward, as its own holistic scheme of Negative and Positive constitutions, occupies a wholly new theoretical space. The ratification conflict between Antifederalist and Federalist paradigms is now an opposition at a higher level. It is a confrontation concerning the basic science of politics or, more properly, about the broader theory of constitutionalism. Here the questions are about more than good and bad (constitutions). They raise more primitive issues about what is possible beyond historical experience and what will work when other

10. Beginning with the basic research of his "Notes on Ancient and Modern Confederacies" paired with his "Vices of the Political System of the United States," in 1787, he reiterates the lessons of these studies over and over again throughout his career: repeating the insights as the basis for conclusions in his numbers of *The Federalist*, for example, and again, at the end of his life, in his preface to the *Notes on the Federal Convention of 1787*. The stuff of this early research furnishes his bedrock facticity.

11. *The Federalist*'s advocacy on behalf of ratification partakes as much of constitution making as constitutional interpretation. It focuses far more on the *description* of a new world to be made than the *meaning* of words to be interpreted.

noble enterprises have failed. Of this new fundamental theory, Constitutional America is henceforward intended to be a practical replica.

In the United States, through these specific terms of the initial constitution making, Negative and Positive constitutions are *built into* the conditions of the country's collective constitutional being. But that is not all. Through the continued constitution making that took place during the ratification arguments, these twofold constitutions are built in doubly, and then these pairs of doubles are set against each other at the level of their opposition—so that the two oppositions, Federalist and Antifederalist, are established in a persistent tension with one another that is itself a permanently defining aspect of the Founding itself.

The effect is that there are four constitutions in play in the America as founded in 1787–89: Positive Federalist, Negative Federalist; and Positive Antifederalist, Negative Antifederalist. And these have a systematic, complexly interactive relationship—a compound structure of logic, as in F:-F:: A:-A, plus --F and --A (the double-negatives of each paradigmatic constitution). This relationship, as a whole, composes the constitutional order of the United States (see diagram), as it encompasses the country's two sets of founders, crediting each with a properly indispensable role in its making.[12]

Thus, in short, if the theoretical arguments of those opposed to ratification had not been so powerful and persuasive (beyond even being compellingly obvious), the second phase of constitution making that occurred in *The Federalist* could not likely have been so transformative of the very character of constitutional thinking itself.[13] While Aristotle displays practical profundity by recommending a *mixed constitution*,

12. If the American constitutional enterprise were as simple as it is sometimes claimed (and as it is implied in the "names" of the two groups of advocates), this set of relationships could be collapsed (across the diagonals shown in the diagram) and replaced by equations: -F = A (what the **Federalists** were **against** is what the **Antifederalists** were **for**); along with F = -A (what the **Federalists** were **for** is what the **Antifederalists** were **against**). Unfortunately, these are the views that usually appear as unquestioned orthodoxy in American civics and history textbooks, as well as many state testing standards in the United States. But these are not equivalences. Nor is F = --F (what the **Federalists** were **for** is the **negative** of what they were **against**), though it may be that A = --A, given the conditions of the ratification debate and the Antifederalists' clearer commitment to the standard law of noncontradiction. Thus, there are fully four constitutions, and possibly five or six.

Much is at stake in keeping these multiple constitutions of our founding conceptually separate and interpretively distinct. For the continuing presence of each one, along with the structured relationships among them—establishing, as they do, a theoretical scheme in the image of a system of logic—provides a legacy of conceptual capital for understanding Constitutional America over time, along with a set of resources for addressing the more vexing problems issuing from the constitutionally generated history of Americans' lives together.

13. As William Blake wrote at the conclusion of *The Marriage of Heaven and Hell* (ca. 1790), "Opposition is true friendship."

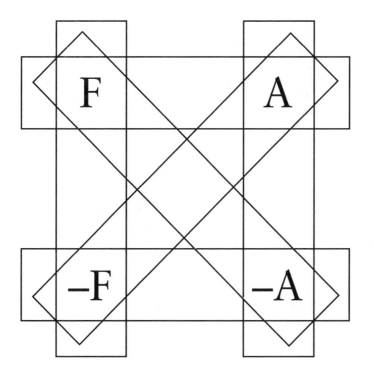

$$--F \qquad --A$$

$$F : -F :: A : -A$$

F = Positive Constitution (Federalist)
−F = Negative Constitution (Federalist)
A = Positive Constitution (Antifederalist)
−A = Negative Constitution (Antifederalist)

the American Founding moves beyond that, to establish an interactive scheme of *multiple constitutions*. And where Hobbes achieves theoretical rigor by generating political authority from the law of noncontradiction, the dual constitutional founders of the United States create a "new order of the ages," organized around a logical multiplicity that embraces the reasonable multivocality in the nature of things, beyond true and false.[14]

Birth of the Nation in Negation

The process of embedding a negative constitution into the genetics of the American Founding begins formally with the Declaration [of Independence]. The core of this document, by its own terms, is configured as a paean[15] to the need for good government, based upon a lament for its absence. This document conducts its advocacy in the negative, providing a comprehensive picture of the bad government that prevails in America, or will eventuate there soon, under the king's "abdication" of government. It composes a portrait of *demise* in the most literal sense of the word, as the termination of a regime. After the "declaration" of the factual existence of "one people," implying that a social compact has occurred at some unspecified point in the past, the building up of attributes of bad government takes on the character of an elaboration of constitutional features. With the detail and order of its negative provisions, the Declaration's constitutional-descriptive portrait for all time establishes one of the two Negative constitutions at the base of the American order. Moreover, and with a simple project of double negation and recomposition, one might induce at least a tentative version of the Declaration's Positive Constitution—largely the same as that subscribed to by the Antifederalists later (and ever after).[16]

The other Negative Constitution of the United States (the Federalists'), however, arises directly from the positive constitutive accomplishment of the Declaration itself and its sustaining Lockean social-compact logic: the establishment at the end of the document of thirteen "free and

14. In this shift of logical ground, of course, a way of governing centered on the single sovereign voice (where Hobbes's covenanted consent of "everyone together" is transformed by a sort of constitutional representation into what is governmentally a "real unitie of them all") is replaced by the multiplicity of a sovereign people whose first nature is mutual differentiation and conflict—as observed in *Federalist* Nos. 10 and 37. As usual, *logos* and *polis* must be kept in synchronicity.

15. A word, associated directly with the name of Apollo, deriving from the term for a hymn of deliverance (from disease).

16. This would produce something very much like George Mason's and Thomas Jefferson's Virginia Constitution of 1776, which incorporates at the beginning of its text the specific language of the negative portrait from the Declaration. The affirmative constitution of Virginia's governmental structure is then set out against this account, with an implication of negative causality.

independent states" or polities. In this manner, the holistic animating *spirit* of "one people" at the very outset of the Declaration (epitomized in the covenantal name given to the new undertaking, the "United" States of America) is balanced, in a parallel section at the end of the document, by the dividedness of that People into multiple political *bodies* (autonomous and equal, separate not only from Great Britain but also from each other). Correspondingly, the very first section of the Declaration, which gives the common name of "Union" to the People of America, is matched by the final section of the document, which arranges the individual signatures of its authors in the North-to-South order of the separate states. Instead of moving from many to one (as in Hobbes's phase shift from holistic covenant to unitary government), this founding document moves from one to many.[17] The negative consequences of the Declaration's pre–constitution making give rise to the theoretical strategy of the Federalists' ratification argument: to pursue their prospect of "happiness" in the world, and to achieve an order of community for themselves, "My fellow citizens" or countrymen need a single body politic (a *constitution* indeed). And in the one proposed by the Convention they will *see* themselves most authentically—*if* they can take a "comprehensive" view (as Alexander Hamilton puts it) of America as a federated union embodying the covenantal spirit of the Declaration's "one people" with a common destiny.

Vices and Constitution

From an analysis of two experimental constitutional zones of accumulated and reiterated failure, Madison induces the initial proposals for the new Constitution (or, rather, on behalf of a *constitution* for the first

---

17. Understanding this, Madison begins his preface to the *Notes on the Federal Convention of 1787* with an explanation of the constitution making, where communities join together to make a federation on the same basis as individuals associate to establish a common authority or government in Hobbes's theory. His very first words:

> As the weakness and wants of man naturally lead to an association of individuals, under a common authority whereby each may have the protection of the whole against danger from without, and enjoy in safety within, the advantages of social intercourse, and an exchange of the necessaries & comforts of life: in like manner feeble communities, independent of each other, have resorted to a Union, less intimate, but with common Councils, for the common safety ag[ain]st powerful neighbors, and for the preservation of justice and peace among themselves. . . .
>
> It remained for the British Colonies, now United States, of North America, to add to those examples [of ancient and modern "confederal associations"], one of a more interesting character than any of them: which led to a system without example ancient or modern, a system founded on popular rights, and so combining, a federal form with the forms of individual Republics, as may enable each to supply the defects of the other and obtain the advantages of both.

time).[18] These proposals appear first tentatively in his letter to Governor Edmund Randolph in 1787 (where he proposes a "new system") and then more substantively in his Virginia Plan (which set the framework of debate in the Federal Convention of 1787). As background for these, he has composed in effect two white papers: "Notes on Ancient and Modern Confederacies" (1787) and "Notes on the Vices of the Political System of the United States" (1787). The first background analysis is laid out structurally as a series of six or seven comparative "constitutions" of the "foederal authority" of attempted confederations,[19] each with a textually corresponding account of the distinguishing "vices of the constitution" that sustain its failure. These "vitiated" constitutions serve as negative examples of laudable but functionally unsuccessful endeavors by others who aimed at achieving what the Americans also aspire to do. They provide specific constitutional attributes, *at the level of federation*, to be avoided systematically in the making of a new American Constitution.

The second analysis focuses primarily on "vices"—in effect, rendering a Negative Constitution of twelve Articles, with initial attributes of an affirmative "constitution" of the American "political system" implicated in its sequence of deficiencies. The affirmative "system" is as yet only an inchoate "constitution," if the term could have been used at all. This document provides a descriptive catalog of the consequences of malconstitution, *at the level of government*. And by so doing, it lays out the space and agenda for its alternative. The detrimental constitutional characteristics that give rise to governmental failure provide specific inducements to positive constitutional provisions that will counter the forces of vitiation. They do not, of themselves, however, fully direct all that a Positive Constitution for the United States should comprise.[20]

18. It is not often remembered that the Constitutional "plan" presented by the Federalists in the 1780s was itself a risky combination of two political forms with distinguishing historical reputations for abject and disastrous failure: republics and federations.

19. His final (seventh) example, the Gryson League (the Indian confederacy in New York), is left without details in his research, though he reserved a page for it.

20. As Madison writes in *Federalist* No. 37:

The novelty of the undertaking immediately strikes us. It has been shown in the course of these papers, that the existing Confederation is founded on principles which are fallacious; that we must consequently change this first foundation, and with it the superstructure resting upon it. It has been shown, that the other confederacies which could be consulted as precedents have been vitiated by the same erroneous principles, and can therefore furnish no other light than that of beacons, which give warning of the course to be shunned, without pointing out that which ought to be pursued. The most that the convention could do in such a situation, was to avoid the errors suggested by the past experience of other countries, as well as of our own; and to provide a convenient mode of rectifying their own errors, as future experiences may unfold them.

There are insights for a real constitutional theory, broader by far than the American constitutional enterprise, that arise from his work in these preparatory documents—comparative constitutions, empirical evaluation of political practice in terms of systemic framework, and structurally parallel negative-positive constitutions. These are taken over, often literally picked up in Madison's subsequent constitutional masterworks, as he incorporates them in his essays for *The Federalist* and in his *Notes on the Federal Convention of 1787*, which was edited at the end of his life and published after his death. In the latter work, as he states in his unfinished preface, his fearful and prudential intent is to preserve the founded constitutional order (under threat, as he sees it, from the Negative Constitution of disunion that is articulated as one of America's two possible futures in *The Federalist*) by demonstrating the historical process of how the Constitution was made through conflictual deliberation. He suggests, as well, that his account can provide the future with a historically elaborated example of effective constitution making (which he laments was not available to him as he investigated the characteristics of other confederations). And he implies that other people can similarly make their own constitutions, or that Americans can now know how they might make their Constitution again if the current one should fail. All of this is quite deliberately dedicated to securing the Constitution's future by consolidating the Founding—at this later time at the end of his career, not in *retrospect* (about the past) but by establishing the original *prospect* (about the future). Madison's final *Notes* are not just *about* the initial constitutional Founding; they are, for him, its concluding stage.

FEDERALIST: FAILURE AND PROMISE

Early on in *The Federalist*, the organizational strategy of argument turns from analysis of experienced failure to future projection of American demise. In a sequence of essays building up major themes of constitution making, it may not be obvious why *The Federalist* would spend such effort to establish an elaborate account of "what would failure look like?" But the agenda itself is laid out with great urgency from the outset

---

The Negative Constitution of the Federalists establishes what is to be preempted. Madison's Positive Constitution is not fully articulated at the Founding. It is unfinished, left to be elaborated by a scientific evaluation of its own mistakes, which it will generate through its proper workings. Thus, the production of error is subsumed into the progress of the Positive Constitution. Quite simply, the product of *The Federalist*'s "new science of politics" will learn from its mistakes, shoring up its own constitutional integrity and contributing new knowledge about the nature of the well-ordered community, quite beyond the constitutional understandings on which it was established. That is to say, the Federalist Constitution is not just *based on* a new science of politics; it *is* that new science.

in *Federalist* No. 1, where Hamilton stipulates that failure—on behalf of the American People and for humanity at large—will be the alternative to ratification of the proposed Constitution. Federalist failure or success is yet to come. Attention is oriented to founding a future, and it can be bad or good.

Overall, as Moses did, *The Federalist* writers put forth two possible eventualities for America. One is a world of comprehensive chaos, terror, and ineptitude; the other, of self-sustaining unity, order, and capacity: Two worlds in the space of one country and for one people—a framework of exposition for the parallel virtual realities of Constitutional America, established then to endure and evolve together for as long as the enterprise lasts.

These two constitutional worlds play off of each other interpretively in the argument, not just rhetorically to encourage ratification but also functionally, as a way to bring about the operative consequences of the American constitutional order. Thus, the Federalists' Negative Constitution is characteristically marked by a *systematicalness*, an essential attribute of "constitution" itself. And it seems clear that this outcome is mandated as a *continuous* possibility alongside the Positive Constitution. But in contrast to Hobbes this time and to the Antifederalists, in this case, the two constitutions are not so much derivative from each other as mutually informing, substantially interleaved in the text of *The Federalist*, though much of the account of the Negative Constitution of Future America is laid out in the first fifteen numbers. These culminate in the matched pair of Madison's No. 14 and Hamilton's No. 15, as variations on the theme. The last paragraph of No. 14 is marked by the same jittery juxtaposition of light and darkness—the co-presence in the text of the twofold constitutions—which one finds in the book of Isaiah. Thus, as members of the always-future present American community, the "fellow countrymen" may be either an aggregation of "aliens, rivals, enemies" or "fellow citizens of one great flourishing respectable empire," the "mutual guardians of our mutual happiness."

Just as there is, for this set of American founders, a *structure of failure* that is not simply the accumulation of detrimental items and traumas, so also is there a structure to the text of Federalist accounts of impending catastrophe, on behalf of ratification. This quality is especially appropriate given their strategy to portray what the affirmative constitutional world would *look* like, instead of primarily advocating why it would be good. (It is a constitutional argument, not a moral one.) Side by side with this world of aspiration is the parallel world of the violated covenant. Readers may be so used to reading the numbers of *The Federalist* in isolation that they do not readily see the pattern of presentation, the theoretical strategy of argument replicated in the order of the text. For example, *Federalist* No. 10, in its treatment of the diseases of factions, is a part of the building up of a picture of systematic chaos, the full-bore Constitution of Failure. Borrowing style from Hobbes, then enhancing it, the comprehensive Negative Constitution of the United States (or the Constitution of the Disunited States) incorporates, in strategic stages, multiple forms of external and internal war: war among European nations transposed to America, war among the regions of the United States, war between the States, war within the States, war among persons (and perhaps even warring confusion within individuals). This hideous Constitution is multifaceted and self-reinforcing, reiterative the way constitutions should be. The Federalists' success in convincing ratifiers that the country faced a present or imminent "crisis" is the consequence of their effectiveness in setting forth this Negative Constitution.

Arrayed against this projected picture of systematic disorder is the Federalists' portrayal of the Positive Constitution, which needed to be matched to the Negative in its completeness. It is quite interesting, though, that the preliminary standards for what a real "constitution" might be—so that it incorporates systematicalness, reiterativeness, and self-replication across levels of political life—are established in the first instance through the Negative Constitution of the Federalists. And, considering the substance of the Positive Constitution, the *complication* (as in a "complicated" Swiss watch) of the Negative Constitution, provides a tacit justification for the complexity of the proposed affirmative Constitution of the Federalists, which would need to be a full match to its negative, at the least.

ANTIFEDERALIST: LOSS AND RECOVERY

Where the founding dread of the Federalists is failure, the original fear of the Antifederalists is loss. While Madison studied the ambitious failures in the establishment and operation of large confederations in Europe and among the Greek city-states, many of the Antifederalists focused on the loss of the Roman republic and Greek democracy. At their most problematic, the Antifederalists evince a nostalgia for what never was but might have been, and now can be for America.

For the Antifederalists, in contrast to the Federalists, *at the level of the charter of governmental institutions*, the Declaration's portrait of bad government (with the later addition of a scheme where government is unrepresentative, nontransparent, and oppressive) displays their apprehensive picture of the negation of the Constitution of a Republic. The proper functioning of this desired form is simple enough for the people to understand (so that they can watch it) and accountable in ways that can be efficiently enforced or punished by a majority. The constitutional recourse of the Antifederalists is conceived of more as a renewal than a remedy. Its aim is to recover the terms of the original enterprise of instituting a republic, recurring to its first animating principles and thereby rejoining the course of the Constitution's history with its precedents in the progress of good government over prior ages of successive elaboration. Antifederalist constitutionalism is a culmination of history, not a new beginning of time.

With increasing focus during the ratification debate, moreover, the distinctive Antifederalist perspective adds a second aspect to its Negative Constitution at the level of the social compact. Where the Declaration had recognized a proper political foundation for good government in "one people" (invoking the "the authority of the good People of these colonies"), the Antifederalists' fear of the potential moral deficiency and social inequality as the distinguishing character of this People becomes the popular basis for their Negative Constitution. These traits may articulate the terms of an "anti-social compact" (perhaps in contrast to the Federalists' "social anti-covenant"). There is no "citizen" in this deformed polity. Its members are solely clients and dependents, bargaining away their liberty and dignity for the illusion of self-gratification, security, or national greatness. Thus, they would return to the level of social compact–making in the course of their routine dealings with government, so as to abuse the fundamental preconditions of political order.

IV

It is not the purpose of this essay to elaborate the substance of the four, five, or six various constitutions in play at the American Founding. The goal here is to sketch the nature of their relationships, as well as to offer support for a conclusion that it is these relationships which are truly constitutive and that all of them are mutually defining. Ever afterward, we draw on this system as the organizing key to map our national political arguments. For what it really means to be *founded* constitutionally as a People is for its citizens to construct the right disagreements—considered as "right" because they arise as interpretive disputes about the meaning of their fundamental commitments—and to have the debate over those differences itself contribute to the reinforcement of the constitutional system.

As such, a successful constitutional system is marked by its capacity to prompt productive problems. Even from within the bounds of a constitutional document, most provisions operate more in the role of posing questions than providing answers. What does it mean, for example, to be committed to "equal protection of the laws" or the "privileges and immunities of citizens of the United States"? It is the task of constitutional citizenship and democratic leadership to figure these things out progressively over the course of the time of our life together.

And so an effective constitutional order will generate inquiry. Modeled on the scientific exploration of nature by experimentation, the constitutional enterprise can be understood *as a scheme of investigation* at three levels—the character of a sovereign people, the nature of political life, and the attributes of good government. The advancement of this Constitution-spurred inquiry adds to knowledge about the well-ordered community that can accelerate a People's progress as a civilization, measured by its contribution to humanity at large (as Hamilton urges in *Federalist* No. 1).

This concept of the *scientific* constitution (an enterprise for inquiring into the nature of the principles it sets out) and its *experimental* polity (a project for working out the structures that sustain the community sketched out by the Constitution) requires a process of trial and error. As anyone who conducts such a practical inquiry realizes, the answers to questions of a *constitutional* character (whether in physics or politics) ineluctably produce more questions. That is a lucky thing for such an enterprise. The design of an effective inquiry is to produce the right questions.

Standing at the Border of Order

The theoretical position I have articulated here should mean that over time and with constitutional practice, the constitutive potential of failure may become more fully *encompassed* by the very order of a particular constitutional enterprise. But it may also mean that constitutional order, the longer it functions effectively (prevailing over its negative), might come to generate *new sorts of failure* as it achieves new sorts of success. That is, it may achieve not just new successes, but new kinds of success; so also with failures.

On the other hand, this founding strategy of elaborating constitutional failure systematically from the outset, as the negative compensatory ground for generating and sustaining a successful constitution (while articulating the inherently potential failure as the ongoing constitutive negative that gives interpretive meaning to a constitution) may leave a constitutional framework vulnerable to forms of failure that show up as unincorporated surprise or unsystematic threats. Thus, its strengths might fatally mask its weaknesses. Or this strategy may leave this constitutional enterprise too effectively resistant against fundamental alternatives to itself—alternatives that may be systematic improvements—and thereby it might suppress a more profound course of constitutional progress.

The success of a constitutional enterprise is to have predefined its *own typical* failure, which it is quite particularly set up to countermand effectively, or at least to negotiate with successfully over time. As complete as this once-new order may purport to be—by accommodating its negative in the very character of its enterprise—there may be other types of failure. Nature, or the world, or history, may refuse to be encompassed by even the most comprehensive of human orders, purporting (as this one in America does) to replicate the deeper constitutional character of knowledge itself: the architectonic knowing of good and bad, of how to make things and how to destroy things, and of the conditions where these negations occupy the same space. To become what it truly is, the Constitution may need to be made new again.

Part II

HOW CAN CONSTITUTIONAL DEMOCRACY
CONTEND WITH EMERGENCY?

5

"In the Name of National Security"

EXECUTIVE DISCRETION AND CONGRESSIONAL LEGISLATION IN THE CIVIL WAR AND WORLD WAR I

BENJAMIN A. KLEINERMAN

IN THE FACE OF PROFOUND SECURITY threats, constitutional republics seem both to require and to rightfully fear powers that threaten
the legal and nonarbitrary political order that they otherwise seek to
maintain. Real political and civil freedom seems to demand that governmental power becomes authority, that is, it becomes legal, only if it
is constrained within certain definitive and well-promulgated boundaries. Walter Murphy defines this as constitutionalism: "Every exercise of
governmental power should be subject to important substantive limitations and obligations."[1] And yet unanticipated exigencies may require
the exercise of power that either could never have been anticipated by
the laws or perhaps, going further, should never have been anticipated
by any system of law that aims to remain within certain boundaries. So
the question becomes: how does a constitutional republic square this
circle? Or, how does it permit the exercise of unanticipated or unwanted
powers given that its very foundation stands in opposition to the exercise of all arbitrary power—and, surely, the exercise of this power, if per-

I would like to thank Mark Largent and Rafael Major for commenting on earlier versions
of this chapter. I would also like to thank my professorial assistant, Maria Bianchi, for her
research on this project.

1. Walter Murphy, *Constitutional Democracy: Creating and Maintaining a Just Political Order* (Baltimore: Johns Hopkins University Press, 2007), 6. Murphy establishes an
important distinction, especially for the purposes of this essay, between what he calls
"constitutionism" and constitutionalism. "Constitutionalism differs from constitutionism
in demanding adherence not to any given constitutional text or order but to principles
that center on respect for human dignity and the obligations that flow from those principles" (ibid.,16). To anticipate the argument of this essay in these terms, one could say that
the anticipation and legalization of all necessary power is "constitutionist" without being
"constitutionalist," while the allowance for an extralegal power capable of exercising that
extraordinary power which sometimes becomes necessary can preserve "constitutionalism"
while abandoning "constitutionism."

mitted, has the potential to become arbitrary? Or, as Lincoln said with his startling eloquence, "Must a Government, of necessity, be too strong for the liberties of its own people, or too weak to maintain its own existence?"[2]

Thus, we ask: how best does a constitutional republic respond to threats to its existence? Should it legalize those new powers that have now become necessary? Or should it merely exercise these powers outside the legal order during the seemingly temporary and extraordinary security threat? When the legal order is put under strain by conditions of insecurity, the legalistic tendency is to look for ways of creating new legal powers. After all, if a constitutional republic insures against arbitrariness by establishing standing laws by which the government acquires the authority to exercise whatever power has now become necessary, then, when new conditions of insecurity arise, these laws seemingly must change. Given its foundational claim that power is acceptable only if exercised according to standing laws, the tendency of a constitutional republic is to change the laws so as to accommodate the new and exceptional state of affairs created by war. If the danger of arbitrariness stems from the unanticipated necessity of power, then the constitutional response would seem to be to choose to anticipate and to provide for the unanticipated.[3]

Of course, in providing for these new powers, one might build into the laws some expectation that the government will exercise discretion. These new powers are made necessary by an exceptional and extraordinary state of war rather than by the ordinary state of peace; thus, one would expect they will be exercised with discretion in accordance with their actual necessity for the conditions of a war. The difficulty is that, precisely by creating the legal authority to exercise extraordinary powers, one runs the risk that they will become both routinized and institutionalized.[4] As David Dyzenhaus warns in another context, "One cannot, as Carl Schmitt rightly argued, confine the exception. If it is introduced into legal order and treated as such, it will spread."[5] In short, once the laws

2. "Message to Congress in Special Session," July 4, 1861, in *Abraham Lincoln: His Speeches and Writings*, ed. Roy P. Basler (Cambridge: Da Capo Press, 2001), 598.

3. Discussing Tocqueville's account of the legalistic ethos, Judith Shklar writes: "If they fear tyranny, it is because it tends to be arbitrary, not because it is repressive." Judith Shklar, *Legalism* (Cambridge: Harvard University Press, 1964), 15.

4. To some degree, Jack Goldsmith's "insider's" account of the Bush administration shows the extent to which this actually did occur. See Jack Goldsmith, *The Terror Presidency: Law and Judgment inside the Bush Administration* (New York: W. W. Norton, 2007).

5. David Dyzenhaus, "Humpty Dumpty Rules or the Rule of Law: Legal Theory and the Adjudication of National Security," *Australian Journal of Legal Philosophy* 28 (2003): 29; see also Mark Tushnet, "Emergencies and the Idea of Constitutionalism," in *The Constitution in Wartime*, ed. Mark Tushnet (Durham, NC: Duke University Press, 2005), 39–54.

provide for it, the exceptional becomes normalized and acceptable. By seeking to provide for the necessity of the exercise of power in certain exigencies, the constitutional regime ends up enlarging the scope of all of its power.[6]

Moreover, during World War I, while the government claimed the war itself had made the legalization of certain powers—otherwise untenable—necessary, this claim seems all-too-often to be nothing more than a cover for repressive authorities that are substantively unrelated to the prosecution of the war. For instance, after having achieved the passage of the legislation limiting dissent that the Wilson administration wanted during World War I, the attorney general said: "May God have mercy on them [dissenters], for they need expect none from an outraged people and an avenging government."[7] Apparently, this legislation had little to do with that which was necessary to win the war and much to do with the feeling that dissent should not be tolerated during a war. Although its advocates claim that war makes the passage of such repressive legislation both necessary and constitutional, the legislation's true intent seems to have little to do with its avowed intent. In other words, war changes everything insofar as it truly does becomes necessary for the government to do certain things that would not and should not be countenanced during peace, but it does not—or, at least, it should not—change everything insofar as the government can now claim any power it wants "in the name of national security."

The lesson of World War I should instead lead us to reevaluate our initial legalistic impulse to legalize all powers that might be necessary. Insofar as a constitutional order claims that power is legitimate only if exercised under and according to the law, unanticipated power, once ensconced, poses an important threat to the constitutional order. But, if we attempt to control this threat by empowering the government to do all that might become necessary in any exigency, we give the government too much power. Instead, as paradoxical as it seems, it is better to embrace something like Lincoln's articulation of a presidential "war power" during the Civil War—that is, to keep the extraordinary powers necessary in a warlike situation outside the legal order. In being outside the legal order, these powers are not necessarily, however, outside the constitutional order. Lincoln claimed the president can exercise powers that Congress cannot. Properly understood, the president has such powers not

---

6. I have examined the problem of exceptional power in constitutionalism at greater length in Benjamin A. Kleinerman, *The Discretionary President: The Promise and Peril of Executive Power* (Lawrence: University Press of Kansas, 2009).

7. Quoted in Paul L. Murphy, *World War I and the Origin of Civil Liberties in the United States* (New York: W. W. Norton, 1979), 95.

as an inherent constitutional right that cannot be abridged, restricted, or overseen by Congress but as an extralegal and thus inherently contestable constitutional possibility. Because their authority can be established only by showing the necessity of discretionary actions, in exercising this power, the executive and his administration always risk themselves. The executive should have this power, in the first place, because he has the active "energy" requisite to respond to unforeseen exigencies. But, in the second place, such power should reside in the executive because the extralegal nature of his activity allows for its exercise when necessary without leading to its normalization.

Again, this is not to say that Congress does not and cannot have an interest in these matters. But, if we can appreciate the exception for what it truly is and allow the executive an inherently contestable authority to respond to the exception, then it allows Congress to legislate for the norm rather than the exception. To anticipate the exigencies of war, the legislature has granted the executive powers either that it might not otherwise feel comfortable with its possessing or that simply go beyond the Constitution; the congressional "war power" has typically been exercised by delegating to and providing for all those powers Congress can imagine the executive might need. By granting to the president a "war power," we can better limit the scope of that power because, in the first place, we now need not claim blithely and with infinite imprecision that Congress has different constitutional powers during war than during peace; Congress's constitutional powers of legislation will now remain the same in war and peace. The necessities that war imposes on the government fall under the extralegal capacities of the executive branch. And, second, we allow Congress to become the overseer of, rather than the co-conspirator with, that branch both most able to respond to the necessities of war and, because its power expands to such a degree in war, most in need of oversight.

To illustrate this contention, I briefly explore the relative experiences of both World War I and the Civil War. While different in a vast number of ways, comparing these two wars is useful because of the dramatically different approaches to the problem of governmental power taken by Woodrow Wilson and Abraham Lincoln. While Wilson, progressive democrat that he was, aimed to legalize all those powers he thought necessary, Lincoln aimed to keep the exercise of his war powers outside the laws. By legalizing all those powers he claimed were necessary, Wilson pursued ends that are much more problematic in a constitutional order, whereas Lincoln, by preserving the extralegal nature of his authority, managed to restrain, to a certain degree, these problematic powers from spreading into areas unrelated to their "constitutional" purpose.

World War I

In an "Address Delivered at the National Democratic Club" in 1908, Woodrow Wilson lamented the increasing reliance on "executive regulation" rather than "legal regulation." He continued: "Have we given up law? Must we fall back on discretionary executive power? The Government of the United States was established to get rid of arbitrary, that is, discretionary executive power."[8] Of course, as president, the exigencies of the war led Wilson to believe discretionary executive power was necessary. But, given his earlier position, it should not be surprising that he sought to legalize this discretion through an expansion of governmental power that had not been seen in the United States since John Adams and the Alien and Sedition Acts of 1798. If the discretionary executive power necessary for the war could be made legal, its arbitrary character would be effaced. Instead of conducting the war utilizing the extralegal discretionary executive power Wilson found so distasteful, he sought instead legal authority for the full range of powers he thought necessary to conduct the war.[9]

Thus, beginning in 1917, when he asked for the "authority to exercise censorship over press" because it was "absolutely necessary to the public safety," Wilson sought, though he did not always get, the legal authority he needed to exercise discretionary executive power.[10] As with other powers he requested during the war, the president related this press censorship provision of his proposed Espionage Act, this part of which Congress did end up resisting, directly to the conduct of the war effort.

8. Woodrow Wilson, *College and State: Educational, Literary and Political Papers*, ed. Ray Stannard Baker and William E. Dodd (New York: Harper and Brothers, 1925), 2:25.

9. It is certainly relevant but beyond the scope of this chapter that Woodrow Wilson had, by the time he became president, managed to reinterpret the presidency such that it could comport with his admiration for the unitary model of government that exists in Great Britain, an admiration he certainly learned from Sir Walter Bagehot. Having at first dismissed the presidency precisely because he thought it had no power beyond the routine execution of congressional law, Wilson came to believe, or, at least, to claim, that he believed that the "President is at liberty . . . to be as big a man as he can." Of course, in coming to this conclusion, Wilson had not also arrived at an embrace of the theory of separation of powers advocated in *The Federalist* by which presidents could be great by excelling in their independent sphere of powers. Instead, Wilson had come to believe that it was possible for presidents to act as prime ministers, deriving from their power from their ability to persuade and lead the people—and thus Congress—to achieve results in their government. For a fuller treatment of the difference between Wilson's understanding of the source of executive power and *The Federalist*'s, see Jeffrey Tulis, *The Rhetorical Presidency* (Princeton: Princeton University Press, 1987).

10. Quoted in Geoffrey Stone, *Perilous Times: Free Speech in Wartime from the Sedition Act of 1798 to the War on Terror* (New York: W. W. Norton, 2004), 149.

He claimed to need the "authority to exercise censorship over the press" because he needed to be able to stifle those "persons in a position to do mischief" by publishing sensitive war news.[11] Wilson connected his desire for this legislation to a very concrete and important military necessity. There are occasions in war when secrecy is essential to the war effort: a secrecy that would be severely compromised if the press were to publish everything related to the war.

But, that being said, Wilson seems to have wanted this legislation for reasons other than a justifiable interest in helping to prosecute the war. Thomas Lawrence asserts that Wilson aimed "to suppress anti-War sentiment and propaganda which might hinder the development of a national pro-War consensus."[12] Wilson sought the censorship of the press not so much to help prosecute the war in a very immediate way—that is, to ensure that the press did not let the Germans know how many ships were going to battle—but to help prosecute the war in a much more nebulous open-ended way that is far more problematic in a constitutional republic. As he said in a speech entitled, "This Is a People's War," "Woe be to the man or group that seeks to stand in our way in this day of high resolution when every principle we hold dearest is to be vindicated and made secure for the salvation of the nations."[13] In seeking legislation that allowed his administration to repress the press, Wilson sought to make good on such promises. If this is a people's war, then the people's democratic power extends as much to speech as anything else. As Justice Oliver Wendell Holmes said in a letter to Learned Hand before the transformation that seemed to occur in his thought on these issues between *Schenck* and *Abrams*: "Free speech stands no differently than freedom from vaccination." It is something that the majority can, if it chooses, decide to override.[14]

The democratic interest in overriding free speech for the sake of national unity during World War I led to what Geoffrey Stone calls a "low point in American history" for speech: "The dominant mood of the public was repressive to a degree that is hard for contemporary Americans to imagine."[15] The first Espionage Act passed in 1917 was used by

11. *New York Times*, May 23, 1917, 1. See also Murphy, *World War I and the Origin of Civil Liberties*, 78.

12. Thomas A. Lawrence, "Eclipse of Liberty: Civil Liberties in the United States during the First World War," *Wayne Law Review* 21 (1974): 40. See also David M. Rabban, *Free Speech in Its Forgotten Years* (Cambridge: Cambridge University Press, 1997).

13. Woodrow Wilson, *The Public Papers of Woodrow Wilson: War and Peace*, ed. Ray Stannard Baker and William E. Dodd (New York: Harper and Brothers, 1927), 5:67.

14. Quoted in Bernard Schwartz, "Holmes versus Hand: Clear and Present Danger or Advocacy of Unlawful Action?" *Supreme Court Review* (1994): 218. See also Stone, *Perilous Times*, 199.

15. Stone, *Perilous Times*, 183–84.

the administration to the full extent of its powers to suppress all criticism of either the war or the administration directing the war. What is interesting, however, is that, in enacting this legislation, Congress had expected and had been told that discretion would be used in its execution. And, in fact, the legislation that it had passed had been intentionally restricted to that authority which seemed necessary for the conduct of the war. As Stone writes,

> The act made it a crime, when the nation is at war, for any person (a) willfully to "make or convey false reports or false statements with intent to interfere" with the military success of the United States or "to promote the success of its enemies"; (b) willfully to "cause or attempt to cause insubordination, disloyalty, mutiny, or refusal of duty, in the military or naval forces of the United States"; or (c) willfully to "obstruct the recruiting or enlistment service of the United States."[16]

But, rather than exercising discretion in a manner that confined prosecution only to those acts which truly did endanger the war effort in a material way, the administration often used the act to prosecute all speech whose "bad tendencies" might have indirect effect on the war effort.

So, in one of the most egregious but nonetheless representative cases, Robert Goldstein was prosecuted, convicted, and sentenced to ten years in prison for promoting insubordination by producing and exhibiting *The Spirit of '76*. While the movie was a fairly standard heroic depiction of the American Revolution, it also included a depiction of the Wyoming Valley Massacre, a massacre of women and children by British soldiers. The trial judge concluded that there was no time for "those things that may have the tendency or effect of sowing . . . animosity or want of confidence between us and our allies."[17] An instance such as this indicates the extent to which this congressional legislation, despite the fact that its intent was limited to that legal authority necessary to prosecute the war, was used to suppress other types of speech that could in some less-immediate way be connected to the public's perception of the war. Though even the attorney general, the same attorney general who had told dissenters to beware of an avenging government, called for discretion from U.S. attorneys in administering the Espionage Act, such discretion was frequently outpaced by prosecutorial excesses of the sort exhibited in the case of Robert Goldstein.[18]

16. Ibid., 151–52.
17. Ibid., 173.
18. Many of these prosecutions illustrate well Montesquieu's contention: "Nothing makes the crime of high treason more arbitrary than when indiscreet speech becomes its material." *The Spirit of the Laws*, trans. Anne Cohler, Basia Miller, and Harold Stone (Cambridge: Cambridge University Press, 1989), XII, ch.12: 198.

Prosecutions under the Espionage Act were both fueled by and provided fuel for a public that seemed intent on using the war to exorcise many of its long-held fears about the new immigrants. Many Americans feared that recent immigrants, some of whom were anarchists, socialists, and other radicals, were fundamentally antithetical to the "American" way of life. And, as John Lord O'Brian shows, there had been enough actual evidence connecting some of these German immigrants to foreign espionage that the public could credibly connect its fears of them to the necessities of the war. He wrote: "It is scarcely necessary to point out how these revelations of activities of foreign agents within our borders steadily accelerated the feeling of alarm throughout the country and the growth of suspicion and fear in local communities everywhere."[19] O'Brian noted such actual activities and the suspicion it fostered in order to justify the laws he, as assistant attorney general, took part in both seeking and implementing. He claimed stronger laws were necessary because they "had no laws adequate to deal with the insidious methods of internal hostile activities."[20] Of course, he does not show how such laws were not adequate, given the fact that actual espionage had been both prevented and prosecuted under the legal code before the passage of the Espionage Act. That is, for the most part, the actual legislation passed contributed materially more to the very "war mania" and "oppression of innocent men" that O'Brian himself would later lament than it did to the prevention and prosecution of actual espionage within the country.[21] For instance, following an instruction by the attorney general, that "citizens should feel free to bring their suspicions and information to the . . . Department of Justice," the department received thousands of accusations of disloyalty every single day. Such accusations and the prosecution that sometimes followed contributed very little to the actual prevention of espionage, a legitimate governmental goal, and much more to the prevention of "disloyalty." And, while such disloyalty may have stood in the way of Wilson's democratic claim that this was a "people's war," it is hard to see how it created a security threat of the sort that required extraordinary governmental intervention beyond that which was countenanced during ordinary times.

Going beyond the initial Espionage Act of 1917, the administration sought even more power in a set of amendments known as the Sedition Act of 1918. Where the initial legislation aimed to restrain governmental

19. John Lord O'Brian, "New Encroachments on Individual Freedom," *Harvard Law Review* 66 (1952): 7. O'Brian shows that there was a series of prosecutions beginning in 1915, indicating German espionage activity in the United States.

20. Ibid., 8.

21. Stone, *Perilous Times*, 158.

suppression to only that speech that was substantively related to the military, this new legislation broadened the scope of governmental power. All speech that brought the form of government of the United States, or the Constitution, or the military, or the flag of the United States into contempt, scorn, contumely, or disrepute was now criminalized and violators were subject again to extensive sentences. To justify such legislation, the administration went beyond citing the necessities of war. Instead, it claimed that such legislation was necessary because of the dangers that, without it, the public would take justice into its own hands and lynch those whose speech offended it.[22] As Zechariah Chafee writes, "Doubtless some governmental action was required to protect pacifists and extreme radicals from mob violence, but incarceration for a period of twenty years seems a very queer kind of protection."[23]

Additionally, Chafee nicely captured the problem with both the first Espionage Act and this second more draconian version of it: it failed to fulfill the ostensible reason for which it was created, that is, the prevention of security threats during the extraordinary occasion of a war. "If Congress had adopted some plan by which persons outside the existing conspiracy statutes whose speeches and writings were really causing trouble could be tried and confined until the actual emergency was passed, and in no case beyond the termination of hostilities, this would have prevented every danger to such men, and, what is more, every danger from them." Chafee contrasted this with the "preventive but not punitive policy pursued by Lincoln in the Civil War toward his most disloyal opponents."[24] The problem is that by passing legislation that has the ostensible aim of controlling otherwise acceptable behavior that might pose a security threat, Congress inevitably invited the view that the behavior itself has become unacceptable. If made illegal, behavior that might need to be prevented in certain instances is transformed into that which must be punished in all circumstances. And the legal order is transformed not actually for the sake of national security but for the sake of the pent-up animosities and suspicions that the claim of national security allows the government and the people to release.

The Civil War

Zechariah Chafee frequently used the Civil War as a point of contrast to criticize the policies pursued by the Wilson administration during World

22. Ibid., 184–85.
23. Zechariah Chafee Jr., *Freedom of Speech* (New York: Harcourt, Brace, 1920), 46.
24. Ibid.

War I. In fact, although Chafee was less concerned with the principle of separation of powers than I am, his criticisms nonetheless serve as a useful point of departure for my own. Chafee noted: "We fought the Civil War with the enemy at our gates and powerful secret societies in our midst without an Espionage Act." Instead, when one of Lincoln's generals, Ambrose Burnside, did curb the press, Chafee noted that he received a sharp telegram from the president. This suppression, Lincoln suggested, is "'likely to do more harm than the publication would do.'"[25] To the extent that Lincoln suppressed the speech of certain men, Chafee suggested that Lincoln was "proceeding against men who were so far within the test of direct and dangerous interference with the war that they were actually causing desertions." Thus, Lincoln's suppressions were much more substantively connected to the necessities of fighting a civil war, and Lincoln, in a way that is connected to this concern for military necessity, "acted to prevent and not to punish."[26]

This same concern for military necessity evinces itself again in one of the most infamous cases of the Civil War: the arrest by the same overzealous General Burnside of Clement Vallandingham. A popular peace Democrat from Ohio, Vallandingham gave a spirited and rousing speech in which he called the war "wicked, cruel, and unnecessary." Much of his speech was directed against General Order no. 38, which had been issued by Burnside without Lincoln's knowledge or approval and declared that "the habit of declaring sympathies for the enemy will not be allowed in this Department." Again, without consulting his superiors, Burnside arrested Vallandingham under the authority of General Order No. 38 and brought him before a military commission where he was charged with "weakening the power of the government in its efforts to suppress an unlawful rebellion" and found guilty.[27] While Vallandingham would certainly have been convicted under the legislation that existed during World War I, Lincoln told Burnside that he doubted the necessity of his arrest.[28] In fact, Nicolay and Hay report that "the arrest, trial and sentence of Vallandingham took the President somewhat by surprise." He chose to commute—by sending him into exile in the Confederacy—rather than to overturn Vallandingham's sentence because, "finding himself in the presence of an accomplished fact, the question now . . . was, whether he should approve the sentence of the court, or by annulling it, weaken the authority of the general commanding the district, and greatly

25. Ibid., 116.
26. Ibid., 117.
27. Stone, *Perilous Times*, 96–101.
28. "To Ambrose E. Burnside," May 29, 1863, in Abraham Lincoln, *The Collected Works of Abraham Lincoln*, ed. Roy P. Basler (New Brunswick, NJ: Rutgers University Press, 1953), 6:237.

encourage the active and dangerous secession element in the West."[29] The question of maintaining Vallandingham's arrest seems to have nothing to do with his "guilt" in violating Burnside's General Order and everything to do with the effect that Lincoln's actions in relation to the arrest would have on the prosecution of the war.

Lincoln emphasizes the importance of military necessity as the controlling question that either justifies or repudiates this arrest, and seemingly all other arrests and suppressions of speech, when he responded in written form to the claim made by some of his critics that Vallandingham was tried "for no other reason than words addressed to a public meeting, in criticism of the course of the administration, and in condemnation of the military orders of that general." Lincoln wrote: "If there was no other reason for the arrest, then I concede that the arrest was wrong." Lincoln claimed, however, that this was not the case with Vallandingham because he was "warring upon the military; and this gave the military constitutional jurisdiction to lay hands upon him."[30] Moreover, in justifying Vallandingham's arrest, Lincoln once again reiterated this important distinction between prevention and punishment:

> The military arrests and detentions . . . including those of Mr. V . . . have been for prevention and not for punishment—as injunctions to stay injury, as proceedings to keep the peace—and hence, like proceedings in such cases, and for like reasons, they have not been accompanied with indictments, or trial by juries, nor, in a single case by any punishment whatever, beyond what is purely incidental to the prevention. The original sentence of imprisonment in Mr. V's case, was to prevent injury to the Military service only, and the modification of it was made as a less disagreeable mode to him, of securing the same prevention.[31]

Because the arrest was connected to that which was necessary to win the war, there should be no punishment attached to it. While the claim of necessity empowered Lincoln to exercise certain powers in a case "of Rebellion or Invasion" that he would not and should not exercise during peace, that claim itself also limited the nature and the extent of these

---

29. John G. Nicolay and John Hay, *Abraham Lincoln: A History* (New York: Century, 1890), 7:338–39.

30. "To Erastus Corning and Others," June 12, 1863, in Lincoln, *Collected Works*, 6:266. Of course, it should be said that his manner of "war" did not reach Hand's "direct advocacy" standard. Instead, Lincoln provides a complicated argument culminating in the claim that "to silence the agitator" whose words encourage, if only implicitly, desertion and "save the boy" who would otherwise fall victim to the agitator and be punished for desertion "is not only constitutional, but withal, a great mercy."

31. "To Matthew Birchard and Others," June 29, 1863, in Lincoln, *Collected Works*, 6:303.

powers.[32] The prevention of certain types of speech and deeds, otherwise acceptable, that would now have a material and damaging effect on the war is an acceptable assertion of power; the punishment of these speeches and deeds is not. In other words, the exception does not have to "spread"; it can be limited so long as one constantly keeps in view the constitutional end—that is, the preservation of the constitutional order itself—that created the exception in the first place. And, given this view of speech and the fact that Lincoln generally thought the suppression of speech hurt the war effort by causing more negative public reaction than it helped the war effort by suppressing criticism of it, it is not surprising that, as Paul Finkelman writes, "during the war a vigorous opposition press constantly criticized Lincoln, military policy, and the whole purpose of the war itself."[33]

The Legalization Model and the Problem with Precedents

Explicating the difference between the respective constitutional approaches in the Civil War and World War I is important not just in examining the short-term question as to which one yields fewer abuses but also in determining the long-term question as to which one has a less deleterious effect on the sustenance of constitutionalism. In his dissent in *Korematsu*, Justice Robert Jackson suggests that the deeper danger from emergency governmental action lies in its long-term effects on the Constitution: "A military commander may overstep the bounds of constitutionality, and it is an incident. But if we review and approve, that passing incident becomes the doctrine of the Constitution." By making it the doctrine of the Constitution that the legislature may overstep the boundaries of the Constitution under the claims of national security, "the principle then lies about like a loaded weapon, ready for the hand of any authority that can bring forward a plausible claim of an urgent need."[34] Although Jackson does not say this, I would say that the temporary, extralegal,

32. For a fuller exploration of the "limits" or "standards" that Lincoln creates for the exercise of discretionary executive power beyond or against the law, see my "Lincoln's Example: Executive Power and the Survival of Constitutionalism," *Perspectives on Politics* 3 (2005): 801–16. For a clarification of my argument there that distinguishes these as a set of standards by which the public should judge the exercise of discretionary executive power rather than what Richard Posner mistakenly calls my "three-factor test" or legal rules by which a president could stretch the limits of discretionary executive power, see my review of Posner's book. "9/11, the Liberty/Security Balance, and the Separation of Powers," *Criminal Justice Ethics* 26 (2007): 59–64.

33. Paul Finkelman, "Review: Civil Liberties and Civil War: The Great Emancipator as Civil Libertarian," *Michigan Law Review* 91 (1993): 1376.

34. *Korematsu v. United States*, 323 U.S. 246 (1944).

nonprecedential, and explicitly impeachable quality of executive discretion prevents it from creating this sort of dangerous principle—so long as we remember those are the characteristics of executive discretion—while the legal, precedential, and representative character of legislative action does create such a principle.

Moreover, legislative action invites judicial rationalization in a way that executive discretion does not. Robert Nagel makes a similar argument to the one I offer here: "The extralegal quality of many of the military's acts of suppression during the Civil War may well have been linked to their short duration." Perhaps because their duration was relatively short and because there were no grand legal and constitutional claims about the power to overrun the Constitution during a war—such claims were made by some radical Republicans in the Civil War Congress but they were contested by other Republicans more friendly to Lincoln—"the courts made no significant attempt to control the military's excesses during the war." For this reason,

> the claim that extreme public exigencies could justify censorship was never addressed, and the public was spared both the implausible conclusion that no amount of emergency can justify suppression and the provocative promulgation of a rule that some amount of emergency can. Instead, the suppressions remained illegitimate and irregular and did not lead to any prolonged, general breakdown of free speech.[35]

By contrast, as Nagel notes in his footnote, "the pattern of suppression during the Civil War was in sharp contrast with that which accompanied World War I." The World War I suppressions "resulted from statutes and judicial enforcement rather than from executive decrees and military actions."[36]

As Nagel implies, it is extraordinarily difficult, if not impossible, to arrive at a principle of suppression that does not either hamper the government too much or constrain the government too little. Thus, although it is the case, as Nagel notes, that "judicial protections of free speech" began after World War I, they did so only after a considerable period of judicial rationalization of governmental suppressions.[37] And, as Nagel argues in his provocative book, the subsequent period of judicial protection may have "done great damage to the public understanding and appreciation of the principle of free speech by making it seem trivial, for-

35. Robert F. Nagel, *Constitutional Cultures: The Mentality and Consequences of Judicial Review* (Berkeley: University of California Press, 1989), 40.

36. Ibid., 173.

37. See, e.g., *Schenck v. United States*, 249 U.S. 47 (1919); *Frohwerk v. United States*, 249 U.S. 204 (1919); *Debs v. United States*, 249 U.S. 211 (1919); *Abrams v. United States*, 250 U.S. 616 (1919).

eign, and unnecessarily costly."[38] This is because the very creation of rules and doctrines by which certain speech is acceptably limited and certain speech is not creates artificial distinctions that cannot possibly do justice to the subtleties of actual politics. In the Civil War, speech was both occasionally more restricted (e.g., Vallandingham's case) and generally much less restricted because there was no principle of acceptable speech.

Moreover, as in the case of both Vallandingham and the public's reaction to the first Alien and Sedition Acts, the lack of judicial "protection" promotes a sense of public responsibility for protecting free speech. As bad as the first Alien and Seditions Acts might have been, the political fallout from them was so great that no political party dared restrict speech again until World War I. These early restrictions did not create the kind of "loaded gun" about which Jackson worries in his *Korematsu* dissent; instead, they did the opposite: they created a long-term commitment to freedom of speech that did not depend on judicial protections. Although it does seem to be the case, as Paul Murphy suggests, that the restraints on speech during World War I spawned a new tradition of civil liberties concerns, especially in the Progressive circles that were initially indifferent to them, the tendency has been to look for judicial support for these civil liberties rather than political support.[39] That is, even if one asserts that the long-term consequence of the suppressions instigated by World War I are good because of the judicial protections instigated by them, that good is not unalloyed insofar as the public remains indifferent to questions of free speech. Because the judicial model of protection seems, in a certain sense, to assume the model of countermajoritarian judicial heroics, it is nearly inevitable that this would be the case. If speech is protected only by courts whose "principles" and "doctrines" preserve it over and against egregious and overbearing majorities, then why would the public not remain indifferent? The model itself assumes not only that it is indifferent but that it remains forever like the public of World War I.

Lincoln's Discretionary Executive versus the Bush Administration's Unitary Executive

There is a striking and, for some, disquieting similarity, however, between Lincoln's articulation of a presidential war power and the Bush administration's. After all, as reported to us by Nicolay and Hay, Lincoln said to some senators late in the war who sought his support for the congressional form of reconstruction legislation: "I may in an emergency

38. Nagel, *Constitutional Cultures.*
39. See Murphy, *The Origin of Civil Liberties.*

do things on military grounds which cannot constitutionally be done by Congress."[40] Is there any difference between this claim and John Yoo's claim in a memorandum written soon after 9/11: "The President has broad constitutional power to take military action in response to the terrorist attacks on the United States"?[41] Besides the inescapable fact that Lincoln seems to have possessed a greater degree of prudence than Bush, is there any principled difference between their claims?

To answer this question adequately, it is useful first to explicate more fully the arguments of the Bush administration. Jack Goldsmith nicely captures the essence of these arguments in relation to executive power: "The President had to do what he had to do to protect the country. And the lawyers had to find some way to make what he did legal."[42] In a document released by the U.S. Department of Justice after the National Security Agency (NSA) revelations, the administration asserts: "The NSA activities are supported by the President's well-recognized *inherent* constitutional authority as Commander-in-Chief and sole organ for the Nation in foreign affairs to conduct warrantless surveillance." It continues: "The President has *inherent* constitutional authority to conduct warrantless searches and surveillance *within the United States* for foreign intelligence purposes."[43] Although the Bush administration's insistence that these discretionary powers belong exclusively to the president resembles Lincoln's similar claims, this resemblance is deceiving. The Bush administration asserts a *legal* right to extralegal and even illegal powers. For instance, in a signing statement released soon after a 2005 law prohibiting torture, President Bush asserts that, to the extent that this prohibition of torture "interferes with the President's direction of such core war matters as the detention and interrogation of enemy combatants," it is unconstitutional.[44] It is unconstitutional and seemingly, by the Bush administration's reasoning, illegal for Congress to attempt to make torture illegal.

In asserting a legal right to illegal measures, the Bush administration has inversed the beneficial constitutional effects of a discretionary

40. Abraham Lincoln, *The Collected Works of Abraham Lincoln*, ed. Roy P. Basler (New Brunswick, NJ: Rutgers University Press, 1953), 9:120.

41. Deputy Assistant Attorney General John Yoo, "Memorandum Opinion for Timothy Flanigan, The Deputy Counsel to the President, Re: The President's Constitutional Authority to Conduct Military Operations against Terrorists and Nations Supporting Them," September 25, 2001, reprinted in *The Torture Papers: The Road to Abu Ghraib*, ed. Karen J. Greenburg and Joshua L. Dratel (New York: Cambridge University Press, 2005), 3.

42. Goldsmith, *The Terror Presidency*, 81.

43. "Legal Authorities Supporting the Activities of the National Security Agency Described by the President," January 19, 2006, United States Department of Justice, http://www.usdoj .gov/opa/whitepaperonnsalegalauthorities.pdf (accessed July 7, 2008, emphasis added).

44. Jay S. Bibbee, "Memorandum for Alberto R. Gonzalez Counsel to the President," August 1, 2002, in Greenburg and Dratel, *The Torture Papers*, 202.

executive. Lincoln's actions outside the law prevent the legalization of powers that are dangerous but necessary. Bush's claim to a legal right to these necessary powers creates what might be called the "worst of both worlds."[45] In its proper constitutional formulation, discretionary executive power provides an essential supplement to the laws, both providing the laws with flexibility if they have not authorized all power that becomes necessary and preventing them from attempting to authorize all powers that might become necessary. Discretionary executive power of the sort exercised by Lincoln allows the government to suppress the press in a particular instance if it plans to publish materials that would be truly damaging to the war effort, such as battle strategies, without creating a problematic law by which the press can be suppressed. The possibility that this discretion will be exercised arbitrarily is offset both by the more problematic situation created if such discretion is legalized, so as not to be "arbitrary," and by the fact that its lack of legal authority means it can always be questioned. But the claim of the Bush administration to possess an inherent right to these sorts of discretionary decisions, a right that can neither be questioned nor circumscribed, obliterates both of the benefits of discretionary executive power. Now, this arbitrary extralegal power can be exercised virtually at will. Woodrow Wilson's vision of a legal effacement of arbitrary power seems, in a certain way, superior to the legalization of arbitrariness itself. While Woodrow Wilson sought continuing legal authority from the laws passed by Congress, Bush seeks continuing legal authority from the Constitution itself.

The key difference between the Bush administration's claim and Lincoln's may lie in the realm of the relationship between judgment and constitutionality. The Bush administration claims an inherently constitutional right to make discretionary judgments about national security. In deriving this power from the Constitution, it also asserts its inherent legality. The administration's claim neither invites nor even contemplates questioning. By contrast, Lincoln writes of executive discretion: "If he uses the power justly, the . . . people will probably justify him; if he abuses it, he is in their hands, to be dealt with by all the modes they have reserved to themselves in the constitution."[46] Like Bush, Lincoln suggests that the president is in sole possession of the power to exercise discretion; but, unlike Bush, he does not suggest that, when exercised, the power is inherently legal. Instead, Lincoln's president has the constitutional power to exercise an inherently extralegal power that, as such, is always subject to judgment. Because the

45. I would like to thank Ian Shapiro who, in his discussion at the conference, formulated my earlier critique of the Bush administration's arguments in this way.

46. "To Matthew Birchard and Others," June 29, 1863, in Lincoln, *Collected Works*, 6:303.

power exercised falls outside the legal order, such judgment is the only possible way of reconciling this extralegal power with the constitutional order it seeks to preserve. In Lincoln's formulation, insofar as the exercise of power itself is inherently contestable, it also begins as extraconstitutional. Through the judgment of the people and Congress, the extraconstitutional or unconstitutional action can become constitutional. As Lincoln writes in a letter to Albert G. Hodges, "measures, otherwise unconstitutional, might become lawful, by becoming indispensable to the preservation of the constitution."[47] Unlike Jefferson's prerogative, which lies entirely outside both the Constitution and the constitutional order, Lincoln's discretion can and should become constitutional.[48] But it can become so only by being indispensable to the preservation of the Constitution from which it departs. The executive has a constitutional power to take actions of questionable constitutionality. Thus, executive discretion, especially if exercised illegally or unconstitutionally, must be judged by a fairly exacting standard of constitutional necessity. In other words, even if the actions depart from the Constitution, they should be judged by standards created by the Constitution itself.[49] Where Bush claims that the executive has a constitutional power to take whatever actions he thinks necessary—a permanent power that precludes the laws of Congress and cannot be questioned—Lincoln asserts only that the president has the constitutional power in certain extraordinary circumstances to take unconstitutional actions for the sake of the preservation of the Constitution itself, a power that neither precludes the law of Congress nor stands as unquestionable.

In understanding executive discretion as extralegal, one also can better understand what should be the function of Congress's statutory frameworks. The World War I Congress, under the prodding of Woodrow Wilson, authorized all those powers Wilson thought might be necessary to fight the war. In so doing, it adopts what might be called the executive perspective because it will be, after all, the executive who conducts the war rather than Congress. Moreover, if the exercise of all necessary power must be authorized by the law, then Congress must legislate with a view to the extreme situation. Because Woodrow Wilson understands political power as essentially unitary, it is not surprising that he would have wanted to force Congress into adopting his perspective in the legislation it passes. The argument I have proposed here as a superior alternative

47. April 4, 1864, in Abraham Lincoln, *The Collected Works of Abraham Lincoln*, ed. Roy P. Basler (New Brunswick, NJ: Rutgers University Press, 1953), 7:281.
48. For a discussion of Jeffersonian prerogative, see Jeremy Bailey, *Thomas Jefferson and Executive Power* (New York: Cambridge University Press, 2007).
49. For a fuller development of this argument, see Benjamin A. Kleinerman, "Lincoln's Example: Executive Power and the Survival of Constitutionalism," *Perspectives on Politics* 3 (December 2005): 801–16.

depends on a conception of the separation of powers that understands each branch as possessing a different perspective on its constitutional function and purpose.[50] Describing the executive function, Mariah Zeisberg writes: "The executive is a unitary office, the most efficient of the three, structured to ensure the capacity to respond to events quickly, provide initiative to the legislature, and protect national security."[51] If every power that the executive exercises must derive from a congressional statute, then it forces Congress to adopt the perspective of the executive. It must conceive and authorize all powers that might be necessary to protect national security. But if Congress knows that the executive possesses an independent constitutional source of power that is responsible for protecting national security, then it need not legalize or authorize dangerous powers. Instead, it can concern itself with demarcating the legitimate range of the executive's independent powers. Instead of adopting a statutory framework that authorizes what the executive can do, it can adopt a statutory framework that delimits what the executive should not do except under exceptional circumstances. If some pressing necessity forces the executive to overrun those limits, then the executive must defend these actions to Congress and to the people. Instead of adopting a perspective by which all necessary power can be authorized "in the name of national security," thus inviting Congress and the people to believe that the Constitution is infinitely flexible so long as one justifies it through a "pressing necessity," a discretionary executive allows Congress and the people to remain constitutionally vigilant, judging, through both reelection and impeachment, the one person who the Constitution can hold responsible for departing from it.[52]

The Bush administration claims a preclusive authority to ignore congressional statutes that "unconstitutionally" aim to limit executive discretion. It does so under what appears to be the same doctrine of executive discretion as Lincoln advocates. But, again, this appearance is deceiving because the difference reveals a yawning gulf between Lincoln's constitutionally conservative position and Bush's constitutionally radical

---

50. For further elaboration of this conception of the separation of powers, see Jeffrey K. Tulis, "Deliberation between Institutions," in *Debating Deliberative Democracy*, ed. James S. Fishkin and Peter Laslett, Politics and Society 7 (Oxford: Blackwell, 2003), 200–11; and Mariah Zeisberg, "Constitutional Fidelity and Interbranch Conflict," *Good Society* 13 (2004): 24–30; Alexander Hamilton, John Jay, and James Madison, *The Federalist*, ed. Jacob E. Cooke (Middletown, CT: Wesleyan University Press, 1961), 331.

51. Zeisberg, "Constitutional Fidelity," 25.

52. For this reason, Jeffrey Tulis argues that we need to reinvigorate a political understanding of the impeachment power. Jeffrey Tulis, "Impeachment in the Constitutional Order," in *The Constitutional Presidency*, ed. Joseph M. Bessette and Jeffrey K. Tulis (Baltimore: Johns Hopkins University Press, 2009), 229–46.

alternative. For Lincoln, the necessity to override either the Constitution or the laws does not stem from some inherent preclusive authority; instead, it stems only from the specific situation in which this discretion must be exercised. The situation, and *only* the situation, justifies the departure; the departure becomes constitutional only through the authority of Congress and the people to judge its necessity. The executive remains bound by the laws except in those situations where he cannot possibly be; because of the executive's power in such extraordinary situations, it is that much more bound by the laws in ordinary times. For Bush, by contrast, the necessity to override these limitations in certain situations transforms into a constitutional right to ignore these limitations at all times. Where this dangerous power is limited to the emergency and always subject to question in Lincoln, this power is neither temporary nor questionable in Bush. Moreover, the executive now stands superior to the laws themselves.[53] The necessity of the exception has destroyed the authority of the very laws from which the exception has been derived. In World War I, the exception normalizes because it seeks legal authority for extralegal action; in this case, the exception normalizes because, in attempting to make the extralegal legal, it seeks entirely to exempt executive discretion from the control of the laws.

Conclusion

In *Schenck v. United States*, Justice Holmes writes:

> We admit that in many places and in ordinary times the defendants in saying all that was said . . . would have been within their constitutional rights. But the character of every act depends upon the circumstances in which it is done. The question in every case is whether the words are used in such circumstances and are of such a nature as to create a clear and present danger that they will bring about the substantive evils that Congress has a right to prevent. It is a question of proximity and degree. When a nation is at war many things that might be said in time of peace are such a hindrance to its effort that their utterance will not be endured so long as men fight.[54]

Holmes here points to the absolute necessity of a certain degree of governmental discretion beyond the ordinary laws, especially in times of crisis. But the argument is both misleading in the direction toward which

---

53. David J. Barron and Martin S. Lederman, "The Commander in Chief at the Lowest Ebb—Framing the Problem, Doctrine, and Original Understanding," *Harvard Law Review* 121 (January 2008): 689–804.

54. 249 U.S. 52 (1919).

it points and useful in the direction toward which, properly understood, it should have pointed. First of all, it should be noted that the "false shout of fire" metaphor that precedes this argument points in a direction different from this argument itself. It is unacceptable and illegal in both the exceptional case of war and the normal case of peace falsely to shout fire and cause a panic in a crowded theater. The wrongness and illegality of this act does not depend on any circumstances beyond the act itself. In connecting this metaphor to this argument, however, Holmes has misled us into connecting the illegality of the "false shout of fire" to the political problems created by certain kinds of speech during war. Wartime "speech" like the revolutionary war film for which the director was prosecuted might create political dangers insofar as it makes us less likely to trust our allies. Or more inflammatory speech such as that for which Eugene Debs was prosecuted might make efforts to recruit for the war effort more problematic. But it is hard to see why it should be illegal and thus punishable. If anything, there might be a need for preventative action against certain kinds of speech—for example, the executive might legitimately close down a newspaper about to publish U.S. war strategy—but it is hard to see why it should be punished. In connecting this speech to a punishable act, Holmes has invited the conclusion that that which can be prevented must also be punished. That Holmes uses the word "prevent" rather than "punish" indicates much about where his second argument actually leads.

Furthermore, Holmes's standard for the necessity of suppression during war seems to hinge not on the actual needs of war but on the fact that other men are fighting. This argument resembles the argument of Senator William Borah who, in supporting the Sedition Act, said it is not "too much to ask complete devotion upon the part of those who remain at home to the things for which our boys are fighting and dying upon the Western Front."[55] But this is not an intelligible *constitutional* principle. It is a principle of patriotic nationalism that ultimately undercuts the principle of constitutional restraint. To demand devotion to a cause and to punish dissent stems not from the necessities of war but from the passions created by war. As Madison suggests in *Federalist* No. 49, the American Constitution aims to temper these passions to insure that reason, not passion, governs us.[56]

Instead, if Holmes's principle means anything, it must hinge on the question of "proximity and degree." As the false-shout-of-fire metaphor does show, all forms of speech are not always acceptable. And, given this

---

55. Stone, *Perilous Times*, 189.
56. "It is the reason, alone, of the public, that ought to control and regulate the government. The passions ought to be controlled and regulated by the government."

fact, it would certainly have been acceptable for the government to have prevented the man they knew would falsely cry fire from doing so before it was done. But the question of "proximity and degree" is much more ambiguous than this metaphor would lead us to believe. The requirements of war will require a wide variety of judgment calls that defy any easy principle, including "clear and present danger," by which to determine them. For this reason, the attempt either to specify what can be suppressed through the laws or to clarify how far the laws can go in their suppression will invariably run afoul of the "proximity and degree" that characterize political life. Holmes's argument points to discretion, but neither the laws nor judicial principles are capable of exercising discretion; only the executive possesses this. And, paradoxically enough in our current times, executive discretion is actually the constitutionally conservative position.

6

The Possibility of Constitutional Statesmanship

JEFFREY K. TULIS

TRUE STATESMANSHIP LIVES IN a space outside of any constitutional order and would be a threat to constitutionalism or to at least to many particular constitutional orders if we actually tried to nourish its possibility. I indicate how and why this is so but also suggest that the American Constitution replaces what I am calling true statesmanship with a much narrower version. What we call statesmanship is an idealized form of a constitutional officer. A constitutional officer is neither a leader nor a statesman but rather something in between.

One simple and straightforward distinction between leadership as understood by political scientists and the idea of statesmanship, which tends to be ignored by modern social science, is that leadership is value neutral regarding the uses of power, whereas the concept statesmanship requires an assessment of the purposes for which power is deployed. All statesmen must be good leaders, in the political science senses of leadership, but many effective leaders fall short as statesmen. Good versus bad leadership, or statesmanship versus leadership, cannot be distinguished by categorizing the array of political skills, tactics, or techniques deployed by the leader. For example, demagogues are sometimes defined as leaders who manipulate the passions of the people rather than attend to the demands of reason and collective deliberation. Some demagogues divide the people by instilling hate or fear. Others offer unrealistic pictures of the future in attempts to trade on feelings of hope. And the most common technique of demagoguery in our time is to flatter the people, to claim that the people know best and that all political wisdom comes from them. Elite policies can sometimes be christened with popular certification by claiming the people as their source. Demagoguery is a term often reserved for some kinds of bad leaders, or for leaders who are not statesmen.[1]

1. See James Ceaser, *Presidential Selection: Theory and Development* (Princeton: Princeton University Press, 1979), 319–27, and "Demagoguery, Statesmanship and the American Presidency," *Critical Review* 19, nos. 2–3 (2007): 257–98. Melissa Lane, "The Evolution of the 'Demagogue' and the Invention of the Statesman," paper presented at a conference on "Statesmen and Demagogues: Democratic Leadership in Political Thought," Yale University, March 31–April 1, 2006.

As a common practice, demagoguery is a style of leadership that should be lamented and contested. But if the cause is just and the circumstances require them, a statesman may justifiably use these very techniques. We cannot know that the statesman is not a demagogue, or whether a leader is not also a statesman, without an account of the purposes and effects of his or her actions. The concept of statesmanship requires background theories of justice and the common good.

The idea of the "common good" opens up interesting questions regarding what is common as well as what is good. We usually think of the common as pertaining to a particular polity at a particular time. But the common good might also refer to the future of a polity, the descendants of a people, and perhaps to the allies of a polity and their descendants. For these reasons, great statesmen like Churchill have been thought great leaders of a large part of the world, of a civilization extended both geographically and temporally. If the idea of the common points to a potentially awesome range of influence and power for a great statesman, the notion of the good points to potential penetration into the particulars of political life that is awesome in a different sense. Herbert Storing referred to this sort of statesmanship as "great, 'way of life' setting, character-forming political leadership." Not only does statesmanship of this sort advance the interests of a people; it actually makes them. It makes them not just in the sense of giving them a collective identity that distinguishes them from others, but it makes or remakes the most private aspects of their constitution—the concepts, categories, feelings, and understandings that order their minds. Storing's point was that American statesmanship did not have this character, scope, or ambition and rightly so because the older, grander notion of statesmanship "was based upon a misapprehension of political life, a failure to understand its decisively instrumental function."[2]

Behind Storing's observation is a familiar narrative in political theory that the shift from preliberal politics that penetrated deeply into all aspects of human life to constitutional liberalism of more limited political scope brings with it appropriately narrower understanding of ideal leadership, or statesmanship. Political life is "decisively instrumental" in the sense that it services a semiprivate realm of freedom, where individuals pursue diverse ideas of the good life rather than inhabit a polity that defines the good for them. A different kind of statesmanship is appropriate for a different kind of politics.[3] Because we still use the term statesmanship for

---

2. Herbert J. Storing, "American Statesmanship: Old and New," in *Toward a More Perfect Union* (Washington, DC: AEI Press, 1995), 413.

3. Storing's view thus blends the ideas of a lawgiver with that of a statesman. One can, of course, distinguish the two, with "statesman" reserved for a narrower role than that of lawgiver. Storing's point, then, would be that liberalism seeks to diminish the role

praiseworthy leadership in modern constitutional settings, we may over-look the fact that constitutional statesmanship is a contradiction in terms. Constitutionalism was invented to replace statesmanship in the old capacious sense of law giving and polity making. Of course, the movement to replace or remake a constitution might require "true statesmanship," but statesmanship under a constitution would be different—something in between a leader and statesman on the ancient model.[4]

Statesmanship most clearly reveals itself in times of political crisis. It is hard to think of well-known statesmen whose reputations were not the product of exceptional political circumstances. Churchill and world war, Lincoln and Civil War, George Washington and other founders in a constitutional revolution, Nelson Mandela and the reconstitution of South Africa, John Churchill, Duke of Marlborough, and the Wars of William and Anne, Golda Meir and the Yom Kippur War, and Franklin Roosevelt and the Great Depression and world war all illustrate the point. Crisis circumstances are interesting because they not only challenge leaders to perform well under stress but also may be occasions in which the very existence of the political order is in question. Crises in which the constitutional order itself is in question can be called "exceptional" circumstances because the political order cannot be sustained without the efforts of a statesman who needs to act outside of law even to sustain it. Normal political and legal processes give way to exceptions.

John Locke called such exceptional power "prerogative." In his account, this exception was actually a product of the norm because all legal practices require interpretation and discretion even in everyday use. We tend to think of law as an invention designed to reign in arbitrary rule, but Locke shows how discretion is an ineluctable consequence of law itself. Legislatures may not provide for all foreseeable contingencies. To cover those contingencies, discretion or "prerogative" may need to fill the gap left by the law's incompleteness. Sometimes the law is incomplete because the legislature fails to provide a rule for a circumstance that is foreseeable; sometimes the legislature fails to provide for a rule because the circumstance is not foreseeable; and finally, and most interestingly, sometimes necessity requires that prerogative be deployed against clear rules because the rules themselves prevent the realization of a common good in unforeseen circumstances. "This power to act according to discretion, for the public good, without the prescription of the law, and sometimes even against it, is that which is called *prerogative*." Prerogative power is

---

and significance of the statesman as lawgiver and privilege a narrower understanding of statesmanship.

4. The best account of this transformation, by far, is Harvey C. Mansfield, *Taming the Prince: The Ambivalence of Executive Power* (New York: Free Press, 1991).

most necessary when the people are least capable of seeing its need. It is assumed by an executive who has a perception of emergency before the people do. According to Locke, the executive or statesman has a better vision of necessity prospectively, but the people are better than the statesman as evaluators of power after its use. Because the acts of statesmanship affect the people, they are attentive to it, and because they have real-world experience of its effects, they are the best judges of it. In Locke's account, the executive has prospective advantage, and the people have retrospective advantage. The people cannot only judge; they can punish and perhaps revolt, which Locke's calls their "appeal to Heaven."[5]

For Locke, prerogative power, a power crucial to true statesmanship, grows out of law and remains in service to it, monitored by the people for whom it is exercised. Locke is the thinker most important to accounts of emergency power in the American Constitution. Before turning to the U.S. Constitution and the way it domesticates this extraordinary power, it is important to see that prerogative is considerably more problematic than Locke indicates. To show this, some discussion of Carl Schmitt's understanding of the "state of exception" is helpful.[6]

Schmitt calls power in the state of exception "sovereignty," not prerogative. "Sovereign is he who decides on the exception."[7] The use of this term indicates considerably more power than prerogative. Indeed, Schmitt seems not to realize that Locke addressed the subject, although he discusses Locke and instead uses him as an example of excessive legalism in the face of necessity.[8] "All concepts of the modern theory of the state are secularized theological concepts," says Schmitt and hence the title of his book on the state of exception, *Political Theology*.[9] Sovereignty originally referred to God's omnipotent power. Schmitt discerns godlike power in the statesmen who rule in the state of exception. "The decision on the exception is a decision in the true sense of the word," because in moments of extreme peril and outside of the legal or constitutional order no norm is available to guide the statesman.[10] It is the fact of the statesman's decision, his actual decisiveness, that is the essence of his

---

5. John Locke, *Two Treatises of Government*, ed. Peter Laslett, 2nd ed. (Cambridge: Cambridge University Press, 1967), Second Treatise, chap. 14, "Of Prerogative." See also, Joseph M. Bessette and Jeffrey K. Tulis, "On the Constitution, Politics, and the Presidency," in *The Constitutional Presidency*, ed. Joseph M. Bessette and Jeffrey K. Tulis (Baltimore: Johns Hopkins University Press, 2009), 20–24.

6. Carl Schmitt, *Political Theology* (Chicago: University of Chicago Press, 2005).

7. Ibid., 5.

8. Ibid., 32. See also Carl Schmitt, *Constitutional Theory* (Durham, NC: Duke University Press, 2007), where Locke is also discussed but with no reference to Lockean prerogative.

9. Schmitt, *Constitutional Theory*, 36.

10. Ibid., 6.

sovereignty, not the content of his decision. For example (and this is my example, not Schmitt's), FDR's decisions in response the Great Depression were more important for the fact that they happened, that they were decisive happenings, than for their merits as public policies. So in the state of exception, in the space outside of the constitutional order, the statesman is sovereign because only his will matters. "What characterizes an exception is principally unlimited authority, which means the suspension of the entire existing order."[11] Statesmanship in the state of exception reveals "the decision in absolute purity."[12] Schmitt does not believe that these decisions can be evaluated because all norms have been suspended and the sovereign is in a position to actually create new norms.

Schmitt developed his argument in 1922, already worrying about the fragility or imbecility of Weimar constitutional politics. A year earlier, Schmitt had written a book on dictatorship in which he distinguished between "commissarial dictatorship," which seeks to save or preserve a constitutional order, and "sovereign dictatorship," which attempts to create a new one. In *Political Theology*, the commissarial notion is dropped as Schmitt thinks through the implications of rule in the state of exception. Because the state of exception cannot be anticipated, norms or expectations to judge or bind a statesman in those circumstances, including obligations to maintain an existing constitutional order, contradict the very premise of the emergency—the premise that unusual, unheard-of exercises of power might be necessary to confront the unforeseen.

Schmitt is useful because he illustrates the kinds of circumstances for which true statesmanship is most necessary and, for us (though not for him), the obvious problems for constitutional democracy that result from such awesome power. It is not just that one might misplace trust in a leader who is not committed to the common good, and so a people might suffer greatly under the yoke of a tyrant, but also that the statesman is not easily distinguished from the tyrant. In Locke's account, the people feel the actions of prerogative power and judge it. In Schmitt's account, the sovereign, like God, makes or remakes a political world and so the people's capacity to judge is itself subject to the power of the sovereign. Or, like God, the purposes and powers of the statesman are inscrutable to the people, and they cannot understand them even after they experience them. An excellent illustration of this point is Winston Churchill's justification for his magnum opus on statesmanship, *Marlborough: His Life and Times*. Winston Churchill regards his forebear John Churchill, Duke of Marlborough, as one of the greatest statesman in all of political history.

11. Ibid., 12.
12. Ibid., 13.

The wars of William and Anne were no mere effort of national ambition or territorial gain. They were in essentials a struggle for the life and liberty not only of England, but of Protestant Europe. Marlborough's victorious sword established upon sure foundations the constitutional and Parliamentary structure of our country almost as it has come down to us to-day. He carried all that was best in the life work of Oliver Cromwell and William III to an abiding conclusion. In no world conflict have the issues, according to modern standards, been more real and vital. In none has the duty to defend a righteous cause been more compulsive on the British nation. In none have the results been more solid, more precious, more lasting.[13]

But for centuries up until Winston Churchill's own time, John Churchill had no fame or reputation as a statesman. "Fame shines unwillingly upon the statesman and warrior whose exertions brought our Island and all of Europe safely through its perils and produced glorious results for Christendom."[14] Winston Churchill writes four massive volumes to attempt "the task of making John Churchill intelligible to the present generation."[15] Schmitt helps us to understand how it could be that greatness would go unrecognized. The true statesman may so alter the world that its inhabitants can no longer comprehend or assess it. The people may instead chastise the successful statesman because their evaluation of him is through the lens of a prior political order rather than the new one he creates. Locke's heralded retrospective judgment of the people might falter in the face of a statesman's greatest accomplishments.

Schmitt thought that deliberative democracy was ill suited to the needs of modern political life. He thought the usual routines of constitutional governance were equivalent to dithering while Rome burned. So he sought to fortify executive power and explored the awe-inspiring terrain of emergency power. I find his account interesting precisely because he brings out so clearly, more clearly than Locke, what fortified executive power looks like in conditions that call for true statesmanship. For me it is not the case for executive power in the face of a weak legal order that is so compelling but rather the picture of statesmanship, its description and its disturbing implications.

In modern constitutional understandings, two strategies have been proposed to contend with the necessity of emergency power, on the one hand, and the dangers of the state of exception, on the other. One strategy, which is closest to Schmitt's thinking, is to protect the Constitution in times of emergency by forcing the executive to go outside of it into

13. Winston S. Churchill, *Marlborough: His Life and Times,* 2 vols. (London: George Harrap, 1947), 16.
14. Ibid., 17.
15. Ibid., 18.

the state of exception. Arthur Schlesinger Jr. in *The Imperial Presidency* and Justice Robert Jackson in his dissent in the Korematsu case urge this course. Jackson argues that separation of the claims of necessity from the authority of the Constitution protects the Constitution by keeping its meaning coherent and intelligible. The Constitution does not mean one thing in times of peace and another in times of war on this view. It does not stretch but instead always maintains its compositional integrity. The striking fact about America, however, is that no president, except Thomas Jefferson, ever adopted this understanding of emergency power. And even Jefferson, who frankly admitted that actions like the Louisiana Purchase were unconstitutional, did not suspend the Constitution to execute his extraordinary decisions.

Every American president who has faced emergency, except Jefferson, has interpreted the Constitution as containing prerogative power.[16] On this view, the Constitution itself authorizes exceptional powers for exceptional circumstances. As Hamilton argued, ours is a Constitution that contains all power necessary to realize its limited purposes. "It would be unwise and dangerous," Hamilton wrote, "to deny the federal government *an unconfined authority* in respect to all those objects which are entrusted to its management" (emphasis added).[17] Later, he tells us that even the purposes are not to be confining. "[T]here ought to be no limitation of a power destined to effect a purpose which is itself incapable of limitation."[18] As in Locke, the exceptional powers of the government migrate to the executive, the president, because he has the structural properties suitable to their deployment. For Locke, and for the American Constitution, the executive-president should have the prerogative power because he does have the prerogative power. The American constitutional tradition allows the instrument to be stretched, sometimes its meaning strained, in order to provide power to meet necessity, on the one hand, while keeping operative a complex governing structure, on the other. Presidents forced to operate in this complex governing structure, forced to find justifications for emergency power within the terms of the Constitution, and forced to respond to challenges to those justifications by competing political actors will come to understand the tasks of

16. In chapter 5 of this volume, Benjamin Kleinerman argues that Lincoln also held an extraconstitutional view of prerogative. However, the closest that Lincoln comes to articulating Kleinerman's view is when he indicates that *if* his intraconstitutional argument were to be found wrong, the extraconstitutional argument from necessity would then be compelling and sufficient to justify his actions. Lincoln calls out the "war power" from the Constitution, not from somewhere else.

17. Alexander Hamilton, John Jay, and James Madison, *The Federalist*, ed. Jacob E. Cooke (Middletown, CT: Wesleyan University Press, 1961), No. 23.

18. *Federalist* no. 31.

statesmanship quite differently than a leader thrust into the open space of the state of exception. Our president has much more power than constitutionalists are usually comfortable granting, but by constitutionalizing power, American presidents are taught to be a new kind of statesman, one considerably less powerful than the original.

It is sometimes thought that a prerogative-as-outside-the-Constitution view descends from the Roman practice of constitutional dictatorship. But it is actually the American-inside-the-Constitution view of prerogative that descends from the Roman model. The Roman model illustrates the ideal of leader as constitutional officer, a notion that replaces statesmanship or alters the meaning of statesmanship in the American political order. The early Roman Republic was a complicated mixed regime with executive power parceled out to myriad offices and deliberative bodies. Clinton Rossiter points out that "the unitary executive was completely alien to the normal scheme of government in Rome."[19] "Beset by desperate wars without and bitter class struggles within," the republic found itself facing a variety of emergencies. To contend with these difficulties the Romans invented the institution of constitutional dictator. In this context, dictator was not a term of disparagement but, in fact, an office that carried "the highest honor which the Republic could confer. Therefore, the man selected was invariably a well-known public figure, one who had prosecuted a successful career and was known for both his ability and devotion to the Republic."[20]

Because the normal activities of governance were suspended and the dictator given almost unlimited authority to contend with the problem for which he was appointed, some think this model an early version of prerogative as an extraconstitutional power. But because there was a metaconstitution that effectively configured the use of constitutional dictatorship, I think this practice is the early model for the American constitutional officer. Dictators were selected in a very formal and ritualized way, given a specific commission (with dictatorial power to fulfill it), were expected to give up the office after a term of six months or earlier if the problem was solved, and were thought of more generally as accountable to the republic for which they worked. Dictators could be prosecuted if they remained in office after the emergency had clearly terminated. There could be only one dictator in a given year, and there were other limits of this sort. "It is instructive to note the complete absence of any violations of these limits," writes Rossiter.[21] If one conjoins the constitution of the

19. Clinton Rossiter, *Constitutional Dictatorship: Crisis Government in Modern Democracies* (New Brunswick, NJ: Transaction Publishers, 2002), 18.
20. Ibid., 21.
21. Ibid., 24.

normal operations of government with the metaconstitution that governs suspension, one gets a logic that is actually similar to Lincoln's account of the transformation of our Constitution during the Civil War. One superior feature to the Roman model is that talent could be selected with a particular emergency in mind, whereas in the American case a president may be elected for his talents for spending a peace dividend domestically, for example, but find himself a prerogative president facing an international crisis for which he wasn't consciously chosen. Some modern theorists, like Georgio Agamben, have also pointed to the Roman era where emergency power was comfortably disbanded, as a contrast to the normalization of emergencies, continuous emergencies, in our time.[22] While there is some merit to that observation, the contrast is not as stark as it might first appear. The Romans selected a dictator once every three years for three hundred years and over that period kept expanding their definition of an "emergency." But the point I want to stress is that the "constitutional dictator" was an executive with considerable power, but that power was tethered to and constrained by a conception of office. Roman constitutional dictators were oriented to the preservation of an existing constitution, not to the fashioning of a new one, as might be a true statesman. While Lincoln comes readily to mind as an American version and is an excellent illustration of the model, George Washington captures the other aspects of the ideal: the distinguished citizen pressed into service, trusted to do whatever he wanted, yet limited by a republican understanding of office inherent to the Constitution and reinforced by self-understanding virtue.

In the American separation-of-powers arrangement, not only are presidents given an office that both empowers and constrains but, unlike the Roman model, the other major institutions of government, Congress and the courts, continue to function in most emergencies. Carl Schmitt's argument was designed to contest an overly legalistic view of constitutionalism. The American system is not as vulnerable to his critique as was the Weimar regime because the core of our arrangement is political, not legal. President and Congress contest the extent of their powers by negotiating the terrain that they cover. Presidents do not have any constitutional power by simple legal authority. Rather they have to convince Congress and the people that their claims to power are more warranted than competing claims by Congress. The result is that the same "legal" power may not exist in changed political circumstances. For example, presidential claims to executive privilege depend not on a legal determination of whether presidents have such a privilege (they do) but more on whether Congress is willing to agree to it given its own competing powers (such

22. Georgio Agamben, *State of Exception* (Chicago: University of Chicago Press, 2005), 9.

as the oversight function). Tied to concrete and particular circumstances, these determinations are political and will vary as political circumstances vary. Citizens and scholars concerned about the scope of executive power in America today would do better to criticize Congress than to worry so much about executive power, per se. Hamilton stressed that the solution to the abuse of executive power was not to cut back the power but to contest particular uses of it with robust power from a competing political institution. The American Constitution does not stint the provision of power. By defending their respective institutional positions, American political actors are pushed to fulfill their offices.

The Constitution and the offices it creates offer politicians and citizens a vocabulary and a set of standards with which to apprehend politics. In the logic of *The Federalist*, "ambition is made to counteract ambition," but by tying the interests of the officeholders to the constitutional responsibilities and rights of the place, political actors are forced to find reasons to cover or justify their motives. Political actors routinely find reasons to justify actions that were not the original motive for them. In my view, this sort of constitutionally induced hypocrisy is the most important constitutive feature of the American separation-of-powers system. As an aspect of institutional design, hypocrisy is a virtue, even though it is obviously a vice in ordinary social circumstances. After rationalizing political action, often with constitutional argument, politics trades on the plane of reason.[23]

The system of institutionally constructed personas put in conflict and dialogue is a substitute for statesmanship in the day-to-day business of government. "Enlightened statesmen" will seldom be at the helm, *The Federalist* warns.[24] For that reason, the interior structure of government is arranged to produce results that are a kind of pale or muted version of what statesmanship would provide if it were at the helm. The occasional enlightened statesman in this American system is not the true statesman, the way-of-life-setting statesman. Rather the model was George Washington, and one can see that fact not just through the historical record of his influence and prominence but also by working backward, theoretically, from the muted leadership of everyday politics to the authentic image for which it is the pale version.

The president, Congress, and the Supreme Court are constituted not just by assigned power but rather by congeries of structures and powers. Plurality or unity of officeholders, extent of the terms of office, modes of

---

23. I illustrate this process in "Deliberation Between Institutions," in *Debating Deliberative Democracy*, ed. James S. Fishkin and Peter Laslett, Philosophy, Politics and Society 7 (Oxford: Blackwell, 2003), 200–11.

24. *Federalist* No. 10.

selection for office, and specified powers and duties combine to create a set of institutions that behave and "think" quite differently from each other. In older "mixed" regimes, these differences could be traced to different social orders. A crucial invention of the new American science of politics was to design institutions to represent different desiderata of democratic governance rather than to represent social orders or alternative regimes. The presidency was designed to counteract and supplement the expressions of popular will in the legislature, to take a longer view, to force deliberation when the Congress was too hasty, and of course, to respond to problems that require speed and decisiveness. American statesmanship is the authentic expression of attributes, like these, constitutive of the office. Thus, in ordinary discourse, we often hear "statesmanly" applied to unpopular decisions. Presidents who wish to appear statesman-like insist that they pay no attention to public opinion polls. While not statesman themselves, such politicians pay homage to the American version of it by putting into words attributes of their office.

Washington and Lincoln were constitutional statesmen because they did not merely pay homage to the American idea; they performed it. They shaped and formed their offices and their Constitution at the same time that they insisted they were acting under it. Washington spent much of his first term worrying about formalities, about customs, because he wished to inscribe the democratic virtues associated with his character in the office that he served.[25] Lincoln insisted that his dictatorial actions were in service of preserving a Constitution. He could be judged, retrospectively, by the people because the categories and standards they needed to do that were provided by the Constitution. Lincoln insisted that his unprecedented actions and his creative interpretations of the Constitution served the Constitution itself.

Lincoln's and Hamilton's understanding of the separation of powers captures the Lockean idea that executives could be an instrument of prospective judgment and energetic action, while the people through a Congress might provide superior retrospective evaluation. Presidents have enormous advantages over the Congress in initiating action, while Congress has the last word, ultimately through the processes of impeachment and conviction. Lincoln also addressed the much deeper problem, revealed by Schmitt, of providing very wide scope for statesmanship in the state of exception, on the one hand, while still maintaining a discourse with which Congress and the people could use to discover standards of evaluation of extraordinary actions, on the other. Lincoln did this by treating the Constitution as an *aspirational* instrument. Gary

25. See James Hart, *The American Presidency in Action: 1789* (New York: Macmillan, 1948).

Jacobsohn, Sotirios Barber, John Agresto, and others have documented the ways in which Lincoln interpreted constitutional purposes as ideals to be approached rather than as fixed by conventional understandings and practices at the founding of the Constitution.[26] By this interpretive move, Lincoln makes it possible for the statesman to advance the common good by changing the inherited understandings or meanings of the Constitution. But Lincoln's changes are also limited in that his Constitution must be a better version of the one replaced. In this way, Lincoln positions the statesmen in the state of exception between a commissarial dictator and a sovereign dictator. Lincoln does much more than merely preserve a problematic constitutional order, yet he also does not seek a genuine alternative to the inherited order. His innovations are still cognizable by the reconstituted people because they can still recognize themselves in their new Constitution.

I should not conclude without making the obvious point that the operation of American politics does not always conform to this stylized picture. Indeed, there are good reasons to argue that two features of our political condition erode, though they do not totally subvert, the separation-of-powers design. The first is the development of political parties, which transfer many of the incentives for ambition and loyalty away from the House and Senate to party leaders, who may simply defer to the presidency and thereby abdicate responsibilities their institutional position was designed to encourage. Second, the legalization of interbranch conflict has meant that both the Congress and the president now routinely defer to Courts over matters about which they had previously contested. And impeachment is not a robust anchor in the separation-of-powers system to the extent that its pretense to be legal process is taken too seriously and thus precludes impeachment's use as the conclusion of a high-stakes political conflict So the stylized picture of separation of powers should not be mistaken for an empirical account of present-day institutional conflict. Rather, I hope it has been useful as a way to explicate the idea of constitutional officer as the solution to the problem of statesmanship and emergency power.

26. Gary J. Jacobsohn, *The Supreme Court and the Decline of Constitutional Aspiration* (Lanham, MD: Rowman & Littlefield, 1986); Sotirios A. Barber, *On What the Constitution Means* (Baltimore: Johns Hopkins University Press, 1984); John Agresto, *The Supreme Court and Constitutional Democracy* (Ithaca: Cornell University Press, 1984). See also Lawrence G. Sager, *Justice in Plainclothes: A Theory of American Constitutional Practice* (New Haven: Yale University Press, 2004).

7

Exceptions That Prove the Rule

EMBEDDING EMERGENCY GOVERNMENT
IN EVERYDAY CONSTITUTIONAL LIFE

KIM LANE SCHEPPELE

TEMPTATIONS TO CUT CONSTITUTIONAL corners are persistent and real in the face of serious (or seriously imagined) threats to the state. When governments must respond to a crisis—a war launched over the border, an enemy within, terrorists who could be anywhere—security seems to take precedence over separation of powers and over rights, the basic elements of constitutional governance. In fully constitutional states, crises eventually give way to normal governance when the threat subsides—or so the story goes. But a review of actually existing emergencies indicates that crisis government does not disappear when those who call it into being have left the government. Crisis government, once established, leaves scars on the body politic.

This is true not just in U.S. history but in the history of other countries as well. Many states have lurched from one crisis to another, with the extraordinary powers institutionalized during one crisis available as ready tools for the next. A recent example from American life can be seen in the exemplary caution Congress showed when it passed the USA PATRIOT Act right after the terrorist attack of 9/11, including five-year sunset clauses on its most controversial provisions. Five years later, however, when the immediate panic was over but the Bush administration insisted that the danger was still imminent, Congress removed the sunset clauses and made the new provisions a permanent part of U.S. law.[1] After 9/11, the Bush administration engaged in extensive warrantless wiretap-

---

1. USA Patriot Act, Pub. L. No. 107-56, 115 Stat. 272, 2001. For a discussion of the specific features of the act and its sunset provisions, see Kim Lane Scheppele, "Law in a Time of Emergency: States of Exception and the Temptations of 9/11," *University of Pennsylvania Journal of Constitutional Law* 6, no. 5 (2004): 1001–83. Of the sixteen controversial provisions originally made the subject of sunset clauses in the 2001 act, fourteen were made permanent when the sunset clause expired in 2005. Norm Abrams, *Developments in Anti-terrorism Law, Journal of International Criminal Justice* 4, no. 5 (2006): 1117–36.

ping, detained and tortured terrorism suspects under cramped interpretations of international and domestic law, and invoked both extraordinary claims of inherent executive power and broad understandings of state secrets to prevent other branches of government from examining the substance of the antiterrorism programs. Many of the most sweeping uses of emergency powers were implemented only three, four, or five years after 9/11. And in the first year of the Obama administration, there were signs that many of the extraordinary powers President Bush claimed to fight the "global war on terror" were being maintained.[2] The "enhanced interrogation" program was ended and the Guantánamo detention camp was ordered closed. But both the use of widespread surveillance within the United States and the invocation of the state secrets privilege to prevent visibility of the rendition, detention, and interrogation programs have continued, and it appears the Obama administration will seek to regularize preventive detention and military tribunals.

The United States was not the only country that saw its constitutional commitments challenged because of 9/11. The "global war on terror" produced constitutional amendments in Pakistan and Colombia, and statutes with constitutional implications in Russia. In Pakistan, the Constitution was amended to permit the president to dissolve the parliament more easily.[3] This was done in the name of fighting terror, but it is a convenient tool in the hands of any president. In addition, the pre-9/11 antiterrorism laws were used politically by Pakistan's president, Pervez Musharraf, after 9/11 to maintain his hold on power. In Colombia, the constitution was amended to alter the term-limit provision for the presidency.[4] This, too, was argued to be essential for fighting terrorism, but ambitious presidents would want this constraint removed in any event. The term-limit debate occurred in the middle of a struggle between Colombia's president Álvaro Uribe and the Constitutional Court as the president continued a pre-9/11 attempt to invoke emergency powers and the Constitutional Court continued to rein him in. In Russia, President Vladimir Putin, himself a clever lawyer, proposed a raft of new statutes that filled in gaps in the Constitution, avoiding the need for constitutional amendments. These new statutes gave the Russian president the power to select governors of the regions and required all members of the Russian Duma to run on party lists. The changes were billed as part of Russia's

2. Charlie Savage, "Obama's War on Terror May Resemble Bush's in Some Areas," *New York Times*, February 18, 2009.

3. Osama Siddique, "The Jurisprudence of Dissolutions: Presidential Power to Dissolve Assemblies under the Pakistani Constitution and Its Discontents," *Arizona Journal of International and Comparative Law* 23, no. 3 (2006): 615–715.

4. Juan Forero, "Colombian Leader, Seeking Re-election, Warns of Catastrophe," *New York Times*, May 28, 2006, 16.

war on terror, because centrally appointed governors would strengthen the "vertical of power" in the Russian Federation and a parliament with fewer fractions would permit speedier passage of legislation to deal with terrorism.[5] The reforms also, not coincidentally, continued a general program to centralize power in Russia after the collapse of the state in the 1990s. In country after country around the world, 9/11 provided a convenient rationale both to strengthen executives at the expense of other branches of government and to limit rights.[6]

As the shock of 9/11 recedes, we should consider how to design constitutional institutions to guard against the emergency changes that alter what once passed for constitutional normalcy. The most obvious solution, to constitutionalize emergencies by bringing them overtly into the constitutional framework, does not work very well in containing actually existing crisis government. In fact, constitutionalizing emergencies on a "toggle-switch model," in which a crisis allows the government to switch into emergency mode and then flip that switch off at the end of the crisis, fails to deal with the reality of crises and therefore is ineffective when crises occur. Instead, at moments of panic, states are tempted to create new institutions and procedures to deal with threats. When states get used to living with these crisis institutions, states make these new institutions permanent and consolidate compromises of constitutional principle.

What can be done to bring emergencies under legal control? We should design constitutional structures from the start so that they can cope with emergencies without altering basic constitutional principles. If the constitution's normal institutions of government are already equipped to cope with emergencies, then emergency management can be accomplished within routine governmental practice. Crisis-capable institutions, then, will not be used only in crisis.

While this may sound deeply dangerous, I believe it is even more dangerous to assume that one will ever see a constitutional polity that avoids crisis government. Given that crises are empirically inevitable, political institutions should be designed with knowledge of what emergencies tend to produce. Institutions generated in the midst of crisis—when populations are panicked and fear wins out over constitutional restraint—already tend toward permanence and are far more dangerous than institutions created before a crisis, when constitutionalism does not seem like an expendable luxury. It is better to design for the dark side of

5. Kim Lane Scheppele, "'We Forgot about the Ditches': Russian Constitutional Impatience and the Challenge of Terrorism," *Drake Law Review* 53, no. 4 (2005): 963–1027.

6. For more detailed analysis of the Pakistani and Russian cases, see Kim Lane Scheppele, "Le droit de la sécurité internationale: Le terrorisme et l'empire sécuritaire de l'après-11 Septembre 2001" (International Security Law: Terrorism and the "Securitarian" Empire after September 11), *Actes de la Recherche en Sciences Sociales* 173 (2008): 28–43.

government and to be pleasantly surprised than to design for a normal government that never operates as such. I argue that we should *normalize* emergency government within the constitutional order rather than *constitutionalize* emergency exceptions to normal government. If we normalize emergencies by designing ordinary constitutional institutions to handle crises, then there will be no need for new powers to cope with emergencies when they arise.

To this radical proposal, critics may pose two sorts of counterarguments. First, a critic might claim that constitutional governments always need additional powers above and beyond normal governmental routines to fight off threats in crises. Creating a constitution that can never implement special powers then leaves such governments defenseless. To this critique, I would reply that the ability of a government to defend itself depends on the powers it has at any given moment, not on whether such powers are new in a crisis. An effective government should not fail if it is effectively designed in the first place. In the moment of crisis, moreover, governments often have a hard time distinguishing legitimate from illegitimate threats. As a result, leaving the invocation of special emergency powers for precisely the moment of crisis will tend to produce a number of false positives that are dangerous for the maintenance of constitutionalism.

The second critique comes from the opposite direction. Building emergency powers into the normal institutions of government to deal with occasional emergencies seems excessive because they will be needed only rarely. If governmental institutions are designed for perpetual crisis, a critic might say, they will tend to make normal constitutional life impossible. To this critique, I would reply that it is not a danger by itself to have institutions that are strong enough to handle crises, if they are also hardwired with a constitutional sensibility. Effective institutions are not necessarily abusive institutions if they have the right constitutional checks.

To set up my argument for the normalization of emergency powers, I review the "inside-outside" debate over emergency powers. Constitutionalists have often argued for—and succeeded in getting—emergency powers built *into* constitutions around the world by setting up special institutions and procedures that should operate *only* in a crisis and not routinely. These powers go into effect at the declared start of a crisis and stop at some predetermined end. Constitutionalists have preferred this strategy to leaving emergency powers *outside* the constitutional order. But these in-built emergency powers have rarely been used when crises have arisen. Instead, governments tend to softly slide into the use of extraordinary powers without formal declaration. This occurs because actually existing emergencies work differently from the way that the "inside-outside" model predicts. Instead, emergencies tend to follow a script that runs from the centralization of political power when a vague threat is emerging through a predictable series of abuses that occur once the threat is full-blown. Once the worst abuses become visible, however, institutions that might provide a check on this centralized power are usually no longer functioning. Emergencies can then operate without meaningful constitutional constraint. Constitutional emergency powers generally rely on sharp beginnings and endings, but the real world rarely provides such clear markers.

Instead, I argue, the way to design constitutions is to assume that emergencies are inevitable and to insert important checks into "normal" and strong constitutional institutions from the start. If crisis powers tend to take effect gradually and do not start with clear declarations, as I will show, then constitutions are helpless unless they prevent stealth emergencies. Only by building strength and checks into normal institutions can we prevent emergencies from overriding constitutional protections.

Constitutionalizing Emergencies

Usually, the debate over the role of the constitution in times of emergency falls along inside-outside lines. The "insiders" argue that crises of state must be met by entirely legal responses. Such responses may be *different* from what they would be in a normal and peaceful situation, but they must be legal all the same. Insiders typically constitutionalize emergency powers by designing a toggle switch in the constitution for turning on emergency powers; once in effect, "insiders" constrain these extraordinary powers and, at the end of the crisis, require that these powers be explicitly switched off. Only in this way, say the insiders, can constitutional government be preserved in the face of serious challenge. To do anything else abandons a constitution just when it may be most needed to ensure that the basic principles of state are safeguarded. Besides, maintaining separation of powers and rights in times of crisis may affirmatively assist a state in fighting the threat.[7]

The "outsiders" argue that serious crises of state must be met with responses that reject law as such. Law, they claim, must operate by rules,

7. Insiders include Bruce Ackerman, *Before the Next Attack: Civil Liberties in an Age of Terrorism* (New Haven: Yale University Press, 2006); Oren Gross and Fionnula Ní Aoláin, *Law in Times of Crisis: Emergency Powers in Theory and Practice* (Cambridge: Cambridge University Press, 2006), 17–85; John Ferejohn and Pasquale Pasquino, "The Law of the Exception: A Typology of Emergency Powers," *International Journal of Constitutional Law* 2, no. 2 (2004): 210–39; Joan Fitzpatrick, *Human Rights in Crisis: The International System for Protecting Rights during States of Emergency* (Philadelphia: University of Pennsylvania Press, 1994); David Cole and Jules Lobel, *Less Safe, Less Free: Why America Is Losing the War on Terror* (New York: New Press, 2007).

but the very nature of serious crises is that they cannot be predicted, rationalized, and normalized by rules. As Carl Schmitt, perhaps the most famous theorist of "the exception," wrote:

> The precise details of an emergency cannot be anticipated, nor can one spell out what may take place in such a case, especially when it is truly a matter of an extreme emergency and of how it is to be eliminated. The precondition as well as the content of jurisdictional competence in such a case must necessarily be unlimited. From the liberal constitutional point of view, there would be no jurisdictional competence at all. The most guidance the constitution can provide is to indicate who can act in such a case.[8]

The argument from the sociological irregularity of the emergency situation—that it is so unanticipated that no one can organize its governance in advance—has a certain appeal. Most major crises do appear as surprises. Given that prevention patently did not work before a crisis materialized, the executive needs more unusual tools to protect and defend the state in order for it to survive, so the outsiders argue. Moreover, bringing emergencies into the law contaminates the law itself by making it accommodate practices that will of necessity spoil the law. It is better to preserve the integrity of law and the normative coherence of the state by keeping the treatment of emergencies in a different realm altogether, the outsiders say, and thus to protect the state itself.[9]

In many ways, the inside-outside debate is not a live issue, however, because the insiders have won for all practical purposes. In fact, even the signature examples of lawless emergency government—the 1930s regimes of Hitler's Germany and Stalin's Soviet Union—did not generally abandon law (or at least the appearance of legality), except in the most extreme moments of political excess.[10] A tyrannical regime bent on harm

---

8. Carl Schmitt, *Political Theology: Four Chapters on the Concept of Sovereignty*, trans. George Schwab (Chicago: University of Chicago Press, 1985), 6–7.

9. Outsiders include Carl Schmitt, ibid.; John Yoo, *The Powers of War and Peace: The Constitution and Foreign Affairs after 9/11* (Chicago: University of Chicago Press, 2005); Giorgio Agamben, *State of Exception,* trans. Kevin Attell (Chicago: University of Chicago Press, 2005), 32–33.

10. Hitler's rise to power was famously accomplished in a purely legal manner, at least up through the Enabling Act of 1933. Clinton Rossiter, *Constitutional Dictatorship: Crisis Government in Modern Democracies* (Piscataway, NJ: Transaction Publishers, 2002 [1948]). And much of the law of the Nazi period remained surprisingly unchanged. Michael Stolleis, *Law under the Swastika* (Chicago: University of Chicago Press, 1998); Ernst Fränkel, *The Dual State* (Oxford: Oxford University Press, 1941). Stalin's terror was conducted at the same time as he brought in a new constitution and professionalized the judiciary by replacing the people's courts. Peter Solomon, *Criminal Justice under Stalin* (Cambridge: Cambridge University Press, 1996). And, of course, Stalin's ruthless justice minister Andrei Vyshinsky not only presided over Soviet show trials but then went on to coordinate the

will still use the law because law is the way that the state talks to itself. A tyrant cannot generally get the state to do his bidding save through the commands that appear as law; it is otherwise impossible to mobilize state officials to carry out whatever the new state program is. The outsiders cannot possibly win the debate over "law versus no law." At times of crisis, there will not be "no law." There will be law, and the only live question is what sort of law it is.

As a result, most modern constitutions that deal with emergency powers offer some variant of the insiders' view on the inside-outside debate. But the usual method for taking the inside position is to regulate emergencies using a toggle-switch approach. Emergencies are supposed to be declared at the start and explicitly stopped at the end, so that they are handled in constitutionally regulated spaces explicitly marked off within the constitutional order but sealed off from normal politics. They are *inside* the constitutional order (so the insiders win) but *outside* normality (hence the toggle switch that marks when the normal stops and starts again). Emergencies have an outsider's status within the constitutional order, but they are definitely inside for the purposes of the inside-outside debate.

After the political catastrophes of the twentieth-century interwar period, constitutional drafters writing new constitutions for democracies have tried to bring emergencies in from the constitutional cold using this toggle-switch method. Drafters know the temptations that have struck leaders in times of emergency, and they try to provide a legal bulwark against the alteration of constitutional principles when emergency strikes by writing emergency powers, with careful limits, into the constitution itself.

In 1968, for example, Germany amended its Basic Law to constitutionally regulate crisis government.[11] While at first the Basic Law eschewed the constitutional legality of emergencies in light of the disastrous experience under Article 48 of the Weimar Constitution,[12] the rumblings of 1968 produced constitutional changes that recognized the

---

Soviet Union's strategy at Nuremberg. Arkadii Vaksburg, *The Prosecutor and the Prey: Vyshinsky and the 1930s' Moscow Show Trials* (London: Weidenfeld and Nicolson, 1990); Francine Hirsch, "The Soviets at Nuremberg: International Law, Propaganda and the Making of the Postwar Order," *American Historical Review* 113, no. 3 (2008): 701–30. If legality, or the appearance of legality, did not matter, then why have tyrants tried so hard to operate according to law or at least the appearance of law? The debate between positivism and natural law takes as central the question of whether the law of tyrants is *really* law at all. One might ask instead why the worst dictators want to *appear* legal.

11. Grundgesetz (GG), Federal Republic of Germany (Basic Law), Art. 80a and Art. 81, available in English at http://www.bundestag.de/interakt/infomat/fremdsprachiges_material/downloads/ggEn_download.pdf, including amendments through June 2008.

12. Frederick Mundell Watkins, *The Failure of Constitutional Emergency Powers under the German Republic* (Cambridge: Harvard University Press, 1939).

inevitability of emergencies but strictly limited what could occur within them. The 1968 amendments created the constitutional condition of a "state of defense," requiring the approval of two-thirds of *both* houses of Parliament. If the Parliament cannot convene, then the "joint committee" (a representative subset of the parliament) may declare a state of defense instead. The Basic Law provides for parliamentary override of executive decisions throughout emergencies. The Federal Constitutional Court may never be disbanded nor the Parliament dissolved during an emergency. Even the Chancellor may not be replaced unless there is a two-thirds vote of the Parliament or the joint committee in favor of an alternative candidate. A lesser sort of emergency, the "state of tension," requires a two-thirds vote of only the lower house of the Parliament for its initiation. Such a declaration may trigger only specific emergency provisions already placed into federal law.

After a long history of the abuse of human rights in the name of emergency, Russia adopted a new Constitution in 1993, one that embeds emergency powers in the text.[13] The Russian Constitution explicitly lists which rights may be modified in times of emergency and which are inviolable even then. It also indicates that the Parliament may not be dissolved in an emergency. And while the Constitution itself does not specify it, the Constitutional Court Act indicates that the operation of the Court may not be altered by any condition not specified in the act, and the act does not allow for the dissolution of the Court in the case of an emergency.[14]

After Canada revised its Constitution in 1982 to more firmly entrench rights as legally enforceable claims in the constitutional order, it shortly thereafter enacted the Emergencies Act of 1985, which explicitly acknowledges that all uses of the act must be compatible with the Canadian Charter of Rights and Freedoms as well as the International Covenant on Civil and Political Rights.[15] The act also creates a detailed typology of emergencies with precise conditions for the use of each. More crucially, the act has constitutionalized emergencies by giving them a regulated home inside the constitutional order. At the same time as Canada brought in the Emergencies Act, Canada also repealed its previously far-reaching War Measures Act that had for most of the twentieth century permitted emergencies with few constitutional constraints.

13. Constitution of the Russian Federation, particularly Art. 56(3), and Art. 106(5), available in English at http://www.kremlin.ru/eng/articles/ConstMain.shtml.

14. Federal Constitutional Law on the Constitutional Court of the Russian Federation, NO. 1-FKZ of July 21, 1994 (as amended through June 2009), Ch. I, Art. 7.

15. Preamble, Emergencies Act (1985, c. 22 (4th Supp.)), http://laws.justice.gc.ca/en/showtdm/cs/E-4.5. I discuss this statute more extensively in Kim Lane Scheppele, "North American Emergencies: The Uses of Emergency Powers in the United States and Canada," *I-CON International Journal of Constitutional Law* 4, no. 2 (2006): 213–43, 230–31.

The South African Constitution also embeds emergency powers so that they are strictly regulated.[16] There is an "escalator" clause requiring a state of emergency to be approved by the Parliament with an ever-increasing majority as the distance from the crisis-triggering event grows. The Constitution also is explicit about which rights can be limited and for how long. Some rights must be fully protected even during emergency; life and human dignity may never be limited and slavery and servitude are never permitted. Other rights may be temporarily squeezed; free speech and liberty rights may be infringed for brief periods to handle the threat. The crucial point is that there are clear constitutional guidelines that determine what officials may do, as well as which rights can be limited, how much they may be limited, and for how long. In addition to the explicit regulation of a state of emergency, the South African Constitution puts strong limits on the use of the military in a "state of defense."

Despite the admirable constitutionalization of emergency powers in these various constitutional systems, none of them has ever been invoked. As a result, we cannot see whether these constitutional restrictions actually worked in a time of crisis, or whether the limitations that they attempted to institutionalize really held executive power to account. We do not know whether in an actual crisis any of these constitutions would hold fast, bend, or break if the emergency provisions were invoked to limit what the executive could do. They have never been put to the test. Of course, one could say that there have not been serious emergencies in these countries since the constitutions were written, but the history tells us differently.

For example, Germany did not use its constitutional emergency powers after 9/11, and so the Federal Constitutional Court struck down as unconstitutional a number of the laws that were passed in robust response to the attacks on the United States, laws that certainly appeared to give emergency powers to the government.[17] In the wars in Chechyna

16. The Constitution of South Africa, Art. 37 and Arts. 200–204, available at the South African government's Web site, http://www.info.gov.za/documents/constitution/1996/index.htm.

17. The Federal Constitutional Court of Germany struck down as unconstitutional the parliamentary adoption of the European arrest warrant after September 11, primarily on the grounds that the law had failed to ensure German constitutional protections. Judgment of the Federal Constitutional Court of Germany, 18 July 2005. On the European Arrest Warrant, available in English at the Constitutional Court's Web site, http://www.bundesverfassungsgericht.de/entscheidungen/rs20050718_2bvr223604en.html. The judgment is analyzed in Simone Mölder, "European Arrest Warrant Act Is Void—The Decision of the German Federal Constitutional Court of 18 July 2005," *German Law Journal* 7, no. 2 (2006): 45–58, http://www.germanlawjournal.com/pdf/Vol07No01/PDF_Vol_07_No_1_45-58_Developments_Moelders.pdf. That same court also struck down post–September 11 data-mining laws that insufficiently protected the constitutionally guaranteed

between 1995 and 2005, the Russian government simply did not invoke constitutional emergency powers (with their associated permissions and limits), though the Constitution seems designed for such uses.[18] Canada did not use its constitutionalized emergency statute as a rubric under which to enact the country's post-9/11 antiterrorism laws, even though scholars noted that the post-9/11 laws were emergency powers without the label.[19] Only South Africa does not seem to have been tempted to use extraordinary powers since the new Constitution went into effect. Each of these cases where emergency powers were used, however, pitted those who wanted government to be effective in a crisis even if constitutional corners had to be cut against those who wanted government to be fully constitutional at all times. But what unifies all of these cases is that governments have stretched and bent their constitutions in times of crisis, without invoking the regime of constitutional emergency powers in the ways that their constitutions envisioned. The mere existence of constitutional emergency powers cannot provide constitutional constraint at times of crisis if they are simply not invoked.

The most famous case where constitutional emergency powers were invoked is interwar Germany, where Article 48 of the Weimar Constitution created a constitutional framework for emergencies. But this constitutionalization of emergencies did not prevent one of the worst falls from constitutional governance the world has seen.[20] Constitutionalizing the

---

privacy of those whose files were reviewed. Judgment of the German Constitutional Court of 22 May 2006, 1 BvR 518/02 available in German at the Constitutional Court's Web site, http://www.bundesverfassungsgericht.de/entscheidungen/rs20060404_1bvr051802.html. The decision is summarized in English at the European Digital Rights Web site, http://www.edri.org/edrigram/number4.10/datascreening. The Court also struck down the law that gave authorization to the German government to shoot down apparently hijacked aircraft with civilians on board on grounds that the government could not deliberately violate the human dignity of people by taking some lives to save others. Judgment of the Federal Constitutional Court of 15 February 2006, 1 BvR 357/05, BVerfG, 1 BvR 357/05 vom 15.2.2006, Absatz-Nr. (1–154), translated at http://www.bverfg.de/entscheidungen/rs20060215_1bvr035705en.html.

18. The European Court of Human Rights was puzzled by this omission. *Case of Isayeva, Yusupova and Bazayeva v. Russia*, European Court of Human Rights, Applications nos. 57947/00, 57948/00 and 57949/00, Decision of 24 February 2005, noted at paragraph 125, http://www.icj.org/IMG/pdf/Isayeva_others.pdf. Had Russia declared a state of emergency and officially derogated from specific rights provisions, this and other Russian cases before the ECtHR might have come out differently.

19. For the constitutional critiques of the post-9/11 laws, see the essays in Ronald J. Daniels, Patrick Macklem, and Kent Roach, eds., *Security of Freedom: Essays on Canada's Anti-terrorism Bill* (Toronto: University of Toronto Press, 2001).

20. On the uses of Article 48 during the Weimar Republic, see Frederick Mundell Watkins, *The Failure of Constitutional Emergency Powers under the German Republic;* on the collapse, see Rossiter, *Constitutional Dictatorship.*

uses of emergency powers does not mean that those constitutional provisions will in fact be used in times of emergency or, when they are used, that they will save the constitutional order.

There are not many examples—in fact, not *any* that I know of—where the use of national constitutional emergency provisions have been effective at maintaining limited emergency powers in a time of crisis by turning on extraordinary measures to operate for a brief time and then turning them off completely when the crisis is over. The more usual route when emergencies strike has been to ignore the constitutional limitations and use emergency powers regardless of what the constitution says. Sometimes states invoke constitutional emergency powers until executives gain enough momentum to overstep the limits, as in Weimar Germany. Sometimes, the courts strike down these emergency laws but often not until the emergency is effectively over. Crucially, however, the constitutional provisions that permit extraordinary measures and then turn them off again have never been used to good effect by the very parliaments that are typically the constitutional guardians of these emergency regimes.

Maybe this is because this "toggle-switch" approach fails to grasp how emergencies actually work. The toggle-switch method may not be effective at stemming abuses of emergency powers because it does not have barriers and constraints in the right sorts of places. To see why this may be the case, we need to examine how emergencies actually work.

The Emergency Script

When we look at actually existing emergencies and the reactions they generate, we will see that in most emergencies the worst abuses tend to appear gradually, not suddenly.[21] This is why it is hard to determine when to flip the constitutional switch on to emergency governance. At the other end, either old emergencies tend to fade out slowly or new emergencies provide a reason to maintain preexisting emergency powers, and so one rarely finds the clean bright line to mark when the switch should be flipped back. If beginnings and endings are hard to perceive at the time by those who need to flip the constitutional emergency switch, then we can better understand why formal regimes of emergency powers rarely work to contain abuses and why emergency powers tend to outlast the threats that brought them into being. In short, it is only in theory and not

---

21. Much of the analysis reported here is elaborated in my forthcoming book, Kim Lane Scheppele, *The International State of Emergency: Crisis, Legality, and Transnationality after 9/11.*

in practice—or in hindsight and not in prospect—that emergencies look like discrete episodes to which emergency measures can be limited.

Though each crisis has elements specific to time and place, there are common features that emergencies tend to share when one examines them empirically. Regardless of whether an emergency is declared by a right-wing dictator or a left-wing insurgent or whether an emergency is brought about by a war, coup, pandemic, or earthquake, emergency government tends to have a predictable "emergency script" that unites these different causes in a common set of tactics. The emergency script generally starts slowly with a hollowing out of governmental institutions apart from the executive branch, and the signature abuses that signal a real crisis are generally rather late in arriving. By the time an emergency is arguably over, these abusive practices have found new rationales for their continued maintenance, and so it is difficult to repeal them.

How can we examine how emergencies actually work? To take a set of emergencies that are removed from our current preoccupation with 9/11 and its aftermath, we can use the series of case studies prepared by the International Commission of Jurists (ICJ) in the early 1980s to see how actually existing states of emergency are constructed through law.[22] The eighteen countries (some with more than one discrete emergency) are Argentina (military coup in 1976), Canada (October Crisis of 1970), Colombia (emergencies from 1947 to the mid-1980s), Czechoslovakia (after Prague Spring in 1968), Ghana (emergencies in the first twenty years after independence), Greece (the coup of the generals from 1967 to 1974), Hungary (after the uprising of 1956), India (the first three emergencies after independence, particularly the national emergency from 1975 to 1978), Malaysia (in the 1960s and 1970s), Northern Ireland (and British emergency rule from 1922 until the 1980s), Peru (emergencies since 1932), Poland (martial law in 1981–82), Syria (the 1962 coup), Thailand (declarations of emergency between 1932 and 1979), Turkey (states of exception from 1960 to 1980), Uruguay (from 1968 to 1982), USSR (from the Revolution to the 1977 Constitution), Yugoslavia (Kosovo in

22. *International Commission of Jurists, States of Emergency: Their Impact on Human Rights* (Geneva: International Commission of Jurists, 1983). The ICJ commissioned these case studies to provide input into an international process, then just beginning, to establish humanitarian standards to be guaranteed even in times of emergency. In particular, the case studies compiled by Jurist were forwarded to Nicole Questiaux, who was the primary rapporteur on the UN Report urging the adoption of human rights standards for emergencies. U.N. Economic and Social Council [ECOSOC], Sub-Committee on Prevention of Discrimination & Protection of Minorities, *Study of Implications for Human Rights of Recent Developments Concerning Situations Known as States of Siege or Emergency,* P 23, U.N. Doc. E/CN.4/Sub.2/1982/15 (July 27, 1982). Though the empirical evidence showing the need for such humanitarian standards was overwhelming, the international effort to develop an equivalent to the Geneva Conventions for emergencies foundered.

1981), and Zaire (1960–80). In many of these cases, emergency powers extended beyond the scope of the study, which ended in 1982.

The case studies provide particularly good materials to work with because the teams of expert authors who documented the details of emergency governance in each country were instructed to note not only what happened on the ground during these emergencies but also what legal authority was invoked for the use of crisis powers. We can therefore analyze these emergency governments not only by seeing what they did but also by examining the legal infrastructures that were built up to respond to the crisis. In the analysis that follows, I list countries that engaged in each of the described behaviors along with approximate dates that indicate when the practice either started or was institutionalized.[23] The common patterns we see in emergencies follow an "emergency script."

Some readers may object that most of the countries analyzed here were not constitutional democracies at the time of their emergencies and therefore do not provide suitable bases for generalization as we think about how to design institutions in constitutional democracies. While it is true that most of the governments in the ICJ case studies were not constitutional democracies when they had their emergencies, many of them have become constitutional democracies since. There was nothing about their legal cultures that made them inherently unable to constitutionalize their politics. In addition, virtually all of the case-study countries demonstrated rather scrupulous attention to the legal bases for what they did during the emergencies, which should tell us that the legal options available to crisis leaders mattered, even when the government did not have a constitutionalist spirit.

By examining these cases studies, we can find an "emergency script" in operation, providing a common set of strategies as the crisis proceeded.

Executive Centralization

In the first step of the "emergency script," power is centralized in the executive. But this does not mean that an executive typically seizes power

23. While the countries listed in parentheses in this section clearly did engage in the conduct listed, the absence of a country from a list does not mean that it did not engage in that particular conduct. The rapporteurs for each country did not necessarily develop a complete catalog of everything done in the name of emergency powers. So, for example, the fact that a government was responsible for mass disappearances may have meant that the reporter failed to note the incursions on free speech or freedom of assembly. Or the fact that the government may have set up special courts may have drawn more attention from the rapporteur than the institution of curfews. That is why I have used this more qualitative method for determining the anatomy of a crisis. Counting how many of the countries used each method would have to rely on comprehensive documentation, which was not a goal of the ICJ project.

from parliament and courts in one obvious move. Instead, the accumulation of executive power often happens over an extended period of time so that the final act that triggers the emergency is simply the last in a long chain. Emergencies can occur when parliaments are already dissolved (Greece 1967) or in recess (Argentina 1976). Alternatively, parliaments may simply give extraordinary standby powers to the executive through ordinary legislation, powers that may be invoked when the executive deems it necessary (Canada 1914; India 1962, 1975). Or parliaments can pass enabling acts that delegate to the executive the power to legislate without further involvement of the parliament (Colombia 1958–74; Ghana 1960s; Germany 1933; India 1975) or the power to act outside of normal legal constraints (Ghana 1964; India 1962, 1975). Submissive parliaments may have their terms extended (India 1975). Unsubmissive parliamentarians may be arrested (Greece 1967). Sometimes, if all else fails, parliaments are dissolved (Argentina 1976; Peru 1930s; Ghana 1972; Syria 1962).

Executives in emergencies often neutralize or bypass courts as well. Courts may be marginalized by the creation of separate tribunals to deal with the specific cases growing out of the crisis (Hungary 1956; India 1962; Northern Ireland 1970s; Ghana 1961; USSR 1917 and on). Sometimes, decisions by the ordinary courts are simply ignored (Ghana 1964, 1975, 1977; India 1966; Argentina 1974) or overridden by administrative edicts (Greece 1967). Sometimes courts marginalize themselves by refusing to rule on whether there is an emergency in the first place (Colombia 1958–74; Canada 1923, 1947, 1950, 1971; Ghana 1968; India 1962) or by being highly deferential to government claims (Colombia 1978; India 1976, 1977; Northern Ireland 1970s). Or courts accept the suspension of certain parts of the constitution as valid and block legal challenges to the emergency government (Malaysia 1980s; Peru 1933; Thailand 1947 but contrast Thailand 1958; India 1976).

As these examples illustrate, while there are occasionally abrupt seizures of power by executives—for example, when they dissolve parliaments and govern by decree—more typically the other branches of government collude in their own marginalization or fail to act decisively to constrain executive centralization. This makes them ineffective at actually participating in the formal declaration of an emergency—or the formal checking of emergency powers once they are invoked.

Militarization

Once the executive has marginalized the other branches enough to operate alone, the next step in the emergency script involves the militarization of the use of executive power. This is often not hard, as most constitutions make the executive the commander in chief of the military and require the intelligence services to report primarily to the executive even in normal times. Sometimes the military is called out by civilian leaders to put down the domestic opposition or to resolve a crisis (Canada 1970; Hungary 1956; India 1975; Kosovo 1981). Often the military just takes over (Argentina 1974; Colombia 1977; Czechoslovakia 1968; Ghana 1966, 1972; Greece 1967; Peru 1962; Poland 1981–82; Syria 1962; Turkey 1960, 1971; Uruguay 1973). As a result, the military may carry out previously civilian tasks like investigating "subversives" (Argentina 1976), detaining suspects (Colombia 1978; Ghana 1966; Greece 1967; Colombia 1958–74), running the economy (Argentina 1976; Poland 1981–82), distributing basic supplies (Colombia 1979), or participating in maintaining order along with (or in substitution for) ordinary police (Colombia periodically between 1886 and 1978; Czechoslovakia 1968; Ghana 1972; Greece, 1967; Kosovo 1981; Poland 1981–82). In addition, military courts are often given jurisdiction to substitute for civilian courts during crises (Argentina 1976; Colombia 1970; Ghana 1967, 1978; Greece 1967; Poland 1981–82; Uruguay 1972, 1976; Zaire 1960). The military may appoint specific civilian judges to handle particular cases (Argentina 1976). Sometimes, martial law is declared (Greece 1975; Hungary 1956; Poland 1981–82; Syria 1948; Thailand 1976; USSR 1918, 1941–45). The crucial element of this step in the emergency script is that the military starts to perform functions customarily reserved to civilians and the military reports to (or becomes) the executive that has already neutralized the other branches.

Procedural Shortcuts

Once power is firmly in the hands of the executive, and the military has been mobilized to handle the threat, the next casualty is robust legal procedure.

New legal forms and institutions use summary procedures to be able to act quickly. Crises may be managed through executive orders rather than ordinary legislation (Argentina 1976; Colombia 1958–74; 1978; Ghana 1972; Greece 1967; Poland 1981–82; Zaire 1964, 1965). New bodies of state that have not been authorized by the constitution or by legislation spring up to govern with the executive (Argentina 1976; Ghana 1961, 1966, 1972; Greece 1967; Hungary 1956; Poland 1981–82; Uruguay 1973–74). Old bodies of state that provide procedural checks are bypassed or neutralized (Ghana 1972; India 1962; Kosovo 1981). New forms of law (institutional orders, constitutional orders; garrison service regulations, and so on) are invented that avoid parliamentary approval and take their authority only from the new military or irregularly appointed councils that issue these new forms of law (Argentina 1976; Ghana 1966, 1972; Greece 1967; Peru 1963; Uruguay 1974–82). New penalties are created, such as fines that depend on the state's assessment of whether the individual in question *will* commit a crime in the future (Colombia 1975).

Old procedural guarantees are eroded. Administrative tribunals with less elaborate procedural protections for suspects substitute for ordinary courts in criminal cases above and beyond the military tribunals that are often also present (Ghana 1961; Greece 1967; India 1975; Hungary 1956; Poland 1981–82; USSR 1917). New laws are applied retroactively (Canada 1970; Greece 1967; Peru 1932; Syria 1980; Turkey 1961; Uruguay 1973; Zaire 1964). New crimes are invented that mask purely political prosecutions (Argentina 1976; Czechoslovakia 1968; Hungary 1956; Kosovo 1981; Poland 1981–82; USSR 1917 and on). Misdemeanors are given the punishments for felonies (Greece 1967).

Investigations of alleged crimes may be carried out with summary procedures. The need to provide evidence of individualized suspicion before someone is detained or tried is a common casualty of crises (Ghana 1972; Greece 1967; Malaysia 1975; Northern Ireland 1970s; Thailand 1979; Turkey 1961; USSR 1917). Property can be searched without warrants (Canada 1970; Colombia 1978; Zaire 1960) or it can be seized (Ghana 1972; Greece 1967; Peru 1963; USSR 1917 and on) or destroyed (Colombia 1978). Habeas review is suspended (Ghana 1961, 1972, 1978; Peru 1939, 1968; Thailand 1977) or ineffective because the government fails to acknowledge it (Argentina 1976; Northern Ireland 1970s). Cases can proceed without a prosecutor's bill of indictment (Hungary 1956) or without informed defense counsel (Czechoslovakia 1968). The presumption of innocence is abolished (Argentina 1976). Police may be given "shoot to kill" orders based on minimal suspicion without the presumption that a trial would be preferred (Colombia 1978).

Criminal procedure may also be "simplified" or abolished during a crisis (Czechoslovakia 1968; Ghana 1963, 1972; Hungary 1956; India 1975; Malaysia 1975; Northern Ireland 1973; Thailand 1958; Turkey 1971–73; Uruguay 1972–81; USSR 1917). Courts may be urged to work from unwritten "rules of natural justice" (Ghana 1978) or "revolutionary legality" (USSR 1917). The burden of proof may be lessened for certain criminal offenses (Czechoslovakia 1968). Appeals from court judgments are eliminated (Ghana 1963, 1972; Greece 1967; Syria 1968; Turkey 1961; USSR 1917). Those acquitted by courts may continue to be detained (Ghana 1978). Death sentences may be carried out immediately after sentencing (Peru 1932; Syria 1968; USSR 1917 and on).

Putting People in Their Places

With formal procedure disabled, emergency governments then "put people in their places." This has two faces—setting up regimes of preventive detention, in effect requiring the presence of certain people in certain places, and at the same time banning demonstrations, assemblies, and associations, requiring the absence of certain people from certain places.

To make people appear in some places, administrative detention becomes common (Argentina 1976; Colombia 1966; Ghana 1960s–1970s; Greece 1967; India 1962, 1975; Malaysia 1960s–1970s; Northern Ireland 1971; Poland 1981–82; Syria 1962; Thailand 1962, 1969; Turkey 1961, 1971; Uruguay, 1971–81; Zaire 1961; USSR 1917). Sometimes administrative detention takes the form of confinement to psychiatric hospitals (USSR 1941 and on). Detainees may be moved from place to place to escape regular court review (Peru 1975). In addition, people may be prohibited from leaving the country (Northern Ireland 1970s; Peru 1965; Thailand 1953–57). Some may be put in camps (Greece 1967; USSR 1917 and on).

To make people vanish from other places, trade unions, political parties, student groups and professional organizations may be dissolved (Argentina 1976; Czechoslovakia 196; Ghana 1977; Kosovo 1981; Poland 1981–82; Uruguay, 1973). Demonstrations may be broken up, curfews may be established, and social establishments may be closed (Argentina 1976; Colombia 1965, 1978; Czechoslovakia 1968; Ghana 1960s; Hungary 1956–57; India 1975; Northern Ireland 1974; Poland 1981–82; USSR 1941–45). The "usual suspects" are eliminated from public space: resistant army officers are "retired"; university professors are fired; school-teachers are dismissed; judges are disciplined; bishops or other religious authorities are replaced (Greece 1967; Kosovo 1981; Poland 1981–82; Peru 1968, 1973; Turkey 1961, 1971). All organizations may be monitored by the government, or dissolved (Ghana 1962; India 1975; Malaysia 1981). Special areas may be designated that no one may enter (Malaysia 1970s). Certain people may be expelled from the country (Ghana 1960; Malaysia 1969; Peru 1968; USSR 1917, 1941–45), banished from certain places (Czechoslovakia 1968), or deprived of citizenship so that they cannot return (Greece 1967). People may be "disappeared," even in the thousands (Argentina 1976).

Inversion of Free Speech

Along with these measures, the protection of free speech is inverted. Some speech, formerly protected, is criminalized as a threat or labeled as action—for example, sedition or incitement (Argentina 1976; Colombia 1978; Greece 1946–50, 1967–75; Malaysia 1969; Northern Ireland 1970; Peru 1948). Newspapers are closed (Czechoslovakia 1968; Peru 1939, 1968–79; Syria 1962; Thailand 1976; Uruguay 1967), nationalized (Peru 1974), or licensed (Ghana 1962). Foreign journalists are expelled (Kosovo 1981). Censorship is instituted (Czechoslovakia 1968; Ghana 1960s; Greece 1967; Ghana 1972; USSR 1917). Books are burned (Thailand 1977). Communication with certain named individuals or groups is criminalized (Argentina 1976; Ghana 1966), as is the spreading of rumors (Ghana 1966, 1973). News broadcasts must receive prior clearance (Colombia 1970). Possession of certain publications is a criminal offense (Argentina 1976).

Other speech, formerly protected under a right to remain silent, becomes mandatory. Interrogation will not stop without confessions, sometimes achieved under torture (Argentina 1976; Colombia 1979; Ghana 1972; Greece 1967; Northern Ireland 1970s; Syria 1970s; Turkey 1971; Uruguay 1972). Police require those who know about conspiracies and crimes to disclose them under pain of penalty (Czechoslovakia 1968; Ghana 1962, 1972; Northern Ireland 1970s; Thailand, 1979; Zaire 1972). Citizens must pledge to support the state (India 1975).

Reversal of Transparency

The reversal of transparency of the government is the next act in the emergency script. If government was formerly open and responsive to citizen requests for information, emergency government becomes more opaque to its citizens (India 1975). During crises, it becomes harder for citizens to see what government is doing because government is blanketed in secrecy (Ghana 1962; USSR 1917 and on), sometimes acting to erase all evidence that there even *is* a political opposition (Greece 1967). Some legal decrees are simply secret (India 1975; Peru 1976–77), as are detentions (Ghana 1957, 1972) or trials (Ghana 1967). Warrants for detention may be signed by anonymous officials (Ghana 1978). State officials who break the law are never investigated or prosecuted (Ghana 1960s; Greece 1967; Hungary 1956) or they are given formal immunity (Colombia 1978; Ghana 1980; Thailand 1959, 1976). Elections are canceled (India 1975–78) or opposition parties are dissolved (Ghana 1969) to prevent the state from becoming accountable again.

At the same time, the surveillance of those who are resident in the territory increases; people become more transparent to the state (Greece 1967; Turkey 1971; Zaire 1960; USSR 1917 and on). Secret police carry out investigations with few legal restraints (Greece 1967; USSR 1917 and on). Homes are searched; electronic surveillance is increased; secret correspondence is breached (Colombia 1979; Czechoslovakia 1968; Greece 1967; Malaysia 1969; Northern Ireland 1970s; Syria 1970s; USSR 1917 and on). The state may regulate details of daily life, down to how much cash people are allowed to possess (Greece 1967; USSR 1917 and on).

Anticipatory Violence

Finally, states that have taken many of these steps may turn to the deployment of anticipatory violence. *They* have or will soon attack us; *we* must attack them in response, claims the government (Argentina 1976;

Colombia 1979; Ghana 1970s; Greece 1967; Peru 1960s). Full-blown emergencies typically deploy violence against real or imagined opponents even before the threatened violence by others emerges (Argentina 1976; Colombia 1979; Czechoslovakia 1968; Ghana 1972; Greece 1967; Uruguay 1968, 1970). Sometimes the government itself stages the apparent opposition as an excuse to crack down (Greece 1967). Plots are rooted out and plotters are tried before military tribunals to demonstrate to the public that opposition is hopeless (Czechoslovakia 1968; Ghana 1977; Hungary 1956; Zaire 1978). Often, the violence used is disproportionate to the threat and is used against a much broader segment of the population than reasonably poses a serious challenge to the existing government (Colombia 1979; Czechoslovakia 1968; Ghana 1960s–1970s; Greece 1967; Thailand 1976). In the end, jails hold thousands of people detained without trials (Ghana 1960s; Greece 1967; Hungary 1956; Malaysia 1960s–1970s) or mass graves hold the bodies of opponents (Argentina 1976; Peru 1932; Syria, 1962; Zaire 1979).

Lingering Powers

Emergency powers often last well beyond the threat that called them into being. For example, emergency laws from colonial Ghana were used for the emergency declared upon independence in 1957. Emergency laws written in Greece for the 1946–50 emergency were used in 1967, even though they were inconsistent with the constitution written in the meantime. Special powers authorized in India for the 1965 emergency were used in the 1975 emergency, which had a very different cause. The state of emergency declared in Argentina in 1974 to deal with a serious military threat was used to legitimate the coup of 1976. The Colombian Parliament in 1962 adopted as permanent all of the temporary emergency decrees issued from 1949 to 1958. At this point, emergency government became normal government.

If this is how emergencies have operated in practice, developing through these stages, then resilient constitutional design needs to guarantee against each of these sorts of practices in anticipation. But this progression of emergency government from one step to another shows us why the toggle-switch approach will generally not work.

First, toggle switches typically require that parliaments take steps to declare the crisis before executives have consolidated their power, but what we see instead is that either parliaments are already not functioning or they delegate their own powers to the executive at the first sign of crisis. Moreover, executive centralization is characteristic of modern administrative states generally, and it is often hard to tell whether a move that brings more power to the executive is designed to generate efficiency or autocracy (or both).

Second, many of the worst abuses one sees in emergencies happen rather late in the process, long after the time to invoke constitutional emergency powers has passed. By the time the government is routinely deploying preventive detention or anticipatory violence, the crisis is far advanced and executive powers are already entrenched. National governments are usually large and cumbersome and do not react quickly in crises; as a result, it often takes months and years for emergency powers to come into effect. By that time, an emergency will certainly not feel new enough to warrant a declaration of emergency even though the worst abuses are starting. Besides, the institutions that might check the emergency are usually neutralized in the early stages of the crisis.

Third, emergencies do not usually end in the prescribed way—when parliaments or courts call them off. Typically, either parliaments are complicit with the use of emergency powers or they have long since been silenced. Neither parliaments nor courts have the intelligence information available to the executive or the military and, as a result, neither parliaments nor courts are willing to trust their own judgment about when a crisis is over.[24] Lodging the powers in parliaments or courts to declare when emergencies end typically provides little constraint in real emergencies.

How can we keep emergency powers within constitutional constraints, then? The most effective sort of constitutional defense will not just put up a barrier to emergency government at one point in the slide into the use of emergency powers but will attempt to guard against these anticonstitutionalist threats at every point.

The way to deal with actually existing emergencies is to figure out how to live with them as a matter of normal constitutionalism. Given that one prominent threat to constitutional democracy comes from terrorism, we should realize that campaigns against terrorism are not over in a day, a week, or even a few months. As long as a threat appears to continue—and terrorist threats are typically of the long-term, grindingly persistent sort—it is hard to end emergency powers quickly. If the United States, and much of the rest of the world, is in the business of fighting terrorists that are likely to be with us for a very long time, then we should not be looking primarily for emergency measures that will be used in the first month or two after an attack and then will be repealed. We need to think

24. Eight years after a state of emergency was declared in the United Kingdom following 9/11, the European Court of Human Rights felt it was in no position to say that the emergency was over. *Case of A. and Others v. United Kingdom,* Application no. 3455/05, 19 February 2009, http://www.statewatch.org/news/2009/feb/uk-echr-a-and-others-judgment.pdf.

about how to maintain a serious fight against a threat over the long haul without destroying our constitutional order in the meantime. We do not need a short-term *exception* to the constitutional order just to handle the threat of a second strike. Instead, we need durable, constitutionally responsible institutions that can fight long-term threats without undermining the constitutional system over a period of years and even decades.

Designing against the Emergency Script

Designing against emergencies means putting particular safeguards in precisely those places where emergencies are most likely to challenge ordinary constitutionalism. Finding ways to make executives share power will be particularly crucial to any effort to prevent emergency abuses. In addition, keeping the military from exceeding its authority, providing procedural safeguards that are hard to eviscerate, building stronger protection for rights (particularly rights of privacy, assembly, and speech), and finding ways to tamp down the use of anticipatory violence are all likely to be useful at making emergencies much less constitutionally dangerous than they might otherwise be. Reviewing actions taken during an emergency to prevent the lingering effects of emergency powers from carrying over into justifying extreme actions in new crises will be crucial. Building these protections deep into ordinary political institutions is the best way to prevent emergencies from overtaking normal governance over the long haul.

Because in a crisis the executive will want and need to gather a great deal of information about potential threats, institutions that gather such information will come under particular pressures to use emergency shortcuts. The most effective way to cut off the slide into emergency government, therefore, will be to prevent the executive from monopolizing the key information that is necessary to evaluate the threat. As a result, the first place to crisis-proof a government should be through the careful design of institutions that collect crucial intelligence so that they are not controlled just by the executive and cannot be overridden in times of crisis. In this section, I review two examples of the constitutional design of key institutions that stand a better chance of holding emergencies at bay precisely because they respond better to the sorts of challenges that occur in actually existing emergencies.

Gathering Intelligence

How can intelligence agencies have the scope they need to detect threats before they materialize while still preserving constitutional protections that protect individual privacy, maintain limits on state action, and insist that no individual be targeted for surveillance or investigation unless there is an individuated suspicion that the target of the surveillance or investigation has done something wrong? The United States has not had a good track record of accomplishing all of these things at once; the imperatives for surveillance and investigation during the enduring and vague threats of the Cold War quickly turned into mass abuse of civil liberties.[25] The controlling statutes that were put in place to prevent such abuses have been bypassed since the beginning of the U.S. "war on terrorism." In particular, the terrorism surveillance program was conducted without following the Foreign Intelligence Surveillance Act.[26] Are there models that have done better?

While no national security apparatus is free of problems, the institution that seems to have had the best track record on both fighting terrorism and preserving civil liberties is the German domestic security service, the Office for the Protection of the Constitution (Bundesamt für Verfassungschutz or BfV).[27] The BfV is responsible for counterespionage activities within Germany and is also charged with monitoring a wide variety of domestically based extremist groups. It is institutionally housed within the Federal Ministry of the Interior and is based in Cologne.

The BfV can serve as a model for several reasons. First, the BfV's statutory mandate is explicit and limited.[28] Unlike the FBI, which has never had a framework statute setting out its powers and mechanisms of accountability, and which instead is guided by a series of Attorney General Guidelines that can be changed without legislative debate or approval,[29] the BfV has a detailed statutory mandate that sets out precisely what it can and

25. The documentation of the abuses of the FBI in domestic spying can be found most authoritatively in Select Committee to Study Governmental Operations with Respect to Intelligence Activities of the United States Senate (the "Church Committee"), Book II: "Intelligence Activities and the Rights of Americans," *Senate Report* 94-755 (1976): 5–20, http://www.aarclibrary.org/publib/contents/church/contents_church_reports_book2.htm.

26. For the law, see Foreign Intelligence Surveillance Act (FISA), Public Law No. 95-511, Title. I, 101, 92 Stat. 1783 (1983) (codified at 50 U.S.C. §§ 1801–11 [2000]). For the violations, see David Sanger, "In Address, Bush Says He Ordered Domestic Spying," *New York Times*, December 18, 2005.

27. For an elaboration of this example, see Kim Lane Scheppele, "Other People's Patriot Acts: Europe's Response to September 11," *Loyola Law Review* 50 (2004): 89–148, 98–117, and Shlomo Shpiro, "Parliament, Media and the Control of the Intelligence Services in Germany," in *Democracy, Law and Security: Internal Security Services in Contemporary Europe*, ed. Jean-Paul Brodeur et al. (Burlington, VT: Ashgate, 2003), 294, 298.

28. The law can be found in German at http://bundesrecht.juris.de/bverfschg/index.html.

29. Attorney General Guidelines are issued periodically by attorneys general of the United States without any formal rule-making procedure. The guidelines may be promulgated and retracted solely at the discretion of the attorney general. They do not even have to be made public. For the apparently current guidelines in force for domestic FBI investigations, for example, see the Department of Justice Reading Room, http://www.justice.gov/ag/reading room/guidelines.pdf.

cannot do. The statute provides the democratically determined guidelines for the institution, outlines a clear legal framework for the operation of intelligence gathering, and allows the public to recognize when and how intelligence gathering may occur. The mandate of the agency is out in the open, and it operates according to publicly vetted and publicly accountable rules. This makes the office harder to undermine in times of crisis.

Second, the office carries out its investigations in the initial stages through the use of publicly available documents and methods available to all (e.g., agents attend public meetings, read newspapers, carry out surveillance of subjects in public places, or conduct voluntary interviews). Only when BfV officials have a clear basis for suspicion may they then use agents to infiltrate groups, engage in postal checks or electronic surveillance, and use surreptitious photography. But each of these more intrusive and worrisome exercises of surveillance powers are themselves subject to strict legal requirements that are monitored by the other branches of government.

Third, the powers of the BfV are strictly separated from ordinary policing powers. The BfV does not have the power to carry out arrests, searches of premises, interrogations, or confiscations. If the BfV requires any of these powers, then it must get the cooperation of the independent federal police who have the sole capacity to act in these ways. This double check on intelligence procedures requires a different set of eyes and priorities to review all requests for the most severely rights-affecting measures that can be taken against particular individuals. Because the BfV is institutionally separated from the federal police but requires their cooperation in certain matters, the BfV cannot conduct unlimited investigations but must justify its requests for more intrusive information or for action to another agency.

Fourth, this organization of intelligence gathering has a substantial system of parliamentary checks.[30] The Parliamentary Control Commission, which supervises the entire intelligence apparatus in which the BfV is one part, has membership almost equally divided between the governing and opposition parties. But most crucially, the chairmanship of the committee rotates at six-month intervals between the government and opposition parties. The government must report all intelligence activities to this committee, which must itself report (leaving out the classified information) to the Bundestag. This system of parliamentary oversight presupposes, among other things, that the opposition parties must be able to check that the majority parties are not using the intelligence services for their own political purposes.

---

30. For the BfV's own documentation of the mechanisms that control it, see Bundesamt für Verfassungsshutz—Control, http://www.verfassungsschutz.de/en/en_about_bfv/control .html.

In addition to the Parliamentary Control Commission, there are two other parliamentary committees that have been established under Article 10 of the Constitution (which protects the privacy of communications). These committees review surveillance practices of both the intelligence services and the police. The Article 10 *Gremium* reviews and directs general policies about interception of mail, wiretaps, and other forms of electronic intercept. The Article 10 Commission consists of legal experts of the various political parties who meet together with representatives from the intelligence services to review the legality of each specific individual domestic communications intercept. This body has the right to suspend any individual intercept if it appears that the evidence sustaining it is weak or if the intercept infringes any law. In addition to these procedures for reviewing surveillance strategies, there is also the permanent possibility for the Bundestag to set up a special investigating committee if any particular surveillance practice generates concern.

Fifth, the judiciary is generally active in controlling the potentially far-reaching powers of the domestic intelligence agencies despite the fact that the 1968 amendment to Article 10 of the Basic Law that permits electronic interception of communications limited judicial review of ongoing surveillance. Even with parliamentary review largely substituting for judicial review in these cases, however, an individual who suspects that she is under surveillance may not only challenge the practice before the parliamentary commission supervising surveillance but may also lodge a complaint directly with the Federal Constitutional Court. The Court may then ask the government for evidence of such surveillance, which the government is required to provide. The government may, however, provide the information in camera to the Court, which may itself decide to make the information public only by a two-thirds vote.[31] The Federal Constitutional Court has been quite aggressive in reviewing the constitutionality of general measures that may infringe on personal privacy, for example declaring that a new wiretapping law that went into effect in 2004 to fight terrorism was unconstitutional.[32]

31. For a description in English of the constitutional remedies available to an individual under Article 10 of the Basic Law, see http://www.iuscomp.org/gla/statutes/GG.htm.

32. Large-scale Wiretapping Judgment of 3 March 2004, Federal Constitutional Court of Germany, http://www.bundesverfassungsgericht.de/entscheidungen/rs20040303_1bvr 237898.html. For a detailed description in English of the ruling of the Court, see Nicolas Nohlen, "Germany: The Electronic Eavesdropping Case," *I-Con: International Journal of Constitutional Law* 3, no. 4 (2005): 680–86. For the context within which the decision was made, see generally Verena Zöller, "Liberty Dies by Inches: German Counter-Terrorism Measures and Human Rights," *German Law Journal* 5, no. 5 (2004): 469–94, http://www .germanlawjournal.com/pdfs/Vol05No05/PDF_Vol_05_No_05_469-494_special_issue_ Zoeller.pdf.

Finally, in addition to these formal mechanisms of checking investigative powers, the press in Germany enjoys substantial constitutional and statutory protection to investigate intelligence and policing practices.[33] Not only is freedom of the press guaranteed in the Constitution, but there is an explicit constitutional prohibition on censorship. By statute, the press is guaranteed confidentiality of sources and informants, as well as immunity from police eavesdropping and searches of editorial offices. As a result, media coverage of the police and intelligence services is quite common, detailed, and critical. The intelligence services have not been scandal-free, and so this media check has been quite useful.

Even with all of the checks that the German system places on surveillance power, however, there are still strong suspicions that this power cannot be controlled in ways that protect constitutional rights adequately. As Verena Zöller has shown, the 80 percent increase in telephone taps between 1996 and 2001 is hard to account for, as is the fact that only 25 percent of these taps ever led to someone being charged with a crime.[34] Nearly 65 percent of those who were convicted of a crime on the basis of telephone tap evidence were sentenced to less than five years in prison, suggesting that the crimes in question were not serious enough to warrant such an intrusion on privacy in the first place. About 75 percent of those placed under surveillance were never formally notified of the fact, which made later judicial vindication of their privacy rights difficult. Zöller takes these statistics as evidence that surveillance power, once granted and even with many constitutional checks, can still run amok.

While the German system is not perfect—and no system, in fact, is likely to be—one can see from this review that the German system has attempted to design into the normal institutions of government precisely the sorts of checks that the "emergency script" would lead us to believe are particularly crucial. First, this system builds in separation of powers between branches of government and also between the governing parties and the opposition. The double guarantee of the parliamentary check on both general policy and specific intrusions as well as the ability of individuals to bring lawsuits for damages after the fact preserve some procedural guarantees. In addition, the requirement that the security services hand off to the civilian police certain kinds of requests means that there are stronger checks on the stronger uses of policing powers, which tends to protect the rights most in danger during emergencies. One might

33. GG, Art. 5(1), translated in http://www.iuscomp.org/gla/statutes/GG.htm. For a detailed description of the press law and examples of press vigilance in reviewing the German intelligence agencies, see Shpiro, "Parliament, Media and the Control of the Intelligence Services in Germany," 294, 298.

34. Zöller, "Liberty Dies by Inches: German Counter-Terrorism Measures and Human Rights," 5.

expect that this system would be better than most on a long-term basis and therefore that its design would not require that a country live in a constant state of exception.

The Concentration of Expertise

How else might a country fight terrorism over time without upending its constitutional sensibility? It is often beneficial both for effectiveness and for civil liberties to concentrate terrorism investigations in a group of experts who are institutionally separated from ordinary criminal investigations and ordinary intelligence gathering and who can therefore concentrate only on terrorism investigations without getting drawn into other matters. Terrorism investigators can use their expertise to separate the information that is crucial from the information that is misleading, a feature of expertise that turns out also to be beneficial for civil liberties. It also helps if these terrorism investigators are not connected directly to the executive branch of government at time of emergency.

After 9/11, however, the United States decided not to concentrate terrorism investigations in small, relatively independent, expert communities that stay on the job a long time. Instead, it did just the opposite. The most experienced antiterrorism prosecutors in the United States, the U.S. attorney's office for the Southern district of New York, had successfully prosecuted nearly three dozen defendants accused of al-Qaeda-connected terror attacks before 9/11. But after 9/11, the prosecutions of Zacarias Moussaoui and John Walker Lindh were moved to the Eastern District of Virginia, a venue where prosecutors without previous experience had to begin gathering basic information about al-Qaeda, its organization, and its reach. The FBI at the time was plagued with inadequate staffing, high turnover, and lack of experienced translators. Five different people held the top terrorism job at the FBI between 9/11 and the end of 2004. At the CIA after 9/11, many senior analysts left. The United States has had such turnover in the top terrorism analyst positions that it has been hard to accumulate and analyze the narrowly relevant information that would be useful in preventing attacks.[35]

At the same time, the Bush administration launched a program that ran directly counter to the development of concentrated expertise. The U.S.

---

35. Mary Jo White, "Transcript # 121700cb.464," interview by The Abrams Report, MSNBC, December 17, 2002; Scheppele, "Law in a Time of Emergency," 1029; Jimmy Burns and Richard Wolffe, "Huge Obstacles in Global Search for Terrorist Paper Trail," *Financial Times*, September 24, 2001, 6; Philip Shenon, "9/11 Panel Criticizes Reform Effort at the F.B.I.," *New York Times*, October 21, 2005; Richard B. Schmitt, "Exodus of Staff Hobbles the FBI," *Los Angeles Times,* December 13, 2004; James Rosen, "Bush Takes Risk with Pick for CIA Boss," Scripps Howard News Service, May 8, 2006.

government created databases that accumulated information on millions of people, when only a few of those under surveillance, at best, would be reasonable suspects. "Data mining" techniques were then employed to find correlated connections between suspects and others who overlapped them. The National Security Agency gathered a huge database of telephone records; the Transportation Safety Authority's Computer Assisted Passenger Prescreening System collected information about all passengers on all commercial airlines regardless of individuated suspicion—or at least it did so before Congress ordered it to be revised (though not eliminated); the Multi-State Anti-Terrorism Information Exchange program (MATRIX) that linked state criminal data to commercial databases with credit card information has also engendered controversy. The Analysis, Dissemination, Visualization, Insight, and Semantic Enhancement (ADVISE) program within the Department of Homeland Security linked information available from a diverse array of sources to create one of the largest databases in the world—all in the service of looking for terrorists. Of the five publicly known data-mining efforts that the U.S. government has conducted in the "war on terror," none complied with federal privacy law by assessing the privacy impacts of their practices, according to a Government Accountability Office (formerly the Government Accounting Office) audit.[36]

The data-mining operation of the U.S. government after 9/11 generated many false positives in identifying terrorist suspects, which raised concerns about civil liberties. Also, because these efforts were concentrated in executive branch agencies, the data mining operations did not benefit from the type of independent oversight that served the BfV.

How can a country design a mechanism for conducting terrorism investigations in ways that protect the rights of procedure, privacy, association and speech? In a number of European countries, terrorism

---

36. On the NSA: *Homeland Security: The Next Five Years: Written Testimony before the S. Comm. on Homeland Security and Governmental Affairs*, 109th Cong., Hearings Conducted September 12, 2006 (testimony of Daniel B. Prieto, Senior Fellow and Director of the Homeland Security Center of the Reform Institute), http://hsgac.senate.gov/public/index .cfm?FuseAction=Hearings.Hearing&Hearing_ID=9f137c90-5424-4bc6-a3eb-f785acc1f82d). The CAPPS system (Computer Assisted Passenger Prescreening System) was shut down by Congress over privacy concerns and replaced by the Secure Flight system. Jeffrey W. Seifert, "Data Mining: An Overview," 7–10, *Congressional Research Service Report*, Order Code RL31798, January 27, 2006, http://www.fas.org/sgp/crs/intel/RL31798.pdf; On MATRIX: Robert O'Harrow Jr. "Anti-Terror Database Got Show at White House," *Washington Post*, May 21, 2004; On ADVISE: Mark Clayton, "US Plans Massive Data Sweep," *Christian Science Monitor*, February 9, 2006. On the GAO report: Matthew B. Stannard, "U.S. Phone-Call Database Ignites Privacy Uproar: Data Mining: Commonly Used in Business to Find Patterns, It Rarely Focuses on Individuals," *San Francisco Chronicle,* May 12, 2006.

investigations are concentrated in the hands of small numbers of special-ists who stay at their jobs for long periods of time, developing a sense for how terrorists operate, how terrorist networks grow and change, and what constitutes a growing threat. In Spain and France, for exam-ple, special investigative magistrates for terrorism are located outside the executive branch and in the judiciary. Their topical focus allows the investigative magistrates to develop expertise in terrorism and also allows information from all terrorism investigations in the country to be fun-neled into a centralized office where clues can be pieced together. In both Spain and France, terrorism investigators work with their own teams of investigators (and sometimes their own teams of police) to investigate terrorist plots.[37]

The independence of the investigating magistrate has a certain advan-tage in antiterrorism campaigns. Antiterror campaigns can quickly devolve into general emergencies in which power is heavily concentrated in the hands of executives. As a result, having the investigative power lodged in a judiciary that is free of direct executive interference can be a check on the concentration of executive power. In addition, if inves-tigative magistrates are to have relatively broad powers of investiga-tion, it is best to detach them from the overtly political executive and legislative branches that might have other agendas for this information. The danger of such positions is that they can become *too* independent, operating without any meaningful control exerted by other government agencies.

In both Spain and France, this logic of specialized jurisdiction concen-trated terrorism investigations in the hands of two long-serving inves-tigative judges: Jean-Louis Bruguière in France and Baltasar Garzón in Spain.[38] Until his retirement in 2007, Bruguière had been investigating Islamist radicals since a series of bombs exploded in Paris in the mid-1980s. Garzón still sits as a judge in the Audencia Nacional, the Spanish "National Court," which is tasked with handling international and orga-nized crime. Garzón began investigating Osama bin Laden and al-Qaeda in 1995 and has handled many terrorism investigations after 9/11.

---

37. Antoine Garapon, "The Oak and the Reed: Counter-Terrorism Mechanisms in France and the United States of America," *Cardozo Law Review* 27, no. 5 (2006): 2041–77; Micah S. Myers, "Prosecuting Human Rights Violations in Europe and America: How Legal Sys-tem Structure Affects Compliance with International Obligations," *Michigan Journal of International Law* 25 (2003): 211–64, 250.

38. See Martin Arnold, "'Le Sheriff' Warns of al-Qaeda Attack in Asia," *Financial Times*, August 26, 2005, 6; Judge Baltasar Garzón, profile, BBC News, September 26, 2005, http://news.bbc.co.uk/go/pr/fr/-/2/hi/europe/3085482.stm; Baltasar Garzón, interview, *Frontline*, July 27, 2004, http://www.pbs.org/wgbh/pages/frontline/shows/front/map/garzon.html.

Both men are controversial, and the sources of controversy must be understood to assess whether their offices should be emulated. Some worry about concentrating too much power in too few hands and about the nature of the powers involved. In both cases, strategic oversight helps prevent abuse. For example, in France, investigative magistrates may indicate that a particular suspect should be charged with a crime, but the charge must be approved by a panel of other judges. The greater concern is about the specific powers investigating magistrates wield. The heavy use of preventive detention, ethnic profiling, and interrogations without counsel have all prompted concern about the way that the French have conducted antiterror investigations. In Spain, incommunicado detention is allowed by law for up to thirteen days in terrorism cases, and this has generated criticism from human rights groups.[39]

But these powers do not necessarily come with the territory of investigative magistrates. Whether investigative magistrates should have these extraordinary powers is a separate question from whether lodging terrorism investigations in the judiciary rather than in an executive branch ministry is a good idea. All investigative institutions come with strong potentials for abuse. Only by designing effective oversight and review mechanisms will the potential for abuse remain unrealized. The element of the investigative magistrate system that can serve as a model, however, is the part that allows a small team of people to specialize in uncovering terrorist activity over a long period of time, separate from direct executive branch control. The concentration of expertise in a relatively apolitical location is likely, in my view, to increase the chances of locating real terrorists while minimizing chances that the investigative powers will expand to reach individuals and subject matters that are not proper objects for such extraordinary powers.

Knowing the "emergency script" helps to see just why lodging investigative powers outside of the executive branch would be a particularly good check on the use of emergency powers. First, executives tend to want unchecked power at times of crisis; with this system, they cannot so easily get it. Then, concentrating expertise like this provides a way for offices outside the executive branch to be able to tell whether the threats that are used as the basis for emergency declarations are real. Finally, the minimization of "false positives" in a large population preserves important personal rights and makes it far less likely that the state will make incorrect judgments about who is a threat.

39. On France: Craig Whitlock, "French Push Limits in Fight on Terrorism: Wide Prosecutorial Powers Draw Scant Public Dissent," *Washington Post*, November 2, 2004. On Spain: "Setting an Example? Counter-Terrorism Measures in Spain," *Human Rights Watch* 17, no. 1 (January 2005): 23–36, http://hrw.org/reports/2005/spain0105/spain0105.pdf.

Conclusion

When terror strikes, constitutional systems are often casualties. Since 9/11, many legal analysts have rushed to propose ways to keep constitutional orders in place while fighting terrorism, often by proposing the sorts of short-term measures to deal with emergencies that assume that governmental crises are always temporary. Most emergency governments, however, lumber into their abusive powers over a rather longer period of time than the emergency models suggest. For example, it is a sobering thought to recall that the visible part of the U.S. government did not rush to engage in extraconstitutional activities on the day of 9/11 itself. Instead, it closed down.[40] The most abusive measures—large-scale preventive detention, torture, warrantless surveillance—went into effect only over several years. This salient example suggests that the biggest threat is not the immediate aftermath of an attack or crisis, but the longer drawn-out struggle that a momentary threat may presage.

Most emergencies, particularly those involving terrorism, are much more enduring than most analysts suggest. They last not months but years and even decades; they poison constitutional systems by normalizing practices that were unthinkable before the dark days of terror. They have a predictable descent into darkness—first executive centralization, then militarization, then a slide through procedural shortcuts, putting people in their places, inverting speech, reversing transparency, engaging in anticipatory violence, and then extending the emergency powers to engage the next emergency. That is why we need to think about practices we can live with for the long haul. We need to design institutions that are effective but not anticonstitutional, that are subject to constitutional constraint from the moment that they appear, and that are capable of being reined in when they exceed their powers. While even the institutions that I have suggested as models here—the German domestic intelligence service and the French and Spanish system of investigative magistrates—are not free from criticism or potential for abuse, they do offer some constructive ways to think about fighting terrorism while maintaining a system of constitutional checks because they force the executive to share power and they provide multiple checks on the use of the most dangerous tools government possesses.

The greatest danger at times of emergency is that all power tends to flow toward the executive. Concentrated power is, as James Madison knew, "the essence of tyranny."[41] The examples that I have suggested here

40. Steve Twomey, "Security Heightened in D.C.: Government Shuts Down, Employees Sent Home; 'It's Traumatizing,'" *Washington Post*, September 11, 2001.
41. Alexander Hamilton, John Jay, and James Madison, *The Federalist*, ed. Jacob E. Cooke (Middletown, CT: Wesleyan University Press, 1961), No. 47.

provide ways to spread power back through the legislative and judicial branches at times of crisis. In so doing, they offer at least some counterweight against the most likely source of internal threat. These institutions, if correctly designed, would also improve effectiveness in detecting terror plots before they hatch because they permit focused and independent investigations based on concentrated expertise.

If after 9/11 the United States can design political institutions that are compatible with constitutional commitments to the separation of powers and the preservation of rights, then the country will not have to give up the Constitution to fight terrorism. Instead, the fight against terror can provide the opportunity to reaffirm that:

> The Constitution of the United States is a law for rulers and people, equally in war and in peace, and covers with the shield of its protection all classes of men, at all times, and under all circumstances. No doctrine, involving more pernicious consequences, was ever invented by the wit of man than that any of its provisions can be suspended during any of the great exigencies of government. Such a doctrine leads directly to anarchy or despotism, but the theory of necessity on which it is based is false; for the government, within the Constitution, has all the powers granted to it, which are necessary to preserve its existence; as has been happily proved by the result of the great effort to throw off its just authority.[42]

42. *Ex Parte Milligan*, 71 U.S. 2, 209 (1866).

Part III

HOW CAN CONSTITUTIONAL DEMOCRACY
CONTEND WITH WAR? _____

8

The Glorious Commander in Chief

ADRIAN VERMEULE

IN A SHORT BUT INTENSELY BRILLIANT discussion in book II, chapter 33, of his *Discourses on Livy*,[1] Machiavelli argues that the Romans' military successes were due, in part, to the Senate's long-standing refusal to exercise any power relating to armed conflict other than that of "starting new wars and of ratifying peace."[2] In brief—and this is the title of Machiavelli's essay—"[T]he Romans Gave Free Commissions to Their Captains of Armies," leaving them uncontrolled in their military operations, and were right to do so. Restricted legislative oversight gave free rein to the executive's propensity for glory seeking, which produced social benefits.

I draw on Machiavelli's discussion in considering the executive's power as commander in chief (CINC) of the armed forces, and the resulting problems for constitutional design and interpretation. In doing so, I make no attempt to place Machiavelli's argument in its historical context[3] or to consider its implications from an originalist perspective.[4] Rather my interest is theoretical and forward looking—to apply Machiavelli's approach to the project of designing constitutional rules and interpreting them in light of our circumstances today. Machiavelli proposes a kind of *economy of*

Thanks to Jack Goldsmith, Daryl Levinson, Stephen Macedo, Ian Shapiro, Jeffrey Tulis, Mark Tushnet, and the conference participants for helpful comments, and to Elisabeth Theodore for helpful research assistance. An initial version of this essay was presented at a Harvard Law School workshop on Commander-in-Chief Powers, November 2, 2007.

1. See Niccolò Machiavelli, "How the Romans Gave Free Commissions to their Captains of Armies," in *Discourses on Livy*, trans. Harvey C. Mansfield and Nathan Tarcov (Chicago: University of Chicago Press, 1996), 206–7. All translations are taken from this work.

2. Ibid., 206.

3. See Harvey C. Mansfield, *Taming the Prince: The Ambivalence of Modern Executive Power* (Baltimore: Johns Hopkins University Press, 1993); Harvey C. Mansfield, *Machiavelli's New Modes and Orders: A Study of the Discourses on Livy* (Chicago: University of Chicago Press, 1979).

4. On the framers' views of glory, fame, and similar concepts, see Douglass Adair, *Fame and the Founding Fathers* (New York: W. W. Norton, 1974). On the question how and how much Machiavelli influenced Hamilton and the other framers, see Karl-Friedrich Walling, *Republican Empire: Alexander Hamilton on War and Free Government* (Lawrence: University Press of Kansas, 1999). See also Karl Walling, "Was Alexander Hamilton a Machiavellian Statesman?" *Review of Politics* 57 (1995): 419–47.

glory: an account of the benefits and costs of executive glory seeking, and an account of how glory-seeking motivations on the part of the CINC can best be harnessed to the public interest. After generalizing that analysis, I then consider the costs and benefits of presidential glory seeking and how the American national constitution can best be interpreted in that light.

The Costs of Glory Seeking

I begin with the dominant tradition or view in American constitutional scholarship, a view that is critical of the glory-seeking executive. In one standard account of the power to initiate armed conflict, for example, the glory-seeking executive is disastrous from the social point of view; glory-seeking presidents will tend to initiate "bad" conflicts (somehow defined) because they pursue personal glory while partially externalizing the expected costs of warfare.[5] Moreover, as to conflicts that are already underway, the glorious path may not be the militarily optimal one. The executive may "gamble for resurrection" by "escalating conflicts with a low probability of victory."[6] Think of Vietnam in the late stages or Iraq circa 2006. In such cases, the glory-seeking president will throw in new troops and throw good money after bad in an attempt to snatch victory from the jaws of defeat. Such gambles may be socially undesirable in expectation even if they succeed, and even if they are perfectly rational from the standpoint of an executive who does not bear the full social costs of his decisions.

Finally, as with its cousin, the passion for fame, the passion for glory is inherently rivalrous. Not everyone on the public stage can simultaneously be glorious; there must be a supporting cast and chorus to throw

5. Walter Murphy gestures toward this account by remarking that because "[m]any, if not most leaders in the Free World deemed great have been leaders in war," there is a "temptation to invoke, or invent, foreign threats." Walter F. Murphy, *Constitutional Democracy: Creating and Maintaining a Just Political Order* (Baltimore: Johns Hopkins University Press, 2007), 388. For an extended version of this account, focusing on the U.S. Constitution, see William Michael Treanor, "Fame, the Founding, and the Power to Declare War," *Cornell Law Review* 82 (1997): 695–772. Treanor implicitly equates glory and fame. Although this equation does not affect the structure of Treanor's argument, I believe that the two are not fully synonymous. Whereas glory entails fame, fame does not entail glory; Paris Hilton is famous but not glorious (at least not in the relevant sense). On the complex relationships among glory, fame, and other concepts in the neighborhood, see Russell Price, "The Theme of *Gloria* in Machiavelli," *Renaissance Quarterly* 30 (1977): 618–19.

6. Paul F. Diehl and Tom Ginsburg, "Irrational War and Constitutional Design: A Reply to Professors Nzelibe and Yoo," *Michigan Journal of International Law* 27 (2006): 1251. I have taken this quote somewhat out of context. Diehl and Ginsburg ascribe gambling for resurrection to the desire to obtain reelection, which is connected to but hardly identical to the passion for glory. Second-term presidents often have the second motivation but cannot have the first.

the main actors into relief. This may cause harmful infighting between candidates for glory. Consider, as possible examples, the tensions between Lincoln and his generals, or between Truman and MacArthur.

Given these costs of glory seeking, the standard institutional prescription is to place institutional checks on the executive's power to initiate or even to conduct conflicts. At the initiation stage, the idea runs, Congress should have the exclusive power to declare war or to initiate substantial armed conflicts.[7] This view is embodied in the War Powers Resolution, which requires congressional approval, after a few months at most, when presidents commit troops abroad.[8] At the stage of fighting as opposed to initiating conflicts, the prescriptions are usually not as precise, because of worries about encroaching on the president's core commander-in-chief authority to direct the movement of troops, but that authority may be construed more or less broadly, and in any event Congress has undoubted authority to refuse to fund ongoing military operations. Even where troops are in the field, a reason to construe congressional power expansively and presidential power narrowly is that glory-seeking presidents will make socially undesirable decisions if left unchecked.

Machiavelli's Argument

So far I have laid out a standard view that is skeptical of executive glory seeking. Machiavelli's essay suggests that executive glory seeking is at least far more complex than this simple view would have it; executive glory seeking has costs, to be sure, but it also has benefits. Machiavelli's argument in book II, chapter 33 of the *Discourses* is not about whether it is desirable to have a unitary commander in chief. A separate essay—book III, chapter 15, arguing that "One Individual and Not Many Should Be Put over an Army; and That Several Commanders Hurt"—addresses that topic, and rejects a plural military executive or war council.[9] The essay on the Roman Senate's restricted role, by contrast, addresses the scope of the powers accorded to a unitary CINC. The substantive thesis is that those powers were broad; "the people and the Senate . . . consigned [the execution of the campaign] to the judgment of the Consul, who could either wage a battle or not wage it, encamp at this town or that other one, as he liked."[10] The Senate's role was to declare *new* wars and ratify treaties of peace; by implication, the termination of old wars was a component of the CINC power.

7. See Treanor, "Fame, the Founding, and the Power to Declare War," 757.
8. P.L. 93-148 (1973).
9. Machiavelli, *Discourses*, at 253–54.
10. Ibid., 206.

But why was this good? Machiavelli is arguing that the Senate's broad deference to the unitary CINC was a significant contributor to Rome's military successes; what mechanisms account for this? Machiavelli offers two arguments—one from information, one from motivation.

The first is an argument from comparative informational advantage: had the Senate attempted to control the consul's decisions in the field, "the Senate would have been obliged to wish to give counsel about a thing that it could not understand, for notwithstanding that in it were men all very much trained in war, nonetheless, since it was not on the spot and did not know infinite particulars that are necessary to know for whoever wishes to give counsel well, it would have made infinite errors in giving counsel."[11] This is a familiar argument about the informational advantages of delegation. It was also, perhaps, a more impressive argument in Machiavelli's day than in our own, given the reduced costs to present-day legislators of acquiring real-time information about the progress and details of a military campaign. I thus put the informational argument aside to focus on Machiavelli's argument from motivation.

Here is the key passage:

> Whoever will consider this limit well [i.e., broad deference to the CINC's operational decisions] will see that it was used very prudently. For if the Senate had wished that a consul should proceed into war little by little according to his commission, it would have made him less circumspect and more slow, for it would not have seemed to him that the victory would have been all his but that the Senate, by whose counsel he was governed, would share in it. . . . Because of this they wished that the consul should act by himself and that the glory should be all his—the love of which, they judged, would be a check and a rule to make him work well.[12]

In standard principal-agent models, the principal must weigh the agent's informational advantages against the agent's motivational disadvantages. The agent may know more than the principal, but the agent may also pursue ends that do not perfectly match the principal's. In general, the principal may respond in one of two ways, not mutually exclusive. The first is to structure incentives and institutions (such as enforceable contracts) in order to maximize the expected benefits of the relationship to the principal, even given an agent whose preferences diverge from those of the principal. The second way is to focus on selecting agents with the best possible motivations (from the principal's perspective).[13]

11. Ibid., 207.
12. Ibid.
13. See Timothy Besley, "Political Selection," *Journal of Economic Perspectives* 19 (2005): 43–60.

Machiavelli's argument takes the former approach; it assumes that glory seeking is endemic to executive office and asks about institutional arrangements. If motivations are fixed and institutions are the choice variable, we can interpret Machiavelli's key claim as follows: *given a glory-seeking CINC, a regime of broad deference by legislators to the CINC's operational decisions best promotes the public interest.* This fits comfortably with a long tradition in political theory in which individual passions (not interests—glory seeking is a passion, akin but not identical to the passion for fame) are harnessed to public ends.[14] What Machiavelli should be taken to suggest, in other words, is that we need a full economy of glory—an account not just of the costs of executive glory seeking, but also of its benefits, and of the conditions under which executive glory seeking is socially desirable or at least preferable to other motivations that are realistically possible in the executive.

The Benefits of Glory Seeking

What exactly are the benefits? We can interpret Machiavelli as making two largely implicit claims about the glory-seeking executive. First is that *glory seeking supplies motivational energy,*[15] which is socially desirable in the executive. The theme of energy in the executive is one that Hamilton of course expounds,[16] and that Hamilton's exegetes have continued; but the unitary-executive theorists do not connect executive energy with glory seeking as Machiavelli does. Rather they suggest that a unitary executive, or CINC, will be energetic because he bears sole responsibility for failure and will suffer political accountability for mistakes.[17] Where the unitary-executive theorists focus on the costs of failure, Machiavelli focuses on the benefits of success, suggesting that the pull toward glory is what matters, not the push from the threat of accountability. If the point is to offer a full positive theory of motivations, Machiavelli's account seems indispensable. Moreover, because the threat of accountability is typically tied to elections, it fails to illuminate the motivations of second-

14. See Albert O. Hirschman, *The Passions and the Interests* (Princeton: Princeton University Press, 1997), 9–11.

15. This is also the theme of *Discourses* I.43 ("Those Who Engage in Combat for Their Own Glory Are Good and Faithful Soldiers"). See Machiavelli, *Discourses*, 91.

16. Alexander Hamilton, *The Federalist,* ed. Jacob E. Cooke (Middletown, CT: Wesleyan University Press, 1961), No. 70.

17. Steven G. Calabresi, "Some Normative Arguments for the Unitary Executive," *Arkansas Law Review* 48 (1995): 37–45. See also Jide Nzelibe and John Yoo, "Rational War and Constitutional Design," *Yale Law Journal* 115 (2006): 2519–26 (listing speed, information, and accountability as executive advantages, but not the propensity to glory seeking).

term presidents, whereas the positive thirst for glory may be the dominant motive of such presidents.

The second benefit is that *glory seeking aligns the CINC's interests with social interests*; the "love of [glory], they judged, would be a check and a rule to make him work well."[18] There is no claim here that glory seeking perfectly tracks the public interest, somehow defined. The private costs and benefits to the executive of military action or other policies will sometimes diverge from public costs and benefits, so that glory seeking will sometimes produce externalities. However, Machiavelli's implicit argument is merely that, *compared to other possible motivations*, glory seeking would be the best regulator of conduct. The comparison is not to an ideally well-motivated executive but to other executive motivations that might exist in fact. The substance of this claim is not spelled out, but it is not difficult to imagine arguments that an executive motivated by the thirst for glory would do better than an executive motivated by, say, the thirst for power; glory at least has a kind of connection to widespread public approval and esteem. The comparative superiority of glory seeking over other possible motivations seems especially plausible at the stage of *fighting* wars as opposed to *entering* them, a point I return to below.

More specifically, it is possible that the thirst for glory provides executives with a long-term perspective that other motivations will lack. The usual idea is that glory seeking induces a short-term perspective, as executives initiate or prolong conflicts that bring personal benefits but that create long-run social costs. But this is not always true; indeed in some cases it may get things backward. Socially desirable conflicts, somehow defined, will sometimes produce high short-run costs in lives lost and in economic disruption. Perhaps only a glory-seeking executive will have a sufficiently powerful motive to initiate such conflicts and to see them through to their conclusion, despite the immediate costs. Whereas the standard view identifies a risk that glory seekers will not know when to fold their hand, this view suggests that only glory seekers will have the motivation not to fold too early. Perhaps the course of the conflict in Iraq illustrates this dynamic; arguably, events have shown that an American decision to withdraw in 2006, rather than to attempt a final push for victory, would have amounted to a premature acceptance of defeat.

To be sure, an ideal executive would be motivated by the long run anyway,[19] but in the real world no executives have ideal social-regarding motivations. Among the motivations found in the real world, glory

18. Machiavelli, *Discourses*, at 207.
19. Or, more accurately, would discount the future at a rate no higher than the correct social discount rate.

seeking might be, in many cases, the least bad of the possibilities. The alternative to glory seeking might be public-spiritedness or a benign form of enlightened self-interest,[20] but it might instead be something more pernicious, such as power seeking that is utterly insensitive to public esteem.

Overall, then, Machiavelli makes two major claims: glory seeking fuels energetic action and thus produces the socially desirable level of executive activity; and glory seeking is the best available proxy for public-regarding motivation. These two claims are interestingly conjoined when Machiavelli says that close supervision by the Senate, by diluting the gains of glory to the consul, would have made the consul "less circumspect and more slow [in his operations]."[21] One might think that the slower, the more circumspect, but Machiavelli suggests the opposite: the glory-seeking CINC is not only energetic but also an optimal risk taker. Indeed, he is an optimal risk taker precisely because and to the extent that he seeks glory. How else can glory be acquired, this optimistic account suggests, except through the rational calculus of risk? Foolhardiness brings only death and shame, not glory.

A final implication of these points is that Machiavelli stands on its head the concern that glory seeking is inherently rivalrous. Precisely because that is so, legislative oversight of field operations dilutes the glory that the CINC can hope to obtain from victory, reducing the social benefits as well as the social costs of executive glory seeking. How these two reductions net out is a factual question in a given setting; depending upon the setting and the facts, the rivalrous character of glory seeking can just as well supply an argument for reduced legislative oversight as for robust institutional checks on the executive.

The Economy of Glory

None of this is to say that the standard view, critical of executive glory seeking, is wrong; it is just overblown. There is no need to choose between that view and Machiavelli's account of the social benefits of glory seeking. Both may hold under certain conditions, so that one identifies the possible benefits of glory seeking, while the other identifies its possible costs. The economy of glory would then be an account that fully states both sides of the ledger. Here is a sketch of such an account.

Simplifying greatly, we might understand the constitutional rules governing the CINC power as encompassing a two-stage game. The first stage is one of *conflict initiation*, encompassing either formally declared

20. See generally Hirschman, *The Passions and the Interests.*
21. Ibid.

wars or various forms of "police action." The second stage is one of *conflict execution*, including the authority to terminate conflicts. What are the optimal constitutional rules? To set a baseline for discussion, suppose for the moment that there is only an executive, no legislature (or, equivalently, that there is a legislature that lacks any real constraining effect).

In this regime, executive glory seeking produces both costs and benefits, at both stages. At the initiation stage, glory seeking motivates bad conflicts but also motivates the decision to enter into good and necessary ones; a higher activity level—more conflicts initiated—will reduce false negatives (good conflicts forgone), whereas a lower activity level will reduce false positives (bad conflicts commenced).[22] At the conflict stage, glory seeking motivates vigorous action and partially aligns executive motivations with the public interest; the social goal is to win the war, and winning the war confers glory. Even at this stage, however, glory seeking is not a perfect proxy for social interests.

Implications for Constitutional Design, and Interpretation

What follows from the economy of glory? The optimal constitutional regime for allocating both conflict-initiating authority and conflict-executing authority will hinge on two further considerations. First, does adding legislative involvement at either the conflict-initiation or the conflict-execution stage increase the net of benefits over costs? (I ignore judicial involvement. If we like, we may simply consider the two players as the executive and as a compound checking institution composed of both legislature and judiciary.) Machiavelli's implicit judgment is that legislative participation is net beneficial at the stage of conflict initiation but not at the stage of conflict execution. In the former arena, the harms of glory seeking predominate over the benefits, whereas in the latter stage, maximal scope must be provided for vigor and the executive's thirst for a triumphant apotheosis. Second, Machiavelli implicitly judges that executive glory seeking should be taken as fixed or inevitable, while institutions are the choice variable.

For whatever it is worth, I record my own judgments that Machiavelli's two judgments are extremely plausible. As to the first, once one is in a fight, the important thing is to win it,[23] and the most powerful

22. Nzelibe and Yoo offer a somewhat similar treatment of the conflict-initiation phase. Nzelibe and Yoo, "Rational War and Constitutional Design," 2517–18. However, they do not focus on glory-seeking motivation, which I take to be a crucial consideration for approaching these questions.

23. Which implies that Truman was correct to use nuclear weapons at Hiroshima and Nagasaki, given the information available at the time.

possible motives must be given free rein to that end even if collateral harms may ensue. If the costs of failing to win a war one has entered are on average greater than the costs of failing to enter wars one ought to fight, then the motivating power of glory seeking may be beneficial on net at the stage of conflict execution, even if it is not at the stage of conflict initiation. Legislative oversight of operational matters dampens the executive's thirst for glory at just the time when executive glory seeking is most desirable.

Moreover, the two stages are sequential. If legislative participation at the stage of conflict initiation ensures that most of the wars that are actually entered are good wars, somehow defined, then it is all the more plausible that the glory-seeking executive should be released from legislative constraints at the stage of conflict execution; "let slip the dogs of war" is the best rule of thumb if most wars are good. The phenomenon of "gambling for resurrection" is certainly possible, but, as we have seen, glory seeking also provides the impetus not to fold one's hand too soon, which is the countervailing risk. Overall, Machiavelli is persuasive that a kind of circumspection will be built in to glory seeking itself, strictly because prudent war fighting itself maximizes the chance of attaining glory. Even at this stage, glory seeking will not necessarily maximize social welfare, but the crucial question is comparative: plausibly, glory seeking will produce greater social welfare than would other possible motives that real presidents might hold.

As to the second issue, most executives will mostly be glory seekers, and fighting wars is the best way to obtain true glory,[24] so most executives will be interested in war making. This results from a selection effect: because glory is the dominant component of the compensation attaching to executive office (a form of in-kind compensation, needless to say), non-glory-seekers will rarely attain the office in the first place. The occasional

24. Consider the finding that twelve presidents ranked in the top tier in a survey of historians were at war for many more years of their terms, on average, than presidents ranked in the bottom tier. Jack E. Holmes and Robert E. Elder Jr., "Our Best and Worst Presidents: Some Possible Reasons for Perceived Performance," *Presidential Studies Quarterly* 19 (1989): 543–44. See also Dean Keith Simonton, "Predicting Presidential Performance in the United States: Equation Replication on Recent Survey Results," *Journal of Social Psychology* 141 (2001): 300–301 (finding wartime tenure to consistently predict high performance in expert rankings of presidential greatness); Jeffrey E. Cohen, "The Polls: Presidential Greatness as Seen in the Mass Public: An Extension and Application of the Simonton Model," *Presidential Studies Quarterly* 33 (2003): 920 (considering a ranking of presidential greatness by C-SPAN viewers and finding wartime tenure to be a less important but still significant predictor of high performance). For the contrary view that "there is no significant correlation between presidential greatness and the use of force," see David Gray Adler, "Presidential Greatness as an Attribute of Warmaking," *Presidential Studies Quarterly* 33 (2003): 467.

Madison, who does not seem to have been very much interested in glory at least of the military variety,[25] is the exception that proves the rule.

To be sure, presidents do not themselves take part in armed combat; they merely direct generals, who in turn direct soldiers, and this means that presidents must share some part of the glory of military success with their subordinates.[26] But Roman consuls rarely engaged in hand-to-hand combat either. In modern times, an occasional general obtains sufficient military glory to leverage himself into the presidency in the short run (an example is Ulysses S. Grant). If that gambit fails, however, the general will fade into obscurity (an example is Wesley Clark), whereas militarily successful presidents obtain enduring glory.

Under modern conditions, then, glory often accrues to executive leadership in time of war, not necessarily to actual combat, which modern generals do not engage in either. The national executive is more likely to be seen by the public as the ultimate leader than are the subordinate generals, who will often be relatively anonymous, especially in modern warfare; this explains why presidents do in fact gain military glory from providing overall direction to a successful campaign.[27] In any event, to the extent that the executive must share glory with subordinate generals, the conclusion would not be that Machiavelli's analysis is obsolete in a modern state. It would be that modern executives do not fully capture and internalize the social benefits of glory seeking, which would imply that there is too *little* executive glory seeking from the social point of view.

The overall conclusion is that the optimal constitutional regime is one in which the executive is constrained in initiating conflicts but not constrained in carrying them out. That conclusion needs further specification along two margins. First, it applies most cleanly to armed conflicts between states, such as the United States' wars against Iraq, rather than to the sort of diffuse conflicts between states and nonstate actors that are central to counterterrorism policy. Even in that setting, the distinction between initiating and executing conflict can be useful, but it takes more work (than I can do here) to cash it out.

Second, the conclusion I have indicated is rather general; it does not quite get down to the level of the very concrete questions ventilated in

25. See, e.g., Robert A. Rutland, *The Presidency of James Madison* (Lawrence: University Press of Kansas, 1990), 81–97, 105–6 (suggesting that Madison entered into the War of 1812 only because he believed it to be unavoidable, that his "temperament was [not] warlike," and that his goals once the war began were "limited").

26. Cf. Machiavelli, *Discourses* I.30, at 67–68 (a republic, unlike a prince, cannot direct warfare in person, and must therefore permit generals to acquire glory).

27. See sources cited in note 24.

recent congressional hearings.[28] Can Congress enact substantive statutes that regulate the "scope, duration or size of a military operation"? Is this question importantly different from the question whether Congress can instruct the CINC as to how he can use or deploy troops "actually already in the theater of operations?" Can Congress enact substantive statutes that regulate the *means* by which the president conducts an otherwise-legal conflict—for example, by prohibiting the use of torture even when necessary to acquire battlefield intelligence?[29]

Machiavelli's argument does not speak precisely to these questions. Moreover, although we can elicit from Machiavelli's essay an argument about optimal constitutional design, we already have a constitution, which may not at all be optimal as fairly interpreted (according to whatever interpretive theory we hold). However, despite its generality, I believe that Machiavelli's argument gives us important help with these concrete questions, in the following way. Suppose our constitution is importantly ambiguous on these topics, and that considerations of optimal constitutional design can then enter the picture as interpretive principles that help to make our constitution work in sensible ways. What Machiavelli's argument does give us is a sort of default principle or clear statement principle: absent a clear constitutional command to the contrary, we should be extremely reluctant to admit any legislative constraint on the executive at the stage of conflict execution.[30]

28. David Barron, Senate Committee on the Judiciary, Exercising Congress's Constitutional Power to End War, 110th Cong., 1st sess. (January 2007), http://www.law.harvard.edu/news/2007/01/ Barron%20Testimony.pdf (accessed October 25, 2009).

29. Jay S. Bybee, Assistant Attorney General, Office of Legal Counsel, to Alberto Gonzalez, Counsel to the President, memorandum, August 1, 2002, http://news.findlaw.com/hdocs/docs/doj/bybee80102mem.pdf (accessed October 25, 2009).

30. This would be a clear statement rule for constitutional interpretation by nonjudicial actors. It is a separate question whether judges should defer to statutes that violate the rule by constraining executive conflict execution even when there is no clear constitutional warrant for doing so. For reasons of institutional capacity, judges might do best by deferring to statutes of that sort, even if Machiavelli's argument is otherwise correct. See Adrian Vermeule, *Judging under Uncertainty* (Cambridge: Harvard University Press, 2006), chap. 8.

9

The Relational Conception of War Powers

MARIAH ZEISBERG

THE U.S. CONSTITUTION'S ALLOCATION of the authority to initiate military hostilities is conspicuously vague. In contrast to its concrete placement of the power to borrow money in the hands of Congress, or of the power to grant pardons in the hands of the president, the war power is distributed between the branches in ways that defy easy categorization. Congress is given authority to "declare war," but it is unclear whether "declaring war" is the same power as authorizing hostilities.[1] And, although the hierarchical structure of the president's office, the fact that it never adjourns, and his role as commander in chief seem to indicate some war authority, the contours of that authority are left unspecified.

All commentators agree that the president may defensively repel attacks on the United States. But the current debate over the authority to initiate aggressive hostilities is divided according to whether one supports the presidency or Congress. Congressional partisans claim that Congress, and Congress only, enjoys the power to authorize hostilities. Partisans of the presidency, on the other hand, claim that the president has the domestic constitutional authority to initiate aggressive military hostilities without any authorizing legislation. But both sides share a common assumption—that the Constitution settles, or should be interpreted so as to settle, this foundational question of institutional authority.[2]

1. Michael D. Ramsey, *The Constitution's Text in Foreign Affairs* (Cambridge: Harvard University Press, 2007), chap. 11.

2. For congressional partisans, see John Hart Ely, "The American War in Indochina, Part II: The Unconstitutionality of the War They Didn't Tell Us About," *Stanford Law Review* 42, no. 5 (1990): 1093–1148; Michael D. Ramsey, *The Constitution's Text in Foreign Affairs* (Cambridge: Harvard University Press, 2007); Louis Fisher, *Presidential War Power* (Lawrence: University Press of Kansas, 2004). Partisans of the Presidency include John Yoo, "War and the Constitutional Text," *University of Chicago Law Review*, no. 69 (2002): 1639–84; Phillip Bobbitt, "War Powers: An Essay on John Hart Ely's War and Responsibility: Constitutional Lessons of Vietnam and Its Aftermath," *Michigan Law Review* 92 (1994): 1364–1400. Because the U.S. Constitution's allocation of war authority is vague, the framers' dilemma about whether the best constitutional allocation of war powers is strict, explicit, and highly procedural replicates itself at the level of constitutional interpretation. See Walter F. Murphy, *Constitutional Democracy: Creating and Maintaining a*

It is not strange to read the Constitution in light of the idea that it should settle basic questions of institutional authority. A dominant model of constitutional authority, the settlement thesis, claims that resolving foundational political questions is precisely the function of a constitution. According to the settlement thesis, constitutions are meant to settle or resolve foundational political questions, and hence constitutional fidelity must involve little or no conflict over constitutional values, institutions, or procedures.[3] A corollary is that political questions not resolved by the constitutional text are open for resolution in a completely discretionary way. Under this view, constitutions establish frameworks for handling ordinary political contestation. A political question can be either settled by the constitution, and hence become a part of the basic framework, or not settled by the constitution, and hence become a matter for discretionary decision making. From this point of view, struggle between the legislature and executive over war authority looks like a constitutional failure or even a crisis. The settlement thesis is perhaps the single most prevalent premise guiding constitutional theory today.

This essay argues that the settlement thesis is strikingly inadequate for understanding the Constitution's allocation of war authority. I instead defend a "relational" account of war authority, one premised on the value of maintaining the branches in relationships of mutual review, even when that review leads to interbranch interpretive conflict. In fact, the relational model does not see struggle over constitutional meaning as necessarily a problem at all.[4] In some cases, interpretive struggle, by clarifying what is at stake in a particular security context, can generate more constitutional authority than would be the case if one branch were highly deferential. In other cases, interpretive struggle can lead the branches to develop governance and interpretive capacities that are useful for broader constitutional aims. While this essay does not develop the full contours of the relational model, it does demonstrate the model's value for understanding two critical war acts: Kennedy's response to the Cuban missile crisis, and Nixon's Cambodian incursion. In both cases, the relational model

---

Just Political Order (Baltimore: Johns Hopkins University Press, 2007), chap. 14, on the relationship between interpretation and maintenance.

3. Larry Alexander and Frederick Schauer, "On Extrajudicial Constitutional Interpretation," *Harvard Law Review* 110, no. 7 (1997) : 1359–87.

4. See Edward S. Corwin, *The President: Office and Powers 1787–1984*, 5th ed. (New York: New York University Press, 1984), and Cecil V. Crabb and Pat M. Holt, *Invitation to Struggle: Congress, the President and Foreign Policy* (Washington, DC: Congressional Quarterly Press, 1980), for a characterization of the Constitution's allocation of foreign policy powers as an "invitation to struggle." The relational account accepts this characterization of the Constitution's text and seeks to develop normative content for guiding the branches in their interpretive claims given this characteristic of the constitutional order.

points us toward criteria of constitutional evaluation that are more illuminating than are those offered by the settlement account. Exploring the relational model through these cases reveals the tremendous difference between the questions raised by a settlement approach and those raised by a relational approach. Ultimately, whereas the settlement model either defends or condemns together the presidential conduct in each case, the relational account reveals subtle yet critical constitutional differences between Kennedy's and Nixon's acts of war.

The Relational Conception of Constitutional War Authority

Settlement understandings of the war power locate war-making authority with either Congress or the executive. Hence, John Hart Ely emphasizes the necessity of congressional authorization of war, and John Yoo emphasizes the vast scope of the executive power.[5] By contrast, the relational account emphasizes that the war authority is shared, that the best answer to the question of who holds war authority varies according to the security context, and that the Constitution equips the branches themselves to make appropriate constitutional judgments on the allocation of the sovereign war power in ways that are intelligently related to the public good.

Three critical conditions support the branches' capacity to make these judgments. First, both Congress and the president are structured so as to enjoy independent political authority. They are elected from different constituencies, and neither holds the power to remove the other from office except under exceptional circumstances. This independence preserves their capacity to make claims on one another without threats of personal reprisal. Second, the branches are structured so as to achieve distinctive values. While the presidency is structured to achieve a capacity for (relatively) quick response and (relatively) univocal communication, Congress is structured to achieve governance that is (relatively) deliberative and which is in (relatively) greater touch with the relationship between general policy commitments and the well-being of particular constituencies.[6] These distinctive structures can be used to support the development of distinctive perspectives on matters of both ordinary politics and constitutional interpretation. Finally, when exercising war authority, the branches are exercising a power that is shared. These three conditions I call the "conditions of conflict." The independence and distinctiveness of the branches create conditions for disagreement; but the

5. Ely, "American War in Indochina, Part II"; Yoo, "War and the Constitutional Text."
6. Joseph M. Bessette, *The Mild Voice of Reason: Deliberative Democracy and American National Government* (Chicago: University of Chicago Press, 1997).

exercise of shared powers makes it possible for that abstract disagreement to turn into outright conflict as the branches vie for the primacy of their own views in the execution of actual policy. These conditions indicate a constitutional vision on behalf of a broad practice of mutual evaluation from each branch's distinctive point of view, a constitutional vision of interbranch deliberation.[7]

Under the relational conception, these three conditions are not facts about the constitutional order to be proved or disproved through empirical research. They are rather a set of capacities that are also legitimating conditions for the creation of constitutional authority. Because they are so important for generating constitutional authority, these conditions are also a set of public goods to be achieved. Congress can fail to achieve a perspective distinctively related to its special governance strengths; when it does so, its assent to a public policy fails to deliver all of the constitutional authority that Congress is capable of mustering. This means that if one of these conditions is not met, even coordinate judgments of Congress and the president suffer from impaired constitutional authority. If we imagine a president getting his way on a war authorization by plausibly threatening to fire those legislators who disagreed with him, or if we imagine a Congress that cowers before a president's representation of a threat rather than basing its decisions upon its own deliberations, we can easily see how interbranch agreement, on its own, is not enough to create real constitutional authority. Agreement must instead be reached in a context where the conditions of conflict are intact; and when those conditions are intact, interbranch agreement is not as important for war authority as many have argued.

Ultimately, the relational account grounds constitutional authority not only on interbranch agreement but also on the relationship between the branches' epistemic and functional capacities and the nature of the security threat. In a context of immediate invasion, the executive's capacity to move quickly and to take initiative means that that branch has more authority. In the context of wars that signify new and broad foreign policy commitments, Congress's special capacities to integrate the perspectives of citizens from multiple regions and with multiple interests, to integrate new information into large policy visions, and to consider the distribution of benefits and burdens of large commitments give that branch more authority. Of course, it is often unclear what the meaning of a particular war act is or would be and whether that act would benefit more from congressional or presidential determination. In these cases, the branches must make

7. See Jeffrey K. Tulis, "Deliberation between Institutions," in *Debating Deliberative Democracy*, ed. James S. Fishkin and Peter Laslett, Philosophy, Politics and Society 7 (Oxford: Blackwell, 2003), 200–211.

their own best judgments about the relationship between the security context and their own constitutional capacities. When the branches disagree, interbranch interpretive conflict can amount to a deliberative process for helping to achieve a constitutionally authoritative response, one that takes into account more rather than fewer relevant dimensions of political concern. Hence, the relational conception of war powers interprets constitutional vagueness as a way of enabling an appropriate form of political judgment as to the location of constitutional authority in a particular context, as opposed to licensing a zone of pure interpretive discretion.[8]

It is important to distinguish the relational conception from classical separated-powers accounts about foreign policy. There is a vigorous debate over the relationship between separated powers and an effective foreign policy. Some have argued that the branches' capacity to pursue divergent tasks may lead to more efficient and intelligent policy regardless of the intent of officials. For example, Aaron Friedberg argues that congressionally imposed tax ceilings (imposed in response to local political pressure, not from an alternate war vision) inadvertently supported U.S. success in the Cold War by allowing the United States to pursue both productivity and defense buildup at the same time, ultimately leading to a more successful defense posture. Others argue that separation of powers can impair U.S. foreign policy by rendering it self-defeating and vacillating.[9] The settlement versus relational account does not track this division, because instead of focusing on the branches' contributions to "governance" broadly defined, the settlement and relational accounts pertain to the branches' specific constitutional practice—their development and articulation of distinctive constitutional visions that are wedded to their foreign policy visions. Hence, although the departmentalist claim that "just about everybody" engages in constitutional interpretation simply by assuming the constitutional validity of their own behavior is true,[10] there is a conceptual difference between Congress's affecting war policy through the unselfconscious exercise of its tax authority and its destabilizing president's initiative by offering a competing war policy under an interpretation of its own war powers. No scholar challenges the constitutional validity of the first exercise of power (but perhaps some

8. This element distinguishes my account from the interpretation-construction account (where constitutional vagueness is seen as enabling a zone of "construction" that should be guided by an appropriate, nonconstitutional political theory) that has gained so much currency. See Murphy, *Constitutional Democracy,* 460 n. 3.

9. Aaron L. Friedberg, *In the Shadow of the Garrison State: America's Anti-statism and Its Cold War Grand Strategy* (Princeton: Princeton University Press, 2000); Henry Kissinger, *Ending the Vietnam War: A History of America's Involvement in and Extrication from the Vietnam War* (New York: Simon and Schuster, 2003).

10. See Murphy, *Constitutional Democracy,* 463.

should). But the second can be very controversial. One reason it is so controversial is because that struggle creates a burden for the elected branches to defend their constitutional judgments in a context where the constitutional text is not crystal clear. In other words, the relational conception creates a burden for constitutional argumentation that is deeply political in nature. This essay shows how such arguments can be built with regards to two specific cases.

The Cuban Missile Crisis and the Cambodian Incursion

Consider two acts of war of two separate presidential administrations: the 1962 Cuban missile crisis of the Kennedy administration and Nixon's intervention in Cambodia (the bombings in 1969). In the fall of 1962, Kennedy had assured Congress that there were no offensive missiles in Cuba, consistent with statements he was receiving from the Soviets and from personal communication from Khrushchev, and consistent with beliefs of U.S. intelligence. When it became apparent in October that missiles were being installed, Kennedy kept the situation secret, notifying even allies before he notified the public or Congress. He kept the situation secret while making preparations for the possibility of a nuclear war and actually initiating an act of war, a blockade that was not announced until it was actually being executed. It is plausible that Kennedy kept the blockade secret for reasons of political calculation; Kennedy was being attacked by Republicans for his failures in Cuba, especially the disastrous Bay of Pigs invasion.[11]

Nixon cited this "finest hour" of the Kennedy administration as precedent for the Cambodian invasion.[12] Nixon's intervention in neutral Cambodia was justified as a way to weaken that country's utility as a supply line and conduit of soldiers into the Vietnam conflict. Although Nixon did not originally defend his actions under international law (emphasizing that "we live in an age of anarchy, both abroad and at home"), the administration did eventually offer a legal defense of its actions.[13] It is

11. For an argument that the choice of a blockade was a response to domestic political pressures, see Fen Osler Hampson, "The Divided Decision-Maker: American Domestic Politics and the Cuban Crises," *International Security* 9, no. 3 (1984): 130–65.

12. Richard M. Nixon, "Address to the Nation on the Situation in Southeast Asia," April 30, 1970, at *Miller Center of Public Affairs Presidential Speech Archive* (University of Virginia, The Scripps Library), http://millercenter.org/scripps/archive/speeches (accessed October 17, 2009).

13. Ibid.; John R. Stevenson, "United States Military Action in Cambodia: Questions of International Law?" *Department of State Bulletin* 62 (1970): 765, reprinted in *American Journal of International Law* 64 (1970): 933–41.

plausible that Nixon, like Kennedy, kept his actions in Cambodia secret to evade domestic political pressure—in this case, against escalating the Vietnam War.

The settlement account has few questions to ask about the constitutionality of these actions. From a pro-Congress settlement position, evaluating the constitutionality of these acts is entirely a question of whether the president was appropriately authorized by Congress. From a pro-executive settlement position, we need only ask whether Congress had taken any constitutionally legitimate action—such as defunding the military—to block what was an inherent executive power. The answers to these questions are similar in the two cases. Neither act of war received explicit authorization from Congress, but in neither case did Congress block the executive's capacity for action. Both were kept secret from the public and from Congress. Both presidents justified their acts by appealing to an inherent executive power, but neither act actually represented a response to an immediate attack or invasion.

From a pro-Congress settlement position, evaluating the Cambodian incursion is entirely a question of whether the president received congressional authorization, which in turn hinges on one's interpretation of the Gulf of Tonkin resolution, which authorized executive action in Southeast Asia.[14] John Hart Ely, a pro-Congress settlement theorist, reads the Gulf of Tonkin resolution as a broad mandate, but argues that the bombing of Cambodia in 1969 was still unconstitutional because the secrecy of the bombing meant that Congress was denied the opportunity to retract its authorization if it so chose when confronted with the consequences of its security decision.[15] For Ely, the constitutionality of a war act is entirely a function of congressional authorization in a context of full knowledge. The context or meaning of the war act does not matter for Ely; authorization is authorization, no matter what bizarre consequences follow. In fact, Ely followed the logic of his position to its full conclusion by arguing that the Gulf of Tonkin resolution would even license bombing supply lines in China if the Congress knew about this action and hence had a

---

14. See William D. Rogers, "The Constitutionality of the Cambodian Incursion," *American Journal of International Law* 65, no. 1 (1971): 26–37, who argued that the incursion was unconstitutional because the Gulf of Tonkin resolution allowed the President only to repel "armed attack," not to disrupt supply lines. The resolution also allowed the president to use armed force to aid a SEATO member or protocol state requesting assistance, but Cambodia had not requested assistance in 1969. Rogers believes that the case of the Cambodian incursion thus rests fully on whether the president has such powers under his sole authority as commander in chief.

15. Ely, "American War in Indochina, Part II."

chance to block it.[16] The meaning of the escalation of the war outside of Vietnam and the incoherence of Nixon's public justifications for his actions are simply insignificant, on this settlement account, because congressional authorization is congressional authorization no matter what. Ely never published commentary on the Cuban missile crisis, other than a footnote noting his astonishment that Robert Kennedy never considered Congress as a possible source of advice.[17] But in all of his work, Ely makes it clear that it is congressional authorization in the context of full knowledge that makes acts of war constitutional. According to that criterion, the naval blockade of Cuba, like the Cambodian incursion, was unconstitutional.

What about the inherent powers of the executive office? Even pro-Congress settlement theorists agree that the president can respond defensively if another country launches an attack on U.S. territory. The Cambodian incursion was an escalation of an aggressive war, and nobody has defended it in terms of presidential defense powers. As for the Cuban missile crisis, it is worth emphasizing that Kennedy had even less statutory authority than Nixon did. Nixon had at least the Gulf of Tonkin resolution, where it is arguable what power Congress had granted; Kennedy had nothing. Hence, according to a settlement account, the only constitutional authority Kennedy could enjoy for the blockade would have been in terms of his pure executive authority to defend the nation from attack. But the existence of missiles in Cuba did not constitute an attack or even an immediate threat. As Kennedy himself appreciated, the USSR already had ample missiles to destroy the Unites States. Although the missiles somewhat enhanced the Soviet first-strike capability, such an enhancement would likely not have an effect on the strength of the retaliatory response—and it was the retaliatory response that was the primary basis for the Cold War security guarantee. Furthermore, the missiles were attractive targets for preemptive strikes given that they did not have rapid launch capabilities (the United States was already considering removing its missiles from Turkey for this very problem).[18] More significant was the

16. See Ely's response to Bork's claim that such action would require additional legislative approval on the grounds that it would involve "a decision to initiate a major war." John Hart Ely, "The American War in Indochina, Part I: The (Troubled) Constitutionality of the War They Told Us About," *Stanford Law Review* 42, no. 4 (1990): 905 n. 125; Robert Bork, "Comments on Legality of U.S. Action in Cambodia," *American Journal of International Law* 65, no. 1 (1971): 79–81.

17. John Hart Ely, *War and Responsibility* (Princeton: Princeton University Press, 1996), 222 n. 20.

18. Arnold H. Horelick, "The Cuban Missile Crisis: An Analysis of Soviet Calculations and Behavior," *World Politics* 16, no. 3 (April 1964): 363–89.

meaning of the introduction of the offensive missiles from the point of view of international political appearance. Kennedy had just assured the public that if Cuba were ever to "become an offensive military base of significant capacity" that the United States would do "whatever must be done to protect its own security and that of its allies."[19] For the Soviets to quickly and secretly insert missiles into Cuba after such remarks by the president represented a threat to U.S. honor but a crisis only from within a Cold War paradigm whereby international security was guaranteed by the willingness of the U.S. president to back up words with force. In other words, the Cuban missile crisis, like the presence of supply lines in Cambodia, was a threat according to a particular security paradigm but did not itself represent an immediate hostile invasion or even the threat of an immediate hostile invasion.

For this reason, pro-Congress settlement scholars will find little to defend in either instance. By contrast, pro-executive settlement theorists can defend both actions according to the president's inherent power to authorize hostilities. John Yoo defended the Cambodian incursion as clearly constitutional, not because of the Gulf of Tonkin resolution, but because the executive power of the president contains an inherent power to initiate hostilities. (Although Yoo emphasizes that "the Constitution does not establish any specific procedure for going to war," it is appropriate to call him a settlement theorist because of his view that insofar as the Constitution does not decisively settle the question of where authority for war resides, the right answer to such a question is completely discretionary.) His analysis easily extends to Cuba. Under Yoo's reading, because Congress never decisively blocked Nixon from the Cambodian incursion or Kennedy from the Cuban blockade through funding restrictions or other measures, these acts were constitutional.[20]

The settlement account has little to ask about an act of war other than which institution authorized the act. And according to the settlement conception of war powers, the constitutionality of Kennedy's blockade in Cuba and Nixon's bombing of Cambodia rises and falls together. Both Nixon's bombing of Cambodia and the naval blockade that Kennedy established in the Cuban missile crisis were acts of war under international

19. John F. Kennedy, "News Conference 43," September 13, 1962, at *John F. Kennedy Presidential Library & Museum: Historical Resources*, http://www.jfklibrary.org/Histor ical+Resources/Archives/Reference+Desk/Press+Conferences/003POF05Pressconference 43_09131962.htm (accessed October 17, 2009).

20. Yoo, "War and the Constitutional Text." See especially his assertions that, because of the paucity of judicial opinions on this question, past practice determines constitutionality (24). Although Yoo criticizes "legalistic" accounts of war powers, the posing of a sharp dichotomy between constitutional determinations resolved by judges and zones of pure political discretion is a core characteristic of the settlement view.

law. Both presidents undertook these acts of war without the consent of Congress—indeed, without notifying Congress at all. And neither of these acts was consistent with an executive power to defend the nation, unless that power is understood quite broadly, as John Yoo does, in which case both acts are justifiable together.

The relational conception, on the other hand, expands the scope of constitutional questions we can ask about these acts of war. Beyond simply asking whether the executive received explicit legislative authorization, the relational conception asks us to consider the relationship of the war act to a legislatively authorized security vision; the meaning of executive secrecy, specifically the relationship of that secrecy to the development of a distinctive institutional perspective; and the retrospective judgment of Congress. Each of these criteria is offered as politicized dimensions of constitutional judgment. The rest of this essay discusses what is valuable in each of the criteria that the relational conception proposes and applies them to the Cuba and Cambodia cases. Ultimately, examining the cases through these expanded criteria reveals that the two acts are constitutionally (although not legally) distinguishable.

Relationship of the War Act to a Legislatively Authorized Security Policy Vision

It is a familiar idea that independent executive action can be warranted when the country faces an emergency threat. The structure of the executive office (which seems well equipped for quick response) and a deeply held, widely shared national consensus undergird this constitutional warrant. Even the most ardent pro-Congress settlement theorist sees a role for independent executive action to defend the country from immediate hostile invasion. Exercising this capacity skillfully is normally seen as one of the main functions of a presidency.

But the language of war, with its accompanying rhetoric of necessity, emergency, and urgency, often conceals the considerable element of judgment that is involved in designating a threat as a threat. What counts as a national interest, and hence what counts as a security threat, far from being self-evident, is always a matter of political construction.[21] For example, although the interruption of trade that led to the Barbary Wars constituted a "threat" that Jefferson used to justify extensive uses of independent executive power, the far more significant and massive interruption of U.S. trade during the lead-up to World War II was not identified

21. Peter Trubowitz, *Defining the National Interest: Conflict and Change in American Foreign Policy* (Chicago: University of Chicago Press, 1998).

as a "threat" by the Congress that passed the Neutrality Acts of 1935. That Congress saw entanglement in European politics as the true threat. This strong element of political judgment is present even in designating attacks on national territory as war threats. The 1993 bombing of the World Trade Center was understood as catastrophic but not as an act of war that would justify a broad executive war power. Few emergencies come neatly labeled as such. Rather, most emergencies are cognizable within a security paradigm that designates the content of the national (or public) good and designates the sorts of events that count as an emergency or warlike disruption of that good.

What counts as an emergency threat depends upon what has been articulated as a national self-interest, and these articulations are not always self-evident. The Constitution itself implies one national self-interest in terms of the preservation of its own institutions. This was the articulation Lincoln relied upon to undergird the extraordinary security powers he assumed during the Civil War. A deeply held and broadly shared general consensus about threat may undergird another articulation. For example, although the identification of a hostile invasion as an emergency threat makes sense only from within a contestable paradigm (the Dalai Lama does not believe China's invasion of Tibet warrants a warlike response), it is a paradigm that is so deeply *un*contested in the United States that it is appropriate to rest on it as a solid touchstone for grounding executive authority. But other public interests are given specific content neither through the Constitution itself nor through deep consensus but rather through the operation of the political processes that the Constitution supports. The national self-interest that counts is not only the self-interest articulated in the Constitution but also the one (or ones) that emerge (or are constructed) from the security politics of a particular time. Hence, the first criterion that the relational conception advances is the relationship of the war act to a security paradigm that Congress has participated in constructing.

Congress has a powerful role to play in articulating these political conceptions of national self-interest not only because of the considerable security-related powers that the Constitution gives Congress but also because of the relationship between its constitutional capacities and the nature of that task. Constructing a security paradigm involves integrating at a minimum both the security concerns of the nation as a whole and the varied meaning of these security commitments for different regions, economies, and interests within the nation. Legislatures are comparatively well equipped to integrate the perspectives of diverse constituencies, to consider the significance of various kinds of threats for those constituencies, and to consider how the public good regarding security should be constructed given these perspectives. Indeed, Congress has the occasion to consider these questions every time it exercises one of its security powers. As an institution that is practiced in debating priorities and experienced in the political questions that lay beneath broad security visions—questions of funding, allocations of costs and benefits, the kinds of risk that are and are not tolerable, and so forth—Congress, as well as the president, has a valuable epistemic role to play in constructing a security paradigm for its particular age. This paradigm, once constructed, can play a role in guiding acts of executive prerogative.

This criterion—the question of the relationship of a war act to a congressionally authorized national security paradigm—allows us to move beyond Lockean prerogative as the sole theoretical framework for guiding judgments about authorized independent executive power. Right now, pro-Congress settlement theorists implicitly rely on Locke to provide the theoretical justification for executives to engage in defensive war without congressional authorization. For, although the Constitution requires the president to vow to "preserve, protect, and defend" the Constitution, we need reference to Lockean notions of executive power in order to construe that oath as an actual grant of independent war-making power.

Lockean prerogative gives the executive power to act without, or even against, the law for the sake of the public good.[22] For Locke, the only limitation on this power is the right of revolution or resistance, powers that are inherently reactive. Locke's failure to offer any specification for the content of the public good renders this power unruly, especially when we take seriously the deep element of political judgment that is involved in designating threats as threats. To make prerogative tractable from a constitutional perspective, we can specify the content of the common good at least in part through reference to the functioning institutions that are given responsibility for defining that good.[23] Understanding legislative authority in terms not only of Congress's power to authorize particular hostilities but also of its power to construct, through legislation, a public conception of the national security interest can be useful as a constitutional discipline to Lockean prerogative. Under this more disciplined, constitutionalist conception, the prerogative power still pertains to action without law (i.e., actual authorization). Yet insofar as it responds to a threat identified as such through Congress's construction of a security framework, it is less constitutionally problematic than is a pure prerogative power, where the content of the public good is left undefined or defined only by the president himself.

22. John Locke, *The Second Treatise of Civil Government* (1690).

23. See Stephen L. Elkin, *Reconstructing the Commercial Republic: Constitutional Design after Madison* (Chicago: University of Chicago Press, 2006), on the general appeal of specifying values in terms of institutional content for constitutional thinking.

One value of this criterion beyond its capacity to discipline Lockean notions of prerogative power is that it draws attention to an element of congressional participation in the construction of war authority that has been too often ignored. Advocates of strong presidential power (even reluctant advocates) speak of the president's advantage in acting as "first responder" to emergency. This gives him the capacity to set the terms of debate and creates a field within which Congress's only plausible role is that of a reactive institution. This first criterion shows us that Congress, too, can act as a "first responder" by defining the field within which events will be categorized, or not, as war or emergency events. If Congress's participation in the construction of a security paradigm is one element of its constitutional agency, there is good reason for Congress to pay deep attention to this part of its security tasks.

Congress did not authorize either Kennedy's or Nixon's act of war. Settlement theorists believe that a failure to offer authorization always counts in one direction, either to curtail executive authority or to supplement his zone of discretion. But when we understand the significance of congressional participation in constructing a public conception of the nation's security interest, then it becomes clear that a failure to achieve legislative authorization is of varying constitutional significance depending in part on the relationship of the war action to a broader security vision that Congress has ratified. If the aggressive war act signals a considerable shift in the nature of threat cognizable by the U.S. government, then a failure to achieve congressional authorization is devastating. But if the aggressive war act is meaningful from within a security paradigm that Congress has participated in constructing, then failure to achieve authorization represents the president's recourse to a form of executive prerogative that, while still potentially risky, is less constitutionally problematic.

What does this mean for Cuba and Cambodia? As mentioned, neither received explicit congressional authorization. In the Cuban case, Kennedy announced his view that his authority as commander in chief was adequate for the blockade and asserted that there was no reason for Congress to grant him that authority, although he would "be very glad to have those resolutions passed if that should be the desire of the Congress."[24] Congress then did pass a resolution expressing determination "to prevent in Cuba the creation or use of an externally supported military capability endangering the security of the United States," but

---

24. Louis Fisher, *Presidential War Power* (Lawrence: University Press of Kansas, 2004), 111, citing U.S. President (Kennedy), "The President's News Conference of September 13, 1962," *Papers of the Presidents of the United States, John F. Kennedy, 1962* (Washington, DC: GPO, 1963), 679.

that resolution indicated that the United States was "determined" rather than that the executive was "authorized."[25]

However, the Cuban missile crisis was easily recognized *as* a crisis from within an astonishingly broad Cold War consensus. The basic tenets of the Cold War, including the identification of the USSR as a threat, the identification of the United States as the only global power able to resist Soviet influence after the Cold War, the division of the world into geographic spheres of influence, and the positioning of the president as the first responder to Soviet threats, had been ratified repeatedly by Congress in everything from the system of weapons that were funded, to the structure of the Cold War military and bureaucratic buildup, to alliance decisions and the structure of foreign aid.[26] According to the system for organizing danger under this repeatedly ratified Cold War ideology, the placement of missiles in Cuba represented a threat because they could be launched with little or no warning to the United States, and because the warheads placed Cuba, otherwise within the U.S. regional sphere of influence, explicitly within the Soviet deterrence system. According to Cold War ideology, tolerating this incursion would create a vulnerability by signaling that Kennedy was willing to tolerate a Soviet lie. Legislators had also been pressuring the executive to "do something" about Fidel Castro, a pressure that had conditioned their mild response after the failed 1961 Bay of Pigs invasion.[27] Finally, although the Cuba resolution was not a legal authorization, it did indicate a political commitment to responding to threats to U.S. interests in Cuba. None of these represent congressional authorization for Kennedy's act of war. But they create a field within which the president's response to the Cuban situation is rendered meaningful according to a broadly shared security ideology which was the template for a Cold War legal (i.e., congressionally authorized) architecture.

Nixon, like Kennedy, lacked explicit legislative authorization for the incursion. Congressional authorization for the Cambodian bombing could only be pursuant to the Gulf of Tonkin resolution of 1964. That resolution stated that "Congress approves and supports the determination of the President . . . to take all necessary measures to repel any armed

25. U.S. Congress, *Congressional Record*, 87th Cong., 2nd sess., Vol. 108, No. 170, September 20, 1962, pp. 18892–951; U.S. Congress, *Congressional Record*, 87th Cong., 2nd sess., Vol. 108, No. 174, September 26, 1962, pp. 19702–53.

26. Philip J. Briggs, *Making American Foreign Policy: President-Congress Relations from the Second World War to the Post Cold War Era* (Lanham, MD: Rowman and Littlefield, 1994); Friedberg, *Shadow*; Robert David Johnson, *Congress and the Cold War* (Cambridge: Cambridge University Press, 2006); Nelson Polsby, *Political Innovation in America* (New Haven: Yale University Press, 1984).

27. David M. Barrett, *CIA and Congress: The Untold Story from Truman to Kennedy* (Lawrence: University Press of Kansas, 2005), 2.

attack against the forces of the United States ... Consonant with the Constitution of the United States and the Charter of the United Nations and in accordance with its obligations under the Southeast Asia Collective Defense Treaty, the United States is, therefore, prepared, as the President determines, to take all necessary steps, including the use of armed force, to assist any member or protocol state of the Southeast Asia Collective Defense Treaty requesting assistance in defense of its freedom."[28] Although this resolution authorized the Vietnam War, contra Ely, the language of the resolution should not be interpreted as a legal authorization for the Cambodian bombings simply because Cambodia had not requested assistance. Hence the terms of the statute simply do not cover the assistance Nixon offered through bombing.

We also should not read the resolution as ratifying a security paradigm to which Nixon could turn as a source of constitutional authority. By 1969 whatever political conception of security lay beneath the resolution was deeply imperiled—and the strife was evident in Congress's actions. Beginning in 1966 and 1967, the Senate Foreign Relations Committee (SFRC) had received information that Johnson had misrepresented the Tonkin attacks. The SFRC leaked this information to the press.[29] Senator William Fulbright, the chair of the SFRC, began holding hearings on the Tonkin resolution in 1966, and those hearings highlighted Congress's emerging strong opposition to that conflict. By 1968 Fulbright and a significant number of other congressional foreign policy elites had begun to characterize the Tonkin resolution as an "overreaction obtained by misrepresentation."[30] By 1969 congressional debates over Vietnam had become polarized, and in 1969, while Nixon actually began the bombings (but before they were made public), U.S. senators John Sherman Cooper (R-KY) and Frank Church (D-ID) were passing legislation prohibiting the introduction of U.S. combat troops into Thailand or Laos. Hence, although Congress had funded the Vietnam War and had passed the Gulf of Tonkin resolution, the foreign policy ideology according to which Vietnam itself—to say nothing of expansion of the conflict to Cambodia—made sense at all was subject to serious divisions within Congress. The president was facing immense pressure to disengage and to reframe American security interests in a more limited way.

28. Southeast Asia Resolution, Pub. L. No. 88-408, 78 Stat. 384 (1964) (also known as the Tonkin Gulf Resolution).

29. Randall B. Woods, *J. William Fulbright, Vietnam, and the Search for a Cold War Policy* (New York: Cambridge University Press, 1998), 165–70; David W. Levy, *The Debate over Vietnam* (Baltimore: Johns Hopkins University Press, 1991), 51; Scott Shane, "Vietnam War Intelligence 'Deliberately Skewed,' Secret Study Says," *New York Times*, December 2, 2005.

30. Levy, *Debate over Vietnam*, 146.

It was not even clear that the president himself supported a security vision that could render meaningful an intervention in Cambodia: Nixon's own public statements had offered a foreign policy vision that would preclude expanding the scope of conflict. In 1969 Nixon had started making serious public commitments to deescalate the war, remove American combat troops, and promote "Vietnamization." Also that year, he had announced the Nixon Doctrine, emphasizing that foreign nations have the direct responsibility for their own defense but that the United States would supply assistance when requested in accordance with treaty commitments.[31] Under this doctrine, Cambodia's neutrality should have protected it from interference at least until Cambodia itself requested assistance. The security vision according to which the intervention in Cambodia made sense was not subject to the kind of broad and deep legislative support that the basic Cold War tenets had provided to Kennedy. Nor was the executive himself able to articulate or defend a coherent vision of the national interest that could reconcile his public statements with his actions. Kennedy's and Nixon's actions are constitutionally distinguishable, then, according to this first criterion of the relational conception.

At this point, an alert reader might wonder whether the criterion ultimately falls back onto some of the settlement assumptions that the relational conception is committed to challenging. Is this criterion, that the prerogative power be disciplined by reference to a security ideology ratified by Congress, just another way of saying that interbranch agreement is what, at bottom, authorizes the initiation of hostilities? Perhaps a relational account that truly valued the epistemic benefits of interbranch interpretive conflict would defend Nixon for advancing, through the Cambodian incursion, an alternative to the security consensus that was beginning to prevail in a Democratic Congress. Nixon, not Kennedy, the critic would argue, represented a true departure from security groupthink. His actions represented a challenge to Congress at the level of both policy and constitutional interpretation. This criticism reveals how the first criterion, taken on its own, ultimately locates constitutional authority in interbranch consensus even as the relevant consensus moves to another level of abstraction—consensus over a security paradigm rather than consensus over a particular policy.

The relational conception is not opposed to consensus-based accounts of authority but rather to the claim that authority is generated *only* through consensus. Hence, the critic is right to notice that this criterion

---

31. Richard M. Nixon, "Address to the Nation on the War in Vietnam," November 3, 1969, at *Miller Center of Public Affairs Presidential Speech Archive* (University of Virginia, The Scripps Library), http://millercenter.org/scripps/archive/speeches/detail/3873 (accessed October 17, 2009).

from the relational conception retains an appeal to the authority of political consensus. Yet we must also notice that broad agreement over security paradigms is consistent with intense and powerful political conflict
over the application of that paradigm in particular cases. The criticism is
wrong, for example, to posit Kennedy and the Democratic Congress as
essentially acting in harmony, even as they both appealed to a broadly
shared Cold War security ideology. In fact, Kennedy was at the time
involved in a contentious relationship with Congress precisely over the
question of Cuba. Congress was urging a more bellicose attitude toward
Cuba than Kennedy was willing to accept. While Kennedy's authority
may be enhanced by the act's interpretability from within a Cold War
security consensus, that is different from Congress actually agreeing to
the content of his policy.[32] Political conflict nested within a security consensus can be as significant as conflict that is structured by reference to
opposing major paradigms.

It is also important to resist the idea that Nixon's actions represent
a distinctive contribution to interbranch deliberation over Vietnam War
authority, because he failed to develop and publicly defend an ideology
according to which the incursion in Cambodia made sense in light of his
previous commitments. The relational account asks the branches to wed
their distinctive judgments about public policy to distinctive conceptions
of security authority. Although the Cambodian incursion represented a
departure from reigning security paradigms, it did not represent a departure that was publicly justified according to a new paradigm through
which the public, and Congress, could make sense of a new context. Nixon
argued that Cambodia had lost the capacity to stay neutral and therefore
had become a part of the Vietnam War. But this reasoning pointed toward
a paradigm of escalation and enlargement of the war, not deescalating
and handing responsibility for its prosecution to Vietnam. Nixon was not
able to reconcile these divergent ideologies into a larger, coherent structure. Departures and deviations, on their own, do not represent contributions to an interbranch system of mutual review. They must be articulated
according to a broader security ideology in order to count as deliberative
contributions. Hence, Nixon's failure to publicly articulate an alternative
security ideology that could compete with the one he was resisting is fatal
to the effort to bolster his constitutional authority through reference to
his participation in a system of interbranch deliberation.

---

32. Presupposing that that consensus is itself constitutionally authoritative. For the purposes of this essay, I presume that it is. But it is important to note that, insofar as the Cold
War consensus can create authority for independent executive war action, it is highly appropriate to evaluate the construction of the Cold War security consensus itself through the
lens of the relational conception of constitutional war authority.

Secrecy and the Possibility of Rebuff

The second constitutional criterion advanced by the relational conception is the meaning of secrecy and the possibility of rebuff. We have already seen that at least one settlement account, that of Ely, considers secrecy as undermining of executive constitutional authority. Under Ely's account, for an executive to act in secret curtails his authority insofar as Congress is blocked from the opportunity to revoke or amend the authorizations available to the president. Hence, secret executive war action, for Ely, always represents a constitutional problem.

Like Ely's settlement account, the relational conception emphasizes the importance of the branches being engaged in practices of mutual review. This generates a strong imperative for the branches to publicize their deliberations to one another. But the relational account also sees that the meaning of secrecy can be different depending on the relationship of that secrecy to the conditions of conflict and security context of the moment. Secrecy, in other words, is of varying constitutional significance depending on its contribution to the system of interbranch deliberation.

In the case of Cuba and Cambodia, both presidents concealed what they were doing both for strategic international reasons and, more troubling, in order to avoid political interference. But there is a critical difference in the meaning of this evasion in each case. In Kennedy's case, avoiding public judgment was in service of his capacity to formulate a distinctive perspective at all. Kennedy's opponents were primed and eager to set a belligerent course with Cuba. Kennedy had reasonable grounds for fearing that once the placement of Soviet missiles was made public, and his deliberations were exposed, that political winds would be so strong that he would be unable to develop a distinctive perspective at all. His secrecy was related to the imperative of developing a plan of action. To immediately publicize the missile buildup when it was not clear what the executive branch's judgment on the situation was could have significantly limited the scope of Kennedy's deliberations.[33] Kennedy thus forestalled the judgment of the other branches (the third condition) in order to shore up his capacity to develop a distinctive perspective (the second condition). Importantly, once this second condition was met and Kennedy had developed a position, he exposed his conclusions to Congress (and the public). He did not avoid congressional judgment any more than

---

33. On the value of privacy for generating high-quality conclusions that include all available private information, see David Stasavage, "Polarization and Publicity: Rethinking the Benefits of Deliberative Democracy," *Journal of Politics* 69, no. 1 (2007): 59–72, and Ellen E. Meade and David Stasavage, "Publicity of Debate and the Incentive to Dissent: Evidence from the US Federal Reserve," *Economic Journal* 118, no. 528 (2008): 695–717.

was necessary for developing his own position. It is also significant that the likely direction of congressional influence—toward more aggressive engagement with the Soviets—remained open for Kennedy, and hence the possibility of Congress enacting an alternate legislative preference was not forestalled by Kennedy's failure to notify Congress earlier.

Nixon's evasion of public judgment, by contrast, was not in service of developing a distinctive executive judgment on what should be done. Kissinger offered, as reasons for the administration's "reticence," the desire to "avoid forcing the North Vietnamese, Prince Sihanouk, and the Soviets and the Chinese into public reactions. A volunteered American statement would have obligated Hanoi to make a public response," risking pushing Cambodia further into the arms of the North Vietnamese.[34] But the Nixon administration's efforts to shield the news from domestic audiences went beyond "reticence." When news of the bombing was leaked, Nixon tapped the phone of one of his security advisers and placed others within his security circle on an enemies list.[35] Nixon refused to acknowledge American combat operations in Cambodia for a year. When he announced the ground incursions in 1970, Nixon simply lied about prior U.S. involvement in Cambodia, claiming that "for five years neither the United States nor South Vietnam has moved against these enemy sanctuaries because we did not wish to violate the territory of a neutral nation."[36] Even after the revelation of troop presence in Cambodia, Kissinger and Nixon refused to acknowledge the significance of their intervention, with Kissinger arguing that "it was not a bombing of Cambodia, but it was a bombing of North Vietnamese in Cambodia."[37] In 1971, when Congress began to investigate Cambodia more seriously, Pentagon officials gave the Armed Services Committee classified information claiming that no B-52 bombing raids had happened in Cambodia before the incursion of ground troops in 1970, exposing a major scandal of pilots listing false coordinates of bombing runs.[38] A witness to the Senate hearings on the matter testified that when he "asked his superior officer from whom the Air Force needed to conceal the bombing raids, the response was, 'Well, I guess the Foreign Relations Committee.'"[39] The secrecy and misrepresentations of the Nixon administration is most

34. Kissinger, *Vietnam*, 66.

35. Seymour M. Hersh, "Kissinger and Nixon in the White House," *Atlantic Monthly*, May 1982.

36. Nixon, "Address to the Nation on the Situation in Southeast Asia," April 30, 1970.

37. William Shawcross, *Sideshow: Kissinger, Nixon, and the Destruction of Cambodia* (New York: Simon and Schuster, 1979), 28.

38. Johnson, *Congress and the Cold War*, 187.

39. Ibid., 188, citing U.S. Senate, Armed Services Committee, *Hearings, Bombing in Cambodia*, 93rd Cong., 1st sess., August 16, 1973, p. 9.

plausibly interpreted as a direct desire to avoid the possibility of rebuff by Congress. Such a strategy represents a direct attempt to remove decision making from ultimate democratic control and accountability rather than a secrecy strategy in service of goals that can be constitutionally defended. Nixon may have needed privacy to form a distinctive position on the expansion of the Vietnam War, but, unlike Kennedy, his use of secrecy went far beyond what was required for only those needs.

Because the relational conception emphasizes how constitutional authority is developed over time as a result of the quality of the branches' responsiveness to one another, executive secrecy cannot be examined at one point in time but rather must be evaluated as part of a developing relationship with Congress. Secrecy contributes differently to the system of interbranch deliberation in different contexts. The relational conception, unlike the settlement account, can be sensitive to the way context changes the meaning of executive secrecy.

Retrospective Judgment

A final criterion for evaluating the constitutionality of aggressive war acts is explicitly retrospective: the post hoc judgment of the branches. This criterion asks us to consider, as constitutionally significant, each branch's judgment about whether it would have or should have authorized the war act. In practice, because we can expect executives to defend their own actions almost regardless of the consequences, the question will be about Congress's retrospective judgment of the president's act of war. But the criterion is phrased with more generality to indicate the equal constitutional significance if a president were to repudiate the constitutionality of his own war act when faced with its consequences.

Retrospective judgment is sometimes understood as distinctively valuable for its capacity to integrate the consequences of a course of action into an account about the authority of that action. For some, it is bizarre to consider the authority of a president's conduct without considering whether that conduct led to good results, and this type of reasoning is certainly consistent with a Lockean conception of prerogative, where the retrospective judgment of the public is the *only* way judgment about the legitimacy of an act of prerogative is carried forth. For this reason, the criterion of retrospective judgment has probably been the place where most efforts to develop political criteria for evaluating executive authority have been lodged.

But we must remember that nothing about a judgment being retrospective necessarily makes it better. Those who judge an action after the fact are certainly looking through a different light; but the presence of more information may not provide an epistemic advantage if the framework they use for analyzing that information is distorted—and some theorists argue that any judgment outside of the context of threat is distorted because it will fail to take the threat as seriously as it ought.[40] Perhaps Congress would be right to repudiate an action after the fact that it was right to approve at the time. For this reason, we should understand Congress's retrospective judgment as one factor for evaluating constitutional authority but not as a criterion that is more important than the others. An act could be deemed appropriate retrospectively but still be constitutionally problematic according to dimensions other than retrospective judgment; an act could be condemned retrospectively and lose constitutional validity, even if at the time it appeared to be constitutionally appropriate. The way an action appears when judged retrospectively is one element to include in a full constitutional evaluation, but not the only one.

The value of including retrospective judgment as an element of constitutional evaluation is that of constructing a constitutional precedent for moving forward. A constitutionally responsible Congress will exercise its power to judge not because the reactive judge is necessarily more accurate than a contemporary judge, but because the prospect of judging can be a disciplining force for a president contemplating such scrutiny in the future, and because retrospective judgments are one way for Congress to contribute to the political construction of defensible constitutional interpretations about the war power. On this dimension, the differences between the two cases are worth investigating for what they reveal about Congress. Kennedy was never repudiated by Congress. Certain elements of Nixon's Cambodian incursion were repudiated, but not, as we shall see, intelligently. Hence, here, too, we see a constitutional distinction between the cases, but, as this section describes, the form of the constitutional distinction that Congress drew was bizarre and arguably misplaced.

The response to the Cambodian incursion in the broader public was massive and hostile; Nixon's announcement about Cambodia spurred the Kent State protests and killings, and a week after those shootings more than 100,000 protesters converged in Washington to protest both the shooting of students and the incursion into Cambodia. Congress itself passed a flurry of legislation indicating policy disagreement with Nixon's Cambodian decision. Congress revoked the Gulf of Tonkin resolution shortly after the public announcement of ground troops in Cambodia; moved to cut off funds for combat operations in Cambodia through the Cooper and Church amendments (although it took until 1973 for both

---

40. Eric A. Posner and Adrian Vermeule, "Accommodating Emergencies," in *The Constitution in Wartime: Beyond Alarmism and Complacency*, ed. Mark Tushnet (Durham: Duke University Press, 2005), 55–92.

houses to actually cut off funds for bombing operations); imposed, by 1974, massive restrictions on funding in aid to Cambodia—a ceiling of $377 million against which every expenditure, military or food, had to be counted; and from the early 1970s onward, emphasized in almost all aid bills for Cambodia that no "commitment" was implied (Nixon had used preexisting American commitments in Indochina to prolong the war).[41] In 1973 Congress passed the War Powers resolution, and although the text of that Resolution said nothing about Cambodia, legislative debate was filled with references to Nixon's abuses there. In March 1974 military aid to Cambodia was cut off completely. A notable gap in Congress's response was a simple declaration of the unconstitutionality of the incursion itself. The charge that Nixon's bombing in Cambodia had been unconstitutional was considered as an article of impeachment, but dropped. Hence, Nixon never faced a direct retrospective condemnation in the text of any congressional bill.

With the exception of the War Powers Resolution, the relational conception does not interpret all of this action as constitutional repudiation, however. To interpret policy action as constitutional repudiation would be to destroy the sensitivity of the register with which we read congressional communication. Constitutional interpretation is a practice that depends upon the capacity to communicate subtle positions. Understanding Congress as a constitutional agent is already rendered difficult by the fact that Congress, unlike the president or court, rarely speaks with a single voice. This may be one reason Congress is so often ignored as an interpreter. To read policy judgments of Congress as constitutional evaluations, when Congress itself has not made that connection, would defeat the capacity of the relational account to register Congress as an interpreter at all. Reading policy decisions as necessarily constitutional decisions would also ignore the difference between a separation-of-powers approach, which emphasizes the relationship of separated powers to governance issues, and a relational approach, which pertains to the specifically constitutional implications of the conditions of conflict.

The War Powers Resolution, however, can be read as a condemnation of a certain kind. It is not exactly a retrospective judgment, because it never actually repudiates Nixon's actions in Cambodia. It is thus possible to read the act as a message for going forward, not as a repudiation of the past. But more important than this narrow conceptual point is to notice how bizarre the content of the "repudiation" actually was. The resolution attempted to rectify the imbalance between the branches by requiring the president to consult with Congress before starting hostilities, and to remove armed forces from hostilities if Congress did not declare war

41. Kissinger, *Vietnam*, 514–16.

within sixty days. Advocates did argue that the resolution would condemn Nixonian conceptions of executive authority. But the text of the act is not quite the condemnation one would hope for. It concedes far too much. It concedes that it is constitutional for a president to commit troops on his own authority, as long as he notifies Congress. It also concedes that an executive has independent constitutional authority to keep offensive troops in combat for sixty days. Even more strangely, the resolution makes it the executive's filing of reports on hostilities that begins the congressional "clock." By not filing, the president can avoid facing Congress for authorization. The resolution was essentially designed to control the president without requiring any action from Congress. The resolution exchanges Congress's constitutional power to authorize war for a role in influencing war policy (but only to the extent that the executive is interested in what Congress has to say). If we interpret the resolution as a retrospective judgment, then the content of the judgment is only that Nixon was wrong not to tell Congress that he was bombing Cambodia sooner. It is plausible as a criticism, but this is not the same as a repudiation of Nixon's actually authorizing the hostilities. The argument that Nixon's bombing of Cambodia was unconstitutional because of the post hoc judgment of the Congress is weaker than it could have been because of Congress's failure to state directly that constitutional grievance, whether in the articles of impeachment or elsewhere.

Nor was the Cuban missile crisis repudiated after the fact. In fact, according to Robert Kennedy, the possibility of impeachment for not responding to the missiles was one reason JKF felt compelled to respond in the first place.[42] There is a robust literature about whether Kennedy took the right course of action, whether his conduct was strategically sound, the significance of the reinstallation of the missiles in Cuba (and Turkey), and more. But there is no academic work criticizing Kennedy from a constitutional perspective, nor did such criticism appear in Congress. The crisis seems not to have left much of a constitutional aftermath at all, except as a political precedent for presidential war.

Political Criteria for Constitutional Judgment

The criteria offered here provide a way of discussing many elements of war authority that constitutional participants may find intuitively significant but which receive no development in any settlement account. These

---

42. Robert F. Kennedy, *Thirteen Days: A Memoir of the Cuban Missile Crisis* (New York: W. W. Norton, 1969), 67.

criteria allow us to register sensitivity to the contexts that officials work within, but to nonetheless make critical evaluations about what officials do in those contexts. Hence, the criteria represent a form of constitutional evaluation that is deeply politicized.

They are politicized forms of constitutional judgment because evaluating the "meaning" of a war act, not to mention identifying the nation's operative "security paradigm," for example, is a deeply interpretive, and hence contestable, task. The answer that an interpreter arrives at is likely to be colored by her political goals and values. Furthermore, we can expect radical divergence in the answers interpreters provide rather than subtle shades of gray. As an example, consider the question of whether the incursion into Cambodia represented an extension of commitments already entered into, or a repudiation of the basic tenets of an operative security paradigm. Although this essay takes a position on that question in order to demonstrate the kind of reasoning that undergirds the relational conception, other positions are to be expected and are consistent with a relational account. Because the answer to this question is so deeply interpretive, so deeply informed by the interpreter's own goals and values, and so deeply dependent on one's conception of the nature, meaning, and context of the security decisions that the branches have entered into, applying these criteria to actual war contexts is a task that is well suited to those officials who are deeply immersed in making the everyday judgments of the security state—that is to say, the legislature and executive themselves. This is a profound strength of these criteria. A constitution cannot live through the courts alone. Yet constitutional interpreters other than courts have suffered from a lack of conceptual work articulating forms of defensible yet politicized constitutional judgment.

If the criteria of the relational conception are "political" in the sense of being interpretive and contestable, what distinguishes a constitutional judgment about the use of the war power from a straightforward political judgment about the desirability of a particular war? A constitutional judgment under the relational account is not the same as a political judgment because the relational account can generate constitutional defenses of behavior that is politically tragic, outrageous, or worse. This essay defends the constitutionality of Kennedy's response to the Cuban missile crisis. But it is plausible that, although Congress had ratified a security ideology according to which the threat of the missiles in Cuba was cognizable, that security ideology itself was troubling. Given the dangers of the Cold War security ideology, the fact that a war act is meaningful within that ideology is not necessarily a source of comfort. And, although many scholars believe Kennedy's handling of the crisis to be masterful from a strategic perspective, it is terrifying that Kennedy's blockade brought the nation to the brink of nuclear war. Behavior that is justifiable within the relational approach to war powers can lead to troubling, terrifying, or even horrific outcomes.

Certain evaluations of the consequences of a war policy are not enough, in themselves, to undermine their constitutional authority from within the relational conception. For example, the effectiveness of Kennedy's blockade, that it represented a limited and defensive posture, that it allowed ships with peaceful cargo to continue through, and so on are not relevant dimensions for constitutional evaluation. Nor is it relevant to consider the extent of Nixon's violence in Cambodia, its disruptiveness for the security context in Southeast Asia more generally, the question of whether the incursion helped pave the way for the rise of the Khmer Rouge, or even the legality of the action under international law. To be sure, apprehension of these policies may motivate legislators and the public toward advocacy or opposition, and their presence as advocates or opponents may change the constitutional landscape. But the consequences of the war act (beyond its consequences for constitutional institutions and practices themselves) are not an evaluative category in the relational account.

This brings us to the relational conception's stance on the nature of constitutional interpretation. Michael Ramsey has argued that policy views about a controversy are not an appropriate basis for choosing war power views, and this view is implicit in judicial rhetoric and the rhetoric of international lawyers.[43] But according to the relational conception, whether this is true depends on the kind of policy view that is at stake. Certainly not all actions that are defensible under a relational conception will be defensible as the best way of proceeding, and sometimes there may be better ways of proceeding (from a strictly policy point of view) that are not consistent with constitutional authority as conceived under the relational conception. But the main mechanism for the cultivation of distinctive perspectives on constitutional meaning is precisely a strong and developed concern for a particular policy. For example, it was Congress's opposition to Nixon's war *policy* that motivated it to mount a constitutional challenge to his use of his powers. Insofar as those policy views are distinctively related to the special charge of the branch—protecting the general welfare, for Congress—they are indeed an appropriate basis for officials to choose their war powers views. Hence, under the relational account, whether or not policy views are an appropriate basis for a war powers view depends on the relationship between the nature of the policy view and the nature of the relevant institution's position within the constitutional framework.

43. Michael D. Ramsey, "Presidential Originalism?" *Boston University Law Review* 88, no. 2 (2008): 353–73.

Conclusion

The relational conception of constitutional war powers insists that the war power is shared and sees war-making authority as a function of the quality of relationship that exists between the two branches. Neither branch has ultimate war-making authority. Rather, the authority of each branch fluctuates according to context and the relationship of that context to the branch's capacities. Because it is the branches themselves that bear primary responsibility for constructing a constitutional order that is faithful to the relational conception in each security situation, neither branch can ever be free from the burden to justify its actions to the other.

But the standards for evaluation they should engage for constitutional evaluation are explicitly contextual and political, not legalistic. What this means is that the right constitutional answer to questions of war authority is tied to context. For example, in the two cases I have explored, one relevant dimension of the context includes the nature of the "crisis" (whether it is an immediate attack or rather a crisis from within a given security paradigm) and the relationship of the president's actions to his own, and to Congress's, previously ratified security commitments. Because the relational conception is so tied to context, political judgment will play a significant role in forming how interpreters apply its criteria. The centrality of political judgment to forming the positions interpreters take within the relational conception does not, however, collapse the relational conception into a *simply* political account. The strength of the relational conception of constitutional war authority is precisely that it supports officials in making claims upon each other that are both appropriately political and appropriately constitutionalist in nature.

10

Confronting War

RETHINKING JUSTICE JACKSON'S CONCURRENCE
IN *YOUNGSTOWN V. SAWYER*

JOSEPH M. BESSETTE

DURING SENATE HEARINGS IN September 2005 on federal judge John Roberts's nomination to serve as chief justice of the Supreme Court, Senator Patrick Leahy (D-VT), ranking minority member of the Judiciary Committee, pressed Roberts on whether the president was bound by congressional statute. Roberts offered that "no one is above the law." He added that when Congress and the president disagree over an exercise of "asserted executive authority," the "framework for analyzing this is in the Youngstown Sheet and Tube case, the famous case coming out of President Truman's seizure of the steel mills." He specifically cited "Justice [Robert] Jackson's concurring opinion, which is the opinion that has sort of set the stage for subsequent cases."[1]

In this landmark 1952 case,[2] the Court ruled 6–3 that President Harry S Truman's seizure of the nation's steel mills, in the face of a strike by unionized workers during the Korean War, was unconstitutional. Although Roberts cited Jackson's concurrence, it was actually Justice Hugo Black who wrote the opinion of the court (for himself and four others). All six members of the majority wrote separate opinions, and three members of the Court joined in a single dissent. Yet it is Jackson's lone concurrence that half a century later is best remembered and, as Roberts's remarks made clear, is accepted by many as authoritative.

In particular, judges have embraced Jackson's three-part schema for analyzing controversies over presidential power. First, "[i]f the president is acting in an area where Congress is supportive," Roberts explained, "the president's power is at its maximum." Second, "[i]f the president is acting contrary to congressional authority, . . . the president's authority is at its lowest ebb." Finally, "there's the vast . . . area where courts

---

1. *Washington Post*, September 13, 2005, http://www.washingtonpost.com/wp-dyn/content/article/ 2005/09/13/AR2005091300876.html (accessed September 14, 2008).

2. *Youngstown Sheet & Tube Co. v. Sawyer*, 343 U. S. 579 (1952).

often have to struggle because they can't determine whether Congress has supported a particular exercise or not." When Leahy asked whether he accepted *Youngstown* as "settled law," Roberts confirmed that "the opinion that everyone looks to [is] the Jackson opinion."[3]

Four months later, the subject arose again during the confirmation hearings regarding the elevation of federal judge Samuel Alito to the Supreme Court. Several senators sought assurances that Alito accepted Jackson's analysis. "I do," Alito told committee chairman Arlen Specter (R-PA). "I think it provides a very useful framework." When questions about presidential power arise in the courts, he explained, "those specific questions have to be resolved, I think, by looking to that framework that Justice Jackson set out."[4]

Then in October 2007, senators on the Judiciary Committee quizzed federal judge Michael Mukasey, nominated to succeed Alberto Gonzales as attorney general of the United States, on Jackson's concurrence and its relevance to the president's obligation to abide by the strictures of the Foreign Intelligence Surveillance Act (FISA). Here they were less successful in eliciting a full-fledged endorsement of the authoritativeness of "Justice Jackson's three-part test," or at least its application to the issue at hand. Mukasey insisted that despite the relevance of the Jackson test, FISA did not settle the issue of the president's independent constitutional power to authorize intelligence gathering. The FISA statute, he told Senator Leahy, "regardless of its clarity, can't change the Constitution." Sensing that Mukasey was suggesting that a president might constitutionally violate a congressional statute, Leahy immediately asked whether the president can authorize illegal conduct. Mukasey answered that if the president acts "within the authority . . . to defend the country," then he "is not putting somebody above the law," for "the law emphatically includes the Constitution." Later, Mukasey told Senator Russ Feingold (D-WI): "I recognize the force of Justice Jackson's three-step approach. But I recognize, also, that each branch has its own sphere of authority that is exclusive to it." Feingold was unpersuaded: "Justice Jackson indicated a three-part test, which your analysis today I think renders essentially meaningless."[5]

In embracing Jackson's concurrence from *Youngstown* as the essential guide for resolving controversies over executive power, the senators on

3. Ibid.

4. *Washington Post*, January 10, 2006, http://www.washingtonpost.com/wp-dyn/content/article/2006/01/10/AR2006011000781.html (accessed September 12, 2008).

5. Jackson's concurrence was addressed on October 17 and 18, 2007. The transcripts for these two days are available at the *Washington Post*, http://www.washingtonpost.com/wp-srv/politics/documents/attorney_general_hearing_101707.html and http://www.washingtonpost.com/wp-srv/politics/documents/transcript_mukasey_hearing_day_two_101807.html (accessed September 12, 2008).

the Judiciary Committee were reflecting a near universal view among constitutional scholars. One of these scholars notes that "virtually all have agreed" that Jackson's "tripartite framework . . . provides the appropriate frame for resolving contests between the U.S. Congress . . . and the president when he claims to be acting pursuant to his commander-in-chief powers." "Jackson's majestic *Youngstown* concurrence," he adds, has become "the widely accepted approach."[6] Another scholar calls it "deservedly famous."[7] And a third writes that although the opinion did not "win immediate acclaim among legal scholars" (receiving "no particularized attention" in the extensive review of the Supreme Court's 1951 term by the *Harvard Law Review*), it has by now "grown ubiquitous in legal discourse." It "retain[s] great prominence in debates on the President's power in wartime," is "deeply ensconced in the canon," and "has transcended consensus to become conventional wisdom."[8] As if to confirm the transcendent importance of Jackson's opinion, the journal *Constitutional Commentary* devoted an entire issue to *Youngstown* on the decision's fiftieth anniversary in 2002, much of which focused on Jackson's argument.[9] And as recently as April 2009, Attorney General Eric Holder said in a speech at the United States Military Academy at West Point that Jackson's concurrence was "perhaps the most important court opinion on presidential power in the last century." It was nothing less than "the gold standard to this day for defining the extent to which the president can operate consistent with the rule of law."[10]

Jackson's opinion is especially attractive to "proponents of congressional authority," for it seems to give Congress the final word on disputed matters.[11] Indeed, one such advocate praises it for "deal[ing] a crushing

6. Mark D. Rosen, "Revisiting *Youngstown*: Against the View that Jackson's Concurrence Resolves the Relation between Congress and the Commander in Chief," *UCLA Law Review* 54 (2006–7): 1704, 1745, 1711.

7. Vicki C. Jackson, "Constitutional Law and Transnational Comparisons: The *Youngstown* Decision and American Exceptionalism," *Harvard Journal of Law and Public Policy* 30 (2006–7): 198.

8. Adam J. White, "Justice Jackson's Draft Opinions in *The Steel Seizure Cases*," *Albany Law Review* 69 (2005–6): 1108 n. 4, 1107, 1133. Neither did Jackson's concurrence impress the eminent constitutional scholar Edward S. Corwin, who called it a "rather desultory opinion [that] contains little that is of direct pertinence to the constitutional issue." "The Steel Seizure Case: A Judicial Brick without Straw," *Columbia Law Review* 53 (1953): 63.

9. *Constitutional Commentary* 19 (Spring 2002).

10. Attorney General Eric Holder, "Remarks as Prepared for Delivery by Attorney General Eric Holder at West Point's Center for the Rule of Law Grand Opening Conference," West Point, New York, April 15, 2009, http://www.usdoj.gov/ag/speeches/2009/ag-speech-090415.html.

11. White, "Justice Jackson's Draft Opinions," 1122.

blow to the doctrine of inherent executive power."[12] Yet even the George W. Bush administration relied on Jackson's concurrence to defend the electronic surveillance program conducted by the National Security Agency, and it apparently accepted the authoritativeness of Jackson's schema in the litigation that overturned the president's plan for military tribunals in *Hamdan v. Rumsfeld* in 2006.[13]

Given the preeminence of Jackson's tripartite scheme in the legal-political community, it is not surprising that members of the Supreme Court have relied upon it in important cases on presidential power, including *Dames & Moore v. Regan* (1981) (upholding President Carter's actions resolving the hostage crisis with Iran), *Hamdan v. Rumsfeld* (2006) (overturning the administration's plans for military tribunals to try suspected terrorists), and *Medellin v. Texas* (2008) (ruling that President Bush had no authority to order a state court to review its conviction and sentence of a foreign national because of a decision by the International Court of Justice).

The use of Jackson's concurrence in *Hamdan* is the most telling. Justice Anthony Kennedy addressed it formally in his concurrence, describing it as "the proper framework for assessing whether Executive actions are authorized."[14] He then found that the military commissions established by the president violated specific provisions of federal law and therefore were unauthorized. On the dissenting side, Justice Clarence Thomas also cited Jackson's concurrence but maintained that the president's actions were consistent with congressional law, thus placing the creation of the military tribunals in Jackson's first category where the president's claims are strongest.[15]

Justice John Paul Stevens, on the other hand, in his opinion for the five-member majority mentioned Jackson's concurrence only in a footnote (n. 23). It reads in full: "Whether or not the President has independent power, absent congressional authorization, to convene military commissions, he may not disregard limitations that Congress has, in proper exercise of its own war powers, placed on his powers. See *Youngstown Sheet & Tube Co. v. Sawyer,* 343 U. S. 579, 637 (1952) (Jackson, J., concurring). The Government does not argue otherwise." In its brief, the administration had developed the argument at some length that even though statute authorized the president to establish military tribunals, he also had independent constitutional authority to do so: "The president's war power under

12. David Gray Adler, "The Steel Seizure Case and Inherent Presidential Power," *Constitutional Commentary* 19 (2002): 204.

13. See Rosen, "Revisiting *Youngstown*," 1712–14.

14. *Hamdan v. Rumsfeld*, 548 U.S. 557 (2006), 638.

15. Ibid., 680.

Article II, Section 2, of the Constitution includes the inherent authority to create military commissions even in the absence of any statutory authorization, because that authority is a necessary and longstanding component of his war powers."[16] In a few sentences, which do not even appear in the body of the decision, the majority asserted that it could ignore the administration's constitutional claim because even if true, congressional statute controlled.

As Stevens explained in some detail, the military commission that would have tried Hamdan, Osama bin Laden's former driver and bodyguard, violated the Uniform Code of Military Justice (UCMJ) by incorporating procedures different from those used in courts-martial and by failing to abide by provisions of Common Article 3 of the Geneva Conventions of 1949 (incorporated by inference into federal law by Article 21 of the UCMJ), which requires that someone in Hamdan's situation be tried by a "regularly constituted court affording all the judicial guarantees which are recognized as indispensable by civilized peoples." Whatever authority the U.S. Constitution might vest in the president to establish military tribunals in an authorized war, such authority could not stand up to Congress acting "in proper exercise of its own war powers." Apparently, constitutional authority vested in Congress trumped constitutional authority vested in the president. Or so the Court interpreted Justice Jackson's concurrence.

At its core, the majority's opinion in *Hamdan* turned on a fundamental disagreement with the administration about military necessity and, implicitly, about how the U.S. Constitution vests the power to meet necessity. The majority noted, for example, the "broader inability on the Executive's part here to satisfy the most basic precondition—at least in the absence of specific congressional authorization—for establishment of military commissions: military necessity." It complained that "Hamdan's tribunal was appointed not by a military commander in the field of battle [which might indeed be necessary in wartime], but by a retired major general stationed away from any active hostilities." Hamdan's alleged offenses did not "even necessarily occur . . . during time of, or in a theater of, war." Moreover, "[a]ny urgent need for imposition or execution of judgment is utterly belied by the record."[17]

In his dissent, Justice Thomas challenged the majority's willingness to contradict the president's judgment about military necessity. In the case at hand, with both the UCMJ and the Authorization for Use of Military Force (2001) demonstrating "complete congressional sanction" of the president's actions, "our duty to defer to the Executive's military and

16. *Hamdan v. Rumsfeld*, Brief for the Respondents ("Government Merits Brief"), 21, available at http://www.hamdanvrumsfeld.com/briefs.

17. *Hamdan v. Rumsfeld*, 612.

foreign policy judgment is at its zenith."[18] Yet the Court "overrule[s] one after another of the President's judgments pertaining to the conduct of an ongoing war."[19] This is "an unprecedented departure from the traditionally limited role of the courts with respect to war and an unwarranted intrusion on executive authority."[20] Thomas particularly criticized Justice Stevens's claim that James Madison's praise of the separation of powers in *Federalist* No. 47 supported the majority's position: "[This] merely highlights the illegitimacy of today's judicial intrusion onto core executive prerogatives in the waging of war."[21] In his own critique, Justice Antonin Scalia sharply criticized his colleagues for their "audacity—to contradict [the] determination" of the president that military commissions were necessary for "the disabling, deterrence, and punishment of the mass-murdering terrorists of September 11."[22]

For the dissenters, the Court's obligation to defer to the president's judgments of military necessity derived from the Constitution's assignment of the conduct of a congressionally authorized war to the executive branch. It is "antithetical to our constitutional structure," Thomas wrote, for the Court to believe "that *it* is qualified to pass on the '[m]ilitary necessity' . . . of the Commander in Chief's decision to employ a particular form of force against our enemies."[23] By creating a unified executive branch with the ability to act decisively in times of war or crisis and by vesting the president with "[t]he executive Power" and the office of Commander in Chief, the framers "confer[red] upon the President broad constitutional authority to protect the Nation's security in the manner he deems fit."[24]

Here, Thomas virtually implored his colleagues to address and debate the large issues of presidential constitutional authority that the case seemed to demand. But they refused to do so. Indeed, in none of the three opinions by the members of the majority is there any exploration of the nature of the president's constitutional powers or their relevance to establishing military tribunals to try combatants who violate the laws of war. The majority justices did not refute the administration's claim; they ignored it. And they believed they could do so because Justice Robert Jackson's lone concurrence in a case on a very different matter half a century before had apparently authoritatively established that the powers that the U.S. Constitution vests in Congress supersede the powers it vests in the president.

18. Ibid., 682.
19. Ibid., 706.
20. Ibid., 684.
21. Ibid., 691.
22. Ibid., 674–75.
23. Ibid., 678 (emphasis in original).
24. Ibid., 679.

As both Michael Mukasey and Senator Russ Feingold recognized in Mukasey's confirmation hearings, and as *Hamdan v. Rumsfeld* clearly illustrates, Jackson's schema prejudices the case against presidential claims of independent constitutional authority. Yet, as will become clear, Jackson's concurrence rests on nothing less than a fundamental misinterpretation of the U.S. Constitution. Even the friends of a strong constitutional presidency have largely failed to recognize both its faulty foundations and its dangerous implications for presidential power under the Constitution.[25]

Parsing Executive Power

In his concurrence, Jackson delineates his tripartite schema after three introductory paragraphs. The first two paragraphs disparage the value of "conventional materials of judicial decision" for resolving issues of presidential power.[26] He notes the "poverty of really useful and unambiguous authority applicable to concrete problems of executive power as they actually present themselves."[27] In an often quoted passage, he compares the historical records one might consult to determine what the framers intended for executive power to "materials almost as enigmatic as the dreams Joseph was called upon to interpret for Pharaoh," and he notes that quotations from authorities on each side of the debate on presidential power "largely cancel each other."[28] This is a striking concession at the beginning of an opinion that runs forty paragraphs long. What, one might ask, is the alternative to "conventional materials of judicial decision" when a Supreme Court justice needs to determine whether a president has acted beyond his authority? On what does Justice Jackson ground his opinion if not on these "conventional materials"?

Jackson further sharpens the issue in his third paragraph, which begins by denying that "[t]he actual art of governing under our Constitution" can "conform to judicial definitions of the power of any of its branches based on isolated clauses or even single Articles torn from context."[29] He moves on quickly from here, but it is useful to pause and ask just what this means. The issue before the Court, after all, is one of presidential power. With the exception of the veto power, the president's constitutional powers and responsibilities are specified in Article II of the U.S. Constitution.

25. A conspicuous exception is "Some Thoughts on Youngstown Steel," an insightful critique posted by attorney John Hinderaker on the "Powerline" blog on January 1, 2006, http://www.powerlineblog.com/archives/2006/01/012513.php.

26. *Youngstown*, 634.

27. Ibid.

28. Ibid, 634–35.

29. Ibid., 635.

Among those that the government cited to justify Truman's seizure of the steel mills were (a) the "executive Power" with which Article II opens—"The executive Power shall be vested in a President of the United States of America"; (b) the oath requiring the president to "faithfully execute the Office of President" and to "preserve, protect and defend the Constitution of the United States"; (c) the power to serve as "Commander in Chief of the Army and Navy of the United States"; and (d) the president's duty to "take Care that the Laws be faithfully executed."[30] Yet, at the beginning of his long and detailed legal opinion, Jackson appears to reject the value of analyzing what these or other individual clauses mean, and even what Article II as a whole means (rejecting judicial definitions of "even single Articles torn from their context"). For reasons not specified, the "actual art of governing under our Constitution *does not and cannot conform*" to a judicial understanding of the meaning of the powers vested by Article II of the Constitution.[31]

Perhaps the key to Jackson's point is the qualification "torn from their context." The "context" here must be the Constitution as a whole. The verb "torn" suggests that some violence is done to the Constitution if the clauses of Article II, and Article II as a whole, are analyzed and interpreted apart from the entire Constitution. Now it is certainly true that one cannot fully understand the president's constitutional powers—and his place in the constitutional order—without considering Congress's powers, and perhaps also those of the Supreme Court. Yet, the converse is also true. One cannot fully understand the Constitution without understanding its individual clauses and articles. Unless one understands, for example, what it means for the president to hold the "executive Power," to be "Commander in Chief," and to have the responsibility to "take Care that the Laws be faithfully executed," one cannot really understand the Constitution as a whole. Moreover, unless one understands the purpose and meaning of Article II, one cannot understand the separation-of-powers system established in the fundamental law. Why, then, begin an analysis of the constitutionality of presidential action by denigrating the value of exploring the meaning of the individual clauses of Article II and the article as a whole? How can such an approach do justice to a presidential claim to act in accordance with powers and responsibilities vested by Article II?

Immediately following, Jackson writes, in a now famous passage: "While the Constitution diffuses power the better to secure liberty, it

30. See the Government's brief in *Youngstown*, esp. 27–29, 96–102, in *Landmark Briefs and Arguments of the Supreme Court of the United States: Constitutional Law*, ed. Philip B. Kurland and Gerhard Casper (Arlington, VA: University Publications of America, 1975), vol. 48.

31. *Youngstown*, 635 (emphasis added).

also contemplates that practice will integrate the dispersed powers into a workable government. It enjoins upon its branches separateness but inter-dependence, autonomy but reciprocity."[32] At one level, such a thumbnail description of American separation of powers hardly seems objection-able. Yet to say that the Constitution "diffuses power" is unnecessarily imprecise, and perhaps even confusing; for what the Constitution does is divide the powers of government into the three great types—legisla-tive, executive, and judicial—and assign each type to an institution spe-cially structured to exercise those powers effectively. As James Madison noted in *The Federalist*, in designing a separation of powers constitu-tion, one begins by "discriminating . . . in theory, the several classes of power, as they may in their nature be legislative, executive, or judiciary."[33] This older and familiar way to describe American separation of powers has the virtue, lost in the "diffuses power" formulation, of reminding us that there is such a thing as executive power by nature and that it was assigned to the presidency.

Jackson's very next sentence reveals the implications of obscuring this traditional understanding of separation of powers: "Presidential powers are not fixed but fluctuate, depending upon their disjunction or con-junction with those of Congress."[34] Few commentators have noted just how problematic this statement is.[35] The presidency is a constitutional office, not an agency of the Congress, and receives its powers directly from the Constitution. This is the standard—and accurate—textbook understanding of the office. As political scientist Richard Pious affirmed in his comprehensive and widely read text, *The American Presidency*, "[Article II] made it clear that the powers of the office, especially the enumerated powers that followed, were derived from the Constitution, not derived from or limited by the legislative powers granted Congress in Article I. The powers of the president were not those of Congress to confer upon the executive, nor could they be modified or rescinded by congressional action."[36] Here the framers were consciously remedying a major defect of most of the new state constitutions, whose authors had

32. Ibid.

33. Alexander Hamilton, James Madison, and John Jay, *The Federalist Papers*, ed. Jacob E. Cooke (Middletown, CT: Wesleyan University Press, 1961), No. 48.

34. *Youngstown*, 635.

35. Two who have are Hinderaker, "Some Thoughts on Youngstown Steel," and Patricia L. Bellia, "Executive Power in *Youngstown*'s Shadows," *Constitutional Commentary* 19 (Spring 2002): 93, 149.

36. Richard M. Pious, *The American Presidency* (New York: Basic Books, 1979), 29. See also Charles C. Thach Jr., *The Creation of the Presidency, 1775–1789: A Study in Consti-tutional History* (Indianapolis: Liberty Fund, 2007; originally published by Johns Hopkins University Press, 1923). As Thach notes in his discussion of the Committee of Detail's draft constitution at the Constitutional Convention, "The executive . . . came out [of the

intentionally subordinated the new governors to the legislative will. As Charles Thach showed nearly a century ago, a "fundamental weakness [of the early state constitutions] was the common practice of expressly submitting the exercise of either certain enumerated powers, the field of enumerated powers, or even the whole of the executive power to the legislative will."[37] Under the U.S. Constitution, by contrast, the executive department had "independent possession . . . of its powers by direct grant of the people."[38]

Whether or not the opening words of Article II—"The executive Power shall be vested in a President"—actually vest power, there can be no question that the specific powers and duties detailed in Sections 2 and 3 of Article II *are* fixed. Indeed, that is why they were written into Article II. The president, for example, possesses the constitutional power "to grant Reprieves and Pardons." This power is fixed in the Constitution and emphatically *does not* fluctuate depending on its "disjunction or conjunction with [the powers] . . . of Congress." The same is true for the president's powers to require written opinions from department heads, to make recess appointments, to recommend measures to Congress, to convene Congress on extraordinary occasions, to receive ambassadors, or to take care the laws are faithfully executed. (Two powers by their very terms—making treaties and appointing judges and high-level executives—are shared with the Senate.)

This is not to deny that some powers might be affected by congressional action. If Congress declares war against a foreign nation with which the United States was previously at peace, the president as commander in chief will have more effective power than he would have had in the absence of the declaration of war. But the commander-in-chief power—fixed in the Constitution—limits what Congress can do. Congress cannot, obviously, appoint some favored general to serve as commander in chief and have that officer report directly to Congress. It cannot interfere with the chain of command. It cannot, as Chief Justice Samuel P. Chase wrote in *Ex parte Milligan* (approvingly quoted by the majority in *Hamdan*), "direct the conduct of campaigns."[39] Congress may, however, bring a war to an end by refusing to fund it.

---

committee] not only with additional powers, but with all of them granted in terms which left no loophole for subsequent legislative interference. What have come to be known as the political powers were now the President's, and the President's alone, so far as the Constitution itself could settle the matter" (103).

37. Thach, *Creation of the Presidency*, 17.

38. Ibid., 104.

39. *Hamdan v. Rumsfeld*, 591–92. Not all scholars agree that the commander-in-chief clause constrains Congress in this way. See especially David J. Barron and Martin S. Lederman, "The Commander in Chief at the Lowest Ebb: Framing the Problem, Doctrine, and

By the terms of the Constitution, each branch has the final say on some matters, including national security actions. In the end Congress gets to decide whether the United States should be at war with another nation; what limits to place on an "imperfect war" (i.e., something less than a "total war"); how large, and what kind of, a military to provide for conducting the war; and what monetary resources to commit to the effort. But in exercising these powers, Congress must respect the president's "final say" as commander in chief to issue the military orders that he believes will most effectively achieve victory in an authorized war. The fundamental point is that Congress is not the arbiter of the president's constitutional powers, even though in some situations it may affect the exercise of presidential powers when it exercises its own constitutional powers.

At this point Jackson introduces his now famous schema: "We may well begin by a somewhat over-simplified grouping of practical situations in which a President may doubt, or others may challenge, his powers, and by distinguishing roughly the legal consequences of this factor of relativity."[40] Here is his sketch in full, with only Jackson's footnotes omitted:

1. When the President acts pursuant to an express or implied authorization of Congress, his authority is at its maximum, for it includes all that he possesses in his own right plus all that Congress can delegate. In these circumstances, and in these only, may he be said (for what it may be worth) to personify the federal sovereignty. If his act is held unconstitutional under these circumstances, it usually means that the Federal Government as an undivided whole lacks power. A seizure executed by the President pursuant to an Act of Congress would be supported by the strongest of presumptions and the widest latitude of judicial interpretation, and the burden of persuasion would rest heavily upon any who might attack it.

2. When the President acts in absence of either a congressional grant or denial of authority, he can only rely upon his own independent powers, but there is a zone of twilight in which he and Congress may have concurrent authority, or in which its distribution is uncertain. Therefore, congressional inertia,

Original Understanding," *Harvard Law Review* 121, no. 3 (January 2008): 689–804, and "The Commander in Chief at the Lowest Ebb: A Constitutional History," *Harvard Law Review* 121, no. 4 (February 2008): 941–1112. Although Barron and Lederman seem to hold that Congress may constitutionally control even battlefield tactics, they concede that the commander-in-chief clause establishes "some indefeasible core of presidential superintendence of the army and navy." "[W]e think it would be hard to deny," they write, "that there is some such superintendence core." Thus, "Congress cannot, even by statute, appoint a federal officer to be the commander in chief of the armed forces" (1102). It follows, then, that even for Barron and Lederman, Presidents have independent constitutional powers, however narrowly defined, that Congress may not infringe.

40. *Youngstown*, 635.

indifference or quiescence may sometimes, at least as a practical matter, enable, if not invite, measures on independent presidential responsibility. In this area, any actual test of power is likely to depend on the imperatives of events and contemporary imponderables rather than on abstract theories of law.

3. When the President takes measures incompatible with the expressed or implied will of Congress, his power is at its lowest ebb, for then he can rely only upon his own constitutional powers minus any constitutional powers of Congress over the matter. Courts can sustain exclusive presidential control in such a case only by disabling the Congress from acting upon the subject. Presidential claim to a power at once so conclusive and preclusive must be scrutinized with caution, for what is at stake is the equilibrium established by our constitutional system.[41]

In the first category are presidential actions "pursuant to an express or implied authorization of Congress." In these situations, the president's authority is at its maximum, and only here—"In these circumstances, and in these only"—can it be said that the president "personif[ies] the federal sovereignty." As with many other passages in Jackson's concurrence, commentators tend to pass over this one without comment. Yet, it is demonstrably *not* true that presidents represent the federal sovereignty only when they act "pursuant to an express or implied authorization of Congress." When, for example, they pardon offenses, negotiate treaties, receive ambassadors, or issue lawful military orders in response to an attack on the United States, they emphatically represent "the federal sovereignty." In doing these things, they require no authorization from Congress, express or implied. Here they represent the federal sovereignty because the Constitution vests them with the requisite authority. To deny that the president ever represents, or personifies, the federal sovereignty is seemingly to deny the essence of American constitutionalism: that each branch derives its powers and duties from the people through the Constitution and is authorized to act independently on their behalf in appropriate ways.

In the second category are presidential actions that Congress has neither authorized nor prohibited. Here the president "can only rely upon his own independent powers." What follows is the famous qualifier: "[B]ut there is a zone of twilight in which he and Congress may have concurrent authority, or in which its distribution is uncertain." The problem here is that Jackson has placed two very different situations (legally and practically) into one category, thus obscuring the difference. In one case, the president acts independently but there is no overlap with congressional authority, as in pardoning offenders. In the other case, the

41. Ibid., 635–38.

president's powers may overlap with those of Congress, resulting in "a zone of twilight" in which the two branches possess "concurrent authority" or the "distribution is uncertain." Distinguishing these two situations clarifies what Jackson's schema tends to conceal: presidents often act on their own independent authority in a way that does *not* overlap with the powers of Congress. When they do so, we are in a zone of sunlight, not twilight. Given Jackson's melding of two different situations into one category, it is no surprise that many simply refer to Jackson's second category as the "twilight zone" category.

Finally, in the third category are presidential actions that are "incompatible with the expressed or implied will of Congress." Although Jackson does not explicitly insist that Congress always wins in such a clash, his standard for resolving such conflicts amounts to as much whenever Congress has some constitutional basis for acting; for in these situations the president "can rely only upon his own constitutional powers minus any constitutional powers of Congress over the matter." Or, as Justice Stevens wrote for the Court in *Hamdan*, "[the president] may not disregard limitations that Congress has, in proper exercise of its own war powers, placed on his powers." It follows that for both Jackson and the *Hamdan* majority, the constitutional powers of Congress trump the constitutional powers of the president.

A visual image makes the point clearly. Imagine a simple Venn diagram with two overlapping circles. One circle represents the constitutional powers of the president and the other the constitutional powers of Congress. Where they overlap, we have concurrent powers. Depending on one's understanding of the Constitution, there may be a lot of overlap or a little, but few would deny at least some overlap. How does the overlap affect the president's powers when the actions of the two branches conflict? Jackson says that we must subtract from the president's "own constitutional powers" "any constitutional powers of Congress over the matter." Thus, on our Venn diagram, remove from the circle of presidential powers the shape formed by the overlap of the two circles. When the two constitutional powers overlap, Congress retains all its authority, while the president loses all overlapping powers to Congress.[42]

Why should this be so? What is the principle of American constitutionalism that would give Congress's constitutional powers preeminence over the president's constitutional powers? The U.S. Constitution does not rank the constitutional powers of the three branches of government. The powers of no one branch are more constitutional, or more authoritative,

---

42. In "Revisiting *Youngstown*," Mark Rosen calls this the principle of "categorical congressional supremacy." He then analyzes in great detail alternative rules for resolving conflicts "when identical authority rests with two or more institutions" (1717–45).

than those of another. It is an old doctrine that each branch is supreme within its own proper sphere.

Despite its widespread acceptance, Jackson's schema for evaluating the constitutionality of presidential actions appears to rest on a very different view. In denying that the president ever represents the federal sovereignty on his own authority, in obscuring the breadth of independent constitutional authority vested in the president, and in maintaining that when they overlap Congress's constitutional authorities trump the president's, Jackson pushes from view the nature and reach of the president's "own constitutional powers."

Perhaps Jackson can be rescued from this conclusion if we revisit a possible qualification we passed over in his sentence that introduces the three categories. The categories cover situations "in which a President may doubt, or others may challenge, his powers." Perhaps the categories do not cover all situations but only those where there is real doubt about the president's claim. No one, for example, doubts that the president alone possesses the pardoning power; so this power, it might be argued, is not even covered by the three categories. But this interpretation is belied by three considerations. First, virtually everyone, including justices of the Supreme Court, interprets Jackson's categories as covering the whole field and not as some subset of a larger range of cases. Second, they do this because Jackson's language by its own terms describes three mutually exclusive and exhaustive categories: the president acts consistently with Congress's will, the president acts in the absence of congressional action either way, or the president acts against Congress's will. Finally, category two itself includes the president relying upon "his own independent powers," which presumably includes the provisions of Article II of the Constitution. So, these powers, whose reach is often undisputed, are within the four corners of the schema, however diminished in importance.

After detailing his schema, Jackson argues that Truman's seizure fell into the third category and thus faced "the severe tests under the third grouping, where it can be supported only by any remainder of executive power after subtraction of such powers as Congress may have over the subject. In short, we can sustain the President only by holding that seizure of such strike-bound industries is within his domain and beyond control by Congress."[43] Lest there be any doubt as to the implications of category three, this formulation directly restates the principle of congressional supremacy. The phrase "remainder of executive power" captures the point clearly. In the absence of congressional action, the president has a certain amount of power under the Constitution; but if Congress asserts its own constitutional authority in a way that conflicts with or overlaps

43. *Youngstown*, 640.

presidential authority, executive power shrinks. A process of "subtraction" reduces the president's authority to act. Thus, the "remainder of executive power" is something less than what the Constitution vested in the president before Congress acted. Later, Jackson argues that Congress had prohibited seizures of the type at issue in *Youngstown*, and therefore Truman's actions were illegal.

Although it is not the purpose here to reargue the specific issues in *Youngstown*, it should be noted that the administration maintained both (a) that no law of Congress expressly prohibited the seizure in question and (b) that many laws and treaties committed the nation, in the face of the Soviet threat, to a robust national defense requiring the uninterrupted production of steel, thereby implicitly authorizing the temporary seizure of steel mills by the one constitutionally obligated to "take Care that the Laws be faithfully executed." Under (a) it can be argued that Truman's seizure was actually an example of Jackson's category two; and under (b) of category one. Indeed, as the intervening decades have shown, when legal disputes arise over presidential actions, it is often not at all clear into which Jackson category they fall, even among those who accept the soundness of the categories themselves.

As noted above, most of Jackson's opinion comes after his schema. Yet it is his three categories and their implications, more than the subsequent analysis, that have proved so powerful in debates on presidential power. Indeed, some commentators see an inconsistency, if not a contradiction, between the schema and the rest of the opinion.[44] In one passage, for example, Jackson seems to endorse a broad interpretation of the president's enumerated powers: "[B]ecause the President does not enjoy unmentioned powers does not mean that the mentioned ones should be narrowed by a niggardly construction. Some clauses could be made almost unworkable, as well as immutable, by refusal to indulge some latitude of interpretation for changing times. I have heretofore, and do now, give to the enumerated powers the scope and elasticity afforded by what seem to be reasonable, practical implications instead of the rigidity dictated by a doctrinaire textualism."[45] Yet even this passage does not deny that congressional power trumps presidential power. Moreover, the overall tone of Jackson's discussion of the president's specific powers and duties is one of constricting their reach.

Most importantly, Jackson denied that the "vesting clause" that opens Article II—"The executive Power shall be vested in a President of the United States of America"—actually vests power: "I cannot accept the view that this clause is a grant in bulk of all conceivable executive power

44. See, for example, Bellia, "Executive Power in *Youngstown*'s Shadows."
45. *Youngstown*, 640.

but regard it as an allocation to the presidential office of the generic powers *thereafter stated.*"[46] (The government had argued that the vesting clause "constitutes a grant of all the executive powers of which the Government is capable.")[47] Although the nature and reach of the vesting clause have been debated since the First Congress, a majority of that body agreed that the clause itself does vest power, including at least the power to fire high-level subordinates. In the words of House member Fisher Ames, "The Constitution places all executive power in the hands of the President."[48] James Madison, whose influence in fashioning the Constitution two years before is undisputed, concurred that "the constitution has invested all executive power in the President."[49] Similarly, in the Senate, Oliver Ellsworth (also a delegate at the Constitutional Convention and later to serve as chief justice of the Supreme Court) claimed, "There is an explicit grant to the President which contains the power of removal. The executive power is granted; not the executive power hereinafter enumerated and explained."[50] (The contrast between the views of Ellsworth and Robert Jackson could hardly be clearer.) Four years later, Alexander Hamilton, defending President Washington's Proclamation of Neutrality of 1793, described the vesting clause as a "comprehensive grant" that, subject to exceptions specified elsewhere in the Constitution, vests in the president general authority over foreign affairs and war and peace. Although Madison disputed such a broad interpretation, he did not deny that the clause itself vests power in the president.[51]

One wonders how Justice Jackson would have ruled on a modern Tenure of Office Act that required Senate concurrence to the dismissal of cabinet-level officials. If the vesting clause is nothing but "an allocation to the presidential office of the generic powers thereafter stated," and no removal power is "thereafter stated," then the president, it seems necessarily to follow, has no such power.[52] The First Congress thought otherwise, and the Supreme Court in 1926, half a century after the passage of the Tenure of Office Act by the Reconstruction Congress, ruled that

46. Ibid., 641 (emphasis added).

47. *Youngstown*, Government's brief, 96.

48. Quoted in Thach, *The Creation of the Presidency*, 131.

49. Ibid., 136.

50. Ibid., 139. This quotation is taken from notes taken by John Adams, who, as vice president, presided over the Senate debate.

51. See *The Pacificus-Helvidius Debates of 1793–1794*, ed. and introd. Morton J. Frisch (Indianapolis: Liberty Fund, 2007), esp. 12–13.

52. Article II does, of course, explicitly vest the appointment power. But for high-level executive officials, this power is shared with the Senate. If the power to remove flows not from the vesting clause but from the appointment power, then it would seem to follow that the Senate would share the removal power as well. A minority in the First Congress took this position. See Thach, *Creation of the Presidency*, 127–30.

even a postmaster first class was not immune from presidential dismissal, though federal law required Senate concurrence. Would Jackson have overruled *Myers v. United States*, despite the precedent of the First Congress and the obvious potential that Senate approval of removals would have, as Madison and others feared, of rendering the heads of executive departments subordinate to a house of Congress?[53]

What, then, of the other provisions of Article II? As shown above, Jackson begins his concurrence by effectively denying that historical research can shed light on the meaning of the powers and duties vested in the president by the Constitution. Later, he notes the "vagueness and generality of the clauses that set forth presidential powers."[54] For example, he describes the "Commander in Chief" language as "cryptic words" and a "loose appellation." Even presidential advisers "cannot say where [the power] begins or ends."[55]

Farther into his opinion, Jackson dismisses in a brief paragraph the administration's reliance on the "broad scope" of the president's duty to "take Care that the Laws be faithfully executed."[56] He does so with no mention of the invocation of the "take Care" clause by President George Washington to put down the Whiskey Rebellion in 1794, by President Andrew Jackson to face down South Carolina in the nullification crisis of 1832, and by President Abraham Lincoln to justify emergency measures after the attack on Fort Sumter in 1861.[57] Nor does Jackson discuss the government's reliance on the broad interpretation of the "take Care" clause by the Supreme Court itself in *In re Neagle* (1890), the leading Court case on the meaning and reach of this constitutional duty. There the Court held that the president's duty was not limited to "the enforcement of acts of Congress or of treaties of the United States according to their *express terms*" but also "include[s] the rights, duties and obligations growing out of the Constitution itself, our international relations, and all the protection implied by the nature of the government under

53. *Myers v. United States*, 272 U.S. 52 (1926). See also Thach, *Creation of the Presidency*, "Chapter VI: The Removal Debate," 126–49.

54. *Youngstown*, 647.

55. Ibid., 641. Hinderaker, "Some Thoughts on Youngstown Steel," argues that although "Jackson's analysis might have some plausibility in domestic affairs, where the President and Congress both have major, and potentially overlapping, areas of responsibility, . . . it has no application to the President's powers as Commander in Chief."

56. *Youngstown*, Government's brief, 98.

57. See Washington's proclamations of September 15, 1792 (http://www.presidency.ucsb.edu/ws/index.php?pid=65427&st=&st1=) and September 25, 1794 (http://www.presidency.ucsb.edu/ws/index.php?pid=65478&st=&st1=); Jackson's proclamation of December 10, 1832 (http://www.presidency.ucsb.edu/ws/index.php?pid=67078&st=&st1=); and Lincoln's Message to Congress in Special Session, July 4, 1861 (http://www.presidency.ucsb.edu/ws/index.php?pid=69802&st=&st1=).

the Constitution."[58] Although one need not conclude that these precedents justified Truman's seizure, they seem to merit at least some attention by anyone interested in evaluating the president's high constitutional responsibilities.

Recovering the President's Powers and Duties

Jackson's concurrence in *Youngstown*, with its "three now-canonical categories that guide modern analysis of separation of powers,"[59] has done much to distort clear thinking about the president's constitutional powers and duties. In legal discourse, it has virtually replaced an older view of the president's constitutional responsibilities with deep roots in American history and in the provisions of Article II of the U.S. Constitution. Robert Jackson, himself, while serving as President Franklin Roosevelt's attorney general, recurred to this older understanding when he defended the president's seizure of the North American Aviation Company in June 1941, six months before the United States was officially at war:

> The Constitution lays upon the President the duty "to take care that the laws be faithfully executed." Among the laws which he is required to find means to execute are those which direct him to equip an enlarged army, to provide for a strengthened navy, to protect Government property, to protect those who are engaged in carrying out the business of the Government, and to carry out the provisions of the Lend-Lease Act. For the faithful execution of such laws the President has back of him not only each general law-enforcement power conferred by the various acts of Congress but the aggregate of all such laws plus that wide discretion as to method vested in him by the Constitution for the purpose of executing the laws.
>
> The Constitution also places on the President the responsibility and vests in him the powers of Commander in Chief of the Army and of the Navy. These weapons for the protection of the continued existence of the Nation are placed in his sole command and the implication is clear that he should not allow them to become paralyzed by failure to obtain supplies for which Congress has appropriated the money and which it has directed the President to obtain.[60]

Not surprisingly, when the administration's lawyers defended Truman's temporary seizure of the steel mills—Truman twice reported to

---

58. *In re Neagle*, 135 U.S. 1 (1890), 64 (emphasis in original). See also the Government's brief in *Youngstown*, 98–102, 144–150.

59. Neal K. Katyal and Laurence H. Tribe, "Waging War, Deciding Guilt: Trying the Military Tribunals," *Yale Law Journal* 111 (2002): 1274.

60. Quoted in *Youngstown*, Government's brief, 149–50.

Congress that he would abide by any action Congress might take[61]—
they embraced these broad interpretations of the "take Care" duty and
the commander-in-chief power. Confronted with his prior statements
during oral arguments, Jackson responded, "I claimed everything, of
course, like every other Attorney General does. It was a custom that did
not leave the Department of Justice when I did."[62] And in the concurrence itself Jackson dismissed his broad defense of FDR's constitutional
authorities as "self-serving press statements of the attorney for one of
the interested parties."[63]

Scholars who embrace Jackson's tripartite scheme have not been much
bothered by the justice's facile disavowal of his previous broad interpretation of the president's constitutional powers and duties. Jackson seems
to say that he did not really believe the earlier arguments but was simply
doing his job as the president's advocate. But this is deeply troubling if
it suggests that an attorney general's highest responsibility is to serve
the president rather than the Constitution and the laws. And, indeed, we
know of at least one case—FDR and the Lend-lease Act—where Attorney General Jackson privately resisted FDR's expansive interpretation
of presidential powers: "As Jackson's description of that episode made
clear, where Jackson felt unable to submit to the President a legal opinion
favorable to the President's position, he simply did not."[64]

More likely, and perhaps truer to the man's character, is that service
for seven years as an attorney in the executive branch, including two as
solicitor general and more than a year as attorney general, had attuned
Jackson to the constitutional arguments in support of an energetic presidency. Indeed, the framers had intentionally designed their institutions to
incline public officials to defend aggressively the constitutional prerogatives of their branch. "The interest of the man," Publius wrote, "must be
connected with the constitutional rights of the place."[65]

Article II is the touchstone of the president's independent powers and
duties. In a recent essay, Gary Schmitt and I urge the recovery of its logic
and meaning.[66] We maintain that the executive article is more tightly

61. See *Youngstown*, Chief Justice Vinson, dissenting (joined by Justices Reed and Min-
ton), 675–77.

62. Quoted in White, "Justice Jackson's Draft Opinions in *The Steel Seizure Cases*,"
1132.

63. *Youngstown*, 647.

64. White, "Justice Jackson's Draft Opinions in *The Steel Seizure Cases*," 1132–33.

65. Madison, *Federalist* No. 51, 319.

66. Joseph M. Bessette and Gary J. Schmitt, "The Powers and Duties of the President:
Recovering the Logic and Meaning of Article II," in *The Constitutional Presidency*, ed. Joseph
M. Bessette and Jeffrey K. Tulis (Baltimore: Johns Hopkins University Press, 2009), 28–53.

drawn, more precise, and less enigmatic than is often thought, and is thus a more reliable guide to the reach and limits of the president's constitutional authority than many recognize. In particular, we argue that Article II is structured, or organized, around the distinction between powers and duties; that, broadly speaking, the former—such as the commander-in-chief power—are the means, or instruments, for achieving the latter; and that consequently it is duty that lies at the heart of the constitutional presidency.

Among the highest of the president's duties are those to "take Care that the Laws be faithfully executed" and to "preserve, protect and defend the Constitution of the United States." Abraham Lincoln understood these provisions to give the president a special responsibility to meet national emergencies. With Congress out of session at the outbreak of the Civil War, he believed that he had authority to act for the government as a whole, that "no choice was left but to call out the war power of the Government."[67] In so doing, he took several actions that exceeded his normal powers, such as increasing the size of the army and navy, blockading southern ports, and suspending habeas corpus. Conceding that some of these actions might not have been "strictly legal," Lincoln defended them as justified by "what appeared to be a popular demand and a public necessity, trusting then, as now, that Congress would readily ratify them."[68]

In the special session convened by Lincoln on July 4, 1861, Congress ratified the president's acts, although it took nearly two years before it passed a statute that regulated Lincoln's suspensions of habeas corpus (the Habeas Corpus Act passed on March 3, 1863). And in the *Prize Cases* of 1863, the Supreme Court ruled that the seizures of ships caught attempting to run the blockade of southern ports had full legal force, even if they occurred before Congress officially ratified the president's military actions.[69] Also, a year and a half after the Civil War began, Lincoln drew on his independent constitutional power as "Commander in Chief of the Army and Navy of the United States in time of actual armed rebellion" to free several million slaves then behind enemy lines. He called this "a fit and necessary war measure for suppressing said rebellion" and "an act of justice, warranted by the Constitution upon military necessity."[70] When some charged that he had no constitutional authority to free slaves, he

67. Abraham Lincoln, "Message to Congress in Special Session," July 4, 1861, available at http://www.presidency.ucsb.edu/ws/index.php?pid=69802&st=&st1=.

68. Ibid.

69. *Prize Cases*, 67 U.S. 635 (1863).

70. Abraham Lincoln, "Emancipation Proclamation," January 1, 1863, http://www.presidency.ucsb.edu/ws/index.php?pid=69880&st=&st1=.

responded that "the constitution invests its commander-in-chief, with the law of war, in time of war."[71]

Throughout the Civil War, Lincoln defended his actions as both necessary and constitutional. Perhaps most controversial were his suspensions of habeas corpus, especially after Chief Justice Roger B. Taney ruled in late May 1861, that the military arrest of John Merryman, suspected of rebellious activities in Maryland, was illegal because only Congress could suspend habeas corpus. Lincoln ignored Taney's order to release Merryman and offered an extended defense of his actions in his message to Congress of July 4, 1861, thereby responding to the charge that the constitutional officer pledged to "'take care that the laws be faithfully executed' . . . [had] himself violate[d] them."[72]

In defending his actions, Lincoln drew on a broad interpretation of the "take Care" clause and the oath of office:

> The whole of the laws which were required to be faithfully executed were being resisted and failing of execution in nearly one-third of the States. Must they be allowed to finally fail of execution, even had it been perfectly clear that by the use of the means necessary to their execution some single law, made in such extreme tenderness of the citizen's liberty that practically it relieves more of the guilty than of the innocent, should to a very limited extent be violated? To state the question more directly, Are all the laws *but one* to go unexecuted, and the Government itself go to pieces lest that one be violated? Even in such a case, would not the official oath be broken if the Government should be overthrown when it was believed that disregarding the single law would tend to preserve it?[73]

Though Lincoln went on to deny that he had broken the habeas corpus clause of the Constitution—"it was not believed that any law was violated"—he stated the broader principle publicly and unambiguously: the president's duties to take care that the laws are faithfully executed and to preserve, protect, and defend the Constitution might justify violating some specific law to preserve the whole body of law. In so arguing, Lincoln embraced the Hamilton–Madison interpretation in *The Federalist* that the national government had sufficient powers to meet every contingency: "The circumstances that endanger the safety of nations are infinite, and for this reason no constitutional shackles can wisely be imposed on the power to which the care of it is committed."[74]

71. Abraham Lincoln, "Letter to James C. Conkling," August 26, 1863, in *Collected Works of Abraham Lincoln*, 9 vols., ed. Roy P. Basler (New Brunswick, NJ: Rutgers University Press, 1953), 6:408.
72. Lincoln, "Message to Congress in Special Session."
73. Ibid.
74. Hamilton, *Federalist* No. 23, 149. See also Nos. 25, 31, and 41.

In *Federalist* No. 70, Hamilton had argued that republican government needs "a vigorous executive" to be successful. "Energy in the executive," he insisted, "is a leading character in the definition of good government."[75] Lincoln's is but the most dramatic example of the vigorous American executive in action. And, as Lincoln's example shows, when American presidents act on a broad understanding of their powers and duties, they (or their subordinates) usually make a constitutional argument in their defense.[76] Though we seem to have forgotten it of late, American history contains a rich vein of constitutional arguments in support of an independent and energetic presidency. In addition to Lincoln's actions and his several public justifications, important early examples include the removal power debates in the First Congress, President Washington's Proclamation of Neutrality of 1793 and its defense by Hamilton in the "Pacificus" essays, and President Jackson's defense of executive power in the early 1830s during the battle over the national bank and the nullification crisis. Later, the Supreme Court endorsed a broad understanding of executive powers and duties in such cases as the *Prize Cases* (1863), *In re Neagle* (1890), and *Myers v. United States* (1926).[77]

American constitutionalism would be well served by recovering the insights of this older tradition and rethinking the application of the powers and duties of Article II to modern exigencies. But whatever one's assessment of the evidence bearing on the nature and reach of the president's

75. Hamilton, *Federalist* No. 70.

76. The notable exception is Thomas Jefferson, who despite numerous vigorous exertions of executive power did not publicly interpret his constitutional powers broadly. In private correspondence, he defended interpreting the Constitution narrowly and going outside it when necessity required: "A strict observance of the written laws is doubtless *one* of the high duties of a good citizen, but it is not *the highest*. The laws of necessity, of self-preservation, of saving our country when in danger, are of higher obligation." Letter to John B. Colvin, September 20, 1810, http://press-pubs.uchicago.edu/founders/documents/a2_3s8.html (emphasis in original). Yet, as Jefferson's approval of the purchase of the Louisiana Territory demonstrates, even acts not necessary for survival and beyond the Constitution might be justified if productive of a great good for the nation. Interestingly, in his *Youngstown* concurrence, Justice Jackson quotes Jefferson's letter in 1803 in which he admits that in authorizing the offer to purchase the Louisiana Territory from France he did "an act beyond the Constitution." If the Congress ratified the treaty and paid for the purchase, the members must, Jefferson said, "throw themselves on their country for doing for them unauthorized, what we know they would have done for themselves had they been in a situation to do it." *Youngstown*, 639.

77. I have omitted *United States v. Curtiss-Wright* (1936), which is sometimes taken as the high-water mark of the Supreme Court's interpretation of presidential power, because the majority opinion turns not on a broad reading of the clauses of Article II but on congressional delegation and the powers of sovereignty not vested by the Constitution itself.

powers and duties, it is time to recognize that Justice Robert Jackson's famous and influential concurrence in *Youngstown v. Sawyer* rests on a principle of congressional supremacy that is foreign to the nation's fundamental law, that distorts modern debates on executive power, and that hinders our efforts to understand how the American Constitution confronts wars and emergencies.

11

War and Constitutional Change

MARK E. BRANDON

> Winston could not definitely remember a time
> when his country had not been at war, but it was
> evident that there had been a fairly long interval
> of peace during his childhood. . . . Since about
> that time, war had been literally continuous,
> though strictly speaking it had not always been
> the same war.
> —George Orwell, *1984*

> The accretion of dangerous power does not come
> in a day. It does come, however slowly, from the
> generative force of unchecked disregard of the
> restrictions that fence in even the most disinter-
> ested assertion of authority.
> —*The Steel Seizure Case* (1952) (Frankfurter, J., concurring)

Thesis

As Walter Murphy has cogently demonstrated, maintaining a constitutional democracy is a subtle, demanding enterprise even under the best
of circumstances.[1] For obvious reasons, the demands of maintenance
can be acute in time of war. This is not to suggest, however, that war is
always to be avoided. An uncertain, dangerous, or threatening international environment can make the use of armed force a rational policy for
a political order aiming to protect, maintain, or strengthen itself. This is
all the more true if the order is attacked or invaded, when physical or
political survival may be at stake. But, even when the pursuit of war is

---

1. See Walter F. Murphy, *Constitutional Democracy: Creating and Maintaining a Just
Political Order* (Baltimore: Johns Hopkins University Press, 2007). In prior work, I have
used the term "constitutionalist" to denominate a form of politics roughly equivalent
to Murphy's "constitutional democracy." For the most part in this essay, I use the terms
interchangeably.

rational, its claims on a nation's resources can be substantial, in terms both fiscal and human, both during a conflict and after its cessation. War may entail other, "constitutional" costs as well. The ironic upshot of these costs is that, in attempting to maintain or preserve itself, a constitutional order can end up substantially altering its constitution. By "constitution" in this context, I have in mind institutional structure, institutional functions, fundamental values, and political ethos.

Still, as we observe the experiences of orders that call themselves constitutional democracies, we can see that some such orders seem to cope with the stresses of armed conflict quite nicely, thank you. Take the experience of the United States, for example. The United States has a long history of warfare, from its war of secession from Britain to its present open-ended and ambiguous wars against terrorism.[2] By "warfare" I have in mind three types of armed conflict: declared wars; actions that, though undeclared, are reasonably classifiable as wars; and significant military actions that fall short of wars. With respect to the third category, "significant" suggests a connection with one or more of several criteria: duration, level of commitment of troops or other resources, form or intensity of conflict, and the historical or strategic importance of the conflict or the location.

In the first type, we may include the United States' six declared wars, from the Revolution to World War II. The second type includes ten undeclared wars, from the Naval War with France in the eighteenth century to the current war in Iraq. The third type refers to a wide range of conflicts, including military campaigns against the native tribes, various invasions of Latin America, and interventions in Africa, Asia, and elsewhere. It does not include, however, limited actions to protect consulates, rescue citizens, or protect trade. Nor does it include a host of isolated retaliations against foreigners abroad for insulting, hurting, or killing Americans. Nor, finally, do I count the Cold War as a war (declared or undeclared) or a significant military action. The Cold War was a long-term strategically significant conflict, characterized by massive mobilization of armaments and armed personnel, but in and of itself, the Cold War did not fit the typology that I have described. To be sure, the Cold War did periodically produce directly visible hostilities, such as the action in Korea, the invasion of Cuba, the Cuban Missile Crisis, and the armed conflicts in Vietnam, Laos, and Cambodia. Thus, although I do not include the Cold War per se, I do count as wars or significant military actions those discrete or "proxy" conflicts that it spawned. I believe, however, that, were we to include the Cold War, it would strengthen my thesis.

---

2. This essay borrows from an earlier article: Mark E. Brandon, "War and American Constitutional Order," *Vanderbilt Law Review* 56 (2003): 1815.

Using these types and criteria, I conclude that, beginning in 1776, the United States engaged in wars or significant military actions for 52 percent of the years of its early national existence in the eighteenth century. In the nineteenth century, that figure rose to 72 percent. In the twentieth century, the figure rose to 94 percent. And so far the United States has been at war during every year of the twenty-first century. In connection with these claims, I should note two things. First, in calculating time, I am not necessarily claiming in any given case that a war or military action was continuous throughout a given year or period. I observe only that a war or military action occurred during a year. Hence, the fact that the percentage of years in which wars or military actions have occurred has risen across the centuries is as much a function of the frequency of discrete conflicts as it is about the duration of conflicts. Second, as I have already suggested, the country has engaged in armed conflicts of several types and for many purposes. It has engaged in conflicts large and small, when the nation has been weak and when strong, when it has initiated conflict and when it has responded to actions of others, and when warfare has been optional and when it has been a practical necessity. In light of this experience, I have described the United States as a warrior state. We need not think of this as a martial state, nor a regime that glorifies war, nor one in which the military controls the administration of state, nor one that is overtly and comprehensively organized for militarist purposes. It is, however, a state in which the pursuit of war has become a way of life.

Intuition might suggest that a nation with such a history of persistent warfare would suffer materially and geopolitically, not to mention constitutionally. But, despite its history, the United States has flourished materially and strengthened its position in the world, and has done so while maintaining some of the most important features of a constitutional democracy: institutions authorized by and accountable to the people, limitations on governmental power (through the designation of purposes for governmental action, the specification of rights, and the diffusion of power), and the rule of law (i.e., the regularization of processes for making and enforcing public norms). The country has also substantially conserved its constitutional text, with the notable exceptions of the addition of the Bill of Rights and of momentous alterations in the period following the Civil War.

There might be any number of reasons the United States has succeeded materially and geopolitically despite the potentially enervating effects of armed conflict. One is the good fortune to occupy a continent that is rich in resources and relatively secure against external invasion. Another (perhaps less plausible) reason is the possibility that the country has regularly enjoyed the leadership of wise and virtuous statesmen. Still another is that war itself has strengthened the nation materially and geopolitically. To the extent that the nation has succeeded militarily, it has acquired advantages of physical security in protecting its borders from external assault and reinforcing its domestic authority. It has strengthened its status and influence in spheres of international relations. And it has promoted domestic prosperity by acquiring massive amounts of new territory, securing outlets for economic products, and preserving access to critical resources. If the hypothesis that war engenders strength is apt, then Thucydides' observation, that "the strong do what they can and the weak suffer what they must,"[3] may be as pertinent to constitutional democracies as to less enlightened polities.

There is one other possible explanation for the country's economic prosperity and geopolitical influence, not to mention its apparent formal political stability—an explanation that does not depend on the assumption that war tends to breed (or preserve) strength. Simply, the United States is a well-constructed political system. The system's advantages are a function of any number of characteristics, including intelligent institutional design (i.e., structure, limits, and processes)[4] and a diverse constitutional culture comprised of citizens who are attached not only to the nation but also to the idea of constitutional democracy. In short, according to this explanation, a well-constructed polity may inhibit the vicissitudes and corrosive qualities of persistent armed conflict. This may also explain the apparent confidence that underwrites the nation's self-conception, as well as its relations with others.

Still, formal stability and self-confidence alone do not necessarily signify that the order is maintaining itself in a manner consistent with the values and practices of constitutional democracy or, for that matter, the values and practices authorized under the order's own constitution. In fact, facial stability and self-confidence sometimes disguise departures from constitutional ways of life.[5] I argue here that the sustained practice of war produces such departures, even when the motives for engaging in armed conflict are constitutionally comprehensible and perhaps commendable. Frequently, departures from constitutional ways are subtle and perhaps on their face insignificant. But, in aggregate and accumulating over time, they can lead to profound alterations of the constitution. As one of Milton Mayer's correspondents put it in another context, "And one day . . . [t]he world you live in . . . is not the world you were born in at all. The forms are all there, all untouched, all reassuring. . . . But the

---

3. Thucydides, *The Peloponnesian War*, Crawley translation, rev., ed. T. E. Wick (New York: Modern Library, 1982). Still, there is reason to believe that even the strong can suffer materially and geopolitically from ill-conceived or incompetently prosecuted warfare.

4. As Murphy points out, one challenge of constitutional design is to devise ways to control the military. This is not the only challenge, but it is a significant one.

5. The rubric "constitutional ways of life" owes a conceptual debt to Sotirios A. Barber, *On What the Constitution Means* (Baltimore: Johns Hopkins University Press, 1984).

spirit, which you never noticed because you made the lifelong mistake of identifying it with the forms, is changed."[6] To sharpen the point, the persistent pursuit of war is corrosive of constitutional democracy. In the context of this brief essay, I cannot prove the thesis, either as a general proposition or in the American case. But I hope to provide at least a persuasive analytic basis for the claim.

Analysis

Change, of course, is part of life, not to mention essential to maintaining a constitutional democracy. To put it in Darwinian terms, changes that serve as adaptations to environmental challenges may well be advantageous from an evolutionary standpoint. For slightly different reasons, William Brennan celebrated change. He insisted that the Constitution—including judicial interpretation of the Constitution—has changed in the centuries since its ratification, and properly so.[7] Brennan's story of the Constitution was one of "progress," in which the country was realizing "the aspiration to social justice, brotherhood, and human dignity." There are ways in which Brennan's happy account is a recognizable description of the American experience. But the history of change in the United States has not strictly been a story of progress. For even if change has been adaptive in terms of promoting physical survival, material advantage, or international influence (and there is reason to think that the record even on these fronts is mixed), it has not consistently promoted or preserved some of the basic prerequisites of constitutional democracy.

I believe there are five areas or aspects of political life that a condition of perpetual war is changing in the United States: national ethos, the protection of constitutional rights, the everyday operation of republican government, the allocation of institutional authority, and the location of sovereignty. The sorts of change that are occurring in these areas might be troubling to a constitutional democrat, because they indicate that certain preconditions for maintaining constitutional democracy are weakening.

National Ethos

The social psychology attendant to keeping a constitutional democracy routinely at war is complex. One challenge is that people in such a polity

---

6. Milton Mayer, *They Thought They Were Free: The Germans, 1933–1945* (Chicago: University of Chicago Press, 1955).

7. William J. Brennan Jr., "The Constitution of the United States: Contemporary Ratification," *South Texas Law Journal* 27 (1986): 433.

have an interest—perhaps a sincere desire—to see themselves as peaceful. The mechanisms for reconciling self-image with discrepant behavior include a version of Karl Schmitt's friend-enemy distinction.[8] This distinction permits the people not only to bifurcate the world but also to moralize the bifurcation and hence to justify aggression against "evildoers" and "evil folks." This simplistic moralization, often reinforced by invocations of the maker of the universe, helps produce what Robert Osgood has identified as the patriotic personality, in which conceptions of self and nation become so thoroughly integrated that the interests of the two cannot be easily distinguished.[9] This integration not only permits a people that perceives itself as peaceful to rationalize aggression but also disables citizens from critically assessing the actions of the very government that is ostensibly their agent. This combination is destructive of the ways of constitutional democracy.

The sort of psychic integration I have described tends not to happen spontaneously and must be refreshed over time. It usually requires, therefore, agents who possess the motive and the means to quicken the public imagination around armed conflict, to moralize the conflict, and to demonstrate the necessity of going to war. ("Necessity" here connotes not physical compulsion but merely compelling desirability.) Democratic systems are often replete with agents who might have a motive to animate the public's will to pursue war. Finding an agent with the means, however, is more challenging, especially where the public is inclined to see itself as peace loving and especially in systems in which political authority is diffuse, as in most constitutional democracies. Thus, a constitutional order in which the legislature predominates in foreign affairs (specifically in the decision to go to war) tends to be structurally inhibited from pursuing war with regularity, unless the legislative body possesses one or more persons with Periclean status and eloquence. But, in a constitutional order that concentrates authority (or permits the accumulation of power) over war and foreign affairs in a single leader like a unitary president, that leader can possess both the motive and the means to incite public sentiment in favor of war. It is sometimes even the case that a president need not be eloquent to do so.

Eloquent or not, Woodrow Wilson was able to persuade a skeptical people, in the wake of the Spanish-American War, to enter World War I. He justified entry into war to promote in the world a "new spirit"

8. Carl Schmitt, *The Concept of the Political*, trans. George Schwab (Chicago: University of Chicago Press, 1996).

9. Robert Endicott Osgood, *Ideals and Self-Interest in America's Foreign Relations: The Great Transformation of the Twentieth Century* (Chicago: University of Chicago Press, 1953).

consistent with "our [American] democracy and civilization." This way of putting the appeal spoke directly to the better angels of the American psyche. Even John Dewey was persuaded, though on reflection he later characterized the institutionalized global form of the new spirit as "the war system," in which the United States eventually came to "occupy its 'rightful' place."[10]

I have heard it suggested that repetition is the heart of modern education.[11] Nigel Tubbs has pushed the suggestion one further, claiming that repetition as an educational method can ultimately alter what Kierkegaard (and a host of others) have called the soul.[12] In moving from the education of the individual to the education of society, if we may translate the notion of the soul as something equivalent to ethos, then we can translate Tubbs's claim in this way: The regular practice, justification, and ethical rationalization of continual war may not only inure or desensitize people to warfare but weave the ethic of the warrior state as a positive good into the public mind.

Rights

It is a commonplace that rights give way to power in time of war. The judiciary, which is an institution that has assumed significant responsibility for enforcing rights against government in the United States, has historically invoked two doctrinal devices for calibrating the relation between rights and power during armed conflict. The first and more dramatic—*inter arma silent leges*—posits that law simply ends for certain purposes in wartime. Despite its extremity, this device has more to commend it than might appear at first glance. I do not pause over the doctrine here, however, for although justices have sometimes recited it, it has largely given way in modern times to a second device: balancing. This latter doctrine resembles the jurisprudential approach to rights in normal times. Using it, courts weigh the exigency of the circumstance (and hence the justification for power) against the claim of right. The standard of review varies across cases, presumably depending on the fundamentality of the right at stake. I say "presumably" because it is not clear that the courts are consistent in applying standards of review. For example, employing the traditional test of "rational basis," the Supreme Court in *Hirabayashi v. United States*[13] upheld a curfew order aimed at persons

10. For an interesting discussion of these dynamics, see Peter T. Manicus, *War and Democracy* (Cambridge, MA: Basil Blackwell, 1989), 338–40.

11. The first person I heard invoke this aphorism was Walter Murphy, though, to be fair, he might have intended it ironically—and in fact might now deny having said it.

12. Nigel Tubbs, *Philosophy's Higher Education* (New York: Springer, 2005), 94.

13. 320 U.S. 821 (1943).

of Japanese descent living on the West Coast during World War II. One year later in *Korematsu v. United States*, the Court, employing this time a standard of "strict scrutiny," upheld a related exclusion order, also aimed at persons of Japanese descent.[14] That same year in *Ex Parte Endo*, purporting to avoid constitutional review entirely, the Court relied instead on a strategy of statutory construction to grant a writ of habeas corpus in a challenge to the detention order that also was aimed at persons of Japanese descent.[15]

The problem of potential inconsistency aside, the larger risk is that, just as persistent warfare desensitizes people to the ethical corrosion that can accompany it, judicial balancing will desensitize judges and lawyers to the impact that exigencies of armed conflict may have on civil liberty. In short, the risk is that, from a legal standpoint, balancing in time of war will normalize and legitimate incursions on rights. If this is a risk, reported decisions of the Supreme Court have tended to be more sensitive to rights than one might expect in light of the commonplace. W.E.B. Du Bois argued in fact that *Brown v. Board of Education*[16] would not have appeared when and how it did but for the Cold War.[17] Put differently, Du Bois's claim was that the Cold War animated for the nation (if not the states) a motive to begin to limit the scope of legal disabilities imposed on account of race. This motive and doctrinal context aside, the Court has in fact protected rights, even during armed conflict.

It is sometimes the case, however, that discrete groups can suffer the brunt of governmental policies without spreading the diminution of rights to the public at large. Most visibly and perhaps understandably, the Court has tended to show less solicitude for the rights of noncitizens than of citizens. But even among citizens, the Court has sometimes permitted the coercive hand of government to fall more heavily on small groups.[18] Outside the realm of reported decisions, there is much room for the contraction of rights. For example, employing passive doctrines for controlling its docket, the Court can avoid deciding cases until it is safe to do so,

14. 323 U.S. 214 (1944).

15. 323 U.S. 283 (1944). Justice Owen Roberts, concurring, urged that the Court should have faced squarely and explicitly the "constitutional issues which are necessarily involved" in the case. Ibid.

16. 347 U.S. 483 (1954).

17. W.E.B. Du Bois, *The Autobiography of W.E.B. Du Bois: A Soliloquy on Viewing My Life from the Last Decade of its First Century* (New York: International Publishers, 1968). See also the subsequent validation of this proposition by Derrick Bell, Mary L. Dudziak, and Lucas Powe.

18. This was the case in *Minersville School District v. Gobitis*, 310 U.S. 586 (1940), though that decision was reversed during wartime in *West Virginia v. Barnette*, 319 U.S. 624 (1943).

if at all.[19] And at times even the general public acquiesces in a variety of intrusions and inconveniences—like searches and surveillance in public places or in telecommunication—that are rarely litigated (at least at the highest judicial level) and in fact come to feel normal and justified, even when they would have been unthinkable a generation before.

Operation of Republican Government

By design, the government of the United States is republican. That is, as James Madison famously pronounced in *Federalist* No. 39, it "derives all its powers directly or indirectly from the great body of the people." The framers' aims in this regard were at least twofold: to create a government accountable to the people (consistent with ancient liberty's precept of self-government) and to secure a background check on government (promoting, among other things, modern liberty's commitment to individual rights). In order for such a system to work as a *republican* system, several conditions must hold. One important condition is that processes of government and reasons for governmental decisions should include at least a modicum of transparency. This condition cuts against secrecy in governmental processes and decision. If secrecy is frequently an enemy to transparency, however, it is just as often a friend to the prosecution of war (in fact, to diplomacy and other aspects of national security as well). And the first cousin of secrecy is deception. Of course, war can defend and protect republican institutions. But, because war usually demands substantial elements of secrecy, it can also erode the element of transparency that is a prerequisite to accountability and to aspects of liberty. This means that, on matters of high importance, the people are constrained from performing their republican functions. And, if leaders deceive, the people are denied many of the tools and resources to discover the deception in a timely fashion, much less to uncover the truth.[20] Moreover, just as war can become a way of life, secrecy can become part of the ordinary course of governmental dealing even on issues not directly related to warfare.[21]

One of Milton Mayer's interlocutors put it this way: "What happened here was the gradual habituation of the people, little by little, to

19. This consideration may well explain the Court's decision in *Ex Parte Milligan*, 71 U.S. 2 (1866).

20. On the problem of deception in the United States' invasion of Iraq, see a recent report sponsored by the Center for Public Integrity. Charles Lewis and Mark Reading-Smith, "False Pretenses," January 23, 2008, http://projects.publicintegrity.org/WarCard/ (accessed October 21, 2009).

21. One recent example involves the Environmental Protection Agency's refusal to explain to the State of California why the agency blocked California's plan to place heightened restrictions on emission of airborne pollutants.

being governed by surprise; to receiving decisions deliberated in secret; to believing that the situation was so complicated that the government had to act on information which the people could not understand, or so dangerous that, even if the people could . . . understand it, it could not be released because of national security."[22] No one has seriously suggested that the United States is becoming Nazi Germany. But even subtle and less dramatic incursions on the people's ability to exercise their republican responsibility can be troubling.

Allocation of Institutional Authority

A notable aspect of the American version of republican government is the attentive precision with which power is allocated among institutions. In the area of war, the Constitution allocates authority to both Congress and the president. A quick scan of the constitutional text suggests that Congress possesses at least as much authority over the armed forces as does the executive. As is often the case, the record of the framers' reasons for this allocation is thin and conflictual. But there is evidence that one motive for the Constitution's allocation was to avoid the observed disadvantages of a monarchical model of war in favor of the perceived advantages of a republican model.[23] The latter model would subject decisions about war to a deliberative process embracing a wide range of interests more likely to produce policies that correspond with the common good, as opposed to the narrow, ambitious interests of a ruling elite.

To be sure, some people have claimed that the Constitution established not strictly a republican system but one that combined the advantages of a republic with those of a monarchy. Proponents of this claim typically invoke Alexander Hamilton's famous defense of the executive power in his essays for *The Federalist*. Hamilton worried that government under the Articles of Confederation had become feeble.[24] He (and others) wanted to create a good and strong government, one that is able to achieve the common purposes for which governments are created and governmental power is authorized. The key, he urged, was energy, and an important repository and source of energy was the executive: "Energy in the executive is a leading character in the definition of good government," he said, for it protects against foreign attacks, promotes "the steady administration of the laws," and helps secure liberty and property.[25]

---

22. Mayer, *They Thought They Were Free: The Germans*.

23. Louis Fisher, *Presidential War Power* (Lawrence: University Press of Kansas, 1995).

24. Alexander Hamilton, *The Federalist*, ed. Jacob E. Cooke (Middletown, CT: Wesleyan University Press, 1961), No. 15.

25. Hamilton, *Federalist* No. 70 (1788).

To argue for an energetic executive, however, is not necessarily to extol the virtues of monarchy. In *The Federalist*, at least, Hamilton seems to have been keenly aware of the difference. For one thing, he took pains to distinguish his executive from the king of England, in terms both formal and substantive. His essay in *Federalist* No. 69 was a virtual catalog of differences between a republican executive and a monarch. Among the differences specified in the proposed Constitution were powers related to control of the military, the prosecution of war, and management of foreign affairs. Like a king, the president was to be commander in chief of the army and navy. Unlike a king, who possessed plenary military authority, the president would possess only occasional command of the militia, as local conditions might justify and supporting legislation might permit. Also unlike a king, the president would lack primary powers to raise and to regulate an armed force and was denied the power to declare war. Each of these powers was to be within the province of Congress. Finally, the Constitution would require that the president obtain approval of the Senate for the appointment of ambassadors and ratification of treaties.

Another indication that Hamilton was sensitive to the difference between a president and a monarch was that he justified his executive in terms of republican values. Why are unity and energy important? One reason, said Hamilton, is that they tend to promote "the PUBLIC GOOD," because they ensure that the system has the means to achieve the Constitution's purposes as articulated in the Preamble and elsewhere.[26] This argument, of course, assumes not only that the president would possess the means but also either that the president would possess the motive to promote the public good or, where public-regarding motive were deficient, that the system would inhibit the corrupting effects of narrowly selfish motives. Hamilton spoke of several solutions to this problem, but the most significant solution—and the second way in which an energetic unitary executive was to be republican and not monarchic—concerned accountability. The Constitution's executive would be accountable; a monarch (even a constitutional monarch) is not. The most important assumption here was that the people would know where the buck stopped if things went awry.[27]

There is one additional reason to believe that the Constitution's executive was not conceived to be the republican equivalent of a monarch, though the logic comes less from Hamilton's essays than from the thinking of others around the time of the founding. The issue concerned not unity or energy per se but independence. Herbert Storing has noted that the president's independence was not designed to be comprehensive. This

---

26. Hamilton, *Federalist* No. 71.
27. Hamilton, *Federalist* Nos. 68, 70.

is to do more than suggest Madison's maxim that the governmental system under the Constitution was to consist of separate institutions sharing powers.[28] It is also to say that the executive was to be subject to (or expressive of) two principles. According to the political principle, the president was to be a coequal participant in the constitutional scheme. In this regard, the executive's formal independence was substantial. According to the administrative principle, however, the executive's basic function—legal administration—necessarily implied subordination to the legislature despite the executive's independence. This subordination was because, with respect to administration, the executive was subject to law and therefore, as part of the job, obliged to carry out law's commands. Storing notes that the concept of the binary character of executive independence was generally understood in 1787, even by proponents of a "vigorous and independent executive." As he observes, "The beginning of wisdom about the American Presidency is to see that it contains both principles and to reflect on their complex and subtle relation" as the nation's history has unfolded.[29]

Despite these considerations, Hamilton's position poses difficulties for republican theory. One difficulty involves his defense and definition of energy. The unitary executive, he urged, would be characterized by "[d]ecision, activity, secrecy, and dispatch."[30] On their face, these characteristics seem unobjectionable, but they are in tension with the principles of reflection, deliberation, and transparency that are at the heart of the American constitutional democracy. Another difficulty is his definition of the power to wage war. This power, he said, not only resides in the nation but also is an "unconfined authority" not subject to limitation. The nationalist aspect of the war power can be reconciled with principles of constitutional democracy, but Hamilton's argument that the war-making power is illimitable is problematic, especially if certain conditions hold. Among those conditions is the concentration of the war power within the executive.

The Constitution includes two ways to check this tendency to concentrate power. The first returns to the notion of accountability to the people. This notion assumes that the people are attentive, reasonably intelligent, and motivated to enforce constitutional purposes and limits. It assumes also that they have the means to do so. Hamilton did little to theorize this assumption. George Mason, in contrast, made it central to his analysis of the executive power. If a muscular executive was in tension with the

28. James Madison, *Federalist* No. 51.

29. Herbert Storing, "Appendix: Introduction," in Charles C. Thatch Jr., *The Creation of the Presidency, 1775–1789: A Study in Constitutional History* (Indianapolis: Liberty Fund, 2007), 166.

30. Alexander Hamilton, *The Federalist*, No. 70.

republican principle, as Mason urged that it was, the only power that could prevent or correct executive overreaching was the attentive attachment of citizens "to their laws, to their freedom, and to their country."[31] In short, constitutional ethos was the solution to the problem posed by an energetic unitary executive, and without this residual check, the enterprise could fail as a constitutional democracy.

James Madison, too, was attentive to the people's constitutional roles, but he suspected that the people could not consistently be relied upon to check constitutional abuses. "A dependence on the people is, no doubt, the primary controul on the government, but experience has taught mankind the necessity of auxiliary precautions." When "recourse to the people" is unavailable or unavailing, he argued, the constitutional order could protect against "a gradual concentration of the several powers in the same department" if the government were structured so that each department had the means and motive to resist encroachment by the others.[32] To put a point on Madison's position, the Congress would guard its powers over the regulation and use of armed force and, in doing so, would inhibit aggrandizement by the executive.

Experience has shown that Madison was both right and wrong. First, George Mason's hope that the people, through a constitutionally animated ethos, would resist the accretion of power in the executive has not been realized. On the contrary, Madison's concern that the people would not be consistently reliable in this role has been well founded. Second, however, his claim that institutional structure and competition would enforce limits to power when the people proved deficient has not been vindicated, at least in the context of war and foreign affairs. In short, and contrary to Richard Cheney's worry before he became vice president,[33] the executive has gradually strengthened its control over the use of armed force (even over the "declaration of war"), while the powers of Congress have largely eroded. There is a constellation of explanations for this trend—including strategic and pragmatic advantages in the executive, systematic and political disadvantages in Congress, and the emergence of a militarist and sometimes imperialist ethos among the citizenry. We may add to these considerations a marked expansion in the United States' role in the world's affairs, in which the use or threat of armed force is perceived now to be a primary instrument for international influence.

If these are the trends (and if they are troubling), one might ask whether "the least dangerous branch" might properly play a role as referee for

31. Quoted in Herbert Storing, introduction, 168–69.
32. James Madison, *The Federalist*, Nos. 10, 39, 50, 51.
33. See Jeffrey Toobin, *The Nine: Inside the Secret World of the Supreme Court* (New York: Doubleday, 2007), 277.

disputes over the exercise of power where the use of armed force is at issue. To put a finer point on it, might the judiciary—especially the Supreme Court—shore up Congress's authority in appropriate circumstances, given the executive's institutional advantages? The answer is that it might and sometimes has. But the Court's record in this regard is uneven. It is tempting to claim that the high-water mark of the Court's protection of Congress's turf was *Little v. Barreme* in 1804.[34] Much later, however, in *Youngstown Sheet & Tube v. Sawyer*,[35] the Court reprised this role. Still more recently, the Court has taken up questions related to the legality of detentions in the "global war on terror," though not solely to protect Congress's authority.[36] To be sure, there have been other decisions in which the Court has stood against the executive in the context of war, but these have frequently arisen in cases in which either hostilities had already passed by the time of decision or the Court has left at least one door ajar for further executive action.

The juristic considerations in this area are complex, and I will not parse them here. Legalistic considerations aside, however, there are at least two sets of prudential concerns that weigh against the Court's insinuating itself into matters of war, peace, and international relations. One is the Court's confessed weakness in this area. The weakness stems partly from the fact that it has little direct power over purse and sword, as Hamilton observed. It is also a function of institutional (in)competence. If the Court lacks command of resources, it also lacks the information, skill, and experience to deal with matters related to armed force, which can often be supremely sensitive (not always to say delicate) from a political perspective and beyond law's sometimes clumsy capacity to adjust. It is awkward enough when the Court decides elections. To have judges involved in running a war—or policing the boundary between the executive and the Congress during a war—might be especially worrisome.

The upshot of this worry might be that Congress alone should protect its turf (and perhaps the people) from executive ambition and encroachment. Certainly, one might think, the Congress has the means and the motive to do so. In fact, however, the Congress has shown little interest

---

34. 6 U.S. 170 (1804).

35. 343 U.S. 579 (1952).

36. In *Rasul v. Bush*, 542 U.S. 466 (2004), the Court held that the judiciary had jurisdiction to consider petitions for the writ of habeas corpus from prisoners being held in the U.S. naval base in Guantanamo Bay, Cuba. In *Hamdi v. Rumsfeld*, 542 U.S. 507 (2004), the Court held that Congress, through its general Authorization for the Use of Military Force in 2001, had authorized the indefinite detention of a U.S. citizen who was being held in a naval brig in Virginia, but that the government's procedures for determining whether continuing detention was justified were subject to constitutional limitations. And in *Hamdan v. Rumsfeld*, 548 U.S. 557 (2006), the Court held that the use of military commissions to authorize the indefinite detention of a noncitizen at Guantanamo Bay violated congressional limitations on the authority of the president.

in protecting its authority. There may be several reasons Congress has not energetically asserted itself in these matters—ranging from the ease with which a deft or decisive president can politically outflank Congress, to a congressional fear of appearing unpatriotic at a time in which commitment to armed conflict is an expression of patriotism, to the difficulty any numerous body has in coordinating collectively, to a heightened aversion to institutional risk in opposing a president during actual or threatened armed conflict, to a simple lack of political will. Whatever the reasons, it seems clear that Congress has been less than proficient in pressing its authority over war.

Far from being an exception to this trend, the War Powers Resolution, perhaps by design but certainly in practice, reinforces it. Through this resolution, which most presidents have simply ignored, Congress seems content merely to have shifted the political risk of military misadventure to the executive.[37] Two former secretaries of state, writing for a nongovernmental commission, have recently declared that the War Powers Resolution is "ineffective at best and unconstitutional at worst" and that it should be replaced with a new law.[38] There are genuine questions about whether it could be adopted without (or despite) a presidential veto and, if adopted, whether the new proposal would be at all better than the existing resolution. But even if the new proposal were to mark an improvement, it is plainly the strategy of a politically weak or indecisive institution.

No court can easily assist such an institution in many of the contexts relevant to armed conflict. As Justice Robert Jackson put it in his concurrence in *Youngstown Sheet & Tube*, "only Congress itself can prevent [its] power from slipping through its fingers." In fact, the Congress sometimes seems complicit in the enlargement of executive authority over armed conflict. I noted that, in *Hamdan v. Rumsfeld*, the Court held that the government's use of military commissions to try detainees at Guantanamo exceeded limits that Congress had imposed by statute. In response to the Court's decision, Congress swiftly enacted the Military Commissions Act of 2006, not only explicitly authorizing the use of military commissions in the precise circumstances at issue in *Hamdan* but also suspending the writ of habeas corpus for detainees. Once again the Court stepped in to limit the executive, though it did so to protect not the Congress but a civil liberty.[39]

37. John Hart Ely, *War and Responsibility: Constitutional Lessons of Vietnam and Its Aftermath* (Princeton: Princeton University Press, 1993).

38. James A. Baker III and Warren Christopher, "Put War Powers Back Where They Belong," *New York Times*, July 8, 2008.

39. The Court struck down the Military Commissions Act of 2006 as an unconstitutional suspension of the writ of habeas corpus. *Boumediene v. Bush*, 128 S.Ct. 2229 (2008).

Sovereignty

In one significant earlier case, however, the Court dramatically expanded the concentration of authority in the executive. The case was *U.S. v. Curtiss-Wright Export Corp.*[40] It is significant, not because of its circumstance, involving a congressional delegation of power to the president to prohibit the shipment of arms to Bolivia and Paraguay in 1934, nor because of its holding that the delegation was permissible. The case is significant because its rationale overthrows the prevailing theory on which the authority of the constitutional order rests and, as a practical matter, weakens the capacity of the people or their agents in Congress to check executive discretion. There is reason to believe, moreover, that the rationale has subtly influenced not only the direction of the Court's thinking in other cases concerning the authority of the executive in matters of war and foreign affairs but also at least one president's conception of the scope of executive power.

The prevailing theory of the authority of the constitutional order is that the people authorized the Constitution. Article VII's procedure for ratification provides textual support for this notion. Article VII does not supply decisive evidence for whether those who ratified were the people of states or of the nation as a whole. But either way, the assumption was that the people were the creators of the order. Justice George Sutherland's opinion for the Court in *Curtiss-Wright* negated this conception of authority in the areas of foreign affairs and armed conflict. Concerning strictly domestic affairs, Sutherland urged, the Constitution carved legislative powers for the national government from the antecedent legislative powers of the states. Because, however, the states never possessed power over foreign affairs and war, the creation of such power in the nation derived from a different source—the Union—which antedated the Constitution. The Union came to possess this power not from a sovereign people but via the law of nations. As a new nation-state, the United States acquired all attributes of sovereignty sufficient for conducting relations with other nations.

This unity of state and sovereign is constitutionally problematic, for safely authorizing and delegating power are possible precisely when and to the extent that there is disjunction between sovereign and state. This proposition suggests a tension between the underlying principles and purposes of constitutional democracy, on the one hand, and the nation-state, on the other. To put it bluntly, statism is not the same as constitutionalism. To say this is not to suggest, as Marx did with communism, that constitutionalism and nation-states are incompatible. As a historical matter

40. 299 U.S. 304 (1936).

in the West, for example, a robust practical constitutionalism arose in the wake of the creation of nation-states. This sequence was not mere happenstance, and in fact aspects of constitutionalism have flourished within nation-states. But certain statist conceptions of politics, law, and power are at odds with constitutionalism. This is especially so when statism supplants the sovereignty of the people, on which depend not only the effective operation of republican government but also the crucial right of the people to resist and replace standing government.

If Sutherland's statism were problematic, however, one additional set of moves in *Curtiss-Wright* was constitutionally dangerous. He designated the president as the sole authority for the nation in international relations—free to act exclusive of Congress (and, by implication, without delegation), to do so secretly, to blend war with diplomacy, and to extend both to matters "domestic." Thus, in a quick stroke Sutherland's president procured the perquisites of sovereignty and the ability to avoid ordinary institutional checks presupposed by both republican theory and the notion of popular sovereignty. These moves went far beyond the authority that even Alexander Hamilton imagined for the executive. And, in conditions of perpetual war, they are subversive of constitutional democracy.

Conclusion

As a political enterprise, the United States has been remarkably successful. It has enjoyed stable institutions that often reflect majoritarian preferences and respect for individuals. It has expanded its borders across a continent and beyond. It has generated the most powerful economic system in the world. It once produced the mightiest armed force in the history of the planet. And the ideas and institutions spawned from its constitutional experiment have influenced people and nations through the years and across the globe, animating the development of international norms and institutions. These areas of American constitutional history—touching on values of democracy and liberty, domestic security, material welfare and prosperity, the common defense, and international influence—are interpenetrating. The relations among them, therefore, are not static but are dynamic and changing. They are not always, however, mutually reinforcing. Perhaps perversely, success in one area does not always produce success in others. It is, to put it too simply, a question of balance. Striking the balance and recognizing hazards involve the art and practice of constitutional wisdom. In this essay I have focused on the hazards associated with one preoccupation: the persistent practice of war and armed conflict.

My position here is neither pacifist nor antimilitary, nor does it assume that constitutional democracies must be weak. But it is constitutionalist. And it posits that preserving a constitutional democracy is more complex than simply providing security against armed aggression or extending material and military influence beyond the nation's borders. Constitutionalism is concerned, among other things, with protecting and nurturing a way of life. This essay has spoken to several (though not all) aspects of the way of life of the American version of constitutional democracy: the ethos that is the basis for the public moral life of the people of the constitutional order; the protection of rights, which promote the autonomy and integrity, if not the dignity, of individuals; the collective role of the people in the effective operation of republican government; the balanced allocation of institutional authority, in order to promote ancient and modern liberty and thus inhibit tyranny; and the conservation of the notion that, ultimately, the people, not the state, are sovereign.

I might have included another aspect—the rule of law—concern for which has been just beneath the surface in this discussion. In much of legal scholarship, the rule of law swallows every other aspect of constitutional government, so that constitutional law becomes the sum and substance of constitutionalism. This emphasis is mistaken. Still, the rule of law is important and even fundamental. As I suggested above, its primary function involves the regularization of procedures by which binding public rules are created and enforced. We may add that a premise of the rule of law in a constitutional democracy is that government and governmental officers act "under law." Again, I want to resist the notion that law extends to every governmental action or decision. But, within proper domains, governmental actors are obliged to obey the law, even when they are acting in their official capacities.

Warfare extracts resources from a constitutional order. This is so whether armed conflict is necessary or optional. The resources extracted are not merely material but nonmaterial, too. Some of these nonmaterial resources are central to sustaining a constitutional democracy *as a constitutional democracy*. The impact of a single war or even several wars need not be "resource-negative" in the sense I have suggested. But continual warfare—the use of armed force as a regular part of the life of a nation— is constitutionally enervating and even disabling.

To be sure, war can be advantageous both materially and nonmaterially. Paul Starr has emphasized this point in recent work. He argues that wars are not always to be evaded, but in fact can strengthen a state; that the American history of warfare demonstrates that liberal states are stronger than nonliberal states; and that if American wars have sometimes diminished civil liberties, they are almost always restored once peace and calm prevail and fear subsides.[41] I do not deny Starr's first claim. To maintain itself, a constitutional democracy in a world of nation-states must be strong enough militarily to defend its borders, to maintain domestic peace, to protect its fundamental interests, and to deter armed aggression against itself and its allies. I would quibble with his second claim. For one thing, I do not believe a constitutional order must be liberal in the sense in which Starr intends it. Constitutionalism and constitutional democracy are not coextensive with Anglo-American liberalism. For another, I suspect that the American order will soon be tested again as to whether a constitutional democracy is in fact always stronger (in both military and "softer" senses of the word) than, say, an authoritarian one. On the third claim, however, there are important ways in which we simply disagree.

War's costs do not merely fall on civil liberties but extend broadly to other areas of public life that are crucial to the long-term health of a constitutional democracy. Even if we focus on civil liberties, however, the record is not quite as happy as Starr suggests. It is true that we can identify specific intrusions on civil liberties that were not long-lived: "the Alien and Sedition Acts of 1798, Lincoln's suspension of habeas corpus, the suppression of free speech during and after World War I, the internment of Japanese Americans during World War II, McCarthyism, and the wiretapping of Vietnam-era dissenters."[42] But the reappearance of some of these intrusions in even our own time suggests that, if lessons were learned from these episodes, the half life of knowledge may be shorter than one might hope. Or perhaps the inventiveness of government is greater than one might expect. Either way, it is sometimes the case that restrictions on civil liberties outlast the needs of a particular war. The Supreme Court's decision in *Woods v. Cloyd W. Miller Co.*[43] is merely one example that is visible because judicially ratified. But there have been others.[44]

The story, therefore, is not simply one of the restriction and restoration of civil liberty. For sometimes the restrictions persist and can even become entrenched in patterns of daily life, such as the thoroughgoing surveillance of persons in many public places. The risk that constitutional change will become entrenched may be all the more pronounced when the novelty involves not rights per se but institutional practices

---

41. Paul Starr, *Freedom's Power: The True Force of Liberalism* (New York: Basic Books, 2007)

42. Quotation from Paul Starr, "George W. Bush vs. the Constitution," February 21, 2006, http://cbsnews.com/stories/2006/02/21/opinion/printable1334435.shtml (reprinted from *The American Prospect*) (accessed September 9, 2008).

43. 333 U.S. 138 (1948).

44. See, e.g., James W. Ely Jr., "Property Rights and the Supreme Court in World War II," *Journal of Supreme Court History* 1 (1996): 19.

and structural modifications. Some of these might well be advantageous evolutionary adaptations. The advantage of others might be doubtful, perhaps because their lives have outlived their utility or original purpose. In either case, the constitutional costs can be far-reaching and frequently are difficult to discern.

The problem of discernibility is substantial for leaders and for people in a constitutional democracy. This is so precisely because some of the factors are nonmaterial, relations are subtle and complex, and measurement is elusive. For practical reasons, the ability to detect costs and benefits is important to sustaining a constitutional order, but it requires an attentive people.

This essay has been largely concerned with constitutional maintenance and change. But connected with these themes is a story also of potential failure. As it happens, the boundaries among constitutional maintenance, change, and failure are surprisingly permeable. This fact heightens the stakes of detection. Hegel famously wrote that "[t]he owl of Minerva spreads its wings only with the falling of the dusk."[45] As change blends into failure, the people in a constitutional democracy will surely hope that dusk is soon enough.

45. G.W.F. Hegel, *Philosophy of Right*, trans. T. M. Knox (Oxford: Oxford University Press, 1942), 13.

Part IV

HOW CAN CONSTITUTIONAL DEMOCRACY
CONTEND WITH GLOBALIZATION?

12

Three Constitutionalist Responses to Globalization

JAN-WERNER MÜLLER

IN RECENT DEBATES ON GLOBALIZATION, constitutionalism has created surprisingly high hopes and astonishingly deep anxieties: some have presented the constitutionalization of international law as a kind of last "realistic utopia";[1] others have been profoundly troubled precisely by the threat that international law and global governance supposedly pose to the project of constitutional self-government.[2] Rather than another specific constitutionalist proposal, this chapter seeks to provide a sober assessment of constitutionalism's potential and limits by describing and evaluating three paradigmatic constitutionalist responses to increased global interdependence.

The responses I have in mind all take constitutionalism seriously as a complex normative concept; they either seek to protect constitutionalism from law and regulation in the realm beyond the nation-state or argue, on the contrary, that constitutionalism needs to be extended beyond the state in order to generate new normative constraints and capacities—in the sense of both protecting existing states from supranational nonstate institutions and strengthening such institutions vis-à-vis states. I should stress that I am concerned here with normative ideals, not with what Walter Murphy has suggested we call "constitutionism," that is, the adherence to the rules and even spirit of an order that is fixed by a written constitution (or an unwritten one), without any reference to specific substantive values.[3] Such constitutionism might have intermittently existed in a world that in some ways has been globalized for a long time, but it is different from the explicit (and normative) constitutionalism that is at issue today.

I am grateful to the audiences at the Princeton conference on "The Limits of Constitutionalism" and at Stanford's Political Theory workshop for questions and suggestions. Particular thanks to Stephen Macedo and Jeffrey Tulis for comments on the chapter.

1. See for instance Jürgen Habermas, *Der gespaltene Westen* (Frankfurt: Suhrkamp, 2004).

2. See above all Jeremy A. Rabkin, *Law without Nations? Why Constitutional Government Requires Sovereign States* (Princeton: Princeton University Press, 2005).

3. Walter Murphy, *Constitutional Democracy: Creating and Maintaining a Just Political Order* (Baltimore: Johns Hopkins University Press, 2006), 15–16.

The three paradigmatic responses are, first, what one might call "constitutional closure," based on an argument about the national democratic legitimation of state-based constitutions; second, an approach that one might term "limited mutual constitutional opening" or also "constitutional tolerance" in the circumstances of dense supranational cooperation or even a freestanding supranational constitutionalism (with the European Union as the prime example);[4] and, finally, a global constitution proper as the prima facie most consistent response to the fact of global interdependence. This last position, I suggest, comes in two different versions: on the one hand, a relatively conventional idea that international law, including customary international law, as well as international bodies, especially regulatory agencies, ought to be constitutionalized (again, with the EU as the most plausible prototype at the regional level). However, there is also the more radical notion that the *object* of a global constitutionalism no longer is, broadly speaking, states or political and legal institutions conventionally understood but dynamic social and economic processes summed up with concepts such as digitalization, privatization, and global networks (much more about this below).[5]

Let me set out a number of criteria for evaluating these constitutionalist responses. I chose ones that are reasonable and broad enough to be acceptable to those already committed to one of the three positions. First, do we find consistent standards for the national and the international (or supranational)? Whatever normative and empirical frameworks inform an account of the domestic context should also hold in areas outside the nation-state. Of course, this is not to say that these realms have to be described as absolutely identical—in many ways it would be strange and surprising if they were. But if there is a claim that these two realms are fundamentally different (normatively and/or empirically), that claim must be made explicit and justified. If, for instance, an ideal-typical (or outright idealized) vision of a united democratic will is presented at the domestic level as the sole foundation of political legitimacy, then the question about the possible existence of such a will above nation-states cannot be answered with reference to today's messy realities of global administrative law but would have to involve a similar idealization. Conversely, if, as often happens in the European context, the vision of

4. J.H.H. Weiler, "Federalism without Constitutionalism: Europe's *Sonderweg*," in *The Federal Vision: Legitimacy and Levels of Governance in the United States and the European Union*, ed. Kalypso Nicolaïdis and Robert Howse (Oxford: Oxford University Press, 2001), 64.

5. Gunther Teubner, "Globale Zivilverfassungen: Alternativen zur staatszentrierten Verfassungstheorie," in *Die Staaten der Weltgesellschaft: Niklas Luhmanns Staatsverständni*, ed. Marcelo Neves and Rüdiger Voigt (Baden-Baden: Nomos, 2007), 118.

a supranational multiculturalism among a persistent plurality of peoples is presented as a normative justification for the EU, the question must be asked whether such a normative vision is plausible within the EU's Member States. The point, I hope, is obvious enough: idealizations must go both ways, as must consciously "realist" descriptions; if they do not, we need an explicit justification as to why not. It seems obvious to me that there is a great deal of bad faith precisely when it comes to contrasts between what is within and what is outside the nation-state.

The second question concerns normative dependency, in particular the background notion of constitutionalism that is at work in the theories under consideration. In other words, what larger normative background theory informs or even drives the account we are given, and, above all, what particular understanding of constitutionalism as a normative ideal do we find at work?[6] Constitutionalism, while perhaps not being an essentially contested concept, nevertheless has allowed for many conceptions that derive from radically different normative theories concerning justice, democracy, and the like but also from different theoretical accounts of modern society. Partially following recent theorizations by Neil Walker, one might see the following as plausible elements (or dimensions, or frames) of constitutionalism:[7] first, a public order element (including a normative ideal of legal orderliness) that allows for the linkage of law and politics, as well as the determination of a specialized system of political rule (above all, the specification of political institutions and the distribution or separation of power), and, in particular, provisions for limiting and checking public power; second, mechanisms for protecting the rights and dignity of individuals, thereby also limiting government; third—and already more controversially—the grounding in (and determination of) a constituent power or, put differently, an element of democratic self-authorization; fourth, and also controversially, a social integrative claim,[8] or, put differently, the possibility of fostering a civic identity that can be defined, revised, and furthered through public debates in a constitutionalist register; and, fifth, perhaps also controversially, an explicit, specific, and self-reflexive constitutionalist discourse, or, in Walker's words, "constitution talk" (which clearly is closely related to the fourth element).[9]

6. For the idea of normative dependence, see Rainer Forst, *Toleranz im Konflikt: Geschichte, Gehalt und Gegenwart eines umstrittenen Begriffs* (Frankfurt am Main: Suhrkamp, 2003), 48–52.

7. See the exceptionally rich theoretical framework developed in Neil Walker, 'Taking Constitutionalism beyond the State," *RECON Online Working Paper* 2007/05.

8. See also Dieter Grimm, "Integration by Constitution," *I-CON* 3, nos. 2–3 (2005): 193–208.

9. Walker, "Taking Constitutionalism beyond the State," 11.

Now, different notions of constitutionalism will include only some of these elements or add others that have not been mentioned here; moreover, they will also specify and link individual elements in quite different ways. What one assumes about constitutionalism in general will obviously be crucial when it comes to the rejection or endorsement of the very possibility (and desirability) of having it outside the nation-state. Consequently, the normative background theories behind the positions I analyze should be made as explicit as possible; in particular, when constitutionalism is projected beyond the nation-state, it has to be explained and justified *how* and *why* elements of constitutionalism might be detached from traditional notions of statehood and democratic self-authorization. If, conversely, the very possibility of post-state or nonstate constitutionalism is denied, or is rejected as normatively undesirable, the question is what version of constitutionalism can plausibly ground such judgments.[10]

Third, there is a question about the likely *efficacy* of the responses to interdependence proposed—and, in particular, whether constitutionalism in the absence of statehood and democratic self-authorization can nevertheless fulfill at least some of the functions conventionally associated with having a constitution within a democratic state, such as the ones just mentioned in connection with the second criterion.

Constitutional Closure

Constitutional closure is an option only for the very powerful or, by default, for the very weak. The very weak have little capacity to engage international markets or international institutions, and if they have anything resembling constitutionalism at all, they might claim that it needs no reinforcement from the outside—that their traditional practices would not benefit from, but be corrupted by, an engagement with the global rule-of-law industry that attempts to standardize conceptions of the *Rechtsstaat* across very different societies. But clearly such isolationism is much more likely among states that are illiberal in the first place and seek to do without any constitutionalism. And there is no question at all here about building constitutionalism outward from such weak polities, though there might be one of how to constrain international nonstate institutions from imposing blueprints on them.

---

10. One might add that, while dependence on a highly eccentric or controversial background theory does not doom a constitutional theory, it makes it prima facie less attractive if one holds that public justifiability remains a crucial requirement of any normative theory.

The very powerful face a completely different situation: they can try to resist foreign entanglements, moods, fashions, and fads; and be selective in their engagement with international law; and cultivate a sense of exceptionalism and practical "exemptionalism" (Michael Ignatieff)—and hope not to suffer significant negative consequences. However, even the very powerful, it seems, are increasingly under pressure from both inside and outside explicitly to justify what one might call normative nonengagement. In the case of liberal democracies, they might try to justify that nonengagement by pointing to a sense of confidence that domestic constitutionalism has a long track record of actually protecting individual rights and effectively limiting government, whereas possible constitutionalist devices beyond the nation-state might yet have to prove their capacity to do so. In particular, they might say that the poor quality of the processes of forming international law suggests a presumption against treating international law as a significant constraint on nation-states—at least as far as what some analysts have called "raw international law" is concerned, that is, law which has not been specifically incorporated into domestic law through legislation.[11]

More likely, they will claim that constitutions are, above all, "depositories of values" (Joseph Weiler)—specific values, that is, of a particular nation that has given itself a particular constitution with constraints and protections that reflect these values (and not ones that are just similar) in a highly specific manner. Thus, even when constitutionalist devices beyond the nation-state might at first sight appear to strengthen constitutionalism inside a country (for instance, by reinforcing individual rights protection), it is imperative not to have the differences between constitutional and international law blurred: the constitution is, in this view, ultimately the emanation of a kind of *Volksgeist*, or at least the expression of a clearly defined and normatively unique social unity that seeks to give itself a political form and resolve to master its fate collectively. This, it seems, is the best rationalization for what Frank Michelman has termed "integrity anxiety"—the concern that a highly specific tradition of constitutionalist thought will become weakened and corrupted through the importation of foreign materials and a blanket acceptance of international law, customary international law in particular.[12] One might even be tempted to say that constitutional closure is the logical corollary of a properly understood constitutional patriotism. Precisely because *we* so much believe in *our* laws as expressions of *our* values, we must ignore the

11. See John O. McGinnis and Ilya Somin, "Should International Law Be Part of Our Law?" *Stanford Law Review* 59 (2007): 1175–1247.

12. Frank I. Michelman, "Integrity-Anxiety?" in *American Exceptionalism and Human Rights*, ed. Michael Ignatieff (Princeton: Princeton University Press, 2005), 241–76.

laws of others (and laws partly made by others), unless they have been incorporated or in some other way mediated by national institutions.[13]

How plausible is an advocacy of constitutional closure, given the criteria I suggest? First, one frequently finds what can only be dubbed double standards: the domestic realm is usually described as one characterized by a single national culture, of which the constitution and a particular form of constitutionalism are an outgrowth; the domestic realm is also invested with passionate political commitment and displays a unique density of political power (i.e., the state), which makes it plausible that, in an all-or-nothing fashion, only the national state can be an object of constitutionalism. In short, very specific descriptions of the state and what happens within it renders constitutionalism beyond the state empirically implausible—and normatively undesirable.

Yet these descriptions are based on highly implausible abstractions and one-way idealizations: the existence of a single self-authorizing nation or *demos* as the actual author of the constitution and constitutionalist provisions; the existence of a single, sealed-off national constitutionalist tradition deeply colored by the national culture; a vision of the political world in which by definition only the nation calls forth true personal investment in the form of tears, sweat, and, at the limit, blood;[14] and a state that monopolizes not just the legitimate means of violence but allegedly concentrates power in a way that makes other potential objects of constitutionalist constraints fade from the picture. Put differently: there is a one-way idealization here of what democracy, peoplehood, and statehood must mean.

Second, an advocacy of constitutional closure is likely to be normatively dependent on a background theory of nationalism—most likely liberal nationalism, but not necessarily so. Liberal nationalism, however, comes with a set of both empirical or sociological and normative assumptions that are highly implausible. Alas, this is not the moment to rehearse criticism of these.[15]

Third, is closure actually likely to lead to something like constitutional success? In one sense, clearly no: it would not allow countries adopting constitutional democracy to further "lock in" their democratic and

13. As Jeremy Rabkin puts it in rejecting "global governance," "Global governance requires us to acknowledge that 'we'—the constituents of a particular legislative authority—do not have different interests from the others, so we don't really need distinct institutions to define these interests." See Rabkin, *Law without Nations?*, 43.

14. Paul W. Kahn, *Putting Liberalism in Its Place* (Princeton: Princeton University Press, 2005).

15. I can only gesture toward my *Constitutional Patriotism* (Princeton: Princeton University Press, 2007).

human rights commitments at supranational level (in the way that, for instance, countries acceding to the European Council try to do); it would also not allow references in a constitution to foreign and international law as normative commitment signals in the way that, for example, the South African constitution famously does.[16] But it might strengthen the role a constitution plays in social integration—if, and only if, it is plausible that constitutions will be more likely to persist and successfully function the more they can be presented as a particular *national* project.

To be sure, not all opposition to the very possibility of constitutionalism beyond the state has to be grounded in a one-way idealization or a normatively dubious theory of liberal nationalism. Some skeptics have argued on purely conceptual—as opposed to normative—grounds. In particular, they have claimed that constitutionalism *necessarily* has to have a state as its object, sometimes adding the further requirement of genuine democratic self-authorization.[17] More subtly, they claim that a constitution, as primary and comprehensive higher law of the land, presupposes clear demarcations between inside and outside, and between public and private. Dieter Grimm, for instance, has argued that while there has undoubtedly been a great deal of juridification beyond the nation-state, such juridification does not amount to constitutionalization. As he puts it, "Not all juridification merits the name of constitutionalization. Rather, constitutionalization has shown itself to be a special form of the juridification of rule that presupposes the concentration of all ruling authority within a territory, and is distinguished by a certain standard of juridification. This standard includes a democratic origin, supremacy, and comprehensiveness."[18] Is saying this merely a matter of more or less arbitrary conceptual stipulation? Grimm clearly holds that constitutionalism ought to designate only a specific constellation of elements that emerged, roughly speaking, in the eighteenth century—in particular, a specialized system of exercising public power and democratic self-authorization in a clearly bounded space. Another way of saying this is that, beyond a certain point, constitutionalism cannot be further disaggregated without losing its core normative meaning, and it makes no sense then to transfer some fragments of constitutionalism to the realm beyond the state and pretend that one has exported the whole package. Constitutionalism, in short, is a matter of all or nothing.[19]

16. Cf. Mattias Kumm, "The Legitimacy of International Law: A Constitutionalist Framework for Analysis," *European Journal of International Law* 15 (2004): 919.

17. Dieter Grimm, "The Constitution in the Process of Denationalization," *Constellations* 12 (2005): 447–63.

18. Ibid., 458.

19. See also Walker, "Taking Constitutionalism beyond the State."

This skeptical position does not so obviously involve a one-way ideal-ization, and it is not grounded in any dubious assumptions about national culture. Nevertheless, it seems somewhat arbitrary to idealize a particular constellation of constitutionalist elements in time and insist that at least processes of constitutionalization—short of leading to regional or global states—must be ruled out on conceptual grounds. After all, "the state" as a locus for concentrating public power is not *one* thing. In particular, it is not obvious why partial supranational extensions of the modern admin-istrative state as it has evolved in the twentieth century in particular could not be subject to entrenched limits on power—either to constrain the exercise of public power by supranational agencies or to limit the exercise of public power by states, or possibly a combination of both. Of course, whether entrenchments actually exist and go beyond any simple juridification has to be determined in individual cases; it will be to a con-siderable degree an empirical question. The experience of the EU as com-monly interpreted by European politicians, jurists, and academics at least suggests that de facto constitutionalization is possible in the absence of direct democratic self-authorization, the establishment of a comprehen-sive legal order, civic identity, and an explicit widespread constitutionalist discourse. This, after all, is the accomplishment of the European Court of Justice in the 1950s and 1960s. Similar observations seem to me plausible as far as the European Convention of Human Rights and the specific role of the European Court of Human Rights are concerned.

Constitutional Tolerance (*plus* Engagement)

The second response to interdependence is what I shall call "limited mutual constitutional opening," with, following Joseph Weiler, "consti-tutional tolerance" as a central value and practice. The prime, perhaps the only, example is the European Union. As has often been pointed out, the EU has acted as a pioneer in transforming an organization based on international treaties into an "unidentified political object" (former com-mission president Jacques Delors), which boasts a form of supranational constitutionalism *without* having become a supranational state. Weiler has spoken of Europe's special path in having federal law without being a federal state. It is worth retracing that path briefly.

The starting point, to be sure, had not been any concern about socio-economic interdependence as such, but the imperative to avoid large-scale political violence. European integration was one part of a wider European constitutionalist ethos, which developed after the Second World War; it contained a deep distrust of popular sovereignty (or, put differently, unre-stricted parliamentary supremacy), which was seen as complicit in the cycles of war and aggression in twentieth-century Europe.[20] Specifically, European states sought to delegate powers to unelected actors domestically and also to supranational bodies in order to lock in liberal-democratic arrangements and to prevent a backsliding toward authoritarianism.[21] They actively searched for—and created—co-guardians of human rights beyond their own boundaries.[22] Supranational constitutionalism was thus a direct response to the fragile liberalism of existing nation-state democracies.

The decisive moment in creating supranational EU constitutionalism occurred when the European Court of Justice more or less bootstrapped itself into a position of extraordinary judicial power—and was, for the most part, accepted as possessing that power by both national courts and national governments, which recognized the supremacy and direct effect of European Community law. Arguably, however, national governments would not have put up with the emergence of a transnational legal order that went considerably beyond international law if they had not retained de facto veto power over legislation. The creation of "hard" European law (or what has sometimes been called normative supranationalism) on the one hand and, on the other, intergovernmentalism, which allowed individual states to promote or at least protect their interests, went hand in hand, rather than one being opposed to each other: integration through law and high-level politics balanced out.[23]

The Court itself explicitly kept promoting the view that the Community was not merely a matter of international treaties—but that the European treaties had over time become constitutionalized; the Court even spoke of the founding treaties as the Community's Basic Constitutional Charter.[24] Thus, constitutionalist discourse clearly also served the purposes of the Court as a kind of supranational "norm entrepreneur," who, among other things, was promoting new constraints and capacities—with, not least, the effect of increasing its own power. Over decades, then, the European Community was slowly constitutionalized, but there was no single foundational—or constitutional—normative moment; and, for sure, there was no single *pouvoir constituant* and comprehensive act

20. Peter Lindseth, "The Paradox of Parliamentary Supremacy: Delegation, Democracy, and Dictatorship in Germany and France, 1920–1950s," *Yale Law Journal* 113 (2004): 1341–1415.

21. See Andrew Moravcsik, "The Origins of Human Rights Regimes: Democratic Delegation in Postwar Europe," *International Organization* 54 (2000): 217–52.

22. I take this expression from Jamie Mayerfeld, "A Madisonian Argument for Strengthening International Human Rights Institutions: Lessons from Europe" (on file with author).

23. J.H.H. Weiler, *The Constitution of Europe: Do the New Clothes Have an Emperor? and Other Essays on European Integration* (Cambridge: Cambridge University Press, 1999), and Ulrich Haltern, *Europarecht: Dogmatik im Kontext* (Tübingen: Mohr Siebeck, 2006).

24. *Les Verts-Parti Ecologiste v Parliament*, Case 294/83.

of democratic self-authorization. In fact, the process appeared as a kind of supranational and quasi-secret "serial constitutionalism."[25]

However, with the acceleration of European integration beginning in the late 1980s—and the increase in majority voting in particular (i.e., the decrease in occasions for vetoing to protect core national interests)—the balance between normative supranationalism and intergovernmentalism appeared to be upset. Outvoted Member States now face the question whether they are willing to give loser's consent ever more often—and, if so, whether they should do so in the absence of a sense of being part of a single overall political community.

It is at this juncture that advocates for a specifically *pluralist* transnational constitutionalism have entered the conversation about the nature of the EU. According to Weiler and others, the EU is precisely *not* on the way to statehood, or complete Union—rather, Europeans constitute a "People of Others," a plurality of peoples who seek to respect and preserve their differences, while cooperating closely in a number of policy areas (and also engaging in mutual learning in the process).[26] In particular, Member States conform to the notion of an open constitutional state, as they add provisions in their constitutions about furthering the process of European integration and respecting European law. But at the same time—and this is crucial—they respect each other's various forms of "integrity anxiety" and grant each other willingly vetoes, reservations, special arrangements, and opt-outs. Flexibility serves to alleviate a political-constitutional integrity anxiety that prima facie is considered legitimate. Thus, Europe has developed a number of specific practices that embody constitutional tolerance: the principle of mutual recognition and the doctrine of margin of appreciation in particular; these take the values of different constitutional traditions seriously and avoid a process of legal homogenization that would be characteristic of supranational state building.[27]

The EU, then, appears to combine the best of both worlds: on the one hand, close, formalized cooperation, entrenched, protected and indeed constitutionalized at the supranational level, and yet, on the other hand,

25. Gráinne de Burca, "The Drafting of a Constitution for the European Union: Europe's Madisonian Moment or a Moment of Madness?" *Washington and Lee Law Review* 61 (2004): 558.

26. See Weiler, "Europe's *Sonderweg*,"; Kalypso Nicolaïdis, "Our European Demoi-cracy," in *Whose Europe? National Models and Constitution of the European Union*, ed. Stephen Weatherill and Kalypso Nicolaïdis (Oxford: Oxford University Press, 2003), 137–52; and Kalypso Nicolaïdis, "The New Constitution as European 'Demoi-cracy?'" *Critical Review of International Social and Political Philosophy* 7 (2004): 76–93.

27. Conforming to Goethe's maxim—and thereby contrasting with constitutional closure: "Tolerance should be a temporary attitude only: it must lead to recognition. To tolerate means to insult."

also an explicit commitment to respect, recognize, and even to celebrate, diversity. The laws of others are in fact not merely tolerated (an approach potentially compatible with constitutional closure and limitation); rather, the laws of others are engaged with, sometimes selectively appropriated in a process of mutual learning and opening, and sometimes, where convergence is to be avoided, actively recognized. And in addition, many new laws are in fact still made *with* others.

In sum, we find here a form of constitutionalism that is beyond a group of states, but not unconnected to them; it constrains them (thereby doing justice to one rather uncontroversial dimension of constitutionalism), but it seeks to avoid a lack of democratic legitimacy through the flexibility described above: Member States cannot have anything like "raw international law" imposed on them that might violate some of their deepest normative commitments. Therefore, the absence of an obvious political act of democratic self-authorization of the political community can also be said not to pose any real normative challenge. Constitutionalism here is limiting and limited; it respects and even contains existing constitutional traditions of the various Member States; and it can exist without an overall European civic identity and a Pan-European constitutionalist discourse.

What are we to make of this rather irenic-sounding picture? First, there is a normative one-way idealization here—but this time it is actually to be found in the realm beyond the nation-state. What appears at first sight like a form of supranational multiculturalism in fact turns out to be what one might call plural, statist monoculturalism. A mouthful, admittedly, which is simply to suggest, however, that in this vision diversity is recognized only among states; the practices of mutual recognition of which defenders of constitutional tolerance and European pluralism are so proud, admit states only as agents and addressees.[28] There is little evidence that this particular approach (as opposed to European rights jurisprudence in general) helps to strengthen the rights of individuals, or that it helps to preserve (let alone increase) the *internal* diversity of Member States. This is, of course, not a problem in itself—diversity is not ipso facto a good thing—but it is a problem for a specifically diversity-based justification of European constitutionalism: it appears to reveal double standards. In particular, within European nation-states tolerance, let alone multiculturalism, which is widely seen as discredited, are hardly popular normative justifications.[29] To be sure, this is not a knockdown

28. Kalypso Nicolaïdis, "Trusting the Poles: Constructing Europe through Mutual Recognition," *Journal of European Public Policy* 14 (2007): 682–98.

29. I do not endorse the more or less standard European view that something meaningfully called multiculturalism has failed in the Netherlands and the United Kingdom; I am merely reporting the common perception.

objection to the picture we are presented with. But it points to a possible form of hypocrisy in trying to dress up a revamped version of de facto intergovernmentalism (as evidence by the stress on vetoes, opt-outs, etc.) with values that not many European citizens actually rank highly, and very few associate with the EU in particular.

Second, the vision of Europe as devoted to the preservation of diversity is normatively dependent on either a theory of liberal nationalism or a theory of multiculturalism. More likely it is the former, as only diversity among preconstituted peoples with distinct cultures is really at issue; while the latter, as just said, appears as widely discredited across the continent. Consequently, this version of post-state constitutionalism very much shares normative foundations with at least some of the advocates of constitutional closure. While we now have mutual engagement and dialogue, it is clear that ultimately existing constitutional (and larger cultural traditions) will stay in place. Once more, this is not a critical objection—but it brings out potentially very problematic underlying normative and sociological assumptions.

Moreover, while advocates of this particular kind of constitutionalism can make a convincing case that constitutionalism is not one thing and that it can at least partially be disaggregated, it also seems that some of the basic elements often associated with constitutionalism disappear here—and that nothing new appears to compensate for their functions. In particular, there is the ordinary function of *clarification*: constitutions clarify, when they allocate powers, specify rights, and set out the parameters of a constitutionalist discourse.[30] Now, the constitutionalism described here certainly does not clarify; rather, the quasi-permanent process of negotiating what Europeans want to share with others and what they do not want to share is, for the most part, not very transparent; it involves highly differential relations among members of the polity; and it can easily empower those who can work an increasingly arcane system of exemptions and opt-outs (or can negotiate new special deals).[31] At the same time, to maintain the possibility of always being able to negotiate or renegotiate something special, a kind of supranationally shared culture of mutual accommodation and consensus needs to be and stay in place.

Furthermore, this constitutionalism has to rely on the assumption that delegated supranational authority will *not* fundamentally clash with national constitutional traditions (of which at least some national constitutional courts regard themselves as the ultimate guardians)—that is,

---

30. See Alexander Somek, "Postconstitutional Treaty," *German Law Journal* 8 (2007): 1121–32.
    31. Ibid.

not clash in a way that cannot be resolved through opt-outs and other such mechanisms. Again, this is an observation more than any kind of conclusive objection—but it shows how potentially fragile the achievements of a constitutionalism of tolerance and mutual engagement are. It cannot and does not want to foster a positive shared civic identity; its answer to questions about democratic legitimacy is purely negative (by pointing to vetoes and opt-outs); and, to some degree, it relies on a continuous shared belief in a kind of "as-if": let European law be adjudicated and treated *as if* it was like domestic constitutional law. Whether in the long run such a partial form of constitutionalization—heavily dependent on a culture of accommodation and compromise within and above states—is a stable political arrangement certainly remains to be seen.

Finally, how plausible is this picture empirically? It seems a hard case to make that the Union is really about the maximization of diversity. After all, European integration is also a mechanism for exporting a particular model of the European state: aspiring Member States have to conform to a given template and demonstrate their commitment to constitutionalism (and, not least, state capacity). Thus, the success of European constitutionalism is based precisely not on a celebration of diversity, but, overall, on at least some *homogenization* of constitutionalist traditions. Celebrating mutual recognition and the principle of margin of appreciation as centerpieces of the European constitutionalist response to interdependence makes an aspect of the process central that is important, but not nearly as important as the fact that Member States have to demonstrate sameness in having democracy, constitutionalism, and, not least, a working state.

Global (and Societal) Constitutionalism

Global constitutionalism comes in two versions: on the one hand, there is the suggestion that international law is becoming constitutionalized and serving as a hard constraint on the behavior of states; it is, even in the absence of an explicitly constitutionalist discourse, the functional equivalent of constitutional law at the domestic level. Such claims rest on the assumption that a single state is neither necessarily the subject nor the single possible object of a constitution. In this sense, the EU experience clearly serves a kind of template for the constitutionalization of international law and international bodies such as the WTO. In particular, it's a reasonable expectation, in line with the European analogy, that an increasingly powerful court or a centralized dispute settlement mechanism will be crucial to such supranantional constitutionalization—which, however, is also conceived as an open-ended process (i.e., without an obvious goal such as a world state).[32] Some, however, go even further and already see the emergence of a constitution of the international community centered on *ius cogens* and *erga omnes*, or at least an international political society.[33] This world constitution also comes with a specific institutional infrastructure centered on the UN, rights protection, and mechanisms for adjudication (most plausibly in the form of the World Court, but also the International Criminal Court).

The second version is much more radical. Here it is suggested that global constitutionalism ought to break *completely* with the state-centric model that developed in the seventeenth and eighteenth centuries. The decisive issue, according to this line of reasoning, has long ceased to be how to tame and constrain absolutist state power; and, by implication, concerns about the constitutionalization of partial extensions of the modern administrative state into the supranational realm are far less important than the discussion around the EU would suggest. Rather, the challenge now is to develop a "societal constitutionalism" which effectively constrains the exercise of power by nonstate actors. Put differently, the hope is not for the emergence of a global constitutionalism that limits the power of states—a vision that according to defenders of societal constitutionalism (Gunther Teubner, drawing on David Sciulli's work) remains caught in a state-centric logic; rather, advocates of such constitutionalism already observe the formation of civil constitutions negotiated by private or semipublic actors, such as corporations, associations, unions, and NGOs. These constitutions will not necessarily cohere or ever establish a global hierarchy of norms; in fact, a unified global law—and thus a global constitutionalism, let alone a global state—will not materialize. Instead, global law is inevitably diffuse and fragmented, and very often contradictory, so that collisions between different legal regimes constantly have to be negotiated in a pragmatic fashion, rather than be resolved in the framework of some neat, coherent world constitution.[34] Put differently: legal pluralism is the norm; we make rules in shifting constellations with different Others, frequently finding legal clashes, and having to negotiate partly constitutionalized, overlapping, and often contradictory orders, some private, some

32. Andreas Fischer-Lescano, "Die Emergenz der Globalverfassung," *Zeitschrift für ausländisches öffentliches Recht und Völkerrecht—Heidelberg Journal of International Law* 63 (2003): 717–60.

33. See the foundational text by Georges Scelle, "Le droit constitutionnel international," in *Mélanges R. Carré de Malberg* (Paris: Sirey, 1933), 503–15.

34. Andreas Fischer-Lescano and Gunther Teubner, *Regime-Kollisionen: Zur Fragmentierung des globalen Rechts* (Frankfurt am Main: Suhrkamp, 2006).

public. The global village turns out to be, as Teubner has put it, "global Bukowina."

What do we make of these two visions, given our criteria? There seems to me to be no way of accusing proponents of either vision that they are using double standards; in fact, both advance coherent arguments for continuity between the domestic and the supranational realm. Both explicitly justify such continuity by pointing to the weaknesses of the overly state-centric perspective from which many constitutionalist theories suffer. It is less clear, however, that at least the second vision is not dependent on highly specific and controversial empirical and normative assumptions—in particular the systems theory of Niklas Luhmann. This does not, of course, doom these positions to failure, but it is at least an uphill battle to argue that politics and the state really are as insignificant as Luhmann's systems theory generally holds.

What about empirical evidence? There is little doubt that a strengthening of international human rights protection has taken place in recent decades, and that—again—the European example has real force in the debate about the very possibility of supranational constitutionalism. At the same time, it would be very difficult indeed to sustain that international law has somehow hardened in the way that EC law did from the 1960s onward. Moreover, in the absence of an effective UN, there is no enforcement mechanism, and there certainly is no culture of mutual accommodation in the way it has developed in the EU. In fact, the recent European experience itself points to a difficulty with trying to constitutionalize a whole range of rules and institutions beyond the nation-state: the failed attempt at establishing a European Constitution (or, to be precise, to ratify an EU Constitutional Treaty) reveals the dangers and unintended consequences associated with inflating the "currency of constitutionalism" and strategic pitfalls for postnational or post-state constitutionalism.[35] Rather than the "c-word" containing a kind of magic that automatically conjures up legitimacy, the very language of constitutionalism appears to raise the political stakes: whatever has been constitutionalized ceases to be easily contestable—so those disaffected with the status quo have an important incentive to prevent constitutionalization (or so the logic of many opponents of a European constitution goes, but also of opponents of constitutionalizing the WTO, for instance).[36] Or, put differently: the prospect of disconnecting law from politics in fact leads

35. Neil Walker, "A Constitutional Reckoning," *Constellations* 13 (2006): 140–50.

36. Robert Howse and Kalypso Nicolaïdis, "Enhancing WTO Legitimacy? Constitutionalization or Global Subsidiarity?" *Governance* 16 (2003): 73–94, and Jeffrey L. Dunoff, "Constitutional Conceits: The WTO's 'Constitution' and the Discipline of International Law," *European Journal of International Law* 17 (2006): 647–75.

to intense politicization. This might be a good thing or a bad thing, but a strengthening of constitutionalism is by no means the obvious outcome (as it was not in the case of the EU).

Finally, whether societal constitutionalism can be effective is an entirely open empirical question. The examples pointed to by its proponents—ICANN, international sports associations, maybe the TRIPS agreement—certainly do not inspire the kind of confidence needed completely to break with established state-centered paradigms. In particular, a large question mark remains about the enforceability of civil constitutions in the absence of states. To be sure, enforceability is always a sensitive issue for constitutionalist thought (and for constitutional courts in particular). But the advocates of societal constitutionalism owe more of an answer to these concerns than they have provided so far.

Conclusion

This essay has found most positions in favor of constitutional closure deeply problematic on a number of levels. Many rely on unconvincing one-way idealizations and on normatively and empirically dubious background theories. More plausible are views that are skeptical of constitutionalism beyond the state on essentially conceptual-historical grounds—although in the end there is little reason to reify one particular idealized eighteenth-century constellation of legal and political elements and deny that constitutionalism could not be broken down into different parts. In particular, a basic notion of constitutionalism as entrenched limits on political power subject to supranational adjudication seems transferable to the realm outside the state without thereby making constitutionalism become incoherent or empirically irrelevant.

The most plausible example of such a partial constitutionalization beyond the state is the EU. The proponents of a particular constitutionalism of tolerance and mutual engagement supposedly embodied in the Union have certainly painted a coherent picture, but they arguably overplay their normative hand when justifying their form of constitutionalism in ways that very often do not square with empirical realities. And they tacitly rely on a background culture of compromise and mutual accommodation, which is a real political achievement but also exacts equally real costs in transparency.

Even less convincing are claims about global constitutionalism and societal constitutionalism outside the state. Both lack any far-reaching empirical evidence, and neither has succeeded in alleviating concerns about a lack of democratic legitimacy and constitutionalism's capacity of actual enforcement in the absence of both states and an EU-style culture of mutual accommodation. Global legal pluralism might be celebrated for the diversity and spontaneity it could possibly foster—but it will be even more lacking in transparency than EU constitutionalism, and it might well turn out simply to be rule by the stronger (or regulation by the savvier expert).[37]

Both propositions for global constitutionalism appear as examples of a kind of normative overinvestment in constitutionalism—as if more constitutionalism were always automatically a good thing and as if "constitution talk" could somehow by itself generate legitimacy. As the experience with the EU Constitutional Treaty in particular has shown, the "c-word" (and the specter of a largely irreversible constitutional settlement it necessarily conjures up) can be just as delegitimizing.

Thus, post-state constitutionalism is hardly the last realistic utopia. But it also is not an automatic threat to constitutional-democratic integrity. Above all, it is not a conceptual impossibility. But that in itself simply says nothing about its desirability on a case-by-case basis, and also says nothing about the particular normative goals that constitutionalism in certain contexts might help to achieve.

37. Martti Koskenniemi, "The Fate of Public International Law: Between Technique and Politics," *Modern Law Review* 70 (2007): 1–30.

13

Constitutionalism in a Theocratic World

RAN HIRSCHL

OVER THE PAST FEW DECADES, principles of theocratic governance have gained enormous public support worldwide.[1] At the same time, the world has witnessed the rapid spread of constitutionalism and judicial review. Constitutional supremacy—a concept that has long been a major pillar of the American political order—is now shared, in one form or another, by more than one hundred countries and several supranational entities across the globe.[2] At the uneasy intersection of two sweeping trends—the tremendous increase of popular support for principles of theocratic governance and the global spread of constitutionalism—a new legal and political order has emerged: constitutional theocracy.

What is constitutional theocracy? In a "pure" theocracy (say, the Islamic state envisioned by the Prophet Muhammad in the early seventh century or its emulation in Mahdist Sudan of the late nineteenth century), the supreme religious leader is also the apex political leader. Law proclaimed by the ruler is also considered a divine revelation, and hence the law of God. In a closely related ecclesiocracy (e.g., the Vatican), an ensconced institutional religious leadership is at the helm; the religious leaders assume a leading role in the state, but do not claim to be instruments of divine revelation.[3] In contrast, formal separation exists in con-

---

I thank the participants of the "Limits of Constitutional Democracy" conference, and especially Steve Macedo, Jeff Tulis, and Ayelet Shachar for their helpful comments on an earlier draft.

1. On the resurgence of religion in world politics, see, e.g., John Micklethwait and Adrian Wooldridge, *God Is Back* (New York: Penguin Books, 2009); Gabriel Almond et al., *Strong Religion: The Rise of Fundamentalisms around the World* (Chicago: University of Chicago Press, 2003); Peter Berger, ed., *The Desecularization of the World: Resurgent Religion and World Politics* (Grand Rapids, MI: Eerdmans, 1999).

2. See, e.g., Tom Ginsburg, "The Global Spread of Constitutional Review," in *The Oxford Handbook of Law and Politics*, ed. Keith Whittington et al. (Oxford: Oxford University Press, 2008), 81–98.

3. Interestingly, the Vatican, the world's undisputed bastion of Catholicism, has recently reformed its legal system so that as of January 1, 2009, Italian laws no longer apply automatically to the Vatican state (Holy See). Instead, Vatican clerics will examine pertinent Italian laws to determine their compatibility with Canon Law and Catholic moral principles.

stitutional theocracy between political leadership and religious authority. Power in constitutional theocracies resides in political figures who operate within the bounds of a constitution rather than from within the religious leadership itself. Basic principles such as the separation of powers are constitutionally enshrined. The constitution also typically establishes a constitutional court that is mandated to carry out some form of active judicial review.

At the same time, constitutional theocracies defy the Franco-American doctrine of strict structural and substantive separation of religion and state. Akin to models of "establishment" or "state religion," constitutional theocracies both formally endorse and actively support a single religion or faith denomination. Moreover, that state religion is enshrined as the principal source that informs all legislation and methods of judicial interpretation. Unlike the handful of European countries that grant exclusive recognition and support to a given state religion, the designated state religion in constitutional theocracies is often viewed as constituting the foundation of the modern state; as such, it is an integral part, or even the metaphorical pillar, of the polity's national metanarrative. In this way, religion often determines the polity's boundaries of collective identity as well as the scope and nature of some or all of the rights and duties assigned to its residents.

Constitutional theocracies, however, do more than grant exclusive recognition and support to a given state religion: laws must conform to principles of religious doctrine, and no statute may be enacted that is repugnant to these principles. In most instances, a well-developed nexus of religious bodies, tribunals, and authorities operates in lieu of, or in tandem with, a civil court system. The opinions and jurisprudence of these authorities and tribunals carry notable symbolic weight and play a significant role in public life. Importantly, however, the entirety of this nexus of laws and institutions is subject to judicial review by a constitutional court or tribunal. This tribunal consists of judges who are often well versed in both general and religious law and can speak knowledgeably on pertinent matters of law to jurists at Yale Law School as well as at the al-Azhar center of Islamic learning in Cairo.

The "ideal" model of a constitutional theocracy can be summarized by outlining four main elements: (1) adherence to some or all core elements of modern constitutionalism, including the formal distinction between political leadership and religious authority, and the existence of some form of active judicial review; (2) the presence of a single religion or religious denomination that is formally endorsed by the state, akin to a "state religion"; (3) the constitutional enshrining of the religion, its texts, directives, and interpretations as *a* or *the* main source of legislation and judicial interpretation of laws—essentially, laws may not infringe upon injunctions of the state-endorsed religion; and (4) a nexus of religious bodies and tribunals that often not only carry tremendous symbolic weight but are also granted official jurisdictional status and operate in lieu of, or in an uneasy tandem with, a civil court system. Most importantly, their jurisdictional autonomy notwithstanding, some key aspects of religious tribunals' jurisprudence are subject to constitutional review by apex courts, often created and staffed by the state.

As of the early twenty-first century, as many as a billion people live in polities that either fall squarely within the definition of a constitutional theocracy or feature many of the substantive characteristics and tensions of such a legal order. The 1979 Islamic revolution in Iran established a paradigmatic modern example of constitutional theocracy.[4] From the 1970s to 2000 alone, at least two dozen predominantly Muslim countries, from Egypt to Pakistan, declared the Shari'a "a" or "the" source of legislation.[5] The more recent new constitutions of Afghanistan (2004) and Iraq (2005) reflect precisely that type of dual commitment to principles of the Shari'a and to principles of human rights, constitutional law, and popular sovereignty. In several other countries, precepts of Islam have been incorporated into the constitution, penal code, and personal status laws of subnational units, most notably in twelve Nigerian states, Pakistan's Northwest Frontier province, and Indonesia's Aceh and to various degrees in five Malaysian states.

Granted, Malaysia or Egypt is a world apart from Iran or the Vatican in terms of how lax or rigid the actual translation of religious principles into public life is. But in virtually all of these countries, religion not only plays a key collective identity role but is also granted a formal constitutional status; serves as a source of law, whether symbolically or practically; and, more importantly, enjoys jurisdictional autonomy in matters extending from personal status or education to essential omnipresence in many aspects of life and politics. A further two billion people live in countries such as India, Ireland, or Turkey where no particular religion is granted formal status but where religious affiliation is a pillar of collective identity. The de facto, as opposed to de jure, boundaries of religion and state in these countries are blurred at best, and are continually contested in both the political and the judicial sphere.

Regimes in these and other countries throughout the new world of constitutional theocracies have been struggling with questions of a profoundly

---

4. See Olivier Roy, "Une théocratie constitutionnelle: les institutions de la République islamique d'Iran," *Politique étrangère* 52 (1987): 327–38.

5. The Khomeini-led revolution in Iran is perhaps the quintessential manifestation of this broad trend. See Said A. Arjomand, "Islamic Constitutionalism," *Annual Review of Law and Society* 3 (2007): 123.

foundational nature, forced to navigate between cosmopolitanism and parochialism, modern and traditional metanarratives, constitutional principles and religious injunctions, contemporary governance and ancient texts, judicial and pious interpretation. More often than not, the clash between these conflicting visions results in fierce struggles over the nature of the body politic and its organizing principles.

Strikingly, despite the growing scholarly interest in and bourgeoning literature on comparative constitutional law and the international migration of constitutional ideas, we still know little about constitutional law and politics in countries where the potentially explosive combination of modern constitutionalism and the fundamentals of theocratic governance come together. Akin to early maps of the world where tracts of emptiness cover much of the non-Western world, the jurisprudential landscape of constitutional theocracies, and the role of courts and religious tribunals in such polities more generally, remains a terra incognita of sorts, almost completely uncharted, let alone theorized.[6]

In this chapter, I explore several key aspects of constitutionalism in a theocratic world and their contribution to understanding the tense relationship between constitutionalism and democracy. I begin by placing constitutional theocracy within the range of constitutional responses to the problem of "religion and state" worldwide. Second, I identify the challenges posed by the theocratic surge toward conventional models of constitutional democracy as well as power-sharing, consociational models that view constitutions as effective means for mitigating tensions in multiethnic polities. Third, I examine a few innovative constitutional and legal means employed by predominantly religious polities to temper the challenge of theocracy. Much like its constraining or stabilizing role in a democracy, constitutionalism becomes a favored domain for antitheocratic forces as they seek to tame the spread of religious fundamentalism and diffuse attempts to establish a full-fledged theocracy.

Constitutional Theocracy in Context

To fully understand the scope, nature, and distinct characteristics of constitutional theocracy, a brief discussion of its place within the range of constitutional responses to the worldwide question of "religion and state" is needed.

As every amateur historian acknowledges, religion and politics were closely allied, indeed often inseparable and unified, throughout much of

---

6. I attempt to address this lacuna in Ran Hirschl, *Constitutional Theocracy* (Cambridge: Harvard University Press, 2010).

human history before the eighteenth century. The separation of church and state was seen by Enlightenment thinkers as a means of confining dangerous and irrational religious passions to the private sphere. In the modern West, the long-standing French policy of *laïcité* is arguably the clearest manifestation of the desire to restrict clerical and religious influence over the state.[7] In several liberal democracies, most notably Canada, a softer version of the formal separation accompanied by a true commitment to multiculturalism and diversity (a "mosaic" or "accomodationist" rather than "melting pot" or "assimilationist" approach) has emerged, whereby state and religion are separated, but the conception of citizenship is not tied to strict secularism. But, as Canadian philosopher Charles Taylor notes, the religious has never been lost in Western culture; it has merely become one among many stories striving for acceptance.[8] Although the separation approach in its several versions is the one most familiar to scholars of constitutional law and politics in the United States, expanding our horizons comparatively reveals several other constitutional-institutional models for delineating the relationship between religion and state; these models are of considerable importance to an analysis of the phenomenon of constitutional theocracy. I briefly discuss each in turn.

The first model involves polities that have separated religion from state in what may be called *separationist reformism*. The secularization of predominantly religious Turkey advanced by Mustafa Kemal Atatürk is perhaps the best-known example of separationist reformism in the twentieth century. Following the demise of the Ottoman Empire, the Kemalist secular-nationalist elite decided to abandon Islamic culture and laws, in favor of secularism and modernism. Accordingly, both the 1961 and the 1982 constitutions established an official state policy of laïcism.[9] In Ethiopia, the Ethiopian Orthodox Church was disestablished as the state church in 1974, and its patriarch was executed by the Marxist Derg military junta in 1979. In a notably more civilized fashion, Portugal (1976), Spain (1978), and Italy (1984) all adopted new constitutions or constitutional amendments that disestablished Catholicism as their state religion.

A second pertinent constitutional model is a *weak form of religious establishment*—for example, establishment through the formal, mainly ceremonial, designation of a certain religion as "state religion." Several

7. See Rex Ahdar and Ian Leigh, *Religious Freedom in the Liberal State* (Oxford: Oxford University Press, 2005), 73.

8. See Charles Taylor, *A Secular Age* (Cambridge: Harvard University Press, 2007).

9. This official policy has been challenged by the AKP-led government, as illustrated by the constitutional amendment of February 2008, effectively lifting the ban on wearing the Islamic headscarf in the public education system. In June 2008 Turkey's Constitutional Court declared that amendment unconstitutional.

European countries illustrate this model.[10] A case in point is the designation of the Evangelical Lutheran Church as the "state church" in Norway, Denmark, Finland, and Iceland—arguably some of Europe's most liberal and progressive polities. In England, the monarch is "Supreme Governor" of the Church of England and "Defender of the Faith." The crown has a role in senior ecclesiastical matters and, by the same token, the church is involved in the coronation of a new monarch, and senior bishops are represented in the House of Lords.

A third model, more a state of affairs than a formal constitutional arrangement, is that of official separation of religion and state with de facto preeminence of one denomination. Here, separation of church and state and religious freedoms more generally are constitutionally guaranteed, but long-standing patterns of politically systematized church hegemony and church-centric morality continue to loom large over the constitutional arena. Many Latin American countries, where the vast majority of the population is Roman Catholic and where the history of Catholic Church dominance dates back to the preindependence era, fall in this category. Despite the considerable variance in the legacy of church preeminence, there is a strong echo of such Catholic morality in the constitutional jurisprudence of all of these countries, as well as in that of other predominantly Catholic polities such as the Philippines, Poland, or Ireland.

A fourth constitutional response to the tension between secularism and religiosity is the *religious jurisdictional enclaves* model. Here, the general law is secular, yet a degree of jurisdictional autonomy is granted to religious communities, on the basis of either substantive, subject-matter jurisdictional boundaries or more conventional spatial or regional boundaries (e.g., federalism). Countries such as Kenya, India, and Israel grant recognized religious or customary communities the jurisdictional autonomy to pursue their own traditions in several areas of law, most notably family law. Kenya, for example, has enacted a set of statutes to recognize the diversity of personal laws pertaining to different groups of citizens. India has long been entangled in a bitter debate concerning the scope and status of Muslim and Hindu religious personal laws, versus the individual rights and liberties protected by the Indian Constitution. Each religious community in Israel, including the Jewish community, has autonomous religious courts that hold jurisdiction over its respective members' marriage and divorce affairs. Religious affiliation, conversion, and the provision of religious services are controlled by statutory religious bodies, whose decisions must comply with general principles of

10. A diluted version of this model is at work in Germany, where the institutional apparati of the Evangelical, Catholic, and Jewish religious communities are designated as public corporations and therefore qualify for state support pursuant to the German church tax.

administrative and constitutional law. Core features of this arrangement originated from the Ottoman millet system of semiautonomous jurisdictional enclaves to religious minorities.

An increasingly prevalent yet seldom discussed fifth model is essentially a mirror image of these "religious jurisdictional enclaves"—what we might call *secular jurisdictional enclaves*. Here, most of the law is religious; however, certain areas of the law, such as economic law, are "carved out" and insulated from influence by religious law. Most Islamic countries maintain criminal and economic codes that are based on French civil law, British common law, or other sources of law introduced by, or otherwise borrowed from, European nations, alongside a variable status for *fiqh* (Islamic law and jurisprudence).[11]

An interesting case in point here is Saudi Arabia, arguably one of the countries whose legal system comes closest to being fully based on *fiqh*. Shari'a law is bad for business, however. Whereas Saudi courts apply Shari'a in all matters of civil, criminal, or personal status, Article 232 of a 1965 Royal Decree provides for the establishment of a commission for the settlement of all commercial disputes. Although judges of the ordinary courts are usually appointed by the Ministry of Justice from among graduates of recognized Shari'a law colleges, members of the commission for the settlement of disputes are appointed by the Ministry of Trade. In other words, Saudi Arabia has effectively exempted the entire finance, banking, and corporate capital sectors from application of Shari'a rules. Foreign investors have not protested the move.

The jurisdictional enclaves model is not limited to economic law. Several countries in the Middle East have enacted laws that exclude certain important aspects of the law from the purview of sacred law, thereby expanding the jurisdictional authority of ordinary courts (whose decisions are subject to scrutiny by the constitutional courts) at the expense of religious tribunals. Several countries in the region (e.g., Egypt in 2000, Morocco in 2004; Algeria in 2005) have also embarked upon family law reforms that involve codification of legal amalgams of moderate Islamic sources and secular legal principles, such as gender equality and procedural justice. These legal reforms erode the interpretive monopoly of religious authorities and make the modernized areas of law justiciable by the ordinary courts.

Finally, an increasingly common approach to governing religion and state relations is a *mixed system of religious law and general legal principles*—a close relative of the ideal type of constitutional theocracy. It

11. See Stephen Schwartz, "Shari'a in Saudi Arabia, Today and Tomorrow," in *Radical Islam's Rules: The Worldwide Spread of Extreme Shari'a Law,* ed. Paul Marshall (Lanham, MD: Rowman & Littlefield, 2005), 20.

is well known that Afghanistan has long been torn between conflicting values of tradition and modernism. From 1994 to 2001, the country was ruled by the radical Islamist Taliban, but the U.S.-led military campaign removed the Taliban from power and installed a more moderate regime representing an array of groups hitherto in opposition: moderate religious leaders and the country's elites and intellectuals in exile. The new Constitution of Afghanistan came into effect in January 2004, and it states that Afghanistan is an Islamic Republic (Art. 1); that the "sacred religion of Islam is the religion of the Islamic Republic of Afghanistan" (Art. 2); and that "[n]o law shall contravene the tenets and provisions of the holy religion of Islam in Afghanistan" (Art. 3). Courts are allowed to use Hanafi jurisprudence in situations of constitutional lacunae (Art. 130). At the same time, the constitution also enshrines the right to private property (Art. 40); and resurrects a woman's right to vote, as well as to run for and serve in office (Art. 22). The 2004 Constitution also establishes a Supreme Court (Stera Mahkama) composed of nine judges appointed by the president for a term of ten years (arts. 116–17). All members of the Court "[s]hall have higher education in legal studies or Islamic jurisprudence" (Art. 118).[12]

The Islamic Republic of Iran is commonly considered a fundamentalist theocracy, with governing principles and practices that bear very little resemblance to prevailing principles of Western constitutionalism. In practice, however, its system of government features many elements of modern constitutionalism. In fact, Iran has a long legacy of constitutionalism dating back to the early twentieth century. The 1906 Imperial Constitution, as it is has come to be known, had been in effect for more than seven decades when the 1979 Islamic revolution came. Much of the institutional nexus it established has been a part of Iranian political life for more than a century now. It stipulated that sovereignty came from the people, symbolized in the person of the monarch. It stated that an elected parliament should ensure that this power is represented through the deputies, and should be implemented through the legislations enacted thereupon. It also established a bicameral legislature and set up detailed electoral rules and procedures. Articles 1 and 2 of the supplementary fundamental laws of 1907 established Islam as the official religion of Iran, and specified that all laws of the nation must be approved by a committee of Shi'a clerics. That the Pahlavi dynasty ignored this directive in the later part of the twentieth century was one of the main reasons for the Islamic revolution of 1979, which among other things replaced the 1906 constitution with a new one.

---

12. The Iraqi Constitution of 2005 or Yemen's Constitution of 1994 offer other variants of this amalgam.

Two distinctly softer, albeit equally fascinating, exemplars of constitutional theocracy are Pakistan and Egypt. Pakistan has a long-standing
tradition of constitutionalism and a British-influenced tradition of legal
education and practice. At the same time, Islam has been a major political force in Pakistan—at least since the early 1970s. These conflicting
trends reflect a complex, if not completely blurred, collective identity,
torn between modernity and tradition, universalism and religiosity, and
has been rapidly translated at both the institutional and jurisprudential
levels of Pakistan's constitutional landscape. In 1973 Pakistani legislators departed from the country's rich British common-law tradition by
enabling the Pakistani judiciary to use Islam as an authoritative source in
constitutional interpretation. From 1978 to 1980, President Muhammad
Zia-ul-Haq established a nexus of Shari'a-based high courts at the pro-
vincial level as well as the Shari'at Appellate Bench at the Supreme Court;
each of these would be responsible for ensuring the appropriate imple-
mentation of Shari'a law. In 1985 president Zia went on to introduce a
set of amendments to the Constitution, in which he effectively stipulated:
"All existing laws shall be brought in conformity with the Injunctions of
Islam as laid down in the Holy Qur'an and Sunna, in this Part referred to
as the Injunctions of Islam, and no law shall be enacted which is repugnant to such Injunctions." In theory, this means that legislation must be
in full compliance with principles of the Shari'a.

At the same time, the Supreme Court of Pakistan, while falling short of
advancing a truly progressive human rights agenda by Western standards,
has nonetheless emerged as a bastion of relative cosmopolitanism in an
otherwise increasingly religious Pakistan. It has managed to skillfully
contain the jurisdictional expansion of Shari'a courts and avoid elevat-
ing Islamization into a *Grundnorm* of the entire Pakistani constitutional
order through the development of the "harmonization theory" according
to which no specific provision of the Constitution stands above any or
all other provisions. The Constitution as a whole must be interpreted
in a harmonious fashion so that specific provisions are read as an integral part of the entire Constitution, not as standing above it. The Court
has also retained its overarching jurisdictional authority, including its de
facto appellate capacity over the Shari'at Appellate Bench at the Supreme
Court. This has proved itself time and again to be a safety valve for moderate or secular interests.

Egypt presents a further telling example, having established a system
of judicial review back in 1979. The criminal penal code is largely nonreligious, as are numerous recently modernized economic, property, and
investment rules. In 1971 President Anwar al-Sadat passed a new constitution that, on the one hand, preserved Egypt's socialist legacy and,
at the same time, stated that Shari'a was a primary source of legislation

in Egypt. In 1980 Article 2 of the Egyptian Constitution was amended so as to establish principles of Islamic jurisprudence (the Shari'a) as *the* (not *a*) primary source of legislation in Egypt. Alongside this amendment, Islamism in Egypt has enjoyed an astounding growth in popularity over the past three decades. Under the guidance of the Muslim Brotherhood, Egyptian Islamism has consistently opposed the modernist-nationalist agenda advocated by the government, the historically powerful National Democratic Party, the "pro-statist" military, and, above all, Egypt's moderate, economically well-off elites. Of course, with this expansion the familiar challenges of constitutional theocracy emerged.

As with its counterpart in Pakistan, the Egyptian Supreme Constitutional Court has emerged as an important forum for dealing with the core question of the status of Shari'a rules—arguably the most controversial and fundamental collective identity issue troubling the Egyptian polity. To address this question in a moderate way, the Court developed an innovative interpretative matrix of religious directives—the first of its kind by a nonreligious tribunal. It departed from the ancient traditions of the *fiqh* schools and has instead developed a new framework for interpreting the Shari'a. Specifically, the Court has developed a flexible, modernist approach to interpretation that distinguishes between "unalterable and universally binding principles, and malleable applications of those principles."[13] Legislation that contravenes a strict, unalterable principle recognized as such by all interpretive schools is declared unconstitutional and void; while at the same time, *ijtihad* (contemplation or external interpretation) is permitted in cases of textual lacunae, or where the pertinent rules are vague or open-ended. This wide scope offers the chance to implement Shari'a in different social environments and to allow jurists, including constitutional court judges who wish to invoke religious law, to choose which school they want to follow in a given instance. In so doing, it provides the closest concrete illustration currently on offer of Noah Feldman's argument that Islamic law is not inherently incompatible with interpretive pluralism or with democracy.

The Theocratic Challenge to Conventional Constitutional Theory

The apparently "oxymoronic" nature of a constitution that features significant theocratic substance does not necessarily mean that such a form of constitutionalism is partial, incomplete, or illegitimate. Principles of

---

13. Nathan Brown, "Islamic Constitutionalism in Theory and Practice," in *Democracy, the Rule of Law and Islam,* eds. E. Cortan and A. Omar Sherif (The Hague, Netherlands: Kluwer Law International, 1999), 496.

divine authority and theocratic governance are often at odds with international human rights regimes and principles, perhaps most tellingly in the contexts of religious freedoms, gender equality, or reproductive liberty. That said, an array of possible interpretations and schools of thought, from the strictest to the most liberal, exist within virtually all major religious traditions. So while certain ultraconservative interpretations of religious precepts defy universal values such as tolerance or equality, liberal interpretations of the same precepts suggest some Van diagram–like common ground between religion and, say, democracy or liberalism, may be found.[14] Reform Judaism, for example, is much easier than Ultra-Orthodox Judaism to reconcile with modern ideals of gender equality or freedom of thought.

It is true that akin to any other intolerant perception of the good, a constitutional theocracy is not a natural companion of liberalism or liberal constitutionalism. But it is not inherently at odds with a plain and simple definition of constitutional democracy.[15] Popular legitimacy is something constitutional theocratic regimes do not take lightly. Unlike a pure theocracy, the *demos* in most constitutional theocracies has some nontrivial say in the choice of government (e.g., by periodic elections). The powers of the government are constrained by a constitution, in which certain basic rules, norms, rights, entitlements, and limitations are granted entrenched status and are therefore not easily amenable to change. True, constitutional theocracy is incompatible with a radical notion of democracy that sees any limitation on the will of the *demos*—for example, through constitutionally entrenched rules or sources of authority other than the people themselves—as violating the ultimate essence of democracy. By that standard, however, no constitutional democracy is indeed purely democratic.

More subtle is the tension between a constitutional theocracy and the view of constitutional protection of certain classic civil liberties as an integral element of democratic (not merely liberal) constitutionalism. The issue, however, seems to be related to the authoritarian or quasi-democratic nature of the regime, not to the theocratic aspect per se. Besides, here too, most liberal constitutions limit the scope and application of the rights they protect to full members of the polity. Not everyone in such polities enjoys the right to have rights. Whereas some provisions apply to "everyone" or "every individual," others apply selectively to citizens and to a variable degree to permanent lawful aliens but not to other classes of

14. See, e.g., Noah Feldman, *After Jihad: America and the Struggle for Islamic Democracy* (New York: Farrar, Straus and Giroux, 2003).

15. See, e.g. Walter Murphy, *Constitutional Democracy* (Baltimore: Johns Hopkins University Press, 2007).

people. Prevalent birthright citizenship principles, be it *jus soli* or *jus sanguinis*, have long been drawn upon in most liberal democracies, thereby excluding millions of people from initial access to collective goods.[16] The existence of de facto two-tier conceptions of citizenship that differentiate between full members and "second class" citizens is certainly not a practice foreign to the history and, in some cases, present-day policies of most Western societies. The exclusion or limitation of certain rights from some theocratic constitutions is therefore not a unique practice, unheard of in other settings.

But perhaps more significantly, the obvious tension between theocracy and religious pluralism or religious neutrality (e.g., free expression and [dis]establishment of religion) is not the same as religion-based differential access to core political rights and access to public goods. This problem is illustrated vividly when a polity draws upon religious ascriptions to establish an "ethnocracy" (or its more mellowed "ethnic democracy" version) where the entire political system and the hegemonic religious or ethnic group's foundational national metanarratives are developed and organized so as to benefit members of that group to the detriment of others, and where few or no members of minority ethnic groups are granted proportional access to wealth, power, and opportunities. The political and legal system of Israel (with respect to Jews), Malaysia (with respect to Muslims), or Sri Lanka (with respect to Buddhists) all feature elements of such religion-based preferential treatment. So while none of these countries is a "constitutional theocracy," the formal constitutional status of a foundational ethnoreligious criterion that determines what members of the polity enjoy preferential access to desired public goods illustrates the tension between religion-based ascriptive traits and fundamental democratic governing principles of participation and representation.

More complex still are the challenges that theocracy poses to less idealist notions of constitutionalism. Arguably one of the most admirable functionalist or results-oriented perspectives sees constitutions as establishing an institutional framework for democratic deliberation and, by extension, as offering an effective mechanism for nation building.[17] Unlike Bruce Ackerman's idealist notion of constitution making that is shaped by and reflects the authentic people's will, a pragmatic vision of constitution making sees it as constituting the *demos* and providing a framework for its establishment and evolution. In its more practical guise, a voluminous body of literature on constitutional design and engineering has evolved. Its canonical tenor suggests that when constitutionalization is seen as a

16. Ayelet Shachar, *The Birthright Lottery: Citizenship and Global Inequality* (Cambridge: Harvard University Press, 2009).

17. See, e.g. Jürgen Habermas, *Between Facts and Norms* (Cambridge: MIT Press, 1998).

pragmatic "second order" measure—as opposed to instances of constitutionalization involving a more principled, first order "we the people" outlook—it may help institutionalize attempts to mitigate tensions in ethnically divided polities through the adoption of federalism, secured representation, and other trust-building and power-sharing mechanisms.[18]

Surprisingly, however, although there are many examples of discussions of the mitigating potential of constitutional power-sharing mechanisms to ease rifts along national, ethnic, or linguistic lines, scholars of comparative constitutional design have given little attention to the increasing divisions along secular and religious lines. From an analytical standpoint, the secular-religious divide differs in at least four respects from these more obvious and commonly addressed markers of identity.

First, more than any other divisions along ascriptive or imagined lines, the secular-religious divide cuts across nations otherwise unified by their members' joint ethnic, religious, linguistic, and historical origins. In this sense, the secularism-religiosity factor, or other closely associated distinctions such as universalism versus parochialism, is closer in nature to less visible categories such as income deciles, social class, or cultural milieu than it is to other kinds of markers, such as race, gender, or ethnicity. Nationalist Catalans, the Flemish, or Quebecers see themselves as autonomous people with a unique cultural heritage, language, and history that is distinct from that of Spaniards, Walloons, or Anglophone Canadians, respectively. By contrast, most cosmopolitan *and* traditionalist Egyptians define themselves as members of the same nation, speak the same language or dialects of it, treasure the Pharaoh dynasty, and share the same ancestral ties. Importantly, however, some Egyptians are close adherents of religious directives, while others follow them more casually.

Second, the territorial boundaries of the secular-religious divide are often blurred. Although residents of certain regions within a given country may be more prone to holding theocratic views than residents of other regions, this divide is not neatly demarcated along territorial lines, as is often the case with ethnic or linguistic boundaries. Proponents of theocratic governance may reside in rural towns or in blue-collar neighborhoods on the outskirts of large urban centers. But they may also reside within a few bus stops from bastions of modernism such as art galleries, universities, shopping malls, or government buildings. So the secular-religious divide manifests itself in a wide range of situations in everyday

18. The works that propose various versions of this "consociational" approach are too numerous to cite. A prominent exponent of this line of thought is Arend Lijphart, *Democracy in Plural Societies: A Comparative Exploration* (New Haven: Yale University Press, 1977). A more "integrationist" version is advanced by Donald Horowitz, *Ethnic Groups in Conflict* (Berkeley: University of California Press, 2000).

life, from the sidewalk to the market and from school to the workplace. Territory-based power-sharing mechanisms—or any other kind of joint-governance structures that are based on the allocation of powers or goods by a regional key—may not be an efficient means for analyzing, let alone reducing, tensions along secular-religious lines.

Third, accounts of religion and state tend to assume firm identities and fixed group affiliations, although in reality this is not always the case.[19] To begin with, people have multiple identities beyond their faith-based affiliation. More importantly, membership in a group is in some instances voluntary and self-professed, whereas in others it is determined by laws external to the group, and in yet other cases it is imposed by intragroup practices and traditions. When it comes to religion, labels such as "Jewish," "Christian," or "Muslim" do not tell us much as there are a variety of schools, from very moderate to ultraconservative, within each of these categories. At certain times, one school or the other may enjoy greater support or become more dominant than others. But as the political kaleidoscope shifts, other voices within each religious community become more prevalent, and different aspects of that religion are emphasized. So, identity and group affiliation are not primordial. They are to a large extent politically constructed by a dynamic interplay between intragroup politics and the political context within which that group operates. And religiosity as a marker of identity may be brought to the fore or relegated to a lesser status as coalitions shift, elites transform, and interests change.

Fourth, the assumption that whole peoples share unified interests is, at best, highly questionable. Akin to early writings about the postcolonial world that tended to view postcolonial countries as a homogeneous block, populist academic and media accounts in the West tend to portray the spread of religious fundamentalism in the developing world as a near-monolithic, ever-accelerating, and all-encompassing phenomenon.[20] The West is largely secular and modernist, whereas the non-West is largely religious and traditionalist is the frequent formulation of this supposed dichotomy. In contrast to the Western portrayal of religion as private and relatively benign, "politicized" religions are depicted as being a threat to reason and a hindrance to progress.[21] The Islamic world in particular has been the target of much of this critique. Whereas the West is portrayed as driven by a constant quest for modernism and progressiveness, Islam and Muslims have increasingly been depicted as insular

19. See Rogers Brubaker, *Ethnicity without Groups* (Cambridge: Harvard University Press, 2004).

20. For an oft-cited illustration, see Samuel Huntington, *The Clash of Civilizations and the Remaking of World Order* (New York: Simon & Schuster, 1998).

21. See, e.g., Talal Asad, *Genealogies of Religion* (Baltimore: Johns Hopkins University Press, 1993), 27–29.

and anticosmopolitan.[22] The post-9/11 popular media followed suit by portraying Islamic societies as united by their religious zeal and antiliberal sentiment.

The reality, however, is more complex and nuanced. The sociopolitical struggles in contemporary Iran are widely reported and need not be replicated here. In several instances, religious parties, perhaps by virtue of their participation in the formal political process, are led by pragmatic moderate leaders, not by fundamentalist zealots. Turkey's Justice and Development Party (AKP) or the similarly named PJD (Parti de la Justice et du Développement) in Morocco illustrates this trend. Egypt, to continue with that example, has witnessed tremendous growth in popular support for the Muslim Brotherhood. But this is the same Egypt that attracts tens of millions of tourists every year, a country that produced Anwar al-Sadat, initiator of the historic peace accord with Israel, Naguib Mahfouz, winner of the Nobel Prize in Literature, and Boutros Boutros-Ghali, former U.N. secretary-general, among other world-class luminaries. And yes, it is also the same Egypt that on December 31, 1999, hosted the world's largest outdoor concert to celebrate the new millennium as well as five thousand years since the Ancient Egyptian civilization—an audiovisual megaspectacle by French electronic music icon Jean-Michel Jarre performed at the Grand Pyramids of Giza.

Principles of theocratic governance may pose a threat to the cultural and policy preferences of secular-nationalist elites, as well as of powerful economic stakeholders in these countries. Theocratic governance has seldom appealed to members of the often-cosmopolitan urban intelligentsia and the managerial class. The scientific community tends to resent it. The struggles between scientists and religionists in the United States and elsewhere over evolution theory and embryonic stem cell research are merely two illustrations. Theocratic governance is also often at odds with principles of modern economy and may threaten the interests of major economic sectors and stakeholders. Pragmatic state bureaucrats may see it as an impediment to progress and modernization. And it would be an understatement to say that theocratic governments are not the type of regimes that find favor with supranational trade and monetary bodies such as the International Monetary Fund, the World Bank, or the World Trade Organization. With few exceptions, theocracy has been and remains detested by the military—a powerful symbol of modern nationalism in many developing polities. The Turkish, Pakistani, and Algerian armed forces are only three among many examples that come to mind

22. For a debunking of this dichotomy, see Roxanne Euben, *Journeys to the Other Shore: Muslim and Western Travelers in Search of Knowledge* (Princeton: Princeton University Press, 2006).

here. Finally, the prospect of theocratic government has potentially far-reaching redistributive implications. In terms of demographic indicators, support for religious parties is often closely associated with the relative have-nots and is distinctly more prevalent among occupiers of the periphery, economic and cultural.

These conflicting pressures and interests have led to intense constitutional maneuvering in predominantly religious polities. All of these countries face the sources of friction inherent in a constitutional theocracy—a potentially explosive combination by its very nature, and one that poses new challenges to conventional constitutional ideas about secularism, religious freedom, and the relationship between religion and the state. How can a polity therefore reconcile the principles of accountability, separation of powers, and the notion of "we the people" as the ultimate source of sovereignty when the fundamental notions of divine authority and holy texts make up the supreme governing norm of the state? Who should be vested with the ultimate authority to interpret the divine text, and on what grounds? What ought to be done when principles of modern constitutionalism and human rights collide with religious injunctions and support for theocratic governance? And, more generally, how can a polity advance principles of twenty-first century government or run a modern economy when it treats ancient texts and pious authorities as a main source of legislation?

Constitutionalism against Theocracy

In a constitutional democracy, the powers of the government are constrained by a constitution, in which certain basic rules, norms, rights, entitlements, and constraints are granted entrenched status and are therefore not easily amenable to change by the political power holders of the moment. Akin to constitutional democracy where the former element establishes a core set of entrenched limitations on the scope, nature, and range of possible outcomes of the latter element, constitutionalism in predominantly religious settings plays a key role in curbing the spread and impact of theocratic governance, with its alternative worldviews, texts, and hierarchies of authority.

The growing popular support for principles of theocratic governance in many developing world countries now poses a major threat to the worldviews, cultural propensities, and policy preferences of secular elites and intellectuals, modernist state bureaucracies, powerful economic stakeholders, and the managerial class in these countries. At the same time, "religious talk" is becoming essential to maintaining these elites' popular legitimacy and political hegemony. These conflicting pressures and interests have led to intense constitutional maneuvering, at times even to the adoption of constitutional norms by political elites as a matter of self-interest. Two increasingly common strategies by those who wield political power—and represent the groups and policy preferences that object to a fully fledged theocratic governance—are a constitutional ban of religion-based parties, in some cases notwithstanding of the constitutional enshrinement of a given religion as the state religion and as "a" or "the" source of legislation, and the establishment of constitutional courts that maintain jurisdictional supremacy over religious tribunals, the expansion of constitutional oversight of religious tribunals, and an accompanying tightened political control over the judicial system. These two strategies allow non- or antitheocratic leaders to talk the talk of commitment to religious values without walking the actual walk of that commitment. Let us consider briefly each of these strategies in turn.

As several shrewd observers note, democracy is beneficial to its participants mainly in cases where political divisions do not cut very much deeper than the marginal issues on which we can achieve democratic compromise.[23] But when the stakes are really high, democracy looses much of its appeal, particularly for the projected losers. Constitutional provisions that prohibit political association based on religion constitute one of the common weapons (its questionable effectiveness notwithstanding) used by regimes to contain the tremendous popular following religious parties in these polities have gained. Algeria, Tunisia, Egypt, and Turkey are obvious examples.

As is well known, a vicious decade-long civil war between the French-backed Algerian army and religious militants erupted after the Islamic Salvation Front party gained tremendous support among Algerian voters. In reaction, the historically hegemonic National Liberation Front party canceled the first multiparty election in Algeria after the first round (December 1991). A military coup introduced a state of emergency, which suspended any electoral processes. In 1996 a revised constitution was introduced, which remains in effect today. Article 2 of Algeria's Constitution states that "Islam is the religion of the State." Article 42 allows for the formation of political parties. However, it also states that the right to form political parties "cannot be used to violate the fundamental values and components of the national identity, . . . as well as the democratic and Republican nature of the State. Political parties cannot be founded on religious, linguistic, racial, sex, corporatist or regional basis." Furthermore, political parties are prohibited from resorting to partisan propaganda based on any of these grounds. No political party can resort to any form of violence or constraint, whatever the nature.

23. See, e.g., Russell Hardin, *Liberalism, Constitutionalism and Democracy* (Oxford: Oxford University Press, 1999).

In a similar fashion, Article 1 of the Tunisian Constitution establishes Islam as the state religion. Article 38 further states that the president of the republic must be a Muslim. Article 8 of the Tunisian Constitution guarantees the right to form political parties, but states that "political parties must respect the sovereignty of the people, the values of the republic, human rights, and the principles pertaining to personal status. Political parties pledge to prohibit all forms of violence, fanaticism, racism and discrimination. No political party may take religion, language, race, sex or region as the foundation for its principles, objectives, activity or programs. It is prohibited for any party to be dependent upon foreign parties or interests." So whereas Islam is the official state religion and must be the religion of its leader, no political party may make Islam as the basis of its principles. The apparent confusion is not merely in the reader's mind.

And, in a blatant move against the Muslim Brotherhood in March 2007, Egypt's President Hosni Mubarak introduced a set of constitutional amendments that effectively give more power to the president, ban the establishment of religious parties, and loosen controls on security forces in its "war on terror." Among the reforms introduced is the removal of judicial scrutiny of electoral lists, ballots, and procedures. In addition, the Political Parties Law (Law 40/1977), as amended in 2005, allows a committee headed by the ruling party to suspend an existing party's activities if the ruling party judges the suspension to be "in the national interest."

Under the 1982 Turkish Constitution, the Turkey's Constitutional Court (TCC) is vested with the power to order the closure of political parties whose agenda is found to be "in conflict with the indivisible integrity of the State with its territory and nation, human rights, national sovereignty, and the principles of the democratic and secular Republic," or when "the internal functioning and the decisions of political parties shall not be contrary to the principles of democracy" (Art. 22). Such closure may take place upon the ruling of the TCC in a suit filed by the Public Prosecutor of the republic. Over the past twenty-five years, the TCC has ordered the closure of political parties on eighteen occasions (seventeen of those since 1991).[24] While some of these closures were based on technical grounds (e.g., parties' failure to comply with certain bureaucratic standards), others were based on ideological grounds: for example, several pro-Kurdish parties and, most notably, two major Islamic parties—the Welfare (Refah) Party (dissolved by the TCC in 1998) and the Virtue (Fazilet) Party (dissolved by the TCC in 2001). The TCC continues to

24. See Hootan Shambayati, "The Guardian of the Regime: The Turkish Constitutional Court in Comparative Perspective," in *Constitutional Politics in the Middle East*, ed. S. A. Arjomand (Oxford: Hart Publishing, 2008), 99–121.

be a guardian of the secular state against the new specter of religiosity advanced by the AKP—a reincarnation of the two dissolved Islamist parties and the decisive winner in Turkey's 2007 general election. In a widely publicized decision in July 2008, the TCC came very close to banning the AKP; six of the eleven judges, one vote shy of a necessary seven votes, found the AKP platform unconstitutional. In so doing, the judges signaled that no further "Islamization" will be tolerated by the Court and by its secular and military establishment backers.

A second strategy drawn upon by opponents of theocratic governance is the establishment of constitutional courts armed with active judicial review powers. As recent work in political science establishes, the arrival of political competition, or the emergence of a new constellation of power may make threatened elites and political power holders discover the charms of judicial review.[25] Influential sociopolitical groups who face challenges to their worldviews, ideology, and policy preferences may support the establishment of judicial review and judicial empowerment more generally, as a hegemony-preserving maneuver. These groups and their political representatives are more likely to divert policy-making responsibility to a relatively supportive judiciary when present or when prospective transformations in the political system seem to threaten their own political status and policy preferences. Likewise, when politicians are obstructed from fully implementing their own policy agenda, they may favor the active exercise of constitutional review by a sympathetic judiciary in order to overcome those obstructions.[26]

Delegation and legitimation are not, however, all that attract certain polity members to the lure of the constitutional court. Rather, the very logic of modern constitutional law with its state-driven legitimacy and authority, procedural rules of engagement, methods and styles of reasoning, and often-measured approaches to politically charged questions seems intrinsically appealing to a moderate approach to issues of religion and state. Most modern constitutions, including those of most Middle Eastern countries, contain some form of constitutional catalog of rights, individual freedoms, formal equality, and procedural justice. No matter how weak or tentative these rights provisions are in practice, they still provide a potentially favorable antireligious platform for universalists and cosmopolitans alike. And much like religion, the language, principles,

25. See, e.g., Ran Hirschl, *Towards Juristocracy: The Origins and Consequences of the New Constitutionalism* (Cambridge: Harvard University Press, 2004); Tom Ginsburg, *Judicial Review in New Democracies: Constitutional Courts in Asian Cases* (Cambridge: Cambridge University Press, 2003).

26. See Keith Whittington, "'Interpose Your Friendly Hand': Political Supports for the Exercise of Judicial Review by the United States Supreme Court," *American Political Science Review* 99 (2005): 583–99.

and practice of modern constitutionalism reflect certain metaconcepts, most notably concerning the rule of law (as opposed to the rule of God), judicial (as opposed to clerical) interpretation, and thoughtful reasoning (as opposed to a "keep and receive" obedience).[27]

What is more, constitutional courts' very conception of the rule of (state) law, with its deep-rooted orientation toward the European legal tradition and what Max Weber characterized as formal and rational reasoning, necessarily weakens the potential accommodation of alternative hierarchies of traditional or religious interpretation. The emergence of proportionality as the prevalent interpretive method in comparative constitutional jurisprudence also makes constitutional courts appealing to relatively moderate or secular elites. By its very nature, proportionality favors middle-of-the-road, balanced, judicious, and pragmatic solutions to contested issues. Extreme or radical positions are not likely to fare well under proportionality. Moreover, a constitutional court's reluctance to grant support to radical religious views may also derive from its interest in retaining its status as the one and only legitimate interpreter of laws vis-à-vis the perceived menace of alternative interpretation systems (e.g., religious interpreters and authorities that are well-established within the circles of supporters of theocratic governance and have been steadily gaining support among new crowds).[28] The deep, near-organic reluctance of constitutional courts to recognize the legitimacy of alternative, primarily religious, interpretation systems is one of the main reasons for their near universal appeal to the urban intelligentsia, the "managerial class," and proponents of civic nationalism.

These considerations are not merely theoretical. Constitutional courts in many countries have become important secularizing or religion-limiting forces in their respective polities. It is hardly surprising that in a number of Middle Eastern polities that lack established traditions of judicial activism, judicial reform has been instigated in order to create and empower state-controlled courts in an attempt to counterbalance the spread of religious fundamentalism. Saudi Arabia, for example, has recently embarked upon a comprehensive modernization of its judicial system. Part of the rationale for the overhaul is the creation of courts specializing in dealing with criminal, commercial, labor, and family issues to replace the existing general judge-made Shari'a-based interpretation

27. The American Constitution, for example, has been described as a pillar of American "civil religion." See Sanford Levinson, *Constitutional Faith* (Princeton: Princeton University Press, 1988).

28. Ran Hirschl and Ayelet Shachar, "The New Wall of Separation: Permitting Diversity, Restricting Competition," *Cardozo Law Review* 30 (2009): 2535–60. On law's tendency to be "jurispathic," see Robert M. Cover, "The Supreme Court 1982 Term—Forward: *Nomos* and Narrative," *Harvard Law Review* 97 (1983): 4–68.

in these matters that has prevailed for many years. Additionally, the judiciary council that used to act as the highest court and was controlled by some of the most reactionary clerics in the kingdom has been relegated to an administrative role. A new ten-member Supreme Court was established in 2009, staffed mostly with royal appointees, not merely with religious clerics, thereby allowing the kingdom to extend a more pragmatic, flexible application of Shari'a to various aspects of public life.

A similar impulse stood behind the attempt to establish a constitutional court in the Palestinian Authority. Shortly after the surprise landslide victory by the religious Hamas movement in the January 2006 parliamentary elections, the Palestinian Legislative Council (PLC) approved the establishment of a constitutional court. This move, undertaken by the secular-nationalist Fatah movement in its last days as a majority in the PLC, was an attempt to constrain Hamas when it took over the Parliament. A new nine-judge court was to be convened with judges appointed by President Mahmoud Abbas of the Fatah, which would have the power to rule illegal those laws judged to violate the Palestinian Basic Law. Theoretically at least, Abbas would have effectively been in a position to veto laws passed by Hamas legislators. In its first legislative move in Parliament, however, Hamas voted to invalidate all legislation passed by the outgoing Fatah following the 2006 election, including the creation of the constitutional court.

Consider also Ayatollah Ruhollah Khomeini's strategic initiative in 1989 to amend the Iranian Constitution in order to institutionalize the Regime's Discernment Expediency Council (*majma-e tashkhis maslahat nezam*) to serve as the final arbiter between the Consultative Assembly (*majlis*) and the Guardian Council (*shoray-e negahban*).[29] This new body—vested with the powers to review national policy-making matters—aids the government in asserting its pragmatist approach to public policy making (based on the concept of "national necessity") over the Guardian Council's more doctrinal, rigid (or "classical") interpretive approach to pertinent religious directives. At the same time, the creation of the Expediency Council was also aimed at aiding the national project of transforming the traditional private law enterprise of Shari'a law into a public law enterprise befitting a constitutional theocracy in the late twentieth century. In short, even in the least likely settings, constitutional courts and tribunals have been established, or reformed, so as to hedge or mitigate the tension between modern-day needs and principles of theocratic governance.

---

29. Kambiz Behi, "Structure and Process of Legal Change in Post-Revolutionary Iran: The Emergence of the Third Globalization" (unpublished manuscript; on file with author). See generally Said Amir Arjamand, *After Khomeini: Iran under His Successors* (New York: Oxford University Press, 2009), 36–55.

Most judges appointed to these courts have received some general legal education and are familiar with some of Western law's basic principles and methods of reasoning. In an increasing number of countries, judges are required to attend courses on the role and functions of the judiciary for several years where they are exposed to international human rights standards and other legal concepts that are not easily compatible with traditional views, pious authority, and sacred texts. Likewise, several pertinent state bureaucracies have tightened their control over the appointment of judges to religious tribunals and require new appointees to have some formal training or background in general legal principles, in addition to their mastery of religious law.

And when these measures do not deliver the goods, harsher measures are taken.[30] A paradigmatic example is the replacement of the Afghan Supreme Court chief justice. Following more than two years of conservative jurisprudence in religious matters by the newly established Afghan Supreme Court, President Hamid Karzai opted for a shake-up of the Court's composition. In 2006 Karzai appointed several new, more moderate members to the court. In addition, the reappointment of the conservative Chief Justice Faisal Ahmad Shinwari—a conservative Islamic cleric with questionable educational credentials—did not pass parliamentary vote. Karzai then chose his legal counsel, Abdul Salam Azimi—a former university professor who was educated in the United States—to succeed Shinwari.

Conclusion

This chapter points to three main lessons. First, despite the general agreement that the world has witnessed a convergence in principles of constitutional supremacy and international human rights alongside an increasingly popular support for principles of theocratic governance, we still know precious little about constitutional law and practices in countries facing the dilemma of constitutional theocracy. As I hope to have shown, any attempt to explore the limits of constitutional democracy in the early twenty-first century must include serious contemplation of the scope and nature of a different and increasingly common model—*constitutional theocracy*. The theocratic challenge has become a significant factor in world politics as well as constitutional law. It stretches well beyond current media hot spots like Iran, Iraq, and Afghanistan, and any attempt

---

30. See Ran Hirschl, "The Judicialization of Mega-Politics and the Rise of Political Courts," *Annual Review Political Science* 11 (2008): 93–118; Ran Hirschl, "The Judicialization of Politics," in *The Oxford Handbook of Political Science*, ed. Robert Goodin (Oxford: Oxford University Press, 2009), 253–74.

to examine the complexities of constitution drafting in postconflict settings without paying close attention to the ever more relevant secular-universal versus religious-particularist divide is bound to come up short.

Second, constitutional theocracy shakes up the traditional affinity between liberalism, democracy, and constitutionalism. It questions canonical literature concerning constitutionalism as an effective means for mitigating tensions in multiethnic or multilinguistic states and claims that it does not adequately address the theocratic challenge. That literature rests on four main presumptions: territorial concentration and demarcation; social and demographic cohesiveness among members of a given group; unified interests, worldviews, and policy preferences among group members; and an underlying vision of constitutionalism as a viable forum of compromise. Although these assumptions provide a plausible set of working hypotheses with respect to dividing factors such as nationality, ethnicity, or language, they are less relevant in capturing the realities of the secular-religious divide. Of particular significance here are the apparent tensions between principles of modern constitutionalism and the rule of law on the one hand and fundamentals of theocratic governance on the other.

Third, the emergence of a new legal order—constitutional theocracy, which is now shared in one form or another by dozens of countries in the developing world—provides important insights into the sociopolitical role of constitutionalism in predominantly religious settings. Regimes throughout the new world of constitutional theocracies have been struggling with these foundational quandaries, forced to navigate between cosmopolitanism and parochialism, modern and traditional metanarratives, constitutional principles and religious injunctions, contemporary governance and ancient texts, judicial and pious interpretation. More often than not, the clash between these conflicting visions results in fierce struggles over the nature of the body politic and its organizing principles.

From this an uneasy alliance emerges, comprising political leaders, state bureaucrats, economic stakeholders and the managerial class, intellectuals, jurists, and the military. Each of these groups necessarily brings to the table its own worldviews, interests, and communities of reference. Consequently, they seek to tame the spread of religious fundamentalism and diffuse attempts to establish a full-fledged theocracy. Constitutional courts find themselves at the forefront of this struggle, as they attempt to address constitutional theocracy and translate its uneasy bundle of contradictory aims and commitments into practical guidelines suited to public life. The turn to constitutional courts, and constitutionalism more generally, has worked, by and large, in favor of secularist or other atheocratic interests. The "constitutional" in a constitutional theocracy thus fulfills the same restricting function it carries out in a constitutional democracy: it brings theocratic governance under check, and assigns to constitutional law and courts the task of a bulwark against the threat of radical religion.

The bottom line is this: constitutional theocracies are a Galapagos-like paradise for scholars of constitutionalism in today's world. They reflect sociopolitical order under constant duress. Striking tensions are often seen between the rule of law and the rule of God, cosmopolitanism and parochialism, economic interests and public will, modern government and religious authorities, new constitutions and ancient texts, judicial and pious interpretation. A unique hybrid of seemingly conflicting world-views, values, and interests, constitutional theocracies thus offer an ideal setting—a "living laboratory" as it were—for studying constitutional law as a form of politics by other means.

14

Constitutional Democracies, Coercion, and Obligations to Include

ROGERS M. SMITH

WALTER MURPHY HAS ARGUED persuasively that the term "constitutional democracy" should be reserved for political systems that do more than provide the rule of law and some system of representation. Constitutional democracies are founded on beliefs in "equal human dignity, defined to include a wide degree of individual liberty"; so constitutionalism demands adherence to "principles that center on respect for human dignity and the obligations that flow from those principles."[1] Here I argue that constitutional democracies should recognize one such obligation that provides a partial guide to the perennial and today often acute issue of who should be included as citizens of a constitutional democracy: a "principle of constituted identities."[2]

The argument is only for this principle as a *partial* guide, because there are many concerns that legitimately bear on decisions to extend opportunities for citizenship, far more than can be reviewed here. My claim is that, whatever other factors may properly inform these judgments, constitutional democracies have obligations to assist and, in some cases, to include as full citizens persons they have coercively affected in specific ways. These obligations flow from the ethical commitments that define constitutional democracies, in combination with their roles in coercively constituting the identities of many persons whom they may not recognize as full citizens or as members at all. This defense of certain obligations to aid and include does not require rejection of any other arguments for offering citizenship or other types of assistance, such as contentions

Thanks to Walter Murphy for his stimulating scholarship, to discussant Robert George and to Stephen Macedo, Jeffrey Tulis, and other contributors to the Princeton conference for which it was written, as well as participants in later discussions at New York University Law School, Georgetown University, and Brown University.

1. Walter F. Murphy, *Constitutional Democracy: Creating and Maintaining a Just Political Order* (Baltimore: Johns Hopkins University Press, 2007), 7, 16.

2. For an earlier version of these arguments, see Rogers M. Smith, "The Principle of Constituted Identities and the Obligation to Include," *Ethics and Global Politics* 1 (2008): 139–53.

that constitutional democracies should work with other states and international agencies to limit the harmful consequences of their economic and environmental practices, or that they have duties to redress historical injustices they have done to particular groups, or that they have moral obligations of "mutual aid" to all persons in need. But the specific "obligation to include" elaborated here does not rest on any such view.

The principle I advance is an alternative to two influential but problematic positions. The first is the argument of David Miller, Matthew Gibney, Stephen Macedo and others, who call for policing the bounds of memberships in constitutional democracies fairly strictly to avoid eroding senses of mutual trust and reciprocal concern among citizens who provide support for public assistance to the least advantaged members of these communities.[3] The principle of constituted identities argues that many who are not legally recognized as full citizens in a constitutional democracy may be owed the opportunity to become citizens if they choose. Unless they decline this opportunity, their voices and their needs should be considered in redistributive policies along with those of disadvantaged persons who are already legally classified as citizens.[4]

The second alternative is what Robert Goodin rightly deems the leading, but widely criticized, answer in recent democratic theory to the problem of "constituting the demos": the principle of "all affected interests."[5]

3. David Miller, *On Nationality* (Oxford: Clarendon Press, 1995) 73–80, 90–98; Matthew J. Gibney, *The Ethics and Politics of Asylum: Liberal Democracy and the Response to Refugees* (New York: Cambridge University Press, 2004), 69–76; Stephen Macedo, "The Moral Dilemma of U.S. Immigration Policy: Open Borders versus Social Justice?" in *Debating Immigration*, ed. Carol M. Swain (New York: Cambridge University Press, 2007), 76–81.

4. A constitutional democracy that makes rapid access to citizenship readily available to such groups may reasonably confine the franchise to those who choose to take up their opportunities for full formal membership. But as I discuss, its legislatures, pertinent executive agencies, and courts should see themselves as obliged to hear the sorts of claims to inclusion I am defending here in appropriate ways and to craft policies responsive to the needs of such claimants when their positions are well founded.

5. Robert E. Goodin, "Enfranchising All Affected Interests, and Its Alternatives," *Philosophy and Public Affairs* 35 (2007): 40, 49–51. Robert A. Dahl has suggested resolving "the problem of inclusion" in part by the apparently similar criterion that "*the demos should include all adults subject to the binding collective decisions of the association.*" But though Dahl has long argued that the "principle of affected interests" is "not a bad principle to start with" in deciding inclusion questions, he has offered his principle focused on "binding collective decisions" as a guide to who among those living *within* a democratic unit should be part of its enfranchised, self-governing *demos*—not as a guide to what the membership boundaries of that democratic unit should be (Robert A. Dahl, *After the Revolution? Authority in a Good Society*, rev. ed. [New Haven: Yale University Press, 1970, 1990], 51; *Democracy and Its Critics* [New Haven: Yale University Press, 1989], 120, 146–47). Dahl has been explicit that he sees the principle of full and equal political rights for all adults who are affected by binding laws as applying to adults who are already "permanently residing in the country and subject to its laws" (Robert A. Dahl, *On Democracy* [New Haven: Yale University Press, 1998], 86).

Analysts deploying that principle tend to focus on whether persons' material interests—their economic welfare, personal liberty and physical well-being, and political powers—have been affected by a political community's laws, policies, and institutions, even if those actions have not directly coerced them.[6] The principle of constituted identities, in contrast, focuses on whether persons' notions of who they are and of what gives their lives ethical worth—their senses of values, purposes, affiliations, and aspirations—have been coercively shaped by a community's laws, policies, and institutions. Some may argue that we should embrace both these principles simultaneously, and some might suggest that ultimately the categories of "affecting interests" and "constituting identities" are indistinguishable. I believe instead that the principle of constituted identities points to different inquiries that lead to more bounded results. It directs attention to normative identities, not material interests, and to coercive policies and institutions, not simply to actions that affect others.

To provide a formula: The principle of constituted identities holds that *every constitutional democracy is obligated to include as equal citizens all persons whose identities have been pervasively constituted, even if not wholly determined, by the democracy's coercively enforced governmental measures, should those persons wish to be citizens.* By "identities" I mean persons' senses of their core personal values and affiliations, which may have political, economic, religious, ethnic, aesthetic, and other dimensions, and which define for them the ways they can pursue fulfilling, ethically worthwhile lives. By "constituted" I mean that a government's laws, policies, and institutions have coercively required persons to be socialized in a certain range of experiences along many of these dimensions, while inhibiting them from being socialized in other ways—thereby making it difficult for them to conceive of values, purposes, aspirations, and affiliations differing from those which governmental policies have sponsored. Mandatory public education systems socialize in these ways, with greater or lesser success; and so do laws and governmental institutions that authorize or at least allow some forms of religious practice, aesthetic expression, economic pursuits, and marital and familial relationships, while prohibiting others.[7] And by "coercively enforced," I mean that gov-

6. See, e.g., the examples discussed by Goodin, "Enfranchising All Affected Interests," 49–50, 52–53, 57, 62–63, 66–67.

7. In the United States, for example, mandatory education systems include extensive exposure to values of democracy and science, while public school teachers cannot advocate theocracy. Religious, expressive, economic, and associational rights are robust, but, even so, religious practices involving certain kinds of ritual human mutilation, forms of expression and employment that include children in sexual activities, and polygamous marriages are illegal, though these have all been elements of cultural traditions in communities with descendants in the United States.

ernments assert the right to fine, incarcerate, or deport those who disobey pertinent governmental laws, policies, and institutions and sometimes do so, thereby discouraging the formation of identities with the sorts of values, aspirations, and affiliations subject to penalty. Though more indirect pressures might also be construed as "coercive," doing so might well make it impossible to distinguish between "constituting identities" and "affecting interests." So I employ a narrower definition of coercion here.

"Coercively enforced" should not be read as holding that the government laws, policies, and institutions in question are necessarily unjust. Coercion is sometimes needed to achieve legitimate governmental purposes. This formula includes obligations to many who have been coerced but to whom no reparations for injustices are owed. Most will indeed have benefited to a greater or lesser extent from, for example, mandatory education or public health programs. Still, societies that value human dignity and liberty must always justify coercive measures constraining liberties, generally in terms of the contributions of those measures to advancing opportunities for lives of meaning and dignity. They therefore have obligations to those they coerce, including, I contend, an obligation to extend the option of full citizenship under some circumstances.

But not all circumstances. The obligation defined here depends on both the quality and quantity of the coercions in question. It concerns coercions that shape peoples' senses of their identities and what is valuable in their identities, and so it is roughly proportional to the extent to which a constitutional democracy has constituted the identities of the persons in question. It is doubtless impossible to determine with certainty how far governmental measures have constituted persons' senses of who they are and what is valuable in those identities. But we can make reasonable objective judgments of what persons are most likely to have been shaped in those ways. People who have been born and raised with their forms of education, religion, sexuality, marriage, reproduction, diet, medicine, art, morals, economic pursuits, and their politics, among other matters, pervasively and coercively regulated by the governmental laws, policies, and institutions of a particular constitutional democracy are more likely to have been so shaped than their kinsmen residing in neighboring communities—even when those communities have suffered from consensual but one-sided economic, political, and cultural relationships with the constitutional democracy over the years. In turn, insofar as those various relationships have in fact been coercively enforced, the latter persons and groups can be presumed to be more extensively constituted than those whose lives have been relatively untouched by the constitutional democracy's coercive actions. It therefore seems feasible to place people and groups at different locations along a spectrum depending upon the degrees and types of participation they have had in institutions and practices coercively regulated by a particular constitutional democracy. The constitutional democracy must offer full citizenship to those at the "pervasively regulated" end of this coercive spectrum, while those at different points along the way might be legitimately offered different civic opportunities, such as priority in immigration and naturalization queues or economic assistance.

Even for those at the end of the spectrum with strong claims to citizenship, this obligation to include is qualified by two limits that stem from what may be required to sustain constitutional democracies in some circumstances. The first limit is that constitutional democracies need not incorporate new members when doing so would create divisions severe enough to destroy the regime. Still, policies that seek to build support for inclusion over time remain obligatory. The second limit arises when adding new members would expand the constitutional democracy so greatly as to render it impossible for the regime's institutions to provide any real semblance of democratic self-governance. It is then obligatory for leaders to seek to devise and support institutional arrangements that can provide defensibly democratic constitutional governance of, by, and for an enlarged populace over time. Because most actual constitutional democracies, including the United States, have long histories of coercively structuring the identities of populations they have not accepted as equal citizens, these limits do not mean that obligations to include can be minimized. Instead, they set continuing tasks for democratic statesmanship that are likely to endure for many generations.

Sources of Obligations to Include

The obligation to be inclusive in these ways is not self-evident. A quarter of a century ago, Michael Walzer argued that in order to sustain "communities of character," members of democracies were entitled to determine for themselves who would be admitted to their ranks—so long as decisions were made by *all* members, including all longtime residents in the society, and so long as exclusionary decisions were consistent with the constraining moral principle of mutual aid.[8] Somewhat similarly, I have argued that because humanity has not yet devised ways that people can flourish without being organized into particular political communities, and we may not be able to do so, we must give moral weight to things that seem necessary for particular political communities to survive. I have also suggested that all long-enduring societies must be held together in

---

8. Michael Walzer, *Spheres of Justice: A Defense of Pluralism and Equality* (New York: Basic Books, 1983), 62.

part by always-contested but often-overlapping "ethically constitutive stories." These are accounts that define membership in a specific community as "somehow intrinsic to who its members really are, because of traits that are imbued with ethical significance."[9] We must therefore give at least *some* moral weight to the desires of those in such communities to extend membership only to persons who share those characteristics, which may include linguistic, religious, cultural, and ethnic identities or loyalty to certain political ideologies, among other traits.

These "ethically constitutive stories" almost always contain mythical elements proclaiming the transcendental worth of the political identities they valorize. But their mythical qualities should not be taken to mean they are somehow unreal, unimportant, or wholly undesirable. Not only are such stories sources of common identity that help to sustain communities and institutions that contribute to the well-being of many people. They also provide senses of meaning and purpose for many who embrace them. When deployed to structure membership rules, socializing institutions, and a range of policies, they provide content that contributes to the substance, significance, and prestige of the legally, politically, and socially recognized identities and statuses people possess.[10]

But crucially, they also play this role for many to whom a constitutional democracy may assign less than equal civic positions. The framers of the U.S. Constitution, for example, not only remade themselves into citizens of a federal constitutional republic with much more centralized power than the league of states that the Articles of Confederation had created, thereby fostering deeper and richer senses of their American nationality. They also reconstituted the recognized political identities, allegiances, and obligations of their wives, sisters, and daughters; their African American slaves as well as resident free blacks; and persons belonging to or descended from the native tribes located on what the new American government regarded as U.S. soil. Over time, the United States also coercively transformed the identities and statuses of territorial inhabitants in the Northwest and Louisiana Purchase territories; (former)

9. Rogers M. Smith, *Stories of Peoplehood: The Politics and Morals of Political Membership* (New York: Cambridge University Press, 2003), 64–65, 101–2.

10. As I have previously stressed, the accounts of communal identity that get institutionalized are inevitably compromises among rival views of that community's character and purposes. Dominant coalitions can shape laws and policies largely in their preferred directions, but rarely if ever without some concessions to opposing positions. It is the complexly compromised institutionalized measures that result that socialize and constitute the identities of those to whom they apply. When the members of an existing society subscribe to such different stories of peoplehood that they cannot reach agreement on common policies and institutions, they may instead separate and form distinct communities, often appropriately (ibid., 50, 160).

Mexicans in the Southwest, in ways that greatly shaped the development of Mexico as well as the United States; the indigenous peoples of Hawaii and Alaska; and the residents of Puerto Rico, the Philippines, Guam, and other Spanish-American War acquisitions, among others. Many U.S. leaders justified these measures via stories of America's religious and racial "manifest destiny" or "civilizing mission." In response to aggression against it, the United States also occupied and literally reconstituted the governments of Japan and Germany in the wake of World War II. In the modern era, with less blatant provocation, the United States has launched military interventions that have dramatically affected the statuses and identities of large numbers of Vietnamese, Cambodian, Laotian, and Iraqi citizens, and others. Many of those who more or less voluntarily assisted the United States then came to be labeled criminals, traitors, and enemies by the regimes the United States fought, in ways that profoundly altered their prospects.

The significance of this history is that to varying degrees, the coercive policies of the United States altered the educational, religious, medical, cultural, economic, and political institutions and practices shaping these groups' identities, making the story of America, including its constitutional principles, its policies allegedly implementing them, and other American values, ambitions, and traditions, central if sometimes troubling components in the formation of the identities and ethical commitments of many of these groups' members. These policies helped constitute them as American men, American women, as African-Americans, as Native Americans, as American territorial and colonial inhabitants, as members of regimes with American-imposed constitutions and other institutions, as American allies with few prospects for security outside of U.S. protection.

Those statuses are not all identical, and they do not all justify claims to full citizenship; but as they are all products of American coercive actions, they all identify groups to whom the United States has obligations. Those obligations are not altered by whether these forms of coercive regulation, exclusion, subordination, and military intervention and conquest were necessary for America's constitutional democracy to be created or to survive, or whether they actually benefited those coerced. It is possibly true that the nation's distinctive development has been partly dependent on its coercively enforced support for commercial production and exchange economies, for mandatory mass civic education, for electoral provisions favoring a two-party system, and other features of American public policies. It is probably true that the Constitution would not have been enacted if its provisions had banned slavery, enfranchised women, and provided the option of full U.S. citizenship to members of the native tribes and to free people of African descent. It is certainly true that the Japanese empire immediately threatened the survival of the United States in 1941;

the Third Reich then did so as well; and perhaps vital American security interests were at stake in others of the wars listed above. It is also probably true that at least some in those groups have in the long run benefited from their coercion by the United States. I do not dispute that a constitutional democracy is entitled to take actions necessary to its creation, preservation, and perfection as a constitutional democracy, even some actions that may render it less perfectly constitutional and less democratic for a time, because those actions may in the long run aid both its citizens and many others. Though failures to include as equal citizens those who have strong claims to that status do represent constitutional failures, they do not necessarily render the broader enterprise of constitutional democratic governance a failure—unless those shortcomings are never addressed.

Why must at least some of these exclusions be deemed failures of constitutional democracy that need to be addressed? My argument proceeds in three steps.

The first stems from my agreement with Murphy's contention that constitutional democracies should justify themselves and define their obligations and goals in terms of beliefs in human dignity, including a broad range of liberties. In my terms, these beliefs form important parts of the ethically constitutive stories that help bind and guide all genuine constitutional democracies. To be sure, the accounts and specifications of equal human dignity and liberty that different members of a constitutional democracy endorse often vary, with some drawing on religious traditions, some on cultural, artistic, or philosophic ones; and the dominant accounts in different constitutional democracies vary as well. I have also argued that every long-enduring political society needs to add to these accounts more particular ethically constitutive stories that valorize membership in that distinctive community. Nonetheless, every constitutional democracy rests on an overlapping set of accounts endorsing the worth of all human lives and the value of extensive liberty, accounts that provide moral legitimation for its principles.[11]

Second, with Will Kymlicka, I agree that the existence of shared cultures and "cultural narratives" are preconditions for persons to be capable of "meaningful" choices, "intelligent judgments about how to lead" their lives in ways they experience as valuable.[12] The power to choose

11. Ibid., 86–87, 91–92, 132–33. Though other types of political societies are bound and guided by their own overlapping sets of ethically constitutive stories, those stories do not necessarily endorse universal human worth or human liberty. If the argument for the obligation to include that I advance here applies to such societies, it is not because their own ethical stories demand it, but because we regard the values of constitutional democracy as universally binding, even on communities that do not embrace them.

12. Will Kymlicka, *Multicultural Citizenship: A Liberal Theory of Minority Rights* (New York: Oxford University Press, 1995), 82–83.

how to live is barren unless people have some notions of how they should live. Those notions are inevitably built upon, though they need not and should not be dictated by, the various cultural traditions that have helped to form (and re-form) persons' senses of their own identities, purposes, and worth. These cultural traditions are always various, because no national government exercises total control to define all the traditions to which those subject to its authority are exposed, however much the government may try to do so. This reality means that persons' capacities to choose include capacities to select which of the traditions that have shaped them they will most fully embrace; but it is difficult if not impossible for persons to choose to live according to traditions to which they have been minimally exposed. The values of constitutional democracies sometimes require them to restrain discriminatory and repressive conduct hostile to human dignity and liberty. But they should also respect and facilitate "cultural narratives" that support values of dignity and liberty, and they should strive to provide persons with meaningful opportunities to decide how to express and pursue those values in their personal and political lives.

Under some circumstances, these obligations acquire overwhelming weight. The final step of my argument is to connect my own claim, that all political societies are bound together by contesting but overlapping ethically constitutive stories that they need to some degree to sustain if they are to endure, with the points just made—that constitutional democracies rest on stories that promise to recognize and advance equal human dignity and liberty, and that persons cannot really lead free lives if the cultures and cultural narratives that provide the resources for their senses of identity, meaning, and purpose are not sustained. I contend that persons whose identities been pervasively constituted by the coercive policies of a constitutional democracy may well find it *impossible* to lead lives of dignity and freedom if they are denied the option of equal membership in that democracy's political culture. Without this opportunity, they are denied access to the particular forms of political and cultural life that they may rightly see as providing their meaningful "context of choice." A constitutional democracy that professes to embody and express ethically constitutive stories valorizing its contributions to human dignity and liberty may well have reason to contend that it cannot make those contributions if it simply opens its doors to all those who decide for whatever reason that they wish to be part of it. But it cannot ignore its responsibilities when it has coercively shaped human identities and statuses in ways that lead people to share many of those values and aspirations, even as it has denied them the opportunities to realize them. Constitutional democracies are instead obligated to provide those opportunities to all they have coercively shaped in these ways, insofar as they can.

This means that all who have grown up as members of the constitutional democracy must have citizenship revocable only through their own consent, as the United States Supreme Court has held.[13] It also means that those who reasonably believe that they cannot tell themselves their own stories about who they are, what they value, and where they belong without drawing on the cultural narratives that the coercive policies of a constitutional democracy have made central to their lives—through political, economic, social, and religious regulation; through education; even through conquest, enslavement, occupation, colonization—all such persons must be offered the chance to have roles in determining how those narratives are continued. Again, the extent of that obligation, and therefore the roles to which persons are entitled, will vary with the degree to which they have been coercively constituted. Those lines will admittedly be difficult to draw, though in cases of doubt, it seems proper to err on the side of inclusion by extending the option of full and equal citizenship. Still, there may be members of less extensively coerced and less pervasively socialized communities to whom it may be sufficient to offer the option of some sort of affiliation, alliance, or assistance that helps them to achieve significant political and cultural autonomy, rather than full membership.

And many may have no desire to accept equal citizenship in what they see as an oppressive regime. Though throughout U.S. history most African Americans have decided that, despite all the injustices perpetrated by American governments against members of their community, they wished to be full and equal U.S. citizens, some have expatriated themselves, and some have sought U.S. governmental acquiescence or even assistance for their efforts to establish their own autonomous communities.[14] The obligations defined here suggest that they have had strong claims to such assistance. Residents of lands conquered by the United States have also generally not wished to become citizens in new American states. The principle of constituted identities suggests they should have been seen as entitled to choose among a range of alternatives, from complete separation to a variety of possible federated or associated statuses, structured to be consistent with the constitutional democratic principles. Otherwise, tales of violations of the commitments that the constitutional democracy has promised to respect and advance will make up much of those persons' individual stories and of that constitutional democracy's collective story. Neither persons nor political societies constituted by such values

---

13. *Afroyim v. Rusk*, 387 U.S. 253 (1967).
14. See John H. Bracey Jr., August Meier, Elliott Rudwick, eds., *Black Nationalism in America* (Indianapolis, IN: Bobbs-Merrill, 1970); Dean E. Robinson, *Black Nationalism in American Politics and Thought* (New York: Cambridge University Press, 2001).

can regard a life of violations of their own basic principles as expressive of human dignity, or as a life they would or should choose to live.[15]

Limits on Obligations to Include

A constitutional democracy, however, is not obligated to destroy itself as a constitutional democracy in order to save itself; so there are limits to these obligations to include. On its face, at least, the argument made so far defines an obligation to include that is already more limited than Goodin's definition of the principle of "all affected interests." That principle holds that ideally, everyone should be enfranchised to help decide all issues that significantly affect any of their interests, coercively or not, which might mean "giving virtually everyone everywhere a vote on virtually everything decided anywhere."[16] Though I am not seeking to refute that principle or the more realistic variations on it that Goodin discusses, the principle of constituted identities that I am defending is confined to those whose normative identities have been substantially and coercively generated by a constitutional democracy, not to all whose interests are affected by its decisions. This obligation will often support the inclusion of many who are not recognized as citizens of a given constitutional democracy, but it does not extend to "virtually everyone everywhere."[17] The United States has, for example, coercively constituted the identities of residents of the Philippines more than it has those of Singapore, even though its policies and practices have arguably affected the interests of

15. My view has similarities to Rainer Bauböck's arguments for incorporating all those who are substantial "stakeholders" in a particular community. See, e.g., Rainer Bauböck, "Political Boundaries in a Multilevel Democracy," in *Identities, Affiliations, and Allegiances,* ed. Seyla Benhabib, Ian Shapiro, and Danilo Petranović (New York: Cambridge University Press, 2007), 85–109. But where Bauböck's analysis, like the principle of affected interests, focuses on the shares that persons have established in a community's social, economic, cultural, and political life and institutions, mine focuses on the share the community has had in establishing the persons themselves—a type of approach he sees as "problematic" because of its potential stress on "the value of societal cultures," seen as unitary entities (100). Because I stress that persons are constituted by varied cultural traditions, the practical difference in these analyses is unclear. As noted below, Bauböck defends limits on community obligations much like those I suggest here.

16. Goodin, "Enfranchising All Affected Interests," 40, 68.

17. Nor does the obligation defended here extend as far as the one argued for by Arash Abizadeh, who contends that decisions about the legitimacy of the borders of a political community must be made by all who are subject to coercion by the democracy enforcing those borders (Arash Abizadeh, "Democratic Theory and Border Coercion: No Right to Unilaterally Control Your Own Borders," *Political Theory* 36 [2008]: 37–65). Such coercion often falls short of significantly constituting persons' identities and legal status in the manner on which my argument relies.

residents of Singapore as much as those of modern Filipinos. Even if some residents of Singapore more passionately desire U.S. citizenship, the principle of constituted identities provides them little claim to it.

As noted, a number of recent writers have stressed one limit on inclusion that the preceding analysis compels me to reject, or at least to treat as inapplicable to the persons claiming inclusion on the grounds just sketched. Miller, Gibney, and Macedo have expressed concern that if constitutional democracies or republics add too many persons whom many citizens see as alien and unworthy, the result will be to undermine the senses of trust and concern that prompt voters to fund public assistance to their least advantaged fellow citizens. Many forms of distributive justice within a constitutional democracy thereby may be thwarted by excessive inclusiveness.

Though this is a legitimate concern, it is difficult to use it to justify exclusion of the persons I am discussing here: those with strong claims to membership based on the fact that the constitutional democracy has coercively provided much of the cultural "context of choice" generating the identities, values, and purposes those persons feel they must realize if they are to lead meaningful, free lives of human dignity. My argument is that by doing so much to "make" these persons, constitutional democracies have *already* effectively made them members, to a greater or lesser degree; and democratic governments are obliged to recognize that reality and act accordingly. What does it mean to "act accordingly"? At a minimum, the legislative, executive, and judicial organs of the constitutional democracy should recognize their obligations to hear claims for full membership or for other forms of recognition and aid advanced by persons so situated (via petitions, testimony at legislative and executive agency hearings, and litigation). A constitutional democracy's government should grant such claims, supplying full citizenship or other appropriate statuses, when honest examination shows them to be well founded. In many cases, individuals may properly be judged already to have a place among the community's disadvantaged, deserving special consideration in policies of distributive justice, along with many of those legally recognized as citizens. Indeed, because they lack citizenship, they may be even more disadvantaged. Again because these obligations exist in rough proportion to the degree to which a constitutional democracy's coercive policies have constituted those persons' identities, there may indeed be many with limited claims to membership who might legitimately be excluded if their presence would undermine support for just policies toward all existing members. Still, my view does not support the sharp boundaries drawn by these writers between the claims of those who are already legally recognized as citizens and many who are not.

My argument is also consistent with Michael Walzer's claim that political societies are entitled to limit inclusion considerably in order to maintain their distinctive "characters." But that limit has less bite in my analysis than in his, because I contend that the "characters," "cultural narratives," or "ethically constitutive stories" of constitutional democracies include commitments to human dignity and liberty that require them to embrace as members all those whom they have coercively shaped in ways that make the pursuit of these values in those societies central to their lives. And again, the justice or injustice of that coercive shaping is not crucial to this obligation: the fact of coercive shaping alone, on the part of a regime committed to the principles of constitutional democracy, is enough to generate a duty to recognize that the stories of those shaped cannot be legitimately kept apart from the community that did so much to make them who they are, unless they decide they wish to live apart.

Still, limits remain, even for excluded persons with very strong claims to full and equal citizenship, like the members of conquered tribes or nations, slaves, disfranchised women, and residents of annexed territories and colonies. If those seeking to create a constitutional democracy face the choice, as the framers of the U.S. Constitution arguably did, between failing to create any sort of approximation of a just system or succeeding in devising a constitutional "democracy" that does not include many whose identities it is profoundly shaping and will profoundly shape, it seems permissible to create a highly imperfect approximation of a just regime. But it then becomes an enduring duty of the leaders and citizens of that regime to make it more perfect, if their stories of devotion to the principles of constitutional democracy are not to be revealed as hypocritical fables. So long as inclusions continue to threaten the very survival of a constitutional democracy, they can be delayed; but the longer the delay, the stronger the obligation citizens have to find sustainable ways to achieve more just boundaries of membership.

On this view, for example, Abraham Lincoln was probably right to favor a gradualist approach to ending slavery, though not to suggest only the prospect of colonization for emancipated slaves. But the legitimacy of gradualism did not mean that it was permissible to postpone indefinitely the obligation to offer full membership to African Americans or to acquiesce to pressures to abandon that endeavor altogether. Thus, Lincoln was also right to respond to southern secession by using coercive force to keep slaves within the Union; then to emancipate them; then to put them on the path to full citizenship, thereby sustaining the promise of inclusion to all whose identities, ideals, and aspirations had been profoundly constituted by the policies of America's putatively democratic regime.[18]

18. Cf. Mark A. Graber, *Dred Scott and the Problem of Constitutional Evil* (New York: Cambridge University Press, 2006).

Similarly, America's constitutional democracy was obligated by its own ethically constitutive principles and its coercive policies eventually to enfranchise American women and to offer full and equal citizenship to members of the native tribes, to those residing on territories conquered in the Mexican-American War, and to the inhabitants of Puerto Rico, Guam, and other Spanish-American War acquisitions. Throughout the twentieth century, many Filipinos have in fact argued in American courts with much moral force, though with no legal success, that the occupation of their country by the United States in 1898 and its status as a U.S. territory until 1946, with a "special relationship" persisting thereafter, entitles them to U.S. citizenship.[19]

Their example highlights the second limit to the obligation to include. It would admittedly have been a challenge to create new democratic institutions incorporating all Filipinos who wished to be U.S. citizens directly into the civic body. Should the Philippines have simply become a noncontiguous state, as Hawaii and Alaska eventually did? Should it instead have sustained some sort of federated status, perhaps the "commonwealth" status Puerto Rico possesses? Would either of those statuses really have been consistent with democratic self-governance in the Philippines and in the United States as a whole, or would they have amounted to new forms of colonial rule, as we who criticize Puerto Rico's current status contend?

The answers are not obvious, and that reality flags the further difficulties that can justify limits on the immediate inclusion as full citizens of all persons with identities constituted by a particular constitutional democracy. In many cases, incorporating excluded groups requires devising new institutional structures so that all involved can see their membership as genuinely democratic. And as inclusions grow, every large-scale constitutional democracy will increasingly face the challenge of a "democratic deficit," as it encompasses populations and territories so vast that meaningful roles in governance seem logistically impossible for all but a small percentage of the citizenry.

Once again, a constitutional democracy is not obligated to adopt policies that would render it not a constitutional democracy. But once again, these difficulties cannot legitimately be treated as reasons to abandon altogether the project of finding appropriate forms of democratic civic inclusion for those who desire it and have legitimate claims to it. Instead, leaders and citizens must accept responsibility for working out defensibly democratic institutional arrangements, perhaps involving decentralization, federation,

---

19. See, e.g., *Palo v. Weedin*, 8 F. 2d 607 (1925); *Summerfield v. U.S. Immigration and Naturalization Service*, 1994 U.S. App. LEXIS 26379 (1994); *Valmonte v. Immigration and Naturalization Service*, 136 F. 3d 914 (1998).

or considerably autonomous regional or local statuses, which can make inclusions consistent with the principles of constitutional democracy possible. Democratic theorists like David Held have explored such arrangements extensively in recent years, many inspired by the as-yet highly imperfect example of the European Union.[20] On the view of the obligations of constitutional democracies advanced here, members of most existing constitutional democracies need to do so as well, as part of efforts to consider how they can develop their systems into more perfect unions.[21]

Some Implications

In that spirit, let me sketch what this obligation to include may imply for the United States in regard to some populations not currently treated as citizens but who have nonetheless been extensively shaped by coercive American policies. I have noted that post–World War II Japan and Germany operate under constitutions extensively written and imposed by their American conquerors, who also contributed to the restructuring of their educational, economic, and political systems in other ways. Both countries have since modified their institutions and policies themselves, in ways not dictated by the United States, but it cannot be denied that all who have grown up in those societies have had their identities, values, and cultures extensively shaped by American coercion. Does this history mean that modern Japanese and German citizens should also be able to claim U.S. citizenship if they wish to do so?

I do not reject this counterintuitive possibility out of hand: if direct American domination of these nations had long continued, at some point their members would have been owed the option of full and equal inclusion. But it matters that the coercion exercised by the United States came in response to acts and declarations of war initiated by these opponents, so that responsibility for their subsequent coercive transformation rests in part with themselves; and it matters more that these communities were and are more likely to achieve constitutional, democratic ways of life if they remain distinct from the United States. Most Japanese and German citizens would probably spurn U.S. citizenship if offered. They have been and are far more likely to embrace constitutional democracy when its principles and institutions are seen as means for their own national self-governance, rather than as their absorption into the United States.

20. David Held, *Democracy and the Global Order: From the Modern State to Cosmopolitan Governance* (Stanford, CA: Stanford University Press, 1995).

21. For a parallel argument stressing more narrowly political claims, rather than claims of cultural identity, see Bauböck, "Political Boundaries," 96–104.

A far more difficult case is contemporary Mexico—for the Mexican-American War dramatically reconstituted both countries, resulting in the shift of California, Arizona, New Mexico, Nevada, parts of Colorado, and (less directly) Texas to the United States. The United States has since often intervened coercively in Mexico's political system and it has enforced policies affecting the development of the Mexican economy. Has American coercion shaped most Mexicans' identities and statuses so extensively that they can claim to be American citizens? Alternatively, have Mexico's own coercive policies, many of which have affected U.S. citizens, done so pervasively enough for those Americans to claim Mexican citizenship? Though the evidence needs to be examined in detail, the answer to both questions is "probably not." But America's long and largely one-sided history of deeply constitutive coercions may well justify giving Mexicans special access to American residency and citizenship, ahead of the residents of the many countries less affected by U.S. policies, and in ways that should justify leniency toward undocumented Mexican immigrants. I doubt that Mexico's coercive impact on U.S. citizens has been sufficient to warrant symmetrical obligations.

Because of the frequency of U.S. interventions in different parts of Latin America under the Monroe Doctrine, it is likely that, to varying degrees, other Latin Americans can also claim some priority in immigration and naturalization policies. I also think the United States has special obligations to grant refugee status and, perhaps in some cases, citizenship to those Iraqis, Afghans, and others whose existence in their home countries has been disrupted, often made virtually impossible, by American military intervention and by their perceived roles as American allies. After much criticism for failing to grant even refugee status to displaced Iraqis, the United States announced in February 2007 that it would facilitate their entry; but it still aimed to admit only roughly twelve thousand in the next year from a country in which an estimated four million people have been displaced since the U.S. invasion.[22] Most of those four million, to be sure, would prefer to return to a peaceful and stable Iraq, and hopeful ones have begun to do so. But those Iraqis who long acted in good faith as U.S. allies, who have good reason to believe that their lives in Iraq have been made untenable there by America's intervention, and who wish to become U.S. citizens, have a strong case for inclusion within the United States The United States probably has not played so central a role in constituting their identities for so long a time as in other examples I have listed. But because its coercive policies have deprived them of the political identities and personal lives they would otherwise have had, it does have

22. Paul Lewis, "U.S. Will Speed Entry of Refugees from Iraq," *Washington Post*, September 22, 2007, A10.

an obligation to aid them, certainly as refugees and perhaps, if their allied roles have been extensive and consequential, as citizens.

These latter claims, and indeed much of the foregoing, are legitimately controversial, and further reflection might indicate that American obligations are different, lesser or greater than I have suggested here. At a minimum, I hope this discussion will convince readers that when we consider the legitimate civic boundaries of constitutional democracies, we must consider the issues of whether they have included as full and equal citizens all persons that their own principles obligate them to include. In pondering those questions, we must ask whether they are obliged to offer membership to all those who have become who they are because, to a considerable degree, the coercive policies of a constitutional democracy have made them so.

15

Omniviolence, Arms Control, and Limited Government

DANIEL DEUDNEY

The Constitution in the Grave New World

Unexpectedly, a grave new world of large-scale terrorism threatens the prospects for the free world project and the United States' role in it. A mere long decade ago, in what now seems like a very different time, the United States and the liberal democracies, after long travails and struggles, seemed poised to realize the modernized Enlightenment vision of a world of free states. In the wake of a violent century of competition with powerful fascist and imperial authoritarian and totalitarian states, the coalition of liberal democratic states lead by the United States stood in a position of global hegemony never before experienced in modern times. The American free world vision of diverse peoples living in peace and prosperity and working together in robust international unions and communities to solve common problems seemed tantalizingly within reach.

Over the first decade of the twenty-first century, these positive trends and possibilities, while not completely extinguished, are increasingly being overshadowed by several ominous new developments that pose fundamental challenges to the free world project and America's leadership in it. Constitutional democracy is tottering in Russia, and the communist party dictatorship of China appears to have harnessed the benefits of capitalism without liberal democracy. The "third wave" of "democratic transitions" has crested and is receding, as antiliberal forces, particularly in petro-authoritarian states, have rolled back fragile democratic and constitutional reforms. The United States seems to have largely abandoned its traditional leadership role in building stronger institutions and on a variety of fronts has emerged as the insurmountable laggard.

An earlier version of this paper was presented at the "Constitutional Empire" panel at the American Political Science Convention, Toronto, Canada, September 2009. Helpful comments were provided by Jack Balkin, David Hendrickson, Steve Macedo, Jamie Mayerfeld, and Jeff Tulis.

More than anything else, however, the terrorist attacks in the fall of 2001, and the American response to them, ended the widespread sense of security and optimism of the unexpectedly brief post–Cold War era. The attacks on the World Trade Center and the Pentagon, coupled with mailings of small quantities of highly lethal anthrax biological weapons to a handful of public figures, deeply traumatized the American people, much of world opinion, and the American national security establishment. The attacks of the fall of 2001 and the ensuing "war on terrorism" have triggered a range of contentious debates about a wide array of fundamental American constitutional issues. Many of the measures initiated by the Bush administration, from open-ended preventive detention (and abuse) of "enemy combatants" captured on the chaotic battlefields of Afghanistan and elsewhere, through its various surveillance programs, to its theory of the largely unchecked "unitary executive," call into question the survival of fundamental constitutional rights and protections of liberty long taken for granted by Americans.[1] These measures of internal state hardening and strengthening were also accompanied by a sweeping assault on liberal international security measures such as the International Criminal Court (U.S. "un-signing" and active opposition), the Biological Weapons Convention negotiations (U.S. withdrawal and collapse), and the Anti-Ballistic Missile Treaty (U.S. withdrawal and termination).[2]

It was not inevitable that the American response would be the Bush administration response, but these measures have deep roots in the near-zero American tolerance for terrorism by nonstate actors long predating 9/11.[3] American foreign policy will not find it easy to escape a protracted war on terrorists and their state sponsors. If this struggle is, as widely held, "the long war," the stresses on the fabric of constitutional government and civil liberties may be both protracted and cumulatively severe. Among the recent developments inimical to the liberal world order, the problem of terrorism is the most profound because it threatens not peripheral and recent gains but rather what is arguably the core of the core, the limited government constitution of the United States itself.

These stresses may become not only chronic but also much more acute. The attacks of 9/11, horrific and psychologically jarring as they

1. For overviews, see Louis Fisher, *The Constitution and 9/11: Recurring Threats to America's Freedoms* (Lawrence: University Press of Kansas, 2008); James P. Pfiffner, *Power Play: The Bush Presidency and the Constitution* (Washington, DC: Brookings Institution, 2008).

2. For critical overviews, see Philippe Sands, *Lawless World: America and the Making and Breaking of Global Rules from FDR's Atlantic Charter to George W. Bush's Illegal War* (New York: Viking, 2005); G. John Ikenberry, *Liberal Order and Imperial Ambition* (London: Polity, 2006).

3. For these continuities, see Paul R. Pillar, *Terrorism and U.S. Foreign Policy* (Washington, DC: Brookings, 2001).

were, pale in comparison to the threat of catastrophic terrorist attacks employing nuclear or other weapons of mass destruction. The leakage of nuclear weapons capability into the hands of nonstate actors produces the situation that has come to be known as "omniviolence." Members of the terrorist group Al-Qaeda have called for killing four million Americans (by his warped reckoning the number of Muslims who have been killed by the United States and its proxies). The detonation of four nuclear weapons in four large U.S. cities would roughly accomplish his goal. There exists enough fissile plutonium to make (depending on design sophistication) somewhere between 300,000 and 500,000 nuclear weapons. This nuclear abundance makes the prospects for nuclear acquisition by a nonstate actor, whether Al-Qaeda or some as yet unknown group, disturbingly high. These facts have led a wide array of well-informed experts to voice the view that it is not a question of whether but when such an attack will occur. If the panicked enactment of the PATRIOT Act after 9/11 is any guide, a catastrophic terrorist is likely to trigger a deep further abridgment of the limited government constitution of the United States. A world in which groups the size of criminal gangs can wield the power of states poses a historically unprecedented security problem which may be particularly challenging to states committed to political liberty.[4]

Theorizing the Constitution and the International System

This article considers the implications of omniviolence for the survival of limited government constitutionalism. I advance the proposition, which I refer to as "nuclear constitutional internationalism," which holds that the survival of limited constitutional government, particularly in the United States, is coming increasingly to depend upon the strength of the international arms control system. Such a system begins with existing (but currently decaying) measures such as the nonproliferation treaty and the strategic arms limitation treaties. It includes the familiar agenda of "deep arms control."[5] And it extends to a regulatory arrangement of global scope for the control of extreme violence capacities that is sufficiently

4. For a wide-ranging account of these challenges, see Philip Bobbitt, *Terror and Consent: The Wars for the Twenty-First Century* (New York: Knopf, 2008).

5. The basic approach was outlined at the beginning of the nuclear era in J. Robert Oppenheimer, "International Control of Atomic Energy" (1946), in *Minutes to Midnight: The International Control of Atomic Energy*, ed. Eugene Rabinowitch (Chicago: Bulletin of the Atomic Scientists, 1959), 53–63. For an authoritative recent statement, see Harold A. Feiveson, ed., *The Nuclear Tipping Point: A Blueprint for Deep Cuts and De-alerting of Nuclear Weapons* (Washington, DC: Brookings Institution, 1998).

authoritative to constitute a world constitutional union.[6] To preserve the constitution and political liberty in the omniviolence era, the United States must make deep nuclear arms control the centerpiece of its international grand strategy.

A great deal has been written about terrorism and antiterrorism, and their erosive effects on limited constitutional government. And a program for responding to omniviolence terrorism by strengthening interstate arms control is a robust (if decidedly minority) presence in debates over post-9/11American grand strategy. Yet there is a deep conceptual disconnect between the worlds of constitutional theory and international arms control. Both are parts of the broadly liberal approach to politics, but they have virtually no intellectual interaction. Constitutional scholars are highly attentive to the impacts of antiterrorism on constitutional government but pay little attention to international arms control. And arms control theorists do not think much about constitutional government. The proposition of nuclear constitutional internationalism flies in the face of conventional wisdom by suggesting that something as long-lived, robustly successful, and deeply institutionalized as the U.S. Constitution could come to depend on deep international arms control, a project widely viewed as historically inconsequential and deeply utopian.[7]

This essay aims to establish the link between limited government constitutionalism and deep international arms control. The unorthodox nuclear constitutional internationalist proposition follows in a fairly straightforward manner from core ideas of Enlightenment constitutional and international thought in general, and the American founding in particular. For more than two centuries, these ideas and practices have evolved and been adapted to new and increasingly globalized circumstances. These American founding theories and their descendants are now of potentially great value in the emerging omniviolence era. They combined from the outset theorizing about the interplay between international and material environments, republican constitutions, and interstate unions in a manner quite alien to the now compartmentalized intellectual worlds of constitutional and international theory.

The argument proceeds in five steps. First, I summarize the theoretical case for the proposition, which rests generally on a larger and older set of arguments about republics, geopolitics, and unions, and the ways in which different international environments support or subvert

6. For recent analysis of a world constitution that would not be a world state, see Jeffrey L. Dunoff and Joel P. Tractman, eds., *Ruling the World? Constitutionalism, International Law, and Global Governance* (Cambridge: Cambridge University Press, 2009).

7. For the skeptical view of arms control, dominant in international security studies, see Colin S. Gray, *House of Cards: Why Arms Control Must Fail* (Ithaca: Cornell University Press, 1992).

constitutional government. The second step is historical, a brief summary of this line of argument from the founding period to the Industrial Revolution and the global state system of rival great powers in the late nineteenth and early twentieth centuries. Third, I briefly consider the crosscutting effects of the nuclear revolution to date on the Constitution of the United States, arguing that nuclear weapons provided an under-appreciated breathing space, which is likely to close in the years ahead. Fourth, I outline reasons to think that the survival of limited government constitutionalism in the omniviolence era will increasingly hinge upon the success of robust international arms control. Finally, by way of conclusion, I briefly compare and contrast the argument of nuclear constitutional internationalism with four major well-known contemporary approaches to American foreign policy that assign primary significance to freedom (neosovereigntism, anti-imperial progressivism, neoconservatism, and liberal internationalism).

Republican Security Theory and Constitutional Internationalism

The most direct way to get to the essential logic of the nuclear constitutional internationalist proposition is by outlining some of the key ideas in republican security theory.[8] Important pieces of this theory appear in the basic constitutional and international ideas of the American founding. They are also prominent in contemporary realist international relations theory (the anarchy problematique, balance of power, and society of states) as well as in contemporary liberal international relations theory (democratic peace, commercial peace, and international unions). Republican security theory advances arguments that connect the prospects for limited constitutional government (in the United States and elsewhere) with material contextual and international systemic features of the external environment. For the limited focus here, there are three main points: a structural understanding of limited government constitutionalism, claims about the prospects for such constitutions in different international systemic and material contextual circumstances, and claims about the ways in which various types of international unions can preserve limited government constitutions.

Republican constitutions are here understood in structural terms and entail particular patterns of capability, authority, and accountability. Structural analysis of limited government constitutions centrally (but not exclusively) addresses the question of violence—of different arrangements

---

8. For further treatment, see Daniel H. Deudney, *Bounding Power: Republican Security Theory from the Polis to the Global Village* (Princeton: Princeton University Press, 2007).

for arms control. All states, including republics, are arrangements of arms control in that they specify who can employ what kinds of violence. This approach also sees a fundamental difference in the political structures of republics and hierarchical polities (whether absolutist monarchies, authoritarian dictatorships, or totalitarian single-party despotisms). There is no single violence control arrangement that is distinctively republican constitutional. Militias, elections, separation of power, and independent courts are among the ways in which centralized power has been restrained. Across the history of republican government, different contexts of violence capability have been governed with different configurations of authority and accountability. Despite this variety, the ordering principle in republics and unions of republics is always marked by mutual restraint among multiple circumscribed authorities with distributed violence capacity.[9]

All republics have also been states in a broader system of states (or other polities) that is anarchical in the sense of lacking authoritative government. Therefore, all republican states, like states generally, have had to conduct successful foreign and military policies in order to survive.

The features of the external or broadly international environments profoundly shape the prospects for limited government constitutionalism. Mapping this environment and its implications has been central to republican security theory. The external environment of any state, whatever its regime principle, is understood as being composed of three parts: the material context (the possibilities given by different configurations of geography and technology); the domestic regime features of the leading states with which the state in question must interact (a rough spectrum running from loose federal states, through constitutional republican states through various partial and incomplete constitutional democracies, to full-blown absolutist, authoritarian, and totalitarian hierarchies); and the international (or system level) arrangement of authority, which for most states is anarchical (not in the sense of chaotic but in the sense of lacking authoritative government).

One material variable, violence interdependence, is particularly important. It sits at the center of the argument for government generally, and it determines the character of the international system. Violence interdependence is a measure of the capacities of actors to wreak damage on one another, independent of the distribution of power. It is a measure of the velocity and volume of violence that can be projected across space. Anarchies marked by very high levels of violence interdependence

---

9. For ordering principles in structural theory, see Kenneth Waltz, *Theory of International Politics* (New York: Random House, 1979). Unfortunately, the structural theory dominant in international theory leaves out republican variations. For correction, see Deudney, "Republican Security Theory," in *Bounding Power*, 27–60.

are Hobbesian "states of nature" in which fundamental insecurity motivates the formation of authoritative government (whether hierarchical or
republican in character). Conversely, an anarchy marked by lesser levels
of violence interdependence is tolerable for security (at least for its largest
members), and there is no expectation that an exit from anarchy is necessary or likely to occur.

All three parts of this external landscape—material context, domestic
regime types, and the international system of authority (or lack thereof)—
have implications for republican constitutions. Life in interstate anarchies
poses demands that are mainly subversive of limited government constitutions. Successful military competition requires centralization of authority
and mobilization of capability. It also tends to produce increased state
autonomy and diminished accountability. How much limited government
constitutions are compromised depends upon the severity and contours of
the military security threat. Threat in turn depends upon the distribution
of power among the units in the system, the aims of other states (presumably rooted in their domestic regime features), and features of the material context. The constitutions of other states matter because they shape
the fundamental foreign policy aims of states, whether they are revision-
ists (seeking expansion at the expense of others), defensive positionalists
(interested primarily in preserving their own security), or confederative
(suited for and interested in various forms of cooperative problem solv-
ing through authoritatively binding international institutions). Overall,
the demands of the often-precarious life of states in international anarchy
have placed a high premium on dispatch and unity of decision making.
These prerogatives of the executive office thus have been in perpetual tension with the aims of limited government constitutions.

Nested within this view of republican constitutions and their interplay
with external factors is constitutional internationalism's claim about the
role of interstate unions in sustaining limited government constitutions.
Unions are understood as encompassing a range of different arrangements but must be significantly authoritative.[10] Authoritative arrangements of international law, organization, and regimes moderate interstate
anarchy and the demands it places upon republican constitutional states.
Union protects republican constitutional orders by eliminating the need
for measures that produce state hardening.[11] The logic of the argument

10. The most complete treatment remains Murray Forsyth, *Unions of States: The Theory
and Practice of Confederation* (Leicester: Leicester University Press, 1981).

11. For the role of strong international human rights institutions in reinforcing democracy at the domestic level, see Jamie Mayerfeld, "The Democratic Legitimacy of International
Human Rights Law," *Indiana International and Comparative Law Review* 19, no. 1 (2009):
49–99; Robert O. Keohane, Stephen Macedo, and Andrew Moravcsik, "Democracy-Enhanc-
ing Multilateralism," *International Organization* 63, no. 1 (Winter 2009): 1–31.

for union as an alternative to state hardening is essentially the reverse of the argument that anarchy compromises republican constitutions. The scope and character of the interstate union or institution necessary to sustain republican constitutions, and the possibilities for their erection, are also shaped by the features of the external environment. The scope of appropriate union increases with the size of the space within which intense violence interdependence is present. The possibilities for the creation of republican unions are shaped by the domestic regime features of other states. Not all states are suitable as partners for union. Law-governed constitutional states not only have a self-protection motive to form interstate unions but also an intrinsic capacity to do so. In contrast, hierarchical polities governed by the potentially capricious will of the supreme ruler provide few possibilities for mutually co-binding institutional arrangements.

The Fortunate Founding, the Garrison State Specter, and Liberal Internationalism

The logic of this very general argument can be further seen by looking at its articulations, applications, and evolutions at key junctures in American political thought about the Constitution and the international system over the past two centuries. There are four steps in the argument: the happy circumstances of the founding, the threatening creation of the global great-power system by the industrial revolution, the consequent specter of the garrison state, and the emergence of constitutional and liberal internationalism as a program to change the world to save the Constitution.

Heirs to a long tradition that viewed republics as rare and precarious, the American founders believed that the survival of limited government depended upon a set of external factors.[12] The theory of the American founding, laid out straightforwardly in *The Federalist,* was as much an international as a constitutional theory. Learning from the often tragic history of earlier republics and from the republican theorists of the European Enlightenment (most notably Montesquieu), the founders thought that the international and material contextual circumstances of the American founding period were particularly conducive to republican constitutional success. Frequent and extensive war and its threat would

12. Among the vast literature on the American founding, these arguments are commonly neglected. Important exceptions include Gottfried Dietze, "The Federalist as a Treatise on Peace and Security," in *The Federalist: A Classic on Federalism and Free Government* (Baltimore: Johns Hopkins University Press, 1960), 177–254, and David C. Hendrickson, *Peace Pact: The Lost World of the American Founding* (Lawrence: University Press of Kansas, 2003).

require a large military, which would, if the Roman republican experience was a reliable guide, lead to Caesarist coups and the erection of a military monarchy or despotism. The records of Venice, Holland, and (most importantly) early modern England suggested that insularity was conducive to republican success. Island polities could defend themselves primarily with a navy, which could not readily be used to seize the state. In contrast, armies were instruments of both interstate war and internal oppression.[13] With this historical and conceptual framing, the founders pointed to the happy circumstance that the United States was relatively isolated and thus could pursue a foreign diplomatic and military strategy of relative isolationism. This meant that the United States could secure itself with a standing military small enough to be readily checked by the capacities of the militias, the armies of the constituent states.

The favorable geopolitical circumstances that facilitated the founding of the United States as a constitutional republic began to erode in the late nineteenth century. The underlying cause of this new security situation was the Industrial Revolution, which profoundly altered the volumes and velocities of violence capability in the international system. With the widely noted "abolition of distance," the moat of the Atlantic Ocean did not change, but the ability to project violence capacity across it did. The security of the United States had always been significantly dependent on the balance of power among the European great powers. But with the dawn of the new global era, the United States came to recognize that its survival was coming to depend on maintaining a balance of power among much larger states within the much larger space of Eurasia, what the great British geopolitical theorist Halford Mackinder dubbed the "world island." The United States was thus thrown by technological change into a situation in which its survival would hinge on the outcomes of a series of titanic world wars.[14]

The Industrial Revolution not only made everything closer and thus potentially more threatening but also gave rise to a new type of potent antiliberal antagonist. The new technologies enabled the scale-up in the size and capabilities of hierarchical states, adding monstrous size to their menacing goals. With the rise of technologically advanced despotisms and dictatorships, most notably the Third Reich and the Soviet Union, the liberal democracies were threatened by a "Genghis Khan with the railroad and the telegraph," as the Russian liberal Alexander Herzen had

13. Felix Gilbert, "Insula Fortunata: The English Pattern for American Foreign Policy," in *To the Farewell Address: Ideas of Early American Foreign Policy* (Princeton: Princeton University Press, 1961) 19–43. See also Deudney, "Maritime Whiggery," in *Bounding Power*, 114–35.

14. For the debates of this era, see Deudney, "Federalist Global Geopolitics," in *Bounding Power*. 215–43.

anticipated.[15] In these dark years, writers such as James Burnham, George Orwell, and Lewis Mumford drew ominous analyses of what the American political scientist Harold Lasswell termed the "garrison state."[16] Eighteenth- and nineteenth-century liberals and democrats, ranging from Smith and Spencer to Marx, had posited that hierarchical polities were remnants of the premodern era, destined to fall by the historical wayside in the race with free states. But by the high era of heavy industrialism, the spectrum of viable industrial polities appeared much wider, and there was serious question whether liberal democracy was as viable as its authoritarian rivals of the left and the right.

The world of the global industrial state system posed fundamental problems for the American practice of maintaining a small standing army and avoiding participation in the wars of the European great powers. This new material context, combined with the despotic and aggressive character of some of the great powers, meant that the American limited government constitution would be subject to fatal stresses. It was feared that successfully competing with these aggressive totalitarian states would require such extensive levels of American state mobilization that the United States would itself become a garrison state. The United States might be big and powerful enough to sustain American physical security and political independence but at the cost of erecting a swollen and permanent national security state that would extinguish the domestic structural bulwarks of political liberty. With this historical and conceptual framing, many supporters of the American limited government constitution feared that the National Security Act of 1947 and related insitutionalizations of the new national security state, massive by historical American standards, ominously marked a major deformation of the constitutional order and a major step toward its ultimate termination.[17]

During these tumults of industrial security globalization, the program of American internationalism was expanded, deepened, and cast globally. American internationalism has many strands, some relating to humanitarian and religious goals, some relating to economics and the needs

15. Cited in Bertram D. Wolf, "The Totalitarian Potentials in the Modern Great-State Society," in *Revolution and Reality* (Chapel Hill: University of North Carolina Press, 1981), 330.

16. Harold Lasswell, "The Garrison State," *American Journal of Sociology* 46 (July 1941): 455–68. A careful sorting of these arguments is provided by Alex Roland, "The Military Industrial Complex: Lobby and Trope," in *The Long War: A New History of U.S. National Security Policy since World War II*, ed. Andrew J. Bacevich (New York: Columbia University Press, 2007), 335–70.

17. Michael J. Hogan, "Magna Carta: The National Security Act and the Specter of the Garrison State," in *A Cross of Iron: Harry S Truman and the Origins of the National Security State, 1945–1954* (Cambridge: Cambridge University Press, 1998), 23–68. See also Herman Belz, "Changing Conceptions of Constitutionalism in the Era of World War II and the Cold War," *Journal of American History* 59, no. 3 (December 1972): 640–69.

of administrative welfare states faced with high levels of "low politics" interdependence, and some related to the prudential operation of American hegemony among liberal states. The American internationalism of the early twentieth century was also partly constitutional internationalist, a strand somewhat neglected by recent commentaries. Constitutional internationalism is logically central to the whole enterprise, because it sought to alter the world in order to preserve constitutional government in the United States. In the new era of great and growing violence interdependence, it was necessary to formulate and execute a grand strategy to reorder the world in ways supportive of the limited government constitution in the United States. This constitutional internationalist agenda had two interrelated parts: change (somehow) the other units into republics; and substantially abridge interstate anarchy with a panoply of international organizations, laws, and "regimes." This program is very ambitious, even world revolutionary, and it amounts to a "liberal one worldism." But its animating motive was domestic-regime conservative, because world transformation was understood to be necessary for the survival of limited government constitutionalism in the United States (and elsewhere).[18] American power enables this project, but constitutional vulnerability motivates it.

The underlying logic of this line of thinking is that American limited government (and, by extension, the limited governments of the handful of other states that were constitutional republics) would be lost if such states remained in a state system that was both increasingly interactive and competitive, because of the rising security interdependence produced by the Industrial Revolution, and populated by increasingly modernized "total" hierarchical states.[19] Given this grim set of trade-offs, the constitutional internationalist program was crafted as a potentially realizable alternative world order. All states (or at least those that mattered) would become constitutional liberal democracies and interstate anarchy would be effectively abridged through an institutional web of authoritative mutual restraints.

18. The Republican statesman Elihu Root sums up the argument: "The world cannot be half democratic and half autocratic. It must be all democratic or all Prussian. There can be no compromise." See "The Effect of Democracy on International Law," in *Miscellaneous Addresses*, ed. Robert Bacon and James Brown Scott (Cambridge: Harvard University Press, 1917): 293.

19. For concise statements, see Thomas I. Cook and Malcolm Moos, "Foreign Policy: The Realism of Idealism," *American Political Science Review* 46, no. 2 (June 1952): 343–56; Thomas I. Cook and Malcolm Moos, "The American Idea of International Interest," *American Political Science Review* 47, no. 1 (March 1953): 8–44. Moos, a professor of political science at Johns Hopkins University, also served as President Eisenhower's speechwriter, helping to formulate the "military-industrial complex" warning in his Farewell Address.

The Ambivalent Nuclear Revolution

The saving grace of the industrial global era may well have been that it did not last very long, thus avoiding the fully telling test case of whether the garrison state hypothesis was correct. The advent of nuclear weapons profoundly altered the material context in which the United States and other states had to secure themselves. The effects of nuclear weapons on limited government occurred in strongly crosscutting ways. On the negative side of the ledger, are the cluster of hierarchy-enhancing effects, captured with the notions of "nuclear despotism" and the "nuclear total-itarian archipelago." On the positive side of the ledger, the effects are probably considerably more powerful: the decline in great-power war (the result in some significant measure of nuclear deterrence); and the sig-nificant reduction in the magnitude of state mobilization of civil society. Overall, life in the nuclear anarchic system hollowed liberal democratic constitutional government but also afforded an important, and largely underappreciated, breathing space.

Nuclear despotism is the notion that all nuclear armed states, whatever their formal constitutional principles, have become a "nuclear monar-chy" or an "absolute monarch" because decision making about nuclear use has devolved into the hands of one individual.[20] Nuclear explosives are intrinsically despotic because of the lack of accountability stemming from the inability of affected groups (including future generations) to have their interests represented at the moment of nuclear use. These des-potic tendencies have been further amplified by the deployment of mili-tary forces with large numbers of very powerful nuclear weapons placed on high-velocity delivery vehicles (particularly missiles) with global range and poised for immediate launch. With this strategic force structure, the time frame for decision making about nuclear use has been compressed into hours if not minutes.

This arrangement was accompanied by a leap in the practices of hierarchical arms control within nuclear states. Exploiting (and often developing) new communication, information-processing, and sen-sor technologies, the nuclear states (particularly the United States), greatly tightened the military chain of command while at the same time greatly expanding the spatial deployment of weapons platforms.[21] Thus

20. Franz Schurman, *The Logic of World Power* (New York: Pantheon, 1974); Arthur Schlesinger Jr., *The Imperial Presidency* (Boston: Houghton Mifflin, 1974), 11. See also H. Bartholomew Cox, "Reason d'Etat and World Survival: Who Constitutionally Makes Nuclear War?" *George Washington University Law Review* 57, no. 6 (August 1989): 1614–35.

21. C. Kenneth Allard, *Command, Control, and the Common Defense* (New Haven: Yale University Press, 1990).

equipped, the executive reigns supreme in the nuclear world, and the nuclear-state-within-the-state is a zone of unhindered hierarchical command authority. There have been, however, important limitations to this state hardening. It falls far short of full-spectrum political despotism because of the circumscribed range of its operation to date and the continued presence of powerful electoral, judicial, and legislative restraints.

A second state-hardening effect of the nuclear revolution to date stems from the need to establish what amounts to a nuclear totalitarian archipelago composed of a network of artificial islands of complete containment. Within the spaces of the nuclear weapons complex, the national security state has pioneered the creation of organizations that totally regulate information, personnel, and materials.[22] This totally hierarchical government of the atom is a major (if underacknowledged) contributor to overall public security and liberty in the nuclear age because it prevents leakage of nuclear capability into unauthorized hands. The realm of nuclear total control remains very spatially segregated. It employs only a small share of total national territory, and it leaves the broader civilian population largely untouched. Time will tell whether these arrangements of the nuclear totalitarian archipelago will come to be seen as the early laboratories and proving grounds of far more pervasive applications.

On the positive side of the ledger are the effects resulting from the decline in great-power war. Despite prenuclear and early nuclear era expectations that great-power war was a chronic feature of world politics, the past six decades have been marked by the "long peace." It is not entirely clear which of several powerful factors are most responsible for this happy outcome, but there are compelling reasons to think that nuclear deterrence and great-power caution about sliding into catastrophic nuclear war played a very calming role. For liberal democracy and constitutional government, this suspension of great-power war has been highly beneficial, helping to make broadly liberal forms of government more viable. The proximate causes in the explosion in the number of democracies over the past half century are the familiar patterns of domestic level change, but the presence of peace among the great powers has lessened the hurdles to overcome.

A second positive effect of the first, state-centric stages of the nuclear revolution results from the lower overall levels of state mobilization made possible by reliance on nuclear weapons. The vast destructive power of nuclear weapons enabled the United States to reply upon a much smaller conventional force for land, naval, and aerial warfare. The fact that the size of the U.S. military since World War II has been vastly greater than

---

22. The best statement remains Russell W. Ayres, "Policing Plutonium: The Civil Liberties Fallout," *Harvard Civil Rights–Civil Liberties Law Review* 10, no. 2 (1975): 369–443.

the norm during the first century and a half of the republic has tended to obscure the fact that without nuclear weapons it probably would have been considerably larger.[23] At the peak of mobilization during World War II, the United States spent nearly half its total economic product on the military, while during the most taxing periods of the Cold War it only spent about 10 percent. The potential of nuclear weapons to lessen the need for much more expensive conventional military forces was quickly appreciated as making the garrison state much less likely.[24] Nuclear weapons, providing "more bang for the buck," sheltered the limited government constitution from the stresses of more comprehensive mobilization.

Omniviolence and the Arms Control versus Limited Government Trade-Off

The omniviolence era is likely to have effects both like and unlike those of the nuclear revolution thus far. Overall, the ambivalent, crosscutting ways in which the nuclear revolution has partially sheltered and partially hollowed limited government constitutionalism are likely to become unambiguously subversive. The sheltering of the constitution is likely to weaken, while erosive pressures are likely to intensify. And a whole new set of challenging problems is likely to emerge. In this situation, the survival of limited government constitutionalism will come increasingly to hinge upon the erection of a much more substantial international arms control arrangement. Such an arrangement, to be responsive to the threat, is probably best thought of as the antistatist core of a world constitutional exit from interstate anarchy. The argument unfolds with three points: the contours of the omniviolence revolution, antiterrorism and state hardening, and the role of arms control as an alternative.

Solutions are judged by their ability to address problems, so having a clear view of the contours of the omniviolence problem is vital. Omniviolence occurs when weapons of mass destruction capabilities, specifically nuclear and biological weapons capabilities, "leak" into the hands of actors that are not territorial states. Omniviolence is not a new postnuclear stage of world politics but rather the next stage in the rolling "progress" of the nuclear revolution.[25] To think that the next stage of the

23. For American Cold War mobilization, see Aaron L. Friedberg, *In the Shadow of the Garrison State: America's Anti-Statism and Its Cold War Strategy* (Princeton: Princeton University Press, 2000).

24. William Borden, *There Will Be No Time: The Revolution in Strategy* (New York: Macmillan, 1946).

25. For a balanced and thorough treatment, see Charles D. Ferguson and William C. Potter, *The Four Faces of Nuclear Terrorism* (New York: Routledge, 2005).

nuclear revolution will be omniviolence is plausible because it follows an extremely well-established pattern in the history of violence capabilities: the eventual diffusion of new and more effective violence capabilities into the hands of more actors. From the time of their invention, nuclear weapons have been slowly but surely proliferating into the hands of more states, and the technological barriers to acquisition continue to decline. Interstate proliferation has not been as extensive as many feared earlier in the nuclear era, owing to some combination of military alliances (particularly with the United States), the norms and practices of the nonproliferation treaty regime, and various other factors. But the number of nuclear states continues to rise, and there could well be a cascade of nuclear acquisition in both the Middle East and East Asia in the near future. Nuclear proliferation adds to the prospects for nuclear leakage because the more nuclear states there are, the greater the chance of diversion. The fact that many of the recent and emerging nuclear states are subject to severe internal political problems makes it increasingly likely that such weapons will be at play in coups, civil wars, and other weak-state patterns widespread in the international system.

In thinking about the contours of this threat, it is as important to look at actors and their motives as at capabilities. The recent focus on violent fundamentalist Islamic groups operating in many parts of the world has been appropriate[26] but should not obscure the fact that the world is filled with other groups with revolutionary, if not apocalyptic, goals. Many of the nonstate actors of potential concern seek (whether plausibly or not) to seize state power, and selective use of weapons of mass destruction could serve as a gambit in such strategies.[27]

Unfortunately, the link between antiterrorism efforts and state hardening is all too easy to make.[28] Like war, antiterrorism campaigns are "the health of the state" and produce significant infringements on individual liberties. Terrorism in something like its current form has been around for at least a century. Over this period, states have been aggressively combating it with measures that are generally accepted to have strengthened state capacities and activities in ways subversive of individual liberties.

---

26. Bruce Reidel, "If Pakistan Fails: Armageddon in Islamabad," *National Interest*, no. 102 (July–August 2009): 9–18.

27. Fred Charles Ikle, *Annihilation from Within: The Ultimate Threat to Nations* (New York: Columbia University Press, 2006). This model roughly is that of Aum Shinrikyo, the Japanese "cult" that used nerve gas and anthrax in Japan. David E. Kaplan and Andrew Marshall, *The Cult at the End of the World* (New York: Crown, 1996).

28. Most recently, see Kim Lane Scheppele, "The Migration of Anti-constitutional Ideas: The Post 9/11 Globalization of Public Law and the International State of Emergency," in *The Migration of Constitutional Ideas*, ed. Sujit Choudry (Cambridge: Cambridge University Press, 2007), 347–73.

Antiterrorism measures also have enjoyed strong popular support. By increasing the violence potential of terrorist acts by multiple orders of magnitude, weapons of mass destruction multiply the subversive impact of terrorism on limited government constitutions.

In thinking about arms control as solution sets to this problem, images of abolition are essentially misleading. The possibility of creating nuclear weapons is an effectively permanent reality, given the natural occurrence of radiological materials and the edifice of modern scientific technology. Given this, there is no one solution set, and the design trade-offs emerge from asking how much fissile material will exist, situated where, with who having access to it under what circumstances. The omniviolence solution sets are essentially the well-conceptualized paths of arms control as it has been practiced during the nuclear era to date. Arms control between states, culminating in the great reductions in deployed nuclear arsenals at the end of the Cold War, is one of the great public security success stories of the nuclear era, as is the less heralded perfection of internal hierarchical arms control within nuclear states.[29] The path to the containment of nuclear capability is essential to further steps in this dual arms control effort. Despite the revolutionary implications of nuclear weapons for many aspects of world politics, the achievement of comprehensive and universal nuclear containment would not entail revolutionary upheavals and changes in the way of life of peoples, because nuclear capabilities are so distinctive from the activities of civil society. And deep nuclear arms control should not be viewed as a program for the creation of world state or government with a monopoly of either violence capacity or authority, but is better conceived as a confederation of states bound together by a constitutional treaty that prohibits possession of violence capacity by any organ constituted by their union of sovereign states.

Constitutional Internationalism and Its Sibling Rivals

The contemporary landscape of American foreign policy debate is populated with many sophisticated realist and liberal positions, all derived largely from republican security theory, but differing in important ways from nuclear constitutional internationalism. There is no agreed typology, or even terminology, for the competing schools, and they overlap in complex ways. Confining the discussion to approaches broadly liberal because of their primary concern for freedom in some form, there are

29. For the end of the Cold War arms controls treaties and their contribution to global security, see Joseph Cirincione, *Bomb Scare: The History and Future of Nuclear Weapons* (New York: Columbia University Press, 2007).

four schools (neosovereigntism, neoconservatism, anti-imperial progressivism, and liberal internationalism) with noteworthy similarities and differences with nuclear constitutional internationalism. The preservation of limited government is a primary concern for neosovereigntists and anti-imperial progressives, but they (along with neoconservatives) largely oppose international institution building. Conversely, liberal internationalists place great emphasis on building international institutions but rarely invoke the preservation of the limited government constitution as a reason to do so.

The *new sovereigntist* school places great value on the survival of limited government constitutionalism and sees many threats to it. This line of thinking wants to reduce American participation in international organizations and to lessen the influence of international law on the conduct of American foreign policy.[30] These theorists voice great concern for constitutional integrity and then advance arguments about how American participation in actually existing international organizations and regimes is subversive of both the Constitution and American sovereignty. This line of argument is the international extension of a widespread and powerful American domestic "conservative" view which opposes the growth of government in the United States. Large government is seen as a fundamental threat and contrary to both the letter and the spirit of the Constitution of 1787. Much of the neosovereigntist's animus is directed against the European Union and the patterns of economic and social life in contemporary Europe, which they fear that the United States will come to resemble. Although their criticisms are cast in very general terms about constitutional consequences, the offending tendencies are remarkably circumscribed and selective, for reasons that have little to do with concern for limited government constitutionalism. Neosovereigntist attacks on international organizations largely ignore international security (NATO, strategic arms limitation, the NPT, and the IAEA) and say very little about economic developments such as the World Trade Organization. Rather, the focus is on cultural, social, and civil rights. This rather bizarre selectivity suggests that neosovereigntism is animated more by American "culture war" concerns than limited government constitutional ones. This school has a strong strain of populist antilegalism and fears that law, particularly international law, suffers from a democracy deficit of public accountability. While democratic accountability is a key feature of limited government constitutionalism, such arrangements intrinsically have

---

30. For a concise statement, see John Fonte, "Democracy's Trojan Horse," *National Interest*, Summer 2004, 117–27. For extended statement, see Jeremy Rabkin, *Law without Nations? Why Constitutional Government Requires Sovereign States* (Princeton: Princeton University Press, 2004).

a majoritarian deficit in that they structurally remove and insulate certain domains of decision making from (immediate) majoritarian democratic control. It is the independence of courts from (conservative) public opinion that is the prime target of these thinkers. Curiously, however, the neosovereigntists express no concern about the national security state, and expanded executive power in foreign and military policy, as threats to American limited government constitutionalism.

Yet another school, the *progressive anti-imperialists*, characterizes American foreign policy over the past century as imperialist and views American "empire" as subversive of the constitution. These theorists build on a long line of reflection on how Roman imperial success created domestic stresses and imbalances fatal to the Roman republican constitution. These critics see an economic and class-based internal American push to expand rather than an American response to external threats.[31] The American external push to dominate others is seen as the result of corruptions and deformations in the American political and economic order, most notably the autonomy and power of the corporations and wealthy capitalists. As the national security state has grown in size, these theorists also indict its vast industrial base, what Eisenhower termed the "military industrial complex," as a further source of American imperialism, militarism, and empire. In contrast to the view that American interaction with a corrupt world corrupts America, the progressive anti-imperial critics see the world as victim or as a passive (or justifiably rebellious) stage for the enactment of an American deformity.[32] Strong versions of these arguments were advanced against the American aggressions of the Spanish-American War. As the United States became enmeshed in global great-power competition, this view came to closely overlap with constitutional internationalist arguments about state hardening. The solution offered by the progressive critics is a twofold program of internal domestic reform (strengthen democratic controls over wayward corporations) and external retrenchment. However, retrenchment in the nuclear era has the severe problem that it would reduce American involvement in the world without reducing the world's violence interdependence, thus running the risk of contributing to the further diffusion of nuclear weapons to states forced to secure themselves in the absence of American alliance protection.

31. The foundational work is Charles Beard, *An Economic Interpretation of the Constitution of the United States* (New York: Macmillan, 1913). A recent restatement is Andrew J. Bacevitch, *American Empire: The Realities and Consequences of American Diplomacy* (Cambridge: Harvard University Press, 2002).

32. A particularly strong recent version of this argument has been offered by the political scientist Chalmers Johnson in several recent volumes, most notably *Nemesis: The Last Days of the American Republic* (New York: Metropolitan Books, 2006).

Particularly influential over the past three decades, *neoconservativism* is a "one legged-Wilsonianism." It embraces one liberal internationalist element (democracy promotion), while strongly opposing another (the interstate agenda of moderating anarchy through international law, organizations, and regimes). Neoconservatives view international arrangements as essentially threatening to the exercise of American power and the promotion of freedom in the world. Existing international organizations, whatever their founding inspiration, are seen to have been captured by antidemocratic states and deployed to hinder American goals. Negotiating mutually binding restraints with despotic regimes that have threatening military capabilities (such as the Soviet Union) is understood to be futile if not dangerous. Such regimes will systematically cheat on their assumed obligations but will be able to do so in ways that lull the gullible, excessively peace-loving Western publics into complacency and passivity. Conversely, negotiating mutually binding restraints among liberal democratic states is viewed as unnecessary. Such polities, by the virtue of their being democracies, are inherently friends of the United States rather than threats, whatever their military capacities. The neoconservatives also place great faith in the ability of the United States to use military force to promote freedom. The benevolent hegemon, America should overthrow despotic states and police threats to world order. Despotic states, prone to regional revisionist agendas as rogue states, and willing to sponsor various terrorist groups, are appropriate targets for both coercive counterproliferation and regime change. The credibility of this approach has been damaged not just by the costly debacle in Iraq but also by an unwillingness to demand democratic openings in states, such as Egypt, that are geopolitical allies of the United States. Thus, the neoconservative program comes to resemble American imperial and great-power interest buttressed and domestically legitimated by the deployment of free world rhetoric.

Among all the schools of American foreign policy, constitutional internationalism and its nuclear application sit most squarely within the broad family of programs and theories of *liberal internationalism*. But among the major branches of liberal internationalism, concern for limited government constitutionalism is almost nonexistent. The main contemporary liberal internationalist concerns are humanitarianism, welfare state management, and hegemonic maintenance. Despite being nearly invisible in the contemporary family of liberal internationalism, the constitutionalist strand is arguably central to the whole free world project because it addresses the core of the core, the limited government constitution upon which American liberty rests. Part of liberal internationalism, the theory and program of nuclear arms control, similarly ignores limited government constitutionalism, despite the fact that arms control is now becoming pivotal for constitutional preservation. Politically, arms control is undersupported and underemployed and is advanced consistently only by the arms control scientists, periodically augmented by short-lived episodes of mass public concern. Coupling constitutional internationalism with the already robust program of nuclear arms control may help this agenda become as central in the high-security agenda of American grand strategy as it deserves to be.

Discussions of American foreign policy customarily conclude with rousing admonitions—usually futile—for greater coherence and consensus in the formation and execution of American grand strategy. But states, even fractious liberal democratic ones, sometimes galvanize themselves in the face of real peril to define and accomplish extraordinary exertions and innovations. If the United States is to navigate the coming storms of the grave new omniviolence era, foundational American political theory, once again updated, again offers its services as a guide to the preservation of freedom.

Conclusion ─────────────────────────────────

Constitutional Engagement and Its Limits

CHRISTOPHER L. EISGRUBER

THE CONTRIBUTORS TO THIS volume appreciate constitutional conflict. I do not mean merely that they recognize that conflict exists and that constitutions must cope with it. Those banal insights would not distinguish the perspectives represented in this book from more conventional accounts that regard constitutions as devices for resolving political disputes. The essays collected here do something more remarkable: they treat durable conflict as a sustaining element, a kind of animating tension, within constitutionalism. Though some conflicts must indeed be resolved, conflict itself must be nurtured or the constitutional project will fail. Thus, Sotirios Barber contends that "the chief measure of constitutional success is the quality of civic debate" and that "consensus about either ends or means hastens constitutional failure by obviating debate through which error about ends and means is revealed and progress maintained." Gary Jacobsohn maintains that "far from being fatal to the inquiry, the contestability of constitutional identity is a crucial element in our attempt to comprehend it." William Harris proposes that "what it really means to be *founded* constitutionally as a People is for its citizens to construct the right disagreements—considered as 'right' because they arise as interpretive disputes about the meaning of their fundamental commitments—and to have the debate over those differences itself contribute to the reinforcement of the constitutional system." Mariah Zeisberg insists that "interbranch interpretive conflict . . . can generate more constitutional authority than would be the case if one branch were highly deferential" to another branch's resolution of a constitutional question.[1]

It would be easy to multiply these examples. We might say that, despite their many disagreements, the authors of the essays collected in this volume agree about the value of disagreement.[2] Indeed, a superficial reading

---

1. My observations about constitutional conflict owe much to Zeisberg, whose dissertation and essays insightfully analyze the importance of conflict to constitutional democracy.

2. I share this perspective. One of my earliest publications contended that impassioned disagreement about justice was a defining virtue of the American regime. Christopher L. Eisgruber, "Disagreeable People," *Stanford Law Review* 43 (1990): 275, 297–98. My most recent book defends the value of institutional conflict over Supreme Court nominations.

of the book might conclude that its unifying theme is an appreciation for interpretive conflict rather than a concern with constitutional limits. Upon deeper analysis, though, the authors' regard for conflict becomes a window that illuminates a distinctive perspective on the limits of constitutional democracy. In this concluding chapter, I will argue that the essays in this volume share a view of constitutionalism as, among other things, an effort to sculpt a generative culture of argument. Constitutionalism's most fundamental limits pertain to its capacity to execute that ambitious cultural project successfully.

This link between conflict and limits emerges if we consider the significance of Lincoln's leadership during the Civil War, an episode that attracts attention in several of this book's chapters. Sotirios Barber, Gary Jacobsohn, Benjamin Kleinerman, Jeffrey Tulis, Mariah Zeisberg, Joseph Bessette, and Rogers Smith all mention Lincoln's constitutional practice, and several of them treat it in detail. The commentators disagree about how best to characterize Lincoln's actions. For example, Barber and Kleinerman argue that Lincoln acted "extraconstitutionally" when he suspended habeas corpus and took other extraordinary actions to preserve the republic. Tulis and Bessette, by contrast, insist (as did Lincoln himself) that Lincoln acted under the Constitution as well as in service of it.

This fascination with Lincoln is hardly surprising in a book about constitutionalism's limits. Lincoln's career encompassed shocks that tested the capacity of the constitutional order. The antebellum constitutional order failed to contain the conflict over slavery, and violence erupted. A changed constitutional order emerged. One might argue that the old constitutional order had collapsed, or that it survived in amended form after a period of nonconstitutional government, or that the constitution remained active and authoritative (at least for the Union government) throughout the war. Lincoln's presidency and the events surrounding it thus provide a kind of historical laboratory for testing theories about constitutional success and failure. In contending with Lincoln, the Civil War, and Reconstruction, we confront obvious limits of constitutionalism.

Yet, this account of Lincoln's constitutional intervention is a close cousin to the conventional view of constitutional limits that Tulis and Stephen Macedo criticize in their introduction to this volume. Tulis and Macedo note that the "usual way of talking about the limits of constitutional democracy is to discuss the variety of indigenous circumstances—ethnic and tribal traditions, lack of commitment to the rule of law, and religious strife—that hinder its development." This familiar perspective

---

Christopher L. Eisgruber, *The Next Justice: Repairing the Supreme Court Appointments Process* (Princeton: Princeton University Press 2007), 13.

on constitutional limits is easily adapted to embrace the American Civil War. The account invites us to ask whether constitutional norms and institutions can be robust enough to cope with deep cultural divisions like those related to race slavery in America, or whether such conflicts must be addressed extraconstitutionally—perhaps even by brute military force, as manifested in Sherman's march through the South. By posing the question of limits in this way, we implicitly reduce the Constitution to nothing more than a set of institutions and rules. As a result, issues about constitutional limits and failures become questions about whether those institutions and rules can withstand shocks and stresses, much like questions we might ask about whether a building or other rigid structure can withstand wind shears, earthquakes, or forty-year floods.

Abraham Lincoln, though, was not William Tecumseh Sherman. He was not, in other words, simply a great military leader or a ruthless exponent of executive power. He was an extraordinary thinker in addition to being a decisive actor. More specifically, Lincoln was a gifted constitutional interpreter who understood, articulated, preserved, and reformed the American constitutional order. Whatever disagreements the authors in this volume may have about Lincoln, they agree that Lincoln had exceptional constitutional vision and insight. It is *that* feature of his leadership, not the naked fact of the functional breakdown of American institutions during the Civil War or Lincoln's forceful action in response to it, that makes his example so riveting to this book's authors. Lincoln exemplified what we might call active constitutional intelligence, a quality that is indispensible to constitutionalism at all times but becomes more visible in moments of functional crisis.

When Barber and Kleinerman engage with Tulis and Bessette about whether Lincoln acted extraconstitutionally, their argument goes beyond a dispute about the legality of Lincoln's orders. They are also disagreeing about how to understand the place of Lincoln's redemptive exercise of constitutional intelligence. One might view Lincoln's interpretive activity as either outside the constitutional system or embedded within it. The external view of Lincoln's contribution emphasizes that America's fate during the Civil War was uniquely dependent on the perspicacity and leadership of a single individual who had great power and was willing to exercise it ruthlessly in apparent disregard of constitutional forms. The internal view stresses that Lincoln rose to power on the basis of shrewd constitutional arguments that won favor with key electoral constituencies and that during his presidency he not only claimed his actions were fully constitutional but submitted them to Congress for judgment.

This volume's authors recognize the need for active constitutional intelligence not just in exceptional circumstances like the ones that Lincoln confronted but, more generally, in the service of what Walter Murphy terms "constitutional maintenance."[3] As James Fleming notes in his contribution to this volume, Murphy's perspective on a constitution is neither a "machine that would go of itself" nor a static system of limits and settlements. It instead requires continual evaluation and reform. So conceived, a constitution sponsors a vital order, though one very different from the insipid and clichéd idea of a "living constitution" whose provisions yield compliantly to the dominant impulses of the times. Murphy's view of constitutional democracy is more demanding. It presupposes a political community that struggles continuously to make progress toward ends that it only imperfectly comprehends. Constitutional maintenance is not reducible to the periodic adjustment of satisfactory institutions to cope with changing conditions or wear and tear, in the way that one might tune-up a car or repair an aging house. Harris observes in his chapter here that "most [constitutional] provisions operate more in the role of posing questions than providing answers." Far from taking issues off the table, they demand continuing engagement. Public recognition of the need for constitutional maintenance, manifested through engaged dispute about constitutional principles, is a sign that a constitution is flourishing, not that it is faltering.

When viewed from the perspective of constitutional maintenance, Lincoln's presidency raises questions not merely about the Constitution's capacity to withstand acute shocks or hardships but also about a more general and pervasive problem: to what extent can a constitution provide for, structure, and contain—*constitute,* in the fullest sense of the verb—the active constitutional intelligence that it presupposes in order to achieve its ends? This question links constitutional limits to constitutional conflict. Conflict is a corollary of engagement; if citizens are bringing active intelligence to bear on constitutional questions and arrangements, they will inevitably disagree with one another, often vigorously and sometimes passionately. Constitutions must create a matrix of argument that simultaneously nurtures and contains such conflicts. Constitutionalism's most profound limits are those relevant to its execution of this delicate assignment.

The need for active constitutional intelligence generates two categories of limits, each of which occupies the attention of some authors in this volume. The limits may manifest themselves in the presence of exogenous shocks to the political system, such as a military attack or natural disaster, but they ultimately stem not from such events but from the dynamic of constitutional government. They are inherent to the constitutional enterprise, entailments of its defining aspirations.

3. Walter F. Murphy, *Constitutional Democracy* (Baltimore: Johns Hopkins University Press, 2007), 332–33.

The first kind of limit we might call *internal*. Internal limits arise because constitutions have only an imperfect capacity to shape the political culture within the regimes they establish. These internal limits have two distinct forms, which correspond to two objectives of liberal constitutions, freedom and security. First, because constitutions aim to promote freedom, they circumscribe governments' abilities to mold the beliefs, morals, and habits of their citizens. People in a constitutional regime are free to make important choices about what to read, how to worship, what to believe, and how to educate their children. In the United States, for example, public decision making about education is delegated almost entirely to a combination of subconstitutional political bodies (such as local school districts), nongovernmental organizations (such as private schools), and families. The existence of widespread choices about education is not a sign that constitutions are failing, corrupt, or unfinished; on the contrary, one purpose of constitutionalism is to make these choices both possible and meaningful.

Of course, even if constitutional regimes have only limited capacities to shape the character of their citizens, those capacities may be potent and important. In his contribution to this volume, Jeffrey Tulis describes a modified, "narrower" kind of statesmanship consistent with a politics that "services a semiprivate realm of freedom, where individuals pursue diverse ideas of the good life rather than inhabit a polity that defines the good for them." According to Tulis, constitutional statesmanship stops short of remaking "the concepts, categories, feelings, and understandings that order their minds"; instead, it involves "the authentic expression of attributes . . . constitutive of the [existing constitutional] office," and it may improve "inherited understandings . . . of the Constitution" without fundamentally remaking them. Sotirios Barber argues that constitutionalists must pay attention to civic education because "Aristotle and the [classic] tradition were right: there's no substitute for 'better motives'" in politics. He calls for renewed attention to Madison's proposal for a national university that could "promote those 'liberal sentiments and those congenial manners' at the 'foundation' of the political system." New expressions of constitutionalism such as those explored by Ran Hirschl and Jan-Werner Mueller challenge conventional ideas about the relationship between constitutions and cultures. Hirschl describes regimes that simultaneously adhere to "some or all core elements of modern constitutionalism" but that also involve "the constitutional enshrining of [a] religion" and the recognition of a constitutionally authoritative set of "religious bodies and tribunals." Hirschl's account raises issues about how far constitutional regimes may go in shaping the religious life of a people while remaining genuinely constitutional. Müller, on the other hand, investigates supranational forms of constitutionalism and, in so doing, questions oft-repeated assumptions about the extent to which constitutions embody or depend upon the "specific values . . . of a particular nation" or a "single national culture."

These varied arguments illustrate the complexity of the relevant constitutional limits without calling into question either their existence or their importance. One may agree with Barber that the Constitution partly constitutes the people it governs while also agreeing with Tulis that its control over political life is incomplete by design. The question of what "partly" means—of which portions of political life are constitutionally influenced and which are not—is important and interesting. Yet, however one resolves that issue, constitutions cannot guarantee the habits of mind they presuppose. There is thus a tension between the civic engagement that constitutions presuppose and the individual freedom at which they aim. That tension is written into the DNA of constitutional systems—it is a consequence of constitutional aspirations, not bad luck—and it is one important internal limit of constitutionalism.

A second set of internal limits is related to another constitutional aspiration, the aim of providing security from violence (which may result from military attack or internal disorder, including crime, unrest, terrorism, or civil war). To achieve this objective, constitutions must establish executive authorities capable of maintaining order. The Hobbesian sovereign, empowered to settle the violent disputes that occur in the state of nature, is the symbolic embodiment of a commitment to security and order. The Hobbesian sovereign, though, fits uneasily in a constitutional order that depends on engaged argument about constitutional ends: the role of the Hobbesian sovereign is to settle disputes, not nurture them. Insofar as security and order require a unitary, decisive sovereign, constitutional commitments are once again in tension with one another.

Several of the essays in this collection focus on this tension between decision and argument. Joseph Bessette, Kim Lane Scheppele, and Mariah Zeisberg all examine how constitutions can preserve healthy conflict about the propriety of particular policies even in circumstances that require decisive executive action. Scheppele observes that "emergencies, particularly those involving terrorism, are much more enduring than most analysts suggest." For that reason, constitutions cannot treat vigorous executive action as a short-term exception to ordinary arrangements and commitments; instead, they must incorporate institutions and procedures that "are effective but not anticonstitutional" and "spread power back through the legislative and judicial branches at times of crisis." To like effect, Zeisberg articulates a view of war-making authority in which neither the legislature nor the executive "can ever be free from the burden to justify its actions to the other." Dynamic institutional strategies of the sort that Scheppele and Zeisberg recommend extend the range of circumstances in which constitutionalists can pursue security and order without sacrificing engaged citizenship and the debate that goes with it.

Even such strategies have their limits, however. For example, Adrian Vermeule suggests in his essay that the "executive should be released from legislative constraints at the stage of conflict execution." He contends that glory-seeking executives' desire for "public approval and esteem" may render them accountable to the public, in the sense of leading them to "produce greater social welfare" than would result from other self-interested motives for executive action or from constitutional restraints on executive power. Yet, as Mark Brandon points out, this kind of "social welfare" may not include—indeed, it may come at the expense of—the habits of civic engagement that constitutionalists are committed to maintain: deference to wartime decision making may disable "citizens from critically assessing the actions of the very government that is ostensibly their agent."

Brandon's essay also illuminates the second fundamental kind of limit on constitutionalism, which we might call *external*. External limits reflect the fact that polities have geographic boundaries. Constitutions attempt to define a domain of political life, what William F. Harris has elsewhere called (borrowing from Ernest Hemingway's famous short story) a "clean, well-lighted space" carved from the chaos of human interaction and conceptual confusion.[4] To construct this space, constitutions distinguish insiders from outsiders and citizens from foreigners. Thus, James Madison referred to Americans as a "family" and insisted that the ultimate test of the Constitution was whether it was "calculated to accomplish the views and happiness of the people of America."[5] Harris describes the Federalists' constitutional enterprise as founded upon the idea that, "to pursue their destiny of 'happiness' in the world, and to achieve an order of community for themselves, 'My fellow citizens' or countrymen need a single body politic (a *constitution* indeed)."[6] If constitutionalism serves the happiness of a "family," a set of "countrymen," or some other subpart of the world's population, it necessarily defines the remainder of the world as outsiders or foreigners whose happiness is less significant from a constitutional standpoint. Yet, these outsiders or foreigners interact, as individuals and through their own political regimes, with the constitutional polity. Such interactions, which constitutions by definition control incompletely at best, are the source of what I am calling constitutionalism's external limits.

4. William F. Harris II, *The Interpretable Constitution* (Baltimore: Johns Hopkins University Press, 1993), 49.

5. Alexander Hamilton, James Madison, and John Jay, *The Federalist,* ed. Jacob E. Cooke (Middletown, CT: Wesleyan University Press, 1961), No. 14, and No. 40.

6. Harris, *The Interpretable Constitution,* 118.

Whereas the internal limits on constitutionalism derive from tensions among aspirations and commitments within the political orders that constitutions establish, the external limits derive from the relationship between that order and the political world surrounding it. These limits are external because they pertain to the exterior of the constitutional domain, but, like internal limits, they arise not from unfortunate circumstances or surrounding conditions but from the defining aspirations of constitutionalism. No polity is an island (not even island polities); polities (and their members) interact with one another (and one another's members) commercially, demographically, culturally, and militarily. Constitutions presuppose an international environment that they neither define nor regulate, and their commitment to participate in that environment is in tension with other constitutional commitments.

Both Brandon's essay and Daniel Deudney's illustrate the interdependence between a constitutional polity's internal culture of argument and its participation in an international environment.[7] As Deudney puts it, "All republics have also been states in a broader system of states (or other polities)" and "have had to conduct successful foreign and military policies in order to survive." Constitutionalism can flourish only if constitutions can create polities that simultaneously conduct effective foreign policies and establish a domestic political culture distinguished by a respect for liberty, human dignity, and civic engagement. These objectives compete with one another insofar as military success "requires centralization of authority [as well as] increased state autonomy and diminished accountability." Deudney argues that "how much limited government constitutions are compromised depends upon the severity and contours of the military security threat."

Likewise, Brandon observes "a tension between the underlying principles and purposes of constitutional democracy, on the one hand, and the nation-state, on the other." This tension is different from a simple opposition; Brandon notes that, by comparison to other forms of international organization, the system of nation-states has been hospitable to constitutionalism: "[A] robust practical constitutionalism arose in the wake of the creation of nation-states." Nevertheless, the statehood of a constitutional regime may entail that it has certain powers or capacities by virtue of being a state—by virtue of "the law of nations" or, more generally, its status within international affairs. The existence of a source of authority independent of the constitution threatens to displace the "sovereignty of the people," including the right of the people to evaluate and then "to resist and replace [their] standing government."

---

7. I follow Daniel Deudney by adopting the usefully vague term "international environment." Deudney's terminology has the advantage of generalizing beyond any particular set of international circumstances, such as the current arrangement of nation-states.

Constitutional borders generate a second set of tensions that pertain to state-to-individual relationships, rather than state-to-state relationships. To define a political regime, constitutions must distinguish members from nonmembers, but, as Rogers Smith points out, they cannot do so arbitrarily. Constitutional democracies must "justify themselves and define their obligations and goals in terms of beliefs in human dignity, including a broad range of liberties." This requirement applies not only to the regime's treatment of its members but to the policies by which it differentiates members from nonmembers. Yet, as Smith also recognizes, a constitutional regime's obligation to add new members may threaten its integrity, by forcing it either to internalize cultural "divisions severe enough to destroy the regime" or to expand "so greatly as to render it impossible for the regime's institutions to provide any real semblance of democratic self-governance." Controlling borders is one mechanism that constitutional regimes use to sustain the culture of constructive argument on which their success depends. Smith proposes a kind of compromise, pursuant to which constitutional democracies can defer full membership until such time as they can accommodate it successfully. Whether or not we find that treatment of the issue persuasive, we should recognize, as Smith does, that the demarcation between members and nonmembers is a chronic site of potential constitutional failure.

Brandon, Deudney, and Smith frame their claims in the idiom of the nation-state, but their insights apply more broadly to any international environment within which constitutional regimes demarcate geographic borders and use them to distinguish members from nonmembers. That generalization is important in light of Müller's arguments on behalf of the idea that basic constitutional commitments are "transferable to the realm outside the state without thereby making constitutionalism . . . incoherent or empirically irrelevant." Unless, however, one is more optimistic than Müller about the prospects for a successful global constitutionalism, the problems associated with constitutional borders will recur at supranational levels, because even supranational constitutional regimes presuppose an international environment that they do not control.

We have thus identified a series of four tensions, two internal and two external: personal freedom—civic virtue, political order—sustained argument, state sovereignty—constitutional sovereignty, and equality—membership. All eight poles of these dyads correspond to essential constitutional aspirations. Two aspirations (freedom and equality) emanate from the constitutional commitment to human dignity; two others (political order and state sovereignty) arise from its commitment to security (what the American Constitution's Preamble calls "domestic tranquility" and "the common defense"). The other four aspirations pertain to the culture of engaged argument required for the constitutional order to flourish. Each of these four dyads represents a distinct possibility for constitutional failure, none of which is dependent on unusual circumstances or acute misfortune. All are persistently present as a result of constitutionalism's defining principles. Constitutionalism cannot exist, much less flourish, without these tensions. They thus add to the plausibility of Harris's initially surprising suggestion that a "*constitutional* fear" of failure might be so pervasive as to be "characteristic of the enterprise."

These internal and external limits arise from a demanding conception of constitutionalism, what we might call the engagement view. It holds that constitutionalism involves, at its core, a set of commitments to the dignity of the individual, prosperity, and security, which commitments are never fully achieved or even perfectly understood but are nonetheless progressively pursued through a transparent and intelligible form of self-governance that requires continuing civic engagement. It is not surprising that so ambitious a project would be rife with limiting tensions and risks of failure.

There is, of course, another conception of constitutionalism, one that serves as foil for many of the arguments in this book. Zeisberg calls this view "the settlement thesis" while Barber refers to it as "negative constitutionalism." It maintains that the point of constitutions is to settle questions, limit governments, and set up institutions that allow diverse people to cooperate peacefully and with a tolerable level of well-being. For the constitution of settlement or limits, passionate disagreement, far from being indispensible to the constitutional enterprise, is a pathology to be prevented or cured.

Can proponents of the settlement view take a kind of perverse comfort from the many possibilities for constitutional failure identified by the essays in this book? "You are right to think that your view of constitutionalism has important limits," they might say, while adding, "and the existence of those limits is yet another reason why people should prefer the settlement view to your demanding, conflict-centered, and ultimately unworkable view." But, of course, the settlement view has its own limits, and it is far from clear that those limits are more easily circumvented than the ones described in this volume. Some of these limits are apparent to settlement theorists themselves. For example, long-running constitutional debates—such as America's debates about abortion rights and affirmative action—count as problems, and maybe even as failures, from the perspective of the settlement view because they suggest that the Constitution is provoking rather than resolving deep arguments of principle.[8] For engagement constitutionalists, by contrast, these pervasive features of

8. For an example of a settlement theorist who expresses a concern of this kind, see Robert F. Nagel, *Constitutional Cultures: The Mentality and Consequences of Judicial Review* (Berkeley: University of California Press 1989), 22.

our constitutional practice are benign. Thus, James Fleming can count the Constitution's failure to enumerate specifically all of the rights it protects as a "successful failure"—successful from the standpoint of the engagement perspective but not the settlement perspective, precisely because the idea of unenumerated rights invites continued conflict about what rights the Constitution protects.

Ultimately, though, the contributors to this book insist that the settlement view suffers from more severe problems. They contend that the engagement view better describes our constitutional practice, is normatively superior, and indeed is conceptually inevitable, given basic aspects of constitutional practice. For the most part, these arguments are referenced rather than elaborated in this volume, which focuses on the limits of the engagement view rather than its merits by comparison to the settlement view. It is on the basis of these arguments, though, that we must choose between the engagement and settlement views. The fact that the engagement view has limits is not a vice of that view—it is rather something that it shares in common with other conceptions of constitutionalism and, more generally, with other theories of political authority.

This volume's elaboration of constitutional limits should thus give all constitutionalists new insight into Alexander Hamilton's famous statement, in the opening paragraph of *Federalist* No. 1, that "it seems to have been reserved to the people of this country, by their conduct and example, to decide the important question, whether societies of men are really capable or not of establishing good government from reflection and choice, or whether they are forever destined to depend for their political constitutions on accident and force."[9] Perhaps the most conventional reading of Hamilton's observation is patriotic and triumphal: "Yes, it fell to us, and we did it! We created a constitution that has endured for more than two centuries, and thus we have demonstrated the possibility of government by reflection and choice." A more thoughtful reading is ironic: given the failures of state governments in the eighteenth century and the absence of other inherited structures of political authority, Americans had no choice but to establish a constitution from reflection and choice. By good fortune (or "accident"), they enjoyed advantages that made it possible for them to do so. This second reading emphasizes the familiar idea that circumstances limit the possibilities for constitutional success. The contributors to this volume suggest a third, more profound reading. They teach us that there are limits inherent in the very commitment to reflection and choice. Reason is fallible, choices can be catastrophic, and governments founded upon a commitment to reason and choice therefore confront specific, durable risks of failure. Read in this light, Hamilton's dictum

9. Alexander Hamilton, *Federalist*, No. 1.

articulates a question not resolved by the events of the late eighteenth century or by the long-term persistence of the American constitution, but rather intrinsic to constitutional democracy and hence renewed daily in every constitutional regime. The possibility of constitutional failure is not some long-vanquished relic but an awesome challenge, one that animates the constitutional enterprise and should be simultaneously daunting and thrilling to citizens who desire to govern themselves through reflection and choice.

*List of Contributors*_____

Sotirios A. Barber is Professor of Political Science at University of Notre Dame. His writings include *On What the Constitution Means*; *Welfare and the Constitution*; *Constitutional Interpretation: The Basic Questions* (with James Fleming); and *Constitutional Politics: Constitution Making, Maintenance and Change* (coedited with Robert George).

Joseph M. Bessette is the Alice Tweed Tuohy Professor of Government and Ethics at Claremont McKenna College. His books include *The Mild Voice of Reason: Deliberative Democracy and American National Government*; *American Government and Politics: Deliberation, Democracy and Citizenship* (with John J. Pitney); and *The Constitutional Presidency* (coedited with Jeffrey K. Tulis).

Mark E. Brandon is Professor of Law, Professor of Political Science, and Director of the Constitutional Law and Theory Program at Vanderbilt University. His writings include the books *Free in the World* and a forthcoming study, *Family and the American Constitutional Order*.

Daniel Deudney is Associate Professor of Political Science at Johns Hopkins University. His publications include *Bonding Power: Republican Security Theory from the Polis to the Global Village* and articles in *Security Studies, International Organization*, and numerous other venues.

Christopher L. Eisgruber is the Provost of Princeton University, where he also serves as the Laurance S. Rockefeller Professor of Public Affairs and the University Center for Human Values. He is the author of *Constitutional Self-Government*; *The Next Justice: Repairing the Supreme Court Appointments Process*; and *Religious Freedom and the Constitution* (with Lawrence G. Sager).

James E. Fleming is Professor of Law and The Honorable Frank R. Kenison Distinguished Scholar of Law at Boston University School of Law. His writings include *Securing Constitutional Democracy: The Case of Autonomy*; *Constitutional Interpretation: The Basic Questions* (with Sotirios A. Barber); and *American Constitutional Interpretation* (with Walter F. Murphy, Sotirios A. Barber, and Stephen Macedo).

William F. Harris II is Principal Scholar at the Center for the Constitution at James Madison's Montpelier in Virginia. He previously served as Founding Director of the Center. An Associate Professor of Political Science at the University of Pennsylvania, he is also a regular member of the adjunct faculty of the Federal Executive Institute. His publications include *The Interpretable Constitution*, and the first edition of *American Constitutional Interpretation* (with Walter F. Murphy and James Fleming).

Ran Hirschl is Professor of Political Science and Law at the University of Toronto where he holds a senior Canada Research Chair in Constitutionalism, Democracy and Development. His books include *Towards Juristocracy: The Origins and Consequences of the New Constitutionalism*; *Constitutional Theocracy*; and forthcoming, *Comparative Matters: Legal Studies for the 21st Century*.

Gary Jeffrey Jacobsohn is the H. Malcolm MacDonald Professor in Constitutional and Comparative Law in the Department of Government at the University of Texas at Austin. His books include *The Wheel of Law: India's Secularism in Comparative Context*; *Apple of Gold: Constitutionalism in Israel and the United States*; *The Supreme Court and the Decline of Constitutional Aspiration*; and forthcoming, *Constitutional Identity*.

Benjamin A. Kleinerman is an Assistant Professor of Constitutional Democracy in James Madison College at Michigan State University. He is the author of the recently published book, *The Discretionary President: The Promise and Peril of Executive Power*, and articles in the *American Political Science Review*, *Perspectives on Politics*, *Review of Politics*, and other venues.

Stephen Macedo is the Laurance S. Rockefeller Professor of Politics and the University Center for Human Values at Princeton University. His books include *Liberal Virtues: Citizenship, Virtue and Community in Liberal Constitutionalism*; *Diversity and Distrust: Civic Education in a Multi-cultural Democracy*; and (as lead coauthor) *Democracy at Risk: How Political Choices Undermine Citizen Participation, and What We Can Do About It*. He is coeditor (with Walter F. Murphy, James Fleming, and Sotirios Barber) of *American Constitutional Interpretation*.

Jan-Werner Müller is Associate Professor of Politics at Princeton University. He is the author of *A Dangerous Mind: Carl Schmitt in Post-War European Thought*; *Another Country: German Intellectuals, Unification and National Identity*; and *Constitutional Patriotism*.

Kim Lane Scheppele is the Laurance S. Rockefeller Professor of Sociology and Public Affairs in the University Center for Human Values and the Woodrow Wilson School at Princeton University, where she is also the Director of the Program in Law and Public Affairs. She is the author of *Legal Secrets* and the forthcoming *International State of Emergency: Legality and Transnationality after 9/11.*

Rogers M. Smith is the Christopher H. Browne Distinguished Professor of Political Science at the University of Pennsylvania. His books include *Civic Ideals: Conflicting Visions of Citizenship in U.S. History*; *Liberalism and American Constitutional Law*; and *Stories of Peoplehood: The Politics and Morals of Political Memberships.*

Jeffrey K. Tulis edited this volume while serving as Laurance S. Rockefeller Visiting Fellow in the University Center for Human Values at Princeton. His home institution is the Department of Government at the University of Texas at Austin. His publications include *The Rhetorical Presidency*; *The Constitutional Presidency* (coedited with Joseph Bessette); and the forthcoming books from Princeton University Press, *Democratic Decay and the Politics of Deference*, and *Legacies of Loss in American Politics* (with Nicole Mellow).

Adrian Vermeule is John H. Watson Professor of Law at Harvard Law School. His books include *Law and the Limits of Reason*; *Mechanisms of Democracy: Institutional Design Writ Small*; *Judging under Uncertainty: An Institutional Theory of Legal Interpretation*; and *Terror in the Balance: Security, Liberty and the Courts* (with Eric Posner).

Mariah Zeisberg is Assistant Professor of Political Science at the University of Michigan. She is completing a book on war powers in the American Constitution and has published a number of articles on constitutional theory.

Index

Dodd, William E., 95n8, 96n13

Does American Democracy Still Work?
  (Wolfe), 13n1, 21n38, 30, 35

Dorf, Michael C., 39n41

Dratel, Joshua, 105n41

Dred Scott v. Sandford, 29, 34n23, 53, 55,
  292n18

Du Bois, W.E.B., 224, 224n17

Dudziak, Mary L., 224n17

Dunoff, Jeffrey L., 253n36, 300n6

Dworkin, Ronald, 13, 15, 18, 21, 30,
  32n13, 36, 41, 55

Dyzenhaus, David, 92

Ebrahim, Hassen, 57n27

ecclesiocracy, 256

Edwards, Owen Dudley, 65n43

Egypt, 258, 262, 264–65, 268, 270–73, 315

Eisenhower, Dwight D., 307n19

Eisgruber, Christopher L., 8, 29n, 32–33,
  36, 317–28

Elder, Robert E., Jr., 165n24

Electoral College, 13, 32, 35, 43, 45–46

Elkin, Stephen L., 15, 21, 179n23

Ellman, Stephen, 58n30

Ellsworth, Oliver, 209

Ely, John Hart, 15, 168n2, 170, 174–75,
  182, 185, 231n37

Ely, James W., Jr., 235n44

emergencies: ADVISE program and, 150;
  anticipatory violence and, 141–42; Bush
  administration and, 149–50; constitutionalizing, 128–34; data-mining and,
  150–51; designing for dark side of
  government and, 127; enhanced interrogation techniques and, 125; exceptions that prove the rule and, 124–54;
  executive centralization and, 136–37;
  executive discretion and, 92–111;
  expertise concentration and, 149–52;
  Foreign Intelligence Surveillance Act and,
  145; governmental power and, 91–109;
  Guantanamo detention camp and,
  125, 230n36, 231; Hurricane Katrina
  and, 21, 45; inside-outside debate and,
  127–30; institutions and, 92, 108n50,
  119–28, 132, 135–38, 143–49, 152–54;
  intelligence gathering and, 144–49;
  inversion of free speech and, 140–41;
  lingering powers and, 142–44; MATRIX
  program and, 150; militarization

and, 137–38; national security and,
  91–111, 145, 150; 9/11 attacks and,
  21, 45, 102n32, 105, 124–26, 129n9,
  132–35, 143n24, 149–54, 270, 298–300,
  311n28; Office for the Protection of
  the Constitution and, 145–46; Pearl
  Harbor and, 21; prerogative and, 4–5,
  107, 114–20, 179–80, 183, 187, 199,
  212, 303; press censorship and, 95–96;
  preventive detention and, 139–40, 153;
  procedural shortcuts and, 138–39; putting people in their places and, 139–40;
  reform and, 126; reversal of transparency and, 141; rhetoric of necessity
  and, 92–96, 100–101, 107–10, 114–18,
  129, 154; script for, 134–44, 144–54;
  statesmanship and, 112–23; term-limits
  and, 125; terrorism and, 124–26, 129n9,
  132–35, 143n24, 145, 149–54, 230, 273,
  298; toggle-switch model and, 126; U.S.
  Congress and, 93–109; wiretapping and,
  124–25, 147, 235

Emergencies Act, 131

Enabling Act, 129n10

England, 81, 95n9, 117, 218, 227, 261, 305

Environmental Protection Agency, 225n21

Eskridge, William N., Jr., 30n6

Espionage Act, 96–98, 100

establishment by contrast, 71–72

Ethiopian Orthodox Church, 260

Euben, Roxanne, 270n22

European Arrest Warrant, 132n17

European Union, 240–41, 245–55, 294

Evangelical Lutheran Church, 261

executive powers: Article II and, 198–203,
  207–15; Authorization for Use of Military Force and, 198–99; Bush and, 104–
  9, 149–50; commander in chief, 157–67;
  enhanced interrogation techniques and,
  125; Espionage Act and, 96–98, 100;
  General Order No. 38 and, 100–101;
  globalization and, 239–49; glory seeking
  and, 157–66; governmental power and,
  93–97, 102n32, 103–11; Guantanamo
  detention camp and, 125, 230n36, 231;
  inherent authority and, 105; Kennedy
  and, 169–70, 173–77, 180–85, 188,
  190–91, 218; legalization model and,
  102–4; Lend-Lease Act and, 212; Lincoln
  and, 92–94, 99–109, 118n16, 178, 178,
  210, 213–15, 318–20; Machiavelli and,